"J. P. Moreland and Scott Rae challenge the conventional wisdom and give a spirited defense of this form of dualism. Their work deserves the attention of every serious student of this topic."

JOHN JEFFERSON DAVIS, Professor of Systematic Theology, Gordon-Conwell Theological Seminary

---

"The critical foundational issue underlying every ethical battle is personhood. Without a clear and communicable understanding of that issue, the battle is lost. That is why *Body & Soul* is to the ethical war what the atomic bomb was to World War II. This book is long overdue and essential reading."

DAVE STEVENS, M.D., Christian Medical and Dental Society

"Moreland and Rae have produced an engaging study in Christian metaphysics. They marry an appreciation of Thomas Aquinas with biblical studies in the service of reexploring bioethical issues from abortion to euthanasia. For better understanding of the deep divisions in our debates on these issues, this volume provides an important key."

H. TRISTRAM ENGELHARDT JR., Ph.D., M.D., Professor, Baylor College of Medicine

---

"In an age when some educated Christians are selling out the soul for a mess of materialistic pottage, Moreland and Rae's *Body & Soul* is a significant restatement and cogent defense of the historic Christian teaching about human nature and responsibility. In contrast to typical antidualistic arguments, this book is grounded in the best exegesis of all the relevant biblical material and well-informed by the grand theological tradition before it proceeds to the metaphysics and sciences of human nature. Indeed, its properly ordered, multidisciplinary methodology is a crucial strength of the book. It first elaborates a detailed and philosophically sophisticated body-soul dualism that at the same time emphasizes the unity and functional holism of human existence. It then builds a formidable case that the traditional view of persons as substantial souls is necessary for a robust Christian understanding of moral responsibility and our obligation toward the unborn, the dying, reproductive technology and genetic engineering. Moreland and Rae defend dualism not so much to reassure us about what happens when we die as to guide us in how we should life. I welcome this timely and substantial volume."

JOHN W. COOPER, Professor of Philosophical Theology, Calvin Theological Seminary

Franz Hermann
1-16-01

love the Lord with
all your 'soul'—

Body & Soul

Human Nature
& the Crisis
in Ethics

J. P. MORELAND & SCOTT B. RAE

InterVarsity Press
Downers Grove, Illinois

InterVarsity Press
P.O. Box 1400, Downers Grove, IL 60515
World Wide Web: www.ivpress.com
E-mail: mail@ivpress.com

InterVarsity Press® is the book-publishing division of InterVarsity Christian Fellowship/USA®, a student movement active on campus at hundreds of universities, colleges and schools of nursing in the United States of America, and a member movement of the International Fellowship of Evangelical Students. For information about local and regional activities, write Public Relations Dept., InterVarsity Christian Fellowship/USA, 6400 Schroeder Rd., P.O. Box 7895, Madison, WI 53707-7895.

All Scripture quotations, unless otherwise indicated, are taken from the Holy Bible, New International Version®. NIV®. *Copyright ©1973, 1978, 1984 by International Bible Society. Used by permission of Zondervan Publishing House. All rights reserved.*

Cover illustration: Sistine Chapel, Vatican, Rome, Italy/SuperStock

ISBN 0-8308-1577-5

Printed in the United States of America ∞

Library of Congress Cataloging-in-Publication Data

Moreland, James Porter, 1948-
  Body & soul: human nature & the crisis in ethics / J.P. Moreland & Scott B. Rae.
    p. cm.
  Includes bibliographical references.
  ISBN 0-8308-1577-5 (pbk. : alk. paper)
    1. Man (Christian theolgoy) 2. Christian ethics. 3. Mind and body. I. Title: Body and soul. II. Rae, Scott B. III. Title.
  BT701.2.M+
  233'.5—dc21

                                                                                    99-086858

15 14 13 12 11 10 9 8 7 6 5 4 3 2 1

11 10 09 08 07 06 05 04 03 02 01 00

Acknowledgments

A heartfelt word of appreciation goes to many people who helped us in the development of this book.

We wish to thank Lisa Vasquez and Robert Garcia for assisting us in researching and in organizing the manuscript for publication.

We also are grateful to our colleagues at Talbot School of Theology, Biola University—particularly to the philosophy department at Talbot—for creating an atmosphere conducive to spiritual and intellectual growth. A special word of gratitude goes to our dean, Dennis Dirks. His leadership and support have been greatly appreciated.

We are thankful for the vision and support of the Discovery Institute, which provided a grant for us to do research for the book. (One of us—J. P. Moreland—is a fellow of the Discovery Institute.) Francis Beckwith, William Lane Craig and Stewart Goetz provided helpful comments on early drafts of the manuscript.

We regret that William Hasker's *The Emergent Self* (Ithaca, N.Y.: Cornell University Press, 1999) reached us too late to be discussed in our book. While our view differs from Hasker's in certain ways, we are in basic agreement with much of what he proposes. In any case, his is an important book on the mind-body problem, and we highly recommend it.

Finally, thanks go to our families—Hope, Ashley and Allison Moreland, and Sally, Taylor, Cameron and Austin Rae. Their patience with us as we worked on this project was substantial, and we greatly appreciate them. Their love is the very substance of our lives.

Introduction

French philosopher Blaise Pascal once remarked that the immortality of the soul is something of such vital importance to us that one must have lost all feeling not to care about knowing the facts of the matter. In this, Pascal was surely correct. It has always been a part of our nature to be curious about what we are, where we are going and how we ought to be treated. Moreover, Christians have a special interest in developing their understanding of human persons since this understanding is so central to the Christian faith.

As Alvin Plantinga has reminded us, when Christians go about developing their views on various things, including human persons, they should keep in mind certain broad intellectual motifs in order to critique those that are obstacles to advancing the kingdom of God. More specifically, Christians must recognize that the rise of scientism has contributed to a situation in which there is now no universal body of ethical and religious knowledge in the institutions of Western intellectual authority—the universities. The implications of this situation have been disastrous, among them being the marginalization of a Christian worldview, an unnecessary revision of Christian theology as science dictates the parameters in which theology must work, and a lowering of the epistemic justification of biblical, theological and philosophical claims relative to those in the hard sciences.

There are several illustrations of these tendencies. In the mid 1930s, philosopher Edmund Husserl pondered the question of just how the most educated society in history (Germany) could have been so easily lead into some of the most barbarous actions and values the world had ever seen. Husserl's work *The Crisis of European Sciences* was as an expression of his reflections on this and related questions. According to Husserl, the main culprit was the emergence of a view of the nature and limits of knowledge that had come widely to occupy culture: knowledge is to be identified with mathematical physics and the hard sciences generally.[1] For Husserl this meant that pressing questions of human significance—those about values, meaning in life, God, the afterlife, the proper nature of the state—could not be answered with answers that would be regarded as items of objective knowledge. The effect of this view was the privatization of ethical and theological issues and the setting up of a cultural context in which people could be manipulated by powerful leaders since there was no knowledge of moral and religious truths that could be raised against them. Part of Husserl's solution to this problem was to advance a form of dualism regarding consciousness and the self that could counter the cognitive authority of naturalism in his day.

In our own time, Dallas Willard's masterful work on spirituality, *The Divine Conspiracy*, warns us that giving up our understanding of humans as spiritual substances in favor of physicalist alternatives will result in a devitalization of the spiritual life among Jesus' followers. Says Willard, "To understand spirit as 'substance' is of the utmost importance in our current world, which is so largely devoted to the ultimacy of matter. It means that spirit is something that exists in its own right—to some degree in the human case, and absolutely so with God."[2]

Speaking of the negative impact of secularism, of which scientism is a part, Willard goes on to say that

> the crushing weight of the secular outlook . . . permeates or pressures every thought we have today. Sometimes it even forces those who self-identify as Christian teachers to set aside Jesus' plain statements about the reality and total relevance of the kingdom of God and replace them with philosophical speculations whose only recommendation is their consistency with a "modern" [i.e., contemporary] mindset. The powerful though vague and unsubstantiated presumption is that *something has been found out* that renders a spiritual understanding of reality in the manner of Jesus simply foolish to those who are "in the know."[3]

Willard concludes that in order to restore spiritual vitality to the church, we must recapture a view of Jesus as an intellectually competent person who knew what he was talking about. For Willard this will include accepting—as absolutely central to the spiritual life—a view of human persons as having substantial, immaterial souls.

In our view, the complementarity approach to integration (roughly, the view that science and religion are noninteracting, complementary descriptions of reality) as practiced by many of its advocates inadvertently contributes to the scientism noted above and, thereby, to the various results of scientism. In Plantinga's sense this approach is not sufficiently critical of the milieu in which we now live and move and have our being. What is needed is a Christian natural philosophy of living things, especially of human persons, that provides two things—a central role for philosophy and theology in contributing to the ontology of human persons and a proper ordering of science relative to philosophy and theology in the ontological task.

The classical understanding of the human person as consisting of body and soul has come under attack for some time. For example, in his review for *Books & Culture* of several books on consciousness and the mind (many of which we will interact with throughout this book), Allen C. Guelzo points out that "it is remarkable how little Christian thinkers have risen to meet it [i.e., the challenge of those who deny the soul]. Philosophers such as Paul and Patricia Churchland—who deny the existence of the soul and hold to a physicalist view of a human person [and with whom we will interact throughout this book]—issue the challenge to dualists such as ourselves in this way: Mind-body dualists, who think the mind or soul is *not* fundamentally dependent on the brain, owe us a plausible account of these functional dependencies—an account that, so far as I know, is not forthcoming."[4] Guelzo continues by throwing down the gauntlet more explicitly to theologians when he suggests that "from the theologians, there is not only a deafening silence, but not even much recognition that a problem is being brewed under their noses. If we are being saved in both body and soul, hadn't we better secure a reasonably good grip on what we mean by the *soul* if the very idea of salvation is to remain coherent? Where is the evangelical theologian writing on the *soul?*"[5]

Though we believe the nature and reality of the soul is the central issue, and not its functional interaction with the brain, with this caveat in mind, our work is an attempt to provide such an account of human personhood and the soul, to answer the challenge of the physicalist and to reflect on certain ethical issues relevant to it. Morality is very much affected by these metaphysical questions. For example, the naturalist Edward O. Wilson has argued for a biological basis for morality in an attempt to construct a system of morality from philosophical naturalism.[6]

We hold that metaphysics and morality are intimately connected and that our dualist view of the body and soul provides the most compelling account of human personhood and its moral dimension. The book is divided into two parts. In part one we clarify and defend our version of substance dualism, and in part two we analyze and argue for crucial ethical positions that follow from the position maintained in part one.

Part one consists of six chapters. In chapter one we analyze several different sorts of dualism and locate our version of Thomistic dualism in this taxonomy. As we make clear, there are different opinions about the precise details of Thomas Aquinas's philosophical-theological anthropology, and we do not claim to offer a version that conforms to Aquinas's in all details. Still, our view shares enough of the important aspects of a Thomistic approach to warrant our using that label for our position. Next, we argue that a proper understanding of God and angels as spirits and a careful exegesis of Scripture present a biblical anthropology that is inconsistent with physicalism and that is most reasonably associated with Thomistic dualism. Finally, we present what we believe to be the best methodology for approaching the task of forming a model of the constitution of human persons. This methodological approach stands in stark contrast to a complementarity approach in that the former places biblical exegesis, theology and philosophy above the hard sciences in order of importance while, arguably, complementarians reverse this order.

In chapter two we lay out a metaphysical framework of central importance for developing an adequate view of human persons, and we compare and contrast two metaphysical analyses of wholes with parts: substances understood in the classic sense and property-things, or ordered aggregates. Regarding the metaphysical framework, we present a brief philosophical analysis of important metaphysical notions that, in keeping with our methodology set out in chapter one, come to center stage in arguments for and analyses of human persons: properties, relations, events, identity and identity statements, different types of reduction, and different sorts of parts and wholes. In the second section of the chapter we compare and contrast substances and property-things in seven different areas. This distinction is crucial for chapters three through six because there we argue that both strict and complementarian naturalists (Christian or non-Christian) typically depict human persons as property-things. By contrast, we claim that they are substances and that this fact is best captured by Thomistic dualism.

Chapter three clarifies the nature of human persons in strict naturalist and complementarian perspectives. The first half of the chapter describes various versions of philosophical naturalism and the view of human persons entailed by them. The second half of the chapter presents a Christian complementarian view of the integration of science and other fields, such as theology, and it centers on the complementarian understanding of human persons. Metaphysically speaking, the Christian complementarian understanding is virtually identical to naturalist depictions of human persons on most of the central metaphysical aspects of human personhood. The chapter closes with a brief presentation of the ethical implications of a Christian complementarian anthropology for certain end-of-life ethical issues. These will be developed in more detail in part two.

In chapters four and five we argue that human persons are identical to immaterial substances, namely, to souls. In chapter six we explain the soul's relationship to the development and functioning of its body. However, in chapters four and five we limit our investigation of human persons to those considerations that support the claim that human persons are essentially immaterial substances. We direct our attention to three important areas:

☐ human agency and freedom (chapter four)

☐ the nature of our conscious, mental lives and what this tells us about the types of things we are (chapter five)

☐ a set of critical considerations about personal identity (chapter five)

In each of these areas of investigation, our argument follows this form:

1. There are certain features about ourselves that we know or at least about which we have a right to be sure (i.e., to take ourselves to be justified in believing). There are adequate grounds for believing these features to be real, and naturalist or complementarian attempts to provide alternative depictions of these features fail to be convincing.

2. The features mentioned above support the claim that human persons are essentially immaterial substances for at least two reasons: (a) when these features are accurately described and reported to others, these descriptions and reports express facts that are best captured by a substance-dualist model of human persons, and (b) the best explanation for the reality of these fea-

tures is a substance-dualist model of human persons.

In chapter four we compare libertarian and compatibilist views of human action and argue that libertarian agency is the better model. We also claim that the existence and nature of libertarian actions and agents are not plausibly harmonized with physicalist views of human persons but, rather, have as their best explanation a substance-dualist view of libertarian agents. Thus libertarian agency provides evidence for substance dualism.

In chapter five we present and defend three basic arguments for substance dualism. First, we argue that mental properties and events are genuinely mental entities not adequately captured by various physicalist (e.g., functionalist) views. We also argue that mental properties are kind-defining properties—that is, they tell us about the essence of the human persons who have them. Second, we present and defend a modal argument for substance dualism that takes as its starting point the conceivability of disembodied existence. Third, we analyze various views of personal identity and argue that substance dualism is the best position. Along the way, we state and offer a brief criticism of a version of physicalism currently gaining ground: the material-composition position.

In chapter six we develop a view of the soul's relationship to the body. It is here that we part company with Cartesian dualism and advocate Thomistic dualism as both of those are frequently understood. In this chapter we do the following:

□ explain our version of Thomistic dualism more fully and indicate the sorts of evidence that support it

□ consider a set of objections to Thomistic dualism

□ apply our model of Thomistic dualism to questions about the origin of the soul in normal and abnormal cases (e.g., twinning, cloning, frozen embryos)

□ briefly indicate certain ethical implications that follow from our form of Thomistic dualism

Part two of this book takes the metaphysical conclusions and applies them to the complex world of bioethics and biotechnology. Many of the most pressing and complicated issues faced by those in academic medicine and by professional bioethicists have a view of personhood at their core. That is, those making moral decisions and public policy in bioethics assume a particular view of a human person. Issues such as abortion and physician-assisted suicide are well publicized in the popular media. Clearly abortion has a view of human personhood at its foundation. But many other important issues have often unspoken assumptions about what a human person is, assumptions that are critical in informing those who must make decisions in these areas.

Chapter seven takes up the ongoing debate over abortion and the equally important, though less publicized, discussion of fetal-tissue research and transplantation. We attempt to show how the Bible suggests a continuity of personal identity from conception to adulthood, which is consistent with the Thomistic substance view we are defending. We analyze many of the arguments for abortion rights and show how they frequently make question-begging assertions about the personhood of the unborn. However, with some abortion-rights advocates this may be changing, for they are forced by better prenatal technology to recognize that the unborn child is not simply a "product of conception" but a living human being. We interact with philosophers in the abortion debate who hold a functionalist view of a person, such as Mary Ann Warren and Bonnie Steinbock. We further interact with the more radical views that attempt to justify infanticide as well as abortion. Finally, we suggest that the use of fetal tissue from induced abortion is morally tainted since the means of obtaining the tissue has a moral dimension, as does the end for which the tissue is used.

Chapter eight takes up the issues revolving around the burgeoning infertility industry. The central issue is the moral status of extracorporeal embryos, particularly those that are created through in vitro fertilization and kept in storage in laboratories. We will argue that these embryos are persons with moral status, and as such, that they should not be discarded or used for experiments after infertility treatments are complete and, similarly, that they should not be created in the lab for purposes of research. Further, selective termination of pregnancies when infertility treatments have been "too successful" cannot be justified. We explore how the couple who views the human person from our perspective can use reproductive technologies without violating moral boundaries.

In chapter nine we enter the brave new world of genetic technologies and human cloning. Here the view of a human person surfaces more subtly, but this view is no less important here than in the above areas of abortion and of fetal and embryo research. Gene therapy, prenatal genetic testing, the Human Genome Project and human cloning are also controversial areas in which the view of a human person makes a difference. Foundational to this discussion is the view that the essence of a human person can be reduced to or taken as emergent upon his or her genetic content. We interact with the new hallowed ground of genetics—genetic reductionism—and argue that a person is much more than one's genetic material. We suggest that human cloning does not involve creating soulless persons and that the concept itself is an oxymoron. Further we maintain that the bias toward abortion in some prenatal genetic-testing areas is problematic, given our view of a human person.

Finally, chapter ten moves us toward the other end of the bioethical spectrum. Here we take up issues at the end of life such as euthanasia, physician-assisted suicide and the treatment of patients in a persistent vegetative state. Though the notion of personhood is not the central concept in the euthanasia debate, some have argued that one who is terminally ill at the end of his or her life is no longer a person and, thus, that euthanasia in this case does not violate the sanctity of life nor the commandment "Thou shall not kill." We reject this argument and interact with some of the leading advocates of such a view. The more difficult area is the moral status of persons in a persistent vegetative state. We maintain that they are still persons but that further treatment of them, including medically provided nutrition and hydration, is futile and thus is not a moral obligation.

In our view this area of metaphysical and ethical reflection is important because it is central to so many of the issues debated today and to developing a fully biblical view of the world. The concept of personhood that we defend and apply to bioethics is largely dismissed in secular academic circles today. Even in some Christian circles, it is considered inconsistent with biblical teaching. We believe that our view of a human person is both intellectually defensible and biblically based. We realize that this is a highly technical work in many places and that some readers may feel it takes sophisticated philosophical training to follow our argument. We have chosen to write the book at what we consider to be a fairly high academic level because we are convinced that the view of a human person we affirm must be articulated and defended at that level for it to gain a hearing both within the Christian community and in the secular academic setting. Still, we hope a nonspecialist will be able to gain much from the pages to follow.

Part One

Metaphysical Reflections on Human Personhood

*Throughout the centuries Christians have believed that each human person
consists in a soul and body; that the soul survived the death of the body;
and that its future life will be immortal.*[1]

H . D . L E W I S

*In terms of biblical psychology, man does not have a "soul," he is one.
He is a living and vital whole. It is possible to distinguish between his activities,
but we cannot distinguish between the parts,
for they have no independent existence.*[2]

J . K . H O W A R D

*How should we think about human persons? What sorts of things,
fundamentally, are they? What is it to be a human, what is it to be a human
person, and how should we think about personhood? . . .
The first point to note is that on the Christian scheme of things,
God is the premier person, the first and chief exemplar of personhood . . .
and the properties most important for an understanding of our personhood
are properties we share with him.*[3]

A L V I N P L A N T I N G A

CHAPTER 1

Establishing a Framework for Approaching Human Personhood

*I*T IS SAFE TO SAY THAT THROUGHOUT HUMAN HISTORY, THE VAST majority of people, educated and uneducated alike, have been dualists, at least in the sense that they have taken a human to be the sort of being that could enter life after death while one's corpse was left behind—for example, one could enter life after death as the very same individual or as some sort of spiritual entity that merges with the All. Some form of dualism appears to be the natural response to what we seem to know about ourselves through introspection and in other ways. Many philosophers who deny dualism admit that it is the commonsense view.

When we turn to an investigation of church history, we see the same thing. For two thousand years, the vast majority of Christian thinkers have believed in the souls of men and beasts, as it used to be put. Animals and humans are composed of an immaterial entity—a soul, a life principle, a ground of sentience—and a body. More specifically, a human being is a unity of two distinct entities—body and soul. The human soul, while not by nature immortal, is capable of entering an intermediate disembodied state upon death, however incomplete and unnatural this state may be, and of eventually being reunited with a resurrected body. Augustine says,

"But the soul is present as a whole not only in the entire mass of a body, but also in every least part of the body at the same time."[4] Similarly, Thomas Aquinas claims "we now proceed to treat of man, who is composed of a spiritual and corporeal substance."[5]

Today, things have changed. For many, the rise of modern science has called into question the viability of dualism. In popular and intellectual cultures alike, many argue that neurophysiology demonstrates the radical dependence and, in fact, identity between mind and brain, that genetics has shown genes and DNA are all that are needed to explain the development of living things, that advances in artificial intelligence make likely the suggestion that humans are just complicated computers and that cloning seems to reduce us to mere structured aggregates of physical parts.

Interestingly, among contemporary Christian intellectuals there is a widespread loathing for dualism as well. We are often told that biblical revelation depicts the human person as a holistic unity whereas dualism is a Greek concept falsely read into the Bible by many throughout the history of the church. Christians, we are told, are committed to monism and the resurrection of the body, not to dualism and the immortality of the soul. In short, dualism is outdated, unbiblical and incorrect.

Concurrent with the alleged demise of dualism is the rise of advanced medical technologies that have made prominent a number of very important and difficult issues about ethics at both edges of life. Central to these issues are questions about the nature of human personhood, about the reality of life after death and about the existence, nature, accessibility and degree of justification of ethical or religious knowledge as compared to scientific knowledge. It is not too dramatic to say that we are facing a contemporary crisis in ethics, a crisis that has lead to a good deal of moral confusion, chaos and fragmentation.

In our opinion the concurrence of the demise of dualism (specifically a Christian form of dualism) and the ethical and religious crisis just mentioned is no accident. We believe that what is needed is a more careful formulation and defense of Christian dualism—a defense that renders intelligible a solid Christian anthropology and that shows the relative importance and specific roles science, theology and philosophy have in the integrative task of developing a model of human personhood that is adequate to what we know or justifiably believe from all the relevant disciplines. Such a task requires a multidisciplinary effort, and even if we were able to take on such a work (which we are not), a fully developed Christian anthropology would be impossible to complete in a single volume. Given these limitations, we shall offer what we hope will be an adequate defense of the most reasonable and biblically accurate depiction of human personhood, and we hope to relate that depiction to crucial ethical concerns that affect us all. This task is important for some of the reasons just mentioned. But it is also relevant because of the general human curiosity and angst about what persons are and wherein lies their destiny. As Blaise Pascal once put it, "The immortality of the soul is something of such vital importance to us, affecting us so deeply, that one must have lost all feeling not to care about knowing the facts of the matter."[6]

In this chapter we shall look at a taxonomy of versions of dualism, investigate the Christian understanding of a human person as it has been traditionally conceived and discuss the broad contours of what a proper approach to human personhood should look like.

What Is Dualism?

As does any broad philosophical and theological notion, dualism comes in several varieties. At its root, *dualism* simply means "two-ism," and it expresses a commitment to the proposition that two items in question are, in fact, two different entities or kinds of entities instead of being identical to one another. *Cosmic dualism* is the view that reality in general is composed of two different entities (e.g., individuals, properties, realms of reality) that cannot be reduced to each other. Cosmic dualists sometimes go beyond this and accept the claim either that these two entities are both metaphysically ultimate—that is, one did not come from or is not dependent on the other for its existence—or that one entity is inferior in value to the other. For example, Zoroastrianism teaches that Ahura-Mazda (the good, wise Lord) and Angra Mainyu (the spirit of evil) are opposites locked in a cosmic struggle between good and evil. In Taoism the yin and the yang are bipolar forces (good-evil, male-female, light-dark, etc.) that constantly react to and with each other in governing all of reality. Gnostic dualism implies that spirit and matter are different and that the latter is of little value compared to the former.

Is Christianity a form of cosmic dualism? The answer is no and yes.

Christianity does not affirm that there are two ultimate, independent realities. Everything besides God owes its existence to him in some way or another. Nor does Christianity teach that spirit is good and matter is evil. Yet there are clear cosmic dualities presupposed by and taught in Holy Scripture: God-creation, good-evil, truth-falsity, immaterial-material world, being-becoming and, we believe, soul-body.

In addition to cosmic dualisms, there are various forms of dualism regarding the constitution of human persons (and animals, though we will focus here only on human persons). These *anthropological dualisms* may be divided into three categories: *metaphysical, eschatological* and *axiological*. Let us take these in order.

Metaphysical. The metaphysical category of anthropological dualism centers on the question of the constitutional nature of human persons. This version of dualism is the chief focus of this book. *Property-event* dualism is the idea that mental and physical properties or events are genuinely different kinds of entities. Thoughts, sensations, beliefs, desires, volitions and so on are mental events in which mental properties are embedded (e.g., they have intentionality—the property of being of or about something—or the property of being self-presenting); various brain events with physical properties are nonidentical to mental events. The rival to property-event dualism (indeed, to any form of anthropological dualism) is *strict physicalism,* or *monism,* the view that all properties, events, relations, individuals and so on are strictly physical entities. Monists believe that there may be an irreducible duality of language: for example, an event that is caused by a pin stick can be described by the two nonsynonymous terms *pain* and *C fiber firing pattern.* Nevertheless, monists insist that these two terms have the same referent and that the referent is a physical state.

Substance dualism is the view that the soul—I, self, mind—is an immaterial substance different from the body to which it is related. In order to adequately understand substance dualism, one must get clear on the nature of a substance, and we shall look at this topic in chapter two. But for now, suffice it to say that the substance dualist is committed to the claim that the soul is an immaterial entity that could, in principle, survive death and ground personal identity in the afterlife.

Two major variants of substance dualism will be the focus of attention in chapter six[7]: *Cartesian* and *Aristotelian/Thomistic* dualism. (Hereafter, the former will be referred to simply as Thomistic dualism.) Cartesian dualism explicates the philosophy of René Descartes. On this view, the mind is a substance externally related by a causal relation to the body, a corporeal substance that is merely physical. For a Cartesian the mind is an immaterial ego that contains the capacities for mental functioning.

By contrast, Thomistic dualism focuses on the soul, not the mind. The mind is a faculty of the soul, but the latter goes beyond mental functioning and serves as the integrative ground and developer of the body it animates and makes alive. For the Thomistic dualist the soul contains capacities for biological as well as mental functioning. Thus the soul is related to the body more intimately and fully than by way of an external causal connection, as Cartesians would have it. Some Thomistic dualists identify the person with the whole body-soul composite whereas others identify the person with the soul, which contains a natural exigency for embodiment even while disembodied. As we will see in the next section, at a minimum a Christian should hold that the human person can sustain identity in a disembodied intermediate state and after the reception of a new resurrection body.

Both versions of substance dualism are consistent with *functional holism* but not with *ontological holism*. According to functional holism, while the soul (mind) is in the body, the body-soul complex is a deeply integrated unity with a vastly complicated, intricate array of mutual functional dependence and causal connection. But functional holism allows for the possibility that the soul (mind) may exist independent of the body with which it is currently functionally integrated or in a disembodied state altogether. It is a serious mistake to take substance dualism as being inconsistent with functional holism.

Ontological holism is the view that the mental constituents of a human person—the mental property-instances, states, relational complexes, fields or self—are inseparable entities (although the self may be identified as some sort of unity of the mental entities just mentioned or as a more substantial, though emergent and dependent, entity). The mental constituents are ontologically dependent upon a properly functioning physical body or brain, and thus disembodiment is not possible. Ontological holism is consistent with property dualism but not with substance dualism in either form.

Eschatological. Besides the metaphysical versions of anthropological dualism, there are versions of eschatological and axiological dualism. Eschatological dualism categorizes versions of dualism according to their view about the immortality of the soul. *Platonic dualism* held that the soul had a natural immortality. Plato's version of dualism is quite sophisticated in its totality, and much of what Plato taught is very much at home in a Christian worldview, though some of his ideas are clearly not compatible with Christianity. Only an issue-by-issue investigation can determine whether Plato's dualism is compatible with Christian teaching. However, this aspect of Plato's thought is obviously inconsistent with the Bible, which teaches that God alone is immortal and that all human persons owe their moment-by-moment existence to the sustaining power of God, whether before death, during the intermediate state or after the final resurrection.[8]

Does a rejection of Platonic eschatological dualism entail that there is no sense in which the soul is immortal according to Christian theology? No, it does not. In fact the most natural way to take the Scriptures—indeed, the way most thinkers in the history of the church have taken them—is to view the soul as immortal in this sense: the individual soul comes into existence at a point in time; it is sustained in existence by God throughout its existence, including a time of temporary disembodiment in the intermediate state; and there will never be a time in which it will cease to be after its creation. In the next section we will look at the biblical support for this view and compare it to two rival depictions of the soul and the intermediate state.

Axiological. Finally, axiological dualism divides anthropological positions according to the relative value placed on the soul and body. According to Gnostic and (on a traditional interpretation) Platonic dualism, the body is inferior to the soul in value, and more generally the material world is inferior to the immaterial world. Indeed, some versions of axiological dualism have claimed that matter, including the body, is evil. Some advocates of this form of dualism have used it to depreciate the value of physical labor, sexuality, physical health and so forth. It should be apparent that these versions of axiological dualism are inadequate and that Christians affirm the value of both the body and the soul and both the material and immaterial world.

This completes our brief survey of varieties of dualism. At this point we must ask the question, does the Bible teach some form of anthropological dualism that ought to be affirmed by Christian intellectuals and integrated into their intellectual work and practical lives? In spite of the fact that a growing number of Christian thinkers would answer this question in the negative, we think the answer is clearly yes.

Does the Bible Teach Anthropological Dualism?

Christian aversion to anthropological dualism. In recent years there has been something of a craze regarding dualism among Christian thinkers that, in our view, has led some to come perilously close to committing the bandwagon fallacy—taking a position against dualism in order to fit in with the majority of secular thinkers. For many Christian scholars the very idea that some form of anthropological dualism is correct and required by Christian teaching is out of the question. Thus Wolfhart Pannenberg asserts that "the distinction between body and soul as two . . . different realms of reality can no longer be maintained. . . . The separation between physical and spiritual is artificial."[9]

In our view, this aversion to dualism is sustained largely by sociological factors (e.g., a widespread distaste for Greek philosophy and its alleged influence on biblical exegesis) or by various confusions (e.g., that dualism is a rival theory to the resurrection of the body, that it is incompatible with a holistic emphasis that treats humans as unities, that science has somehow shown that dualism must be rejected). However widespread Christian monism is, we believe that it cannot be sustained by a careful exegesis of the biblical text. Holy Scripture clearly teaches some form of anthropological dualism. It will be impossible to justify adequately this claim in the short space of one section of this chapter. For a definitive defense of the biblical affirmation of anthropological dualism, we recommend John W. Cooper's excellent work *Body, Soul and Life Everlasting.*[10] In this section we offer a brief summary and defense of the biblical and theological issues.

An argument from the nature of the paradigm cases. Before we turn to biblical exegesis, there is a theological argument for dualism that should be considered. John Calvin once remarked that "no man can survey himself without forthwith turning his thoughts towards the God in whom he lives and moves."[11] Along similar lines, the great Old Testament scholar Franz Delitzsch claimed that "in order to apprehend the nature of the . . . human soul, it is first of all essential to apprehend the nature of God."[12] More recently, Alvin Plantinga has argued that Christians ought to take the commitments that constitute Christian theology as items of knowledge to be employed in forming an integrated worldview, in doing research and so forth. Among the things that Plantinga takes to be central to theological knowledge is the proposition that God is a person:

> How should we think about human persons? What sorts of things, fundamentally, *are* they? What is it to be a human, what is it to be a *human* person, and how should we think about personhood?. . . The first point to note is that on the Christian scheme of things, *God* is the premier person, the first and chief exemplar of personhood . . . and the properties most important for an understanding of our personhood are properties we share with him.[13]

In the spirit of Calvin, Delitzsch and Plantinga, we offer the following argument for dualism.

God is the paradigm case (i.e., clearest example) of a person, and arguably angels are as well. Now it is clear that God is an immaterial reality (Jn 4:24), most likely an immaterial substance. Moreover, we know angels are immaterial beings from the following examples:

☐ They are explicitly referred to as "ministering spirits" (Heb 1:14; cf. vv. 5, 13).

☐ Our struggle is not against flesh and blood but against principalities, powers, rulers of this present darkness and "spiritual hosts of wickedness in the heavenly places" (Eph 6:12 RSV).

☐ Demons are fallen angels and are regularly described as spirits (cf. Mt 8:16; Lk 11:26; Acts 19:12; Rev 16:14).

☐ Alleged embodiments of angels who appear to people can be explained on the grounds that these were examples of temporary abilities to manifest themselves sense perceptively and that this temporary ability may or may not imply temporary embodiment. In the Old Testament the angel of the Lord appears to have been God himself (cf. Gen 31:11, 13; Ex 3:2, 6), and like angels, God was capable of the same sort of temporary manifestation. Traditional Christians do not think that this makes God a physical being, so the mere fact that angels are capable of temporary sense-perceptible manifestations does not imply that they are essentially or permanently bodily creatures.

If God and, perhaps, angels are paradigm-case persons and since they are immaterial spirits, then it is at least consistent that something be both a person and an immaterial spirit. But more than this, if the paradigm-case persons are immaterial spirits, then this provides justification for the claim that anything is a person if and only if it bears a relevant similarity to the paradigm cases. Arguably, the relevant similarity between other (kinds of) persons and the paradigm cases is grounded in something all persons have in common and that constitutes that which makes the paradigm cases to be persons in the first place, namely, personhood. Personhood is constituted by a set of ultimate capacities of thought, belief, sensation, emotion, volition, desire, intentionality and so forth. As we will argue later in the book, none of these ultimate capacities is physical, and therefore neither is personhood itself. Nor is an individual person qua person. As Boethius (c. 480-524) said, "A person is an individual substance with a rational nature."[14] The rational nature to which Boethius referred is what we are calling *personhood*. Neither the rational nature nor the individual constituted by it is physical qua person. None of this rules out the possibility that certain kinds of persons—for example, human persons—can be *more* than immaterial (e.g., a unity of body and soul). But human persons qua persons are immaterial substances and not material ones.

In our view this argument is a good one, but the monist does have a response to it.[15] He can say that personhood is not a nature that an individual exemplifies; rather, it is a set of functional states that an individual realizes. Either personhood or a soul/spirit is much like software, and it can be realized by different kinds of individual hardwares. For example, Warren S. Brown, Nancey Murphy and H. Newton Malony claim that a soul is "a functional capacity of a complex physical organism, rather than a separate spiritual essence."[16] Roughly, a functional state is something characterized not by its intrinsic features but by its inputs and outputs that constitute its role in a system. Now God and angels are immaterial substances that realized the functional state we call personhood, and the human brain/body realizes personhood even though it is, strictly speaking, a physical entity. We cannot pursue this issue further here except to make two brief points. First, it seems fairly apparent that in scriptural descriptions of God as a thinking, feeling, acting, desiring and conscious being, Scripture is describing attributes God possesses, not functional states external to him and that he somehow realizes. Second, if various mental states are really functional states whose description is neutral to whether the entity realizing that state is a spirit or a brain, then just exactly what is the content of "spirit" when we say that God is a spirit? We believe that the functionalist will have real difficulty answering this question.

In the next few chapters we will examine further problems with functionalism. If there is an adequate rebuttal to this monist argument, then in the absence of a more compelling response, the fact that God and angels are immaterial spirits qua persons gives grounds for claiming the same thing of human persons.

Arguments from biblical exegesis. Before we look at biblical exegesis, it is important to note that an important issue in biblical teaching is the Bible's view of the intermediate state. Currently, there are three views of the intermediate state. The first view is the traditional *temporary-disembodiment position* that we defend below: A person is an immaterial soul/spirit deeply unified with a body that can enter a temporary intermediate state of disembodiment at death, however unnatural and incomplete it may be, while awaiting a resurrection body in the final state. This view is clearly dualistic in nature.

The second view advocated by thinkers like Bruce Reichenbach is monistic and is called the *extinction/re-creation position*[17]: Persons are identical to properly functioning bodies (or brains); when the body dies the person ceases to exist since the person is in some sense the same as his or her body. At the future, final resurrection, persons are re-created after a period of nonexistence either ex nihilo or by reforming either the very same body that died prior to extinction or by taking some subset of parts of that body and re-creating a new body around that subset.

Murray Harris is a major advocate of the third view, the *immediate-resurrection position*[18]: At death each individual is immediately given his or her resurrection body, thus eliminating a disembodied intermediate state as well as a future, general resurrection. We will discuss issues involved in debates about personal identity in chapter five, but suffice it to say here that the immediate-resurrection view seems to be dualistic. Why? Because it claims that the very same person can have two different bodies, and thus the person is not identical but only contingently connected to each body. As Harris admits, "the link between the Christian's successive forms of embodiment—the physical and the spiritual—lies in the same identifiable *ego*. . . . There are two dwellings but only one occupant. There is an identity of occupant but not of dwelling."[19]

Space considerations forbid us to critique directly the extinction/re-creation and immediate-resurrection positions. However, our treatment of the key passages, though unfortunately brief, will indicate the superiority of the temporary-disembodiment position vis-à-vis the other two.

Old Testament Exegesis

The main emphasis in Old Testament theology is on the functional, holistic unity of a human being. But the Old Testament depiction of this unity includes an ontological duality of immaterial-material components such that the individual human being can live after biological death in an intermediate state while awaiting the future resurrection of the body. There are two main lines of argument for this claim: an analysis of Old Testament anthropological terms and of Old Testament teaching about life after death. Let us look at these lines of argument in order.

Biblical anthropological terms exhibit a wide field of meanings, and Old Testament terms are no exception to this rule.[20] Perhaps the two most important Old Testament terms are *nephesh* (frequently translated "soul") and *ruach* (frequently translated "spirit").

The term *nephesh* occurs 754 times in the Old Testament and is used primarily of human beings, though it is also used of animals (Gen 1:20; 9:10) and of God himself (Judg 10:16; Is 1:14).[21] When the term is used of God, it certainly does not mean physical breath or life. Instead, it refers to God as an immaterial, transcendent self—a seat of mind, will, emotion, and so on (cf. Job 23:13; Amos 6:8). According to *A Hebrew and English Lexicon of the Old Testament* (by F. Brown, S. R. Driver and C. A. Briggs), the term has three basic meanings: the life principle, various figurative usages and the soul of a human that "departs at death and returns with life at the resurrection."[22]

To expand on this, in some places *nephesh* refers to a body part—for example, the mouth (Is 5:14) or the neck (Ps 105:18)—and it can even be used to refer to a dead human corpse (Num 5:2; 6:11). It sometimes refers to a desire of some sort: for example, a desire for food or sex.

On other occasions, *nephesh* refers to either life itself (Lev 17:11 KJV: "the life *[nephesh]* of the flesh is in the blood") or to a vital principle or substantial entity that makes something animated or alive (Ps 30:3 KJV: "Thou hast brought up my soul *[nephesh]* from the grave"; cf. Ps 86:13; Prov 3:22: "So shall [wisdom and discretion] be life *[hayyim]* unto thy soul *[nephesh]*"). *Nephesh* also refers to the seat of emotion, volition, moral attitudes and desire or longing for God (Deut 6:5; 21:14; Prov 21:10; Is 26:9; Mic 7:1).

Finally, there are passages in which *nephesh* refers to the continuing locus of personal identity that departs to the afterlife as the last breath ceases (Gen 35:18; cf. 1 Kings 17:21-22; Ps 16:10; 30:3; 49:15; 86:13; 139:8; Lam 1:1). Death and resurrection are regularly spoken of in terms of the departure and return of the soul. Indeed, the problem of necromancy throughout Israel's history (the practice of trying to communicate with the dead in Sheol; cf. Deut 18:9-14; 1 Sam 28:7-25) seems to presuppose the view that ancient Israel believed people continued to live conscious lives after the death of their bodies.

It is sometimes said that in these and other contexts *nephesh* is simply a term that stands proxy for the personal pronoun "I" or "me," and as such it simply refers to the person as a totality. One way of putting this objection is to claim that, frequently, the term *nephesh* is used in a figure of speech known as a synecdoche of part for whole, that is, when a part of something is used to refer to the whole (e.g., "All hands on deck!"). Thus, *nephesh* does not refer to a part of the person but to the person as a whole psychophysical unity.

In our view this claim assumes its conclusion prior to making the argument because it fails to take seriously that it is in virtue of the *nephesh*—and not the body per se—that the individual human is a living, sentient being capable of the various states of emotion, volition and so on. Thus, even if certain passages use *nephesh* to refer simply to the whole person (Ps

103:1: "Praise the LORD, O my soul *[nephesh]*"), it is the whole person as a unified center of conscious thought, action and emotion, that is, as an ensouled body to which reference is being made. Further, in cases of synecdoche of part for whole, implicit in the employment of the figure of speech is an acknowledgment of the reality of the part, even though the whole may be the intended referent of the term. When we say, "All hands on deck!" we may be referring to entire persons, but we do so by way of a part—hands—that exist and are literal constituents of the wholes of which they are parts. The same is true of the *nephesh* when it is used in a synecdoche of part for whole.

Another argument against the dualistic construal of *nephesh* has been raised by Hans Walter Wolff. Speaking of the Old Testament use of *nephesh* to refer to a principle of life that can depart or return, Wolff says, "We must not fail to observe that the nephesh is never given the meaning of an indestructible core of being, in contradistinction to the physical life, and even capable of living when cut off from that life. When there is a mention of the 'departing' (Gen. 35:18) of the nephesh from a man, or of its 'return' (Lam. 1:11), the basic idea . . . is the concrete notion of the ceasing and restoration of the breathing."[23]

Unfortunately, Wolff gives no adequate argumentation for this claim. Indeed, the clear reading of texts like Genesis 35:18 and 1 Kings 17:21-22 implies that here *nephesh* is both a substantial principle of life and a ground of consciousness and personal identity that leaves, continues to exist after biological death and can return. This seems evidently to be how *nephesh* (as the immaterial, conscious, living ground of personal identity) is used when it is employed to refer to God himself. In our view Wolff's inadequate understanding of a functionally holistic form of substance dualism—that is, an inadequate understanding of philosophical issues—is turning his exegesis into isogesis.

Moreover, when the Old Testament speaks of blood atonement to redeem the *nephesh* (Lev 16), the soul cannot merely refer to physical breath or life alone. A person's soul transcends mere physical or biological life, and thus it has a form of significant, intrinsic value that goes beyond mere physical breath or bodily functioning taken simply as a set of physical processes. Similarly, when the Old Testament contains injunctions for people to inflict their souls (Lev 16:29; 23:27), they were not being commanded to torture their physical bodies or their biological life. They were to experience grief and sorrow in their transcendent selves. Finally, the term *nephesh* is always translated *psychē* and never *bios* in the Septuagint. The term *bios* is the Greek word for mere biological or physical life, and the regular avoidance of this term by the translators of the Septuagint is best explained by their recognition that *nephesh* refers to a transcendent, irreducible aspect of living things that goes beyond mere breath or physical life.

The other key Old Testament term is *ruach,* frequently translated as "spirit." The term occurs 361 times, and the breakdown of some of the specific translations in the King James Version are as follows: the Spirit of God (105 times), angels (23 times), the spirit in humans (59 times), the wind (43 times), an attitude or emotional state (51 times), mind (6 times) and breath (14 times).[24] *A Hebrew and English Lexicon of the Old Testament* lists nine meanings for the term:

1. God's Spirit
2. angels
3. the principle of life in humans and animals
4. disembodied spirits
5. breath
6. wind
7. disposition or attitude
8. the seat of emotions
9. the seat of mind and will in humans

Definitions 1, 2 and 4 seem to have straightforward dualist implications; and definitions 3, 7, 8 and 9 do as well when we realize that if dualist arguments are successful, the principle or seat of life and consciousness is a transcendent self or immaterial ego of some sort. *Ruach* clearly overlaps with *nephesh.* However, two differences seem to characterize the terms. First, *ruach* is overwhelmingly the term of choice for God (though it is also used of animals; cf. Gen 7:22; Eccles 3:19). Second, *ruach* emphasizes the notion of power. Indeed, if there is a central thread to *ruach,* it appears to be "a unified center of unconscious (moving air) or conscious (God, angels, humans, animals) power."

Ruach often refers to the wind insofar as it is an invisible, active power standing at God's disposal (Gen 8:1; Is 7:2). In this sense, the *ruach* of

God hovers over the waters with the power to create (Gen 1:2). The term also signifies breath itself (Job 19:17) or, more frequently, a vital power that infuses something, animates it and gives it life and consciousness. In this sense the *ruach* in humans is given or formed by Yahweh (Zech 12:1); it is that which proceeds from and returns to him, and it is that which gives humans life (Job 34:14-15). In Ezekiel 37 God takes dry bones, reconstitutes human bodies of flesh, tendons, skin and so on and then adds a *ruach* to these bodies to make them living persons. Ezekiel 37 is parallel to Genesis 2:7 in which God breaths *neshama*—a virtual synonym to *ruach* that means "the breath of life"—into an already formed body. In both texts the entity God adds is that which animates and makes alive, and it is something that is added by God and is nonemergent. The *ruach* is something that can depart upon death (Ps 146:4; Eccles 12:7). There is no *ruach* in idols of wood or stone; thus they cannot arise and possess consciousness (Jer 10:14; Hab 2:19).

Ruach also refers to an independent, invisible, conscious being, as it does when describing how God employs a spirit to accomplish some purpose (1 Sam 16:14-16, 23; 2 Kings 19:7). In this sense Yahweh is called "the God of the spirits of all flesh" (Num 27:16; cf. 16:22 NASB). Here, *spirit* means an individual, conscious being distinct from the body. Moreover, *ruach* also refers to the seat of various states of consciousness, including volition (Deut 2:30; Ps 51:10-12; Jer 51:11), cognition (Is 29:24), emotion (Judg 8:3; 1 Kings 21:4) and moral or spiritual disposition (Prov 18:14; Eccles 7:8).

In light of our brief study of *nephesh* and *ruach*, it should be obvious that belief in some form of Old Testament anthropological dualism is prima facie justified. Indeed, the burden of proof is on the monist, a burden made even more difficult when we turn to a direct examination of Old Testament descriptions of the intermediate state in Sheol.

The Old Testament on life after death. The Old Testament evidently depicts individual survival after physical death, however ethereal that depiction may be, in a form that seems to be disincarnate, that is, without flesh and bones. The dead in Sheol are called *rephaim*, or shades. As with most Old Testament terms *Sheol* has a variety of meanings, including simply the grave itself. But there is no question that a major nuance of *Sheol* is a shadowy realm of all the dead (with the exception of Enoch and Elijah).

For a number of reasons Old Testament teaching about life after death is best understood in terms of a diminished though conscious form of disembodied personal survival in an intermediate state. First, life in Sheol is often depicted as lethargic, inactive and resembling an unconscious coma (Job 3:13; Ps 88:10-12; 115:17-18; Eccles 9:10; Is 38:18). However, the dead in Sheol are also described as being with family and as awake and active on occasion (Is 14:9-10). Second, the practice of necromancy (communicating with the dead) is understood as a real possibility and, on some occasions, an actuality (cf. Lev 19:31; 20:6; Deut 18:11; 1 Sam 28; Is 8:19). Third, we have already seen that the *nephesh*—a conscious person without flesh and bone—departs to God upon death (cf. Ps 49:15). Finally, the Old Testament clearly teaches the hope of resurrection beyond the grave (Job 19:25-27; Ps 73:26; Is 26:14, 19; Dan 12:2). It is possible to interpret these resurrection texts in a way that denies a conscious intermediate state, and we will look at this possibility shortly when we turn to the New Testament teaching about the intermediate state. However, it seems apparent that the most natural interpretation is to see the soul-spirit as the locus of personal identity that survives death in a less than fully desirable state and to which a resurrection body will some day be added.

John Hick has objected to the disembodied-soul view of the afterlife on the grounds that throughout primitive cultures, as well as in the Old Testament, the entity that survives in the afterlife is not an immaterial soul but rather an ethereal surviving being—a shadowy, insubstantial, counterpart to the body, a quasibodily being.[25] In response, it must be admitted that the dead in Sheol are, in fact, depicted in sense-perceptible language and that the ethereal-body view cannot be ruled out absolutely.

But for at least four reasons, we think that the ethereal-body view of the intermediate state is much weaker that the disembodied-soul view.

☐ The *nephesh* or *ruach* is viewed in Old Testament teaching as something that can depart at death, continue to exist and return; and the *nephesh* or *ruach* seems to be an immaterial, unifying locus of personal identity and ground of various mental and living functions.

☐ Throughout Scripture, sensory imagery is used in a nonliteral way to describe immaterial, invisible realities, including heaven and hell, angels and demons, and God himself. In these cases, the visual imagery is not taken literally, especially in descriptions of spirits and God. Moreover, it is possible to understand the various visitations of angels, of Moses and Elijah in the transfiguration and of the Angel of Yahweh (God himself) as either temporary embodiment or the power to manifest sense-perceptible qualities without being physical.

☐ Old Testament teaching implies that the soul or spirit is added to flesh and bones to form a living human person (Gen 2:7; Ezek 37) and that the resurrection of the dead involves the reembodiment of the same soul or spirit (Is 26:14, 19). This is more consistent with the disembodied-soul view than with the ethereal-body position.

☐ John W. Cooper has shown that intertestamental Judaism used *nephesh* and *ruach* to refer to deceased, immaterial persons in a disembodied intermediate state and that the best way to explain this usage is to see it as expanding on and clarifying ideas already contained in Old Testament teaching.[26]

In sum, the Old Testament teaches that the soul/spirit is an immaterial entity that grounds and unifies conscious, living functions; that constitutes personal identity; that can survive physical death in a diminished form in the intermediate state; and that, eventually, can be reunited with a resurrection body.

New Testament Exegesis

When we turn to the New Testament, this dualistic view of human persons becomes even more compelling. However, before we look at the New Testament, four preliminary remarks should be made.

First, we acknowledge that the New Testament does not attempt to develop a philosophical anthropology as its primary focus. It does not follow, however, that New Testament data do not provide sufficient evidence to rule out certain anthropological models (i.e., monism) and to justify others (i.e., some form of dualism). Second, we acknowledge that certain New Testament texts use *psychē* (soul) or *pneuma* (spirit) as a synecdoche of part for whole (cf. Lk 12:19). However, there are obvious texts where these terms are most naturally taken to refer to an immaterial self. And as we saw in conjunction with Old Testament synecdoches, their employment still affirms the ontological reality of the part (soul/spirit) that stands for the whole. Third, New Testament anthropological terms possess wide fields of meaning, and the precise usage of such terms should be determined on a text-by-text basis.

Fourth, in intertestamental Judaism, the intermediate state was widely understood as follows (cf. *1 Enoch* 22; 2 Esdras 7)[27]:

☐ The dead were evidently referred to as "souls" or "spirits," and these terms were widely employed to refer to disembodied persons.

☐ The dead were considered conscious and active in the intermediate state.

☐ Resurrection was depicted as the reunion of soul and body in a transformed, revivified bodily existence, though there were differences of opinion about the precise nature of the resurrection body.

☐ The Pharisees were among the groups that accepted the three points above. The Sadducees appear to be the major exception to the rule, but opinion is divided about the precise nature of their beliefs. Some interpret them as believing in anthropological monism and annihilationism; others take them to have held to Old Testament teaching about Sheol in which the dead are cut off from God and usually unconscious and inactive. These insights about intertestamental Judaism clearly place a burden of proof on anthropological monists, since New Testament teaching ought to be interpreted in terms of what the original audience would have understood unless there is evidence to the contrary.[28]

New Testament non-Pauline anthropology. Key non-Pauline New Testament passages appear to use the term *spirit* in a dualistic sense. In 1 Peter 3:18-20 we are told that when Jesus was killed, being alive in spirit he went and made proclamation to the spirits in prison who had been disobedient during the days of Noah. This text has two points of relevance for the anthropological debate.

First, we must determine to whom Jesus preached. There are three main interpretations. Some argue that this text refers to the preincarnate Christ's preaching to the wicked during the days of Noah. This interpretation is not likely, however, because it breaks with the chronological order of the passage: Jesus died (v. 18), he preached (v. 19), and he ascended to heaven (v. 22). Verse 18 contains two aorist participles ("having been put to death," "being made alive in the spirit") that present actions occurring at the same time as does the main verb ("Christ died"), so the events described occurred at the time of the crucifixion. The second and third interpretations imply that between his death and resurrection Christ preached either to disembodied spirits in the intermediate state or to imprisoned angels, respectively. The former view entails anthropological dualism, though the text is too ambiguous to allow dogmatism toward either interpretation.

The second point of relevance centers on Christ himself. Between his death and resurrection, he continued to exist as a God-man in the intermediate state independently of his earthly body. Whatever it was about Jesus that allowed him to continue to be a human, it could not be his earthly body. The most reasonable solution is that Jesus continued to have a human soul/spirit, a solution consistent with "being made alive in the spirit" (v. 18).

Hebrews 12:23 refers to deceased but existent human beings in the heavenly Jerusalem as "the spirits of righteous men made perfect." *Spirits* is used to refer to human beings either in the intermediate state or after the final resurrection. Either way, deceased human beings are described as incorporeal spirits, a description fitting the context in which the heavenly Jerusalem is contrasted with what can be touched and empirically sensed (Heb 12:18-19). When this language is used of angels, it seemingly entails the idea of an angelic person who is identical to a substantial spirit, and the same implication for human persons is most naturally seen in this text. Moreover, the verbs of Hebrews 12:18-24 are in the present tense, so it is highly probable that the verse is referring to disembodied persons in the intermediate state who await a final resurrection (cf. Heb 11:35).

Several texts refer to death as "giving up the spirit" (Mt 27:50; Lk 23:46; cf. 24:37; Jn 19:30; "giving up the soul" *[ekpsychō]* is used in Acts 5:10; 12:23). Most likely, this phrase expresses the idea of the departure of the person into the intermediate state and not simply the cessation of breathing because Jesus committed himself, not his breath, to God (Lk 23:46); because this was a standard way of referring to the disembodied dead in intertestamental Judaism; and because Luke 24:37-39 clearly uses *spirit* much like *rephaim* is used in the Old Testament, namely, as a disincarnate person without "flesh and bones" (v. 39 NRSV).

There are also key non-Pauline New Testament passages that appear to use the term *soul* in a dualistic sense. In Revelation 6:9-11, dead saints are referred to as the "souls" of the martyrs who are in the intermediate state awaiting the final resurrection (cf. Rev 20:5-6). Here the intermediate saints are depicted as conscious and alive, and they are described metaphorically with sense-perceptible imagery in a way we have already described in our discussion of Old Testament imagery of Sheol. Further, Matthew 10:28 says, "Do not be afraid of those who kill the body but cannot kill the soul. Rather, be afraid of the One who can destroy both soul and body in hell." In this text *psychē* seems to refer to something that can exist without the body. Thus *soul* and *body* cannot simply be two different terms that refer to the person as a psychosomatic unity. The most natural way to take Jesus' view here is to see it as an expression of a Jewish form of anthropological dualism.

Non-Pauline teaching on the intermediate state. A number of non-Pauline passages are most reasonably taken to affirm a disembodied intermediate state between death and final resurrection. In Jesus' debate with the Sadducees (Mt 22:23-33; Mk 12:18-27; Lk 20:27-40), Jesus specifies the time of the resurrection as a general future event in the age to come (Lk 20:35). This understanding of the resurrection was embraced by the Pharisees of that time, and as the context shows (Lk 20:39) they approved of Jesus' teaching about the intermediate state and resurrection. In John 5:28-29 and 11:23-24, Jesus also affirms that the final resurrection is a future event. Further, Jesus asserts that the patriarchs, as representatives of all people, are currently alive in the intermediate state because "to him all are alive" (Lk 20:38). Matthew 22:32 clarifies this remark and shows that it does not mean that the patriarchs were alive to God's memory, for here Jesus grounds his argument about the intermediate state in the continuous present tense of the verb that he takes to be implicit in the Old Testament text he cites: God *is*—that is, *continues to be*—their God, and thus they continue to be.

Furthermore, in the transfiguration (cf. Mt 17:1-13) Elijah (who never died) and Moses (who had died) appear with Jesus. The most natural way to interpret this text is to understand that Moses and Elijah have continued to exist—Moses was not re-created for this one event—and they have been made temporarily visible. Thus the transfiguration passage seems to imply an intermediate state; though taken alone, it does not rule out the view that persons have bodies in that state.

In the parable of Lazarus and the rich man in Luke 16:19-31, we have a description of the intermediate state in Hades (not the final resurrection in Gehenna). It is hard to know how far to press this parable and, specifically, how much to make of the bodily, visual imagery in the text. But it seems safe to conclude from it that Jesus is at least teaching the existence of conscious, living persons in the intermediate state prior to the final resurrection.

In Luke 23:42-43 Jesus promises the thief on the cross that "today you will be with me in paradise." The word *today* should be taken in its natural sense: the man would be with Jesus that very day in the intermediate state after their deaths. In intertestamental Judaism paradise was understood as the dwelling place of the faithful dead prior to the final resurrection. This text (coupled with other New Testament teaching on Christology) implies that Jesus continued to exist as a fully human person after his death and prior to his bodily resurrection. That is, he was a disembodied human soul with a full human nature united with a divine nature during the period between his death and resurrection. This would seem to imply that the thief existed in a disembodied intermediate state just as Jesus did, which is possible only if the thief was more than his body.

New Testament Pauline anthropology. When we turn to Pauline teaching, we find that several strands of evidence unite to justify the claim that he taught a dualistic anthropology. In Acts 23:6-8 Paul affirms his solidarity with the Pharisees over against the Sadducees in affirming the reality of angels, spirits and the final resurrection. When Paul refers to his acceptance of the "resurrection of the dead," he means to affirm the Pharisaic teaching of the afterlife, which included the notion of the person as a disembodied spirit awaiting the final resurrection.

Paul affirms the idea (1 Thess 5) that at the parousia of Jesus, the dead shall be resurrected and gathered prior to the gathering of those alive at that future time. This seems to teach that individual deceased believers await a future, general resurrection. Moreover, Paul's depiction of those in the intermediate state as "asleep" describes persons who, while conscious and active, are not active in an earthly, bodily way. First Thessalonians 5:10 refers to those who are "asleep" as being alive together with Christ, a description that does not allow for an extinction/re-creation view of the afterlife.

First Corinthians 15 reaffirms the general teaching of 1 Thessalonians

4:13-18: there will be a future general resurrection at the end of the age (cf. 1 Cor 15:20-24, 51-52) following a period of sleep (1 Cor 15:18, 20, 51)—a period of conscious and active, though diminished, survival in a disembodied intermediate state. Moreover, verse 35 seems to make a distinction between persons and their bodies for Paul questions which sort of body the dead have at the resurrection.

The traditional way of understanding 2 Corinthians 5:1-10 is as follows: Paul desires to live until the parousia because this would mean that he would have his earthly body immediately replaced with his resurrection body and thus that he would not have to go through an unnatural state of disembodiment in the intermediate state. Paul refers to the earthly body as the "earthly tent" (v. 1), and he describes the resurrection body as a "building from God," a phrase that cannot refer to a heavenly dwelling since it is something that can be put on (cf. vv. 2-3). Further, Paul refers to the disembodied intermediate state as a state of nakedness or of being unclothed (vv. 3-4), and he explicitly says that to be absent from the body is to be present with the Lord (v. 8), thereby affirming the real possibility of disembodiment.

The passage's previous context adds further weight to this interpretation. In 2 Corinthians 4 Paul's theme is that, given the ministry of the new covenant, we should not lose heart in the face of hardship. The progression of Paul's thought is quite important. In 2 Corinthians 4:7-11 he addresses the issue of persecution, especially bodily persecution, by claiming that one should continue to manifest the life of Jesus in one's "mortal body" (v. 11). Part of our endurance comes from our future hope of our resurrection—which he compares to Jesus' resurrection—from the value of the new covenant ministry and from the assurance that though outwardly we are decaying, inwardly we are being renewed (vv. 12-18). (In regards to Paul's comparison of our resurrection to Jesus', it should be noted that Jesus was not re-created at his resurrection; he continued to exist consciously as a God-man between the crucifixion and the resurrection, at which time he was reunited with his body, now a resurrection body.)

The natural question this raises is, what sort of hope do we have if the body itself is destroyed? In 2 Corinthians 5 Paul addresses this by teaching about the intermediate state and its relationship to the future resurrection. If this interpretation is correct, then it has obvious dualistic implications.[29] Philippians 1:21-24 provides a parallel teaching to 2 Corinthians 5: Paul contrasts living in the body with temporary disembodiment with Christ in the intermediate state.

In 2 Corinthians 12:1-4 Paul describes a visionary experience he had lived through fourteen years earlier. In verse 3 he says that he does not know whether he was still in his body during the experience or whether he was in a state of temporary disembodiment. It doesn't really matter for our argument which was correct. The simple fact that Paul allows for the possibility of his own temporary disembodiment is sufficient to show that he did not take himself to be identical with his body. It is because Paul understands himself as a soul/spirit united to a body that this was a real possibility for him.

In Romans 8:18-23 and Philippians 3:20-21 Paul seems to affirm a future general resurrection associated with the restoration of all things—a view that stands in stark contrast to an immediate personal resurrection position.

In our view, the Bible clearly teaches some form of anthropological dualism, and in the next four chapters we will spell out a version of substance dualism that we claim does the best job of accounting for the biblical data. We will try to show that our version of dualism is a reasonable inference from philosophical and commonsense things we have a right to believe about ourselves. We will argue that our version of substance dualism solves certain ethical dilemmas. We will also argue that it is consistent with, and perhaps more in line with, scientific data than the most popular current rival view when addressing those rare cases in which the findings of science are at all relevant to the formation of a model of the human constitution. In our view, Christian intellectuals have a moral and intellectual obligation to theorize about human persons in light of some version of substance dualism or at least in light of a view like substance dualism that preserves the biblical teaching cited in this chapter.

We have already given some reasons why a number of contemporary Christian thinkers regularly eschew substance dualism—for example, they (mistakenly) think it is a Greek notion eisogetically read into the Bible. However, there is one further objection against substance dualism one finds repeated over and over in the literature[30]: the belief that dualism fragments the unity of the human person and that various biblical terms like *body, soul* and *spirit* do not pick out separable faculties of human persons but rather express different ways of referring to the same holistic unity. J. K. Howard expresses this objection nicely: "In terms of biblical psychology, man does not have a 'soul,' he is one. He is a living and vital whole. It is possible to distinguish between his activities, but we cannot distinguish between the parts, for they have no independent existence."[31] In our view, this objection expresses a very simplistic view of substance dualism and a deep misunderstanding of the metaphysical issues involved, as we will make evident in the next chapter. For now, we close this chapter by asking this question: What is the proper way to approach the question of the constitutional nature of human persons?

What Is the Proper Method of Approach in Forming a Model of the Constitution of Human Persons?

Among Christian thinkers there is a widely accepted approach to the relationship between science and theology in general. This is sometimes called the *complementarity approach,* and it entails certain ideas about the nature of human persons that we find inadequate. Since we will take up the complementarity view in chapter three, our purpose here is simply to state its features that are relevant to the question of methodology. To get at these features, consider the following statement from Arthur R. Peacocke: "The aim of this work is to rethink our 'religious' conceptualizations in the light of the perspectives on the world afforded by the sciences."[32] Peacocke also writes that

> there is a strong *prima facie* case for re-examining the claimed cognitive content of Christian theology in the light of the new knowledge derivable from the sciences. . . . If such an exercise is not continually undertaken, theology will operate in a cultural ghetto quite cut off from most of those in Western cultures who have good grounds for thinking that science describes what is going on in the processes of the world at all levels. The turbulent history of the relation of science and theology bears witness to the impossibility of theology seeking a peaceful haven, protected from the sciences of its times, if it is going to be believable.[33]

For Peacocke this means that we formulate our view of human persons by starting with natural scientific descriptions of human beings—apparently because science has more cognitive authority than theology when it comes to describing what is real in the "natural" world—and that we adjust theology to come in line with science by adding theological descriptions as complementary perspectives to what natural science requires. On this view, it would be inappropriate to require science to adjust its views or limit its anthropological claims if theology seems to require it. For Peacocke this approach requires the adoption of anthropological monism and an extinction/re-creation view of the afterlife.[34]

Along similar lines, Karl Giberson claims that "science, after all, is but one limited perspective on the world, although I would argue that it is the most epistemologically secure perspective that we have."[35] Apart from the fact that Giberson's claim expresses a self-refuting form of scientism, this naive and inadequate theory of knowledge does not do justice to the variegated texture of the intellectual life. More specifically, Giberson's approach has the effect of placing theology in some upper story where it deals with meaning and significance; theology is to be accepted by an act of faith, but it is not allowed to offer a metaphysics of entities like human persons, which might carry enough epistemological authority to require certain scientific claims to be readjusted.

For thinkers such as Peacocke and Giberson the complementarity approach is a sort of default position because of the low epistemological authority of theology vis-à-vis science. On this view, prima facie, certain areas of biblical teaching or theological reflection may seem to imply propositions that run contrary to scientifically justified beliefs as in, for example, the areas of creation and evolution or theological affirmations of a substantial soul. When this happens, the area of theology should be revised so as to make it complementary to science. In this way theology retains its credibility in light of the scientific requirements of intellectual respectability even if the price to be paid is a revision of theology beyond what seems recognizable by normal exegesis of the biblical text.

In our view, when it comes to addressing the nature of human persons, science is largely incompetent either to frame the correct questions or to provide answers. The hard sciences are at their best when they describe how physical systems work, but they are largely incompetent when settling questions about the nature of consciousness, intentionality, personal identity and agency, and related matters. Recently, philosopher and scientific naturalist John Searle has argued that fifty years of focus on philosophy of mind, artificial intelligence and cognitive psychological models of consciousness have been a waste of time in a number of ways. Says Searle:

> How is it that so many philosophers and cognitive scientists can say so many things that, to me at least, seem obviously false? . . . I believe one of the unstated assumptions behind the current batch of views is that they represent the only scientifically acceptable alternatives to the antiscientism that went with traditional dualism, the belief in the immortality of the soul, spiritualism, and so on. Acceptance of the current views is motivated not so much by an independent conviction of their truth as by a terror of what are apparently the only alternatives. That is, the choice we are tacitly presented with is between a "scientific" approach, as represented by one or another of the current versions of "materialism," and an "unscientific" approach, as represented by Cartesianism or some other traditional religious conception of the mind.[36]

We do not agree with everything Searle says here, but he is correct in claiming that various disciplines studying the nature of human persons have been mired in chaos and confusion for at least a half a century. In our view, the reason for this chaos has been the assumption that science is the best way to approach the relevant questions. However, it is easy to see that this is not the case. Consider the following groups of assertions:

1a. The essence of a pain is its intrinsic, felt quality available to first-person introspection.

1b. A pain is whatever brain state realizes the correct functional role—that is, whatever is caused by certain inputs (e.g., a pin stick), causes certain other "internal" states (e.g., tendencies to feel self-pity) and causes certain bodily outputs (e.g., grimacing and shouting "Ouch!").

2a. A certain type of thought is a type of mental state with intrinsic meaning and intentionality, and it is regularly correlated with a specific type of brain state.

2b. A certain type of thought is a type of mental state with intrinsic meaning and intentionality, and it is regularly caused by a specific type of brain state.

2c. A certain type of thought is to be understood according to some physicalist perspective and, thus, is identical to something physical.

3a. A human person is a properly functioning brain that emerges when a certain level of physical complexity appears.

3b. A human person is a soul that God creates at the time of fertilization (creationism).

3c. A human person is a soul that comes to be according to certain metaphysical laws or powers at the time of fertilization (traducianism).

In each set of propositions different views are presented, and it is hard to see how science could adjudicate among the competitors.[37] One of the burdens of chapters two through six of this book will be to formulate and address a number of issues relevant to the nature of human persons. These issues are not pseudo-problems, nor are they incapable of being rationally discussed in spite of the fact that, with the exception of certain issues in chapter six, science has little to offer in their formulation and resolution. If you do not agree with this statement, we hope you will ask yourself this question as you read the chapters to come: How would natural science be able to formulate this issue and provide a resolution to it? We believe it will become obvious that science is of secondary importance to the main desiderata relevant to the nature of human persons.[38]

If the hard sciences are not the proper starting point for the formulation of an adequate ontology of the human person, how shall we proceed? We think the following four steps amount to the best approach:

Step one. Plantinga has urged Christian scholars to bring everything they know to the task of formulating an adequate Christian worldview—specifically, to bring their theological *knowledge* into the process.[39] Plantinga's suggestion expresses the idea that Christianity is a knowledge tradition; that is, its central theological claims provide us with *knowledge* of their subject matter. By way of application we should try to get clear on biblical teaching about human persons by doing careful exegesis. As a part of formulating a biblical and systematic theology of human persons, the main contours of church history should be consulted, and a burden of proof should be placed on any view that is at odds with what the majority of great thinkers have held throughout church history. We are not suggesting that the voice of church history is univocal or infallible, but in our view, the teachings of the great intellectual leaders of the past provide insights that should be taken seriously. Thus we concur with Christian philosopher Stephen T. Davis: "Respect for Christian tradition must (or so I would argue) grant great weight to views held by virtually all the fathers of the church unless there is serious reason to depart from what they say."[40] We believe that step one supports some form of substance dualism as the correct model of human persons in which the soul is an immaterial continuant that can survive in a disembodied intermediate state.

Step two. The field of philosophy is the proper discipline to play the central role in formulating, clarifying and defending the anthropology of step one. By its very nature philosophy studies precisely those issues that are central to an ontology of the human person. Moreover, as George Bealer points out, philosophers do not seek what merely happens to be the case—for example, what physical states are contingently correlated with certain states of consciousness or the "coming to be" of persons—they seek what necessarily must be the case; they employ their methods to get at the nature or essence of things like life, mind, soul, agency, personal identity and so on.[41] We recognize that philosophers do not agree about the correct model of human persons. But the main issues in debates about these models are largely philosophical in nature, an observation that becomes obvious when the details of the relevant anthropological issues are laid bare. Like it or not, philosophy is at the core of this area of study.

In employing philosophy to formulate an adequate ontology of human persons, special emphasis should be placed on scriptural teaching. We should also be guided by commonsense beliefs we inevitably hold, especially those due to our own first-person awareness of ourselves and our inner states. We ought to preserve these beliefs if possible. We agree with philosophers Joshua Hoffman and Gary S. Rosenkrantz, who say that "if entities of a certain kind belong to folk ontology [the ontological presuppositions of our commonsense conceptual scheme], then there is a *prima facie* presumption in favor of their reality. . . . Those who deny their existence assume the burden of proof."[42]

In this way, step two follows the advice of philosopher Roderick Chisholm: "I assume that, in our theoretical thinking, we should be guided by those propositions we presuppose in our ordinary activity. They are propositions we have a right to believe. Or, somewhat more exactly, they are propositions that should be regarded as innocent, epistemically, until there is positive reason for thinking them guilty."[43]

Among the propositions we have a right to believe are these:

☐ A pain is essentially something that has a certain felt texture of which I can be aware by attending to the pain.

☐ This pain I am now feeling is necessarily such that it could not have been someone else's pain, though someone else could have a pain just like this one.

☐ I can be aware of and gain knowledge about myself and my conscious states through first-person acts of attending to myself and my states.

☐ I was a teenager, I am now forty-nine years old, and I will be fifty years old next year if I live long enough.

☐ I have a personality and a body, but I could develop a different personality (and I could have had a different one than I currently possess). And even if life after death is false, I am necessarily such that disembodied existence is at least metaphysically possible for me; more generally, even if it is false, out-of-body survival is coherent and metaphysically possible.

☐ Sometimes I myself intentionally and freely raise my arm or move my body for various reasons that constitute the ends for the sake of which I act.

☐ The heart functions for the sake of pumping blood. Hearts that do not so function are dysfunctional; that is, they are not functioning the way they (irreducibly) ought to function.

Among other things, in the next five chapters we shall clarify and defend these propositions.

The combined effect of steps one and two is to provide a philosophy or theology of natural organisms, specifically, of human persons. So understood, steps one and two express the idea that philosophy and theology are properly suited to provide knowledge about the ontology of living things, including human persons—a form of knowledge that is largely (though not entirely) independent of, conceptually prior to and epistemically foundational for scientific insights about human persons.

Step three. Insights from other disciplines, including the various sciences, should be incorporated into the model where relevant. This step will be of special importance to the issues discussed in chapter six. The fact that step three places the hard sciences below philosophy in integrative importance captures the following two principles expressed by Bealer:

> I wish to recommend two theses. [1] *The autonomy of philosophy*. Among the central questions of philosophy that can be answered by one standard theoretical means or another, most can in principle be answered by philo-

sophical investigation and argument without relying substantively on the sciences. [2] *The authority of philosophy.* Insofar as science and philosophy purport to answer the same central philosophical questions, in most cases the support that science could in principle provide for those answers is not as strong as that which philosophy could in principle provide for its answers. So, should there be conflicts, the authority of philosophy in most cases can be greater in principle.[44]

Applied to integration, this approach claims that philosophy is autonomous from and more authoritative than science even in some areas that are properly within the domain of science itself (e.g., the nature of time, space, causation, consciousness, the person). More specifically, philosophy, not science, is the primary tool for getting at what is real in many areas relevant to theology, and the limited role of science in integration requires philosophical evaluation and clarification before it can be appropriated. Nowhere are these insights more appropriate than in the study of the nature of human persons. As philosopher Alvin Goldman notes:

> Philosophical accounts of mental concepts have been strongly influenced by purely philosophical concerns, especially ontological and epistemological ones. Persuaded that materialism (or physicalism) is the only tenable ontology, philosophers have deliberately fashioned their accounts of the mental with an eye to safeguarding materialism. . . . According to my view, the chief constraint on an adequate theory of our commonsense understanding of mental predicates is not that it should have desirable ontological or epistemological consequences; rather, it should be psychologically realistic. . . . Its depiction of how people represent and ascribe mental predicates must be psychologically plausible.[45]

Step four. Use ethical knowledge as a source of information for adjusting the ontological model when appropriate and relevant. We assume that Scripture and natural law (roughly, the existence of objective ethical values and truth rooted in the way things are made and knowable to humans without special revelation) provide ethical knowledge, though we do not claim that various ethical issues are always easy to resolve. But if there are some items of ethical knowledge—say, that all humans have equal and intrinsic value as such—then this knowledge can be used to help adjudicate between alternative ontologies. For example, if some model of human persons has as a natural consequence the proposition that some human persons have more intrinsic value than others, perhaps by implying that human personhood is an emergent property that can be realized to a greater or lesser degree, then this implication tends to count against the truth of that model. In a theistic universe ethics is grounded in ontology and thus can be a relevant factor in getting at what is real.

In the chapters to follow, our approach to anthropology is an expression of what Thomas V. Morris calls theological realism:

> The Judeo-Christian religious tradition is not just a domain of poetry, imagery, mystical transport, moral directive, and noncognitive, existential self-understanding. Interacting especially with the philosophically developed tradition of Christian theology, [I] join the vast majority of other leading contributors to contemporary philosophical theology in taking for granted *theological realism,* the cognitive stance presupposed by the classical theistic concern to direct our thoughts as well as our lives aright. It has been the intent of theologians throughout most of the history of the Christian faith to describe correctly, within our limits, certain important facts about God, human beings, and the rest of creation given in revelation and fundamental to the articulation of any distinctively Christian world view. In particular, reflective Christians throughout the centuries have understood their faith as providing key insights into, and resources for, the construction of a comprehensive metaphysics.[46]

In the remainder of this book we shall seek to apply a theological realist stance to the task of developing a metaphysical and ethical view of human persons that is responsive to the teachings of special revelation and to the most important information from outside special revelation relevant to the task at hand. In our view, the theological-realist stance, as expressed in our four-step methodology, differs from a widely practiced employment of the complementarity approach in at least this regard: our approach does not result in an inappropriate reinterpretation of Christian theology under the demands of an inadequate scientism, however well intentioned it may be.

[A substance is such that] (1) it has the aptitude to exist in itself
and not as a part of any other being; (2) it is the unifying center
of all the various attributes and properties that belong to it at any one moment;
(3) if the being persists as the same individual throughout a process of change,
it is the substance which is the abiding, unifying center of the being across time;
(4) it has an intrinsic dynamic orientation toward self-expressive action.[1]

W. NORRIS CLARKE

That which is a whole and has a certain shape and form is one in a still
higher degree; and especially if a thing is of this sort by nature,
and not by force like the things which are unified by glue or nails or
by being tied together, i.e., if it has in itself the cause of its continuity.

ARISTOTLE METAPHYSICS
1052a.22-25

[Property-things] are not one entity per se but many that are joined to make an
accidental unit, an entity per accidens. The sensory impression given by a
[property-thing] that is enclosed in a housing, or that is locally moveable only
as a unit by reason of its linkages, must not cloud the issue, for a [property-thing]
is no more an entity per se than the kettle and the stove.[2]

RICHARD J. CONNELL

To be alive is a systems property of a particular type of material system composed
of suitable parts arranged in a suitable pattern of interactions.
To be human is a systems property of a particular type of living material system
composed of suitable parts arranged in a suitable pattern of interactions.[3]

RICHARD H. BUBE

CHAPTER 2

Human Persons
as Substances
or Property-Things

....

W HAT DOES IT MEAN TO BE A HUMAN PERSON? IS BEING A
person the same thing as being a human? If not, how are the
two related? How does one's view about these questions
inform ethical reflection at the edges of life? Are people reducible to or
emergent upon their genetic makeup? Is this the essence of a human
person? Do genetic links or predispositions imply that humans have no
free choice or moral responsibility? Does gene therapy literally change
one's identity?

During the last decade or so, a burgeoning corpus of literature about
these issues has emerged, and while there is no clear agreement about
crucial problems in this literature, nevertheless, there is something of a
consensus among secular and many Christian thinkers that has arisen,
perhaps unconsciously and implicitly at times, regarding how to view a
cluster of crucial metaphysical themes relevant to the ethical issues just
mentioned—the nature of personhood, humanness and personal identity. To be sure, this consensus is currently confined to the scholarly
world, but it is beginning to filter down to the culture at large. For
example, philosopher and popular columnist Tibor Machan recently

wrote a widely printed commentary on abortion. Among other things, Machan argues that it is not clear that fetuses have rights—including a right to life—nor that the violation of fetal rights should be compared to the rights violations exemplified in slavery because the latter is a straightforward case of such a violation whereas the former is at best a borderline case. Machan's case rests on his view of human person-hood:

> The killing of a zygote or fetus prior to the development of the cerebral cortex, the higher or thinking portion of the brain, is arguably not a case of homicide because, just as in the case of whether one is fully human when the brain has died, it raises the issue of whether one is human if the brain has not yet been born. It has been central to our conception of what it is to be human that a human being must have the capacity to think, to form ideas, something that can only be done when the higher functions of the human brain have set in.[4]

As noted above, it is interesting to observe that a number of Christian thinkers have embraced a very similar view of human persons. Thus Christian ethicist Robert N. Wennberg affirms that "it is the maturing of the nervous system that more than anything else renders the fetal organism a unity and not a collection of cells"—a unity that is, for Wennberg, necessary for the entity in question to count as a person.[5]

As we pointed out in chapter one, philosophical clarity and, especially, careful metaphysical distinctions are crucially relevant to the task of assessing various views of human persons and the ethical positions that follow from those views. In this chapter we shall spell out some of those metaphysical distinctions, beginning with a set of general metaphysical issues and moving to a comparison and contrast of two different views of living organisms, including human persons: substances and property-things.

Before we proceed, a word of encouragement is in order. The first half of this chapter may be rough going for those with no philosophical background, and it may be difficult to see how some of the topics are relevant to the metaphysics and ethics of human persons. We assure you that these topics will surface over and over again. Moreover, given the centrality of philosophy in our four-step methodology for approaching human personhood, we must lay out the relevant philosophical distinctions to be true to our view of how these things should be tackled. However, if you get bogged down, you may wish to skip directly to the section of this chapter entitled "Substance Versus Property-Things" (pp. 78-85). Either way, you will wish to refer back to the next section frequently in reading latter chapters.

Crucial Metaphysical Distinctions Relevant to Anthropology

Properties. The first important metaphysical notion is property (attribute, characteristic, quality). A property is an existent reality, examples of which are brownness, wisdom, painfulness and triangularity. In English we often use words that end in -*ness* or -*ity* to refer to properties. Properties have a number of important features. First, a property is a universal that can be in more than one thing at the same time. Redness can be in a flag and an apple at once. Second, a property is immutable and unchanging. When a leaf goes from green to red, the *leaf* changes by losing an old property and gaining a new one. But the property of redness does not change and become the property of greenness. Properties can come and go, but they do not change in their internal constitution. Third, properties can, or perhaps must, be *had by* other things more basic than they. They are *in* the things that have them. For example, redness is in the apple. The apple has the redness. This is also put by saying that redness is exemplified by or predicated of the apple. The apple stands in the relation of predication to the universal, redness. In general, particulars have properties, and properties are had by particulars. Properties are genuine constituents of a thing. By describing a thing's properties, we are describing real features of the thing itself.[6]

There are subgroups of properties relevant to philosophical anthropology. For example, some properties are nondegreed. They either are or are not exemplified; they are either completely present or not present at all. The mathematical properties of being even or odd are nondegreed. Historically, natural kind or species properties,—for instance, being human, lioninity, oakness—have been regarded as nondegreed. Some properties are degreed in that they can be qualified by "greater than" or "less than." Such properties can be exemplified to various degrees. Being cloudy, having mass or size, or being painful, sweet or rational—these are degreed properties. Some degreed properties can be possessed to varying degrees in a quantitative way that can be mathematically measured (having mass or size). Others vary to a greater or lesser degree of qualitative intensity (being loving, being sour). By way of application, here is a question of central importance to this book: *Is human personhood a degreed or nondegreed property?*

Another important distinction among properties is the accidental-essential division. If something (say Socrates) has an accidental property (e.g., being white), then that thing can lose the property and still exist. For example, Socrates could turn brown and still exist and be Socrates. Essential properties constitute the nature or essence of a thing; and by referring to essential properties, one answers in the most basic way this question: What kind of thing is *x*? Socrates is a human kind of thing. In general, if *x* loses its essential properties, *x* ceases to exist.

Another way to get at the distinction between accidental and essential properties is through the language of *possible worlds*. A possible world is a total way things could have been, including, of course, the way things actually are. For every state of affairs, *s* (e.g., apples being red, unicorns being in Montana), a possible world *w* either includes *s* (if possible world *w* obtains or is actual, then *s* must obtain as well) or precludes *s* (if *w* obtains, then *s* cannot obtain). So a possible world is a maximal state of affairs, a total way things could be. One way to think of this is to picture God having before him a number of total alternative ways he could create a world, each alternative representing a possible world, one that is broadly logically possible in that it contains no state of affairs whose description is not self-consistent.[7] By way of application, property *P* is essential to *x* just in case *x* has *P* in every possible world in which *x* exists (there is no possible world in which *x* exists but fails to have *P*). Property *P* is accidental for *x* just in case there is a possible world in which *x* exists and fails to have *P*. An individual pain has a certain hurtful, felt qualitative texture essentially, but the role it plays in behavior is (arguably) accidental.

While we are on the subject of possible worlds, necessity and essential-accidental properties, we should point out that metaphysical necessity is different from and deeper than mere physical necessity. Something is physically necessary just in case it obtains in all possible worlds with the same laws of nature or the same features of matter. But the laws of nature or matter itself could have been different. Indeed, the existence of matter itself is contingent—God could have made worlds with no material objects at all. For example, there are possible worlds with a different law of gravity or no gravity at all. By contrast, metaphysical necessity (e.g., two is an even number; if p is taller than q and q is taller than r, then p is taller than r; or Socrates is human) refers to a type of necessity that obtains in all possible worlds whatever (e.g., two is an even number) or in all possible worlds in which a specific entity exists (e.g., Socrates is human in all possible worlds in which he exists, but since he is not a necessary being, there are possible worlds without Socrates).

When a property is exemplified by something, it forms and enters into the being of a property-instance. To understand this, suppose we have before us two exactly resembling red, round spots on a sheet of paper. Let us call these spots a and b. Each spot has the very same property, redness, in it. The redness of a is identical to the redness of b. Forgetting for a moment the other properties of a and b, there are two spots but only one property, redness. However, there is another sense in which a has its own redness different from the redness of b. After all, a's redness is where a is; and such is the case with b's redness. We can express this by saying that a and b each has its own instance of red. Let us call these red_1 and red_2, respectively. Redness is in red_1 and red_2 in that redness is the nature of each property-instance: "Redness" answers the question, what kind of thing is red_1 or red_2? Each is a red kind of thing. Now, the redness in red_1 is identical to the redness in red_2, but red_1 is not identical to red_2. In fact, if we consider spot a by itself, we can say that each discernible surface area of a has the same property, redness. But each of the variously located places of the surface of a has its own property-instance.

Relations. Relations are universals that require two or more entities (e.g., properties, particulars) in order to be exemplified.[8] Put differently, a relation is any real, discernible aspect of two or more things *taken together.* Relations obtain between or among entities. Examples are "being to the left of" between two balls or "being lighter than" between two colors. Relations are what constitute the structure of the other things that exist. There are various kinds of relations that exist: part-whole relations, causal relations, spatiotemporal relations, the laws of mathematics and logic and so on.

An important subcategory of relation draws a distinction between internal and external relations. To understand this distinction, suppose we have two entities, *a* and *b,* that are standing to each other in some relation *R.* There are two things true of internal relations as they are usually construed. First, if the *R* of *a* to *b* is internal to *a,* then anything that does not stand in *R* to *b* is not identical to *a.* If the relation "brighter than" between yellow and purple is internal to yellow, then any thing that is not brighter than purple cannot be the color yellow. Second, internal relations are not primitive; rather, they are grounded in the natures of the entities they connect. As Gustav Bergmann put it, "The ontological ground of an internal connection lies wholly 'in' the two or more entities it connects. More precisely, it lies in their natures. The notion is so crucial that I reword it. *The ontological ground of an internal connection is the natures of the entities it connects and nothing else.* Still differently, an internal connection has no ontological ground of its own."[9]

More recently, D. M. Armstrong has defined an internal relation as a relation that is logically determined by the nature of the related terms.[10] Armstrong goes on to point out that we can explain why internal relations are such that given two internally related entities a and b, there is no possible world in which the objects remain unaltered but in which the internal relation fails to obtain; we do so by recognizing that internal relations are derived from and grounded in the natures of the entities so related.[11] In fact, these internal relations are called *internal* because they actually enter into the being of—they partly constitute—the entity to which they are internal. If the relation between a heart and a living human body is internal to the heart, then at least part of what it is to be a heart is to stand in certain relations to the circulation system and, indeed, to the organism as a whole. If the heart ceases to be so related to the organism, it is no longer a heart, strictly speaking.

External relations are those that are not internal. If two entities, *a* and *b,* stand in external relations to each other, then *a* and *b* can cease to stand in that relation to one another and still exist. For example, the relation "to the left of" between a desk and lamp is external to both. The lamp can be placed on top of or to the right of the desk—indeed, the lamp can be destroyed—and the desk can still exist and be identical to itself. These relations are called *external* because they do not enter into the very being of the entities they relate in that those entities (e.g., the desk and lamp) can exist and be themselves whether or not they enter into the external relation.

Before we move on to consider the nature of events, one crucial point needs to be made in light of our treatment of relations. It is sometimes said that the world is a hierarchy of systems of parts in ascending levels of generality. More specifically, living organisms are sometimes called systems of structured parts. What is almost always left unclear about such talk is this: *In what sense are living organisms to be counted as systems? Just exactly what do we mean by "structure," and what kind of structure is it in which the parts of a living organism stand? Is the structure a unity of internal or external relations?* We will look at this issue in more detail later in the chapter.

Events. Our understanding of properties and relations puts us in a position to offer an analysis of an event.[12] Examples of events are a flash of lightning, the dropping of a ball and the having of a thought. According to a widely accepted view of events called the *property-exemplification theory,* events are temporal states or changes of states of or among particular things, especially substances. *An event is the coming, continued possession or going of a property by a particular (e.g., a substance) or among particulars at or through a particular time.* This shirt's being green now, that acorn's changing shape then—these are examples of events. This book's moving from on top of to underneath the desk is an event involving a change among particulars.

Identity and identity statements. The nature of identity is among the most important metaphysical notions in all of philosophy.[13] When philosophers talk about the problem of identity, they usually have one of these four issues in mind:

1. When x and y are contemporaneous, what is it for x to be identical to (be the same entity as) y? In general, what is it for anything to be identical to itself?

2. When x and y are noncontemporaneous, what is it for x to be identical to (be the same entity as) y? Are there continuants? Do things remain the same through change, and if so, how are we to understand what accounts for this?

3. What kind of evidence or criteria are there that enable us to know that a given x and y are identical?

4. What are the different kinds of identity statements? How are we to understand sentences containing two or more linguistic expressions that refer to the same thing?

Questions 1 and 2 are basic metaphysical questions. Question 2 focuses on sameness through change and is especially relevant for discussing the metaphysics of substance and questions about personal identity. Question 1 is the most basic metaphysical question about identity, and it will be our focus shortly. Question 3 is basically an epistemological question, not a metaphysical one. Often question 3 is confused with questions 1 and 2, as we will see in our treatment of personal identity in chapter five. Finally, question 4 is a matter of the philosophy of language. Its main concern is not identity itself but identity *statements*—linguistic expressions that assert identity. We will look at this question later in this section. Let us begin our study of identity by looking at the issue surfaced in question 1.

The general nature of identity itself. Suppose you wanted to know whether J. P. Moreland is identical to (is the same thing as) Eileen Spiek's youngest son. If "they" are identical, then, in reality, there is only one person: J. P. Moreland who *is* (identical to) Eileen Spiek's youngest son. If they are not identical, then there are two people, not one. There is a general law of identity known as *Leibniz's law of the indiscernibility of identicals:*

$$(x)(y)[(x = y) \rightarrow (P)(Px \leftrightarrow Py)]$$

Put in nonsymbolic terms this principle states that for any x (e.g., that person who is J. P. Moreland) and for any y (that person who happens to be Eileen Spiek's youngest son), if "they" are identical to each other ("they" are, in reality, the very same entity), then for any property P (being five feet, eight inches tall; being human), P will be true of x (J. P. Moreland) if and only if P is true of y (Eileen Spiek's youngest son). In general, everything is what it is and not something else. Everything is identical to itself and thus shares all properties in common with itself. This implies a test for nonidentity or difference: if we can find one thing true (or possibly true) of x not true (or possibly not true) of y or vice versa, then x is not identical to y.

We can further illustrate the nature of identity if we think about how it applies to events. If e, s, P and t refer to an event, a substance, a property and a time, respectively, then Leibniz's law of the indiscernibility of identicals, applied to events, becomes this:

$$(e_1 = e_2) \rightarrow [(s_1 = s_2) \text{ and } (P_1 = P_2) \text{ and } (t_1 = t_2)]$$

If e_1 and e_2 are identical, then the substances, properties and times constituting "those" events will be identical as well. If the substances, properties and times of the two events are not identical, then the events are different. For example, a case where s_1 is different from s_2 would be where two apples become red simultaneously; a case where P_1 is different from P_2 would be where a specific apple became red and sweet at the same time; a case where t_1 and t_2 are different would be when an apple became sweet at noon, turned sour overnight and became sweet again the next day.

A different way of formulating the law of identity gives a different insight into its nature:

$$(x)(y)[(x = y) \rightarrow \Box \, (x = y)]$$

For all x and y, if x is identical to y, then, necessarily, x is identical to y. There is no possible world where the thing that is x is not identical to the thing that is y. For instance, a cat may happen to be yellow and weigh twenty pounds, but it doesn't happen to be identical to itself. It is necessarily identical to itself. The fact that something is identical to itself is a necessary feature of everything. Suppose the person who is J. P. Moreland and the person who is Eileen Spiek's youngest son are different, but both are five feet, eight inches tall. Then in the actual world, they do not differ in height. However, if it is just possible for them to differ in height—if there is a possible world where one is five feet, eight inches tall and the other is six feet tall, then they are not identical.

Again, if disembodied existence for human persons is metaphysically possible—if there is a possible world in which a human person has disembodied existence—then a human person cannot be identical to his or her body because there is no possible world where the person's body exists in a disembodied state. Since it is possible for a person to exist disembodied but it is not possible for a body to exist disembodied, then a person is not identical to his or her body. Why? Because something is true of the person (the possibility of disembodied existence) that is not true of his or her body.

The identity relation is a relation that everything has to itself and to nothing else. This relation should be kept distinct from three other notions with which it is often confused: *cause-effect, coextensionality* and *inseparability*. If *a* causes *b*, then *a* is not identical to *b*. Fire causes smoke as its effect, but smoke is not identical to fire. Further, two things can be coextensional; that is, one obtains if and only if the other obtains. For example, the property of being triangular is coextensive with the property of being trilateral. One obtains if and only if the other obtains; no object has one without the other. But the two properties are not identical because the property of triangularity has something true of it, namely, being an angle, that is not true of the property of being trilateral.

Finally, two entities can be parts of some whole and can be inseparable from each other or that whole and yet still not be identical. For example, the individual white instance of color in a sugar cube cannot be separated from the individual square instance of shape in that cube and still exist— unlike how the leg and back of a chair can be separated from each other or from the chair taken as a whole. But the instance of whiteness in the cube is an instance of color, and the cube's instance of shape is not; thus, they are not identical. In general, property-instances are inseparable parts of the things that have them. Again, a person's emotions cannot be separated from the person or from the person's beliefs and then be placed in different locations of the room like the top and leg of a table can. But one's various emotions and beliefs are all distinct and not identical to other emotions or beliefs.

In sum, the identity-difference distinction is not the same as the cause-effect distinction, the coextensionality distinction or the insepara-ble-separable distinction. Before we look at identity statements, we should ponder some points made by the great medieval philosopher Francisco Suarez (1548-1617) in his work *On the Various Kinds of Distinctions*. Suarez discussed certain distinctions that shed light on identity and identity statements. First, he described the *real distinction*. Two entities differ by means of a real distinction just in case they can be separated and still exist. For example, the different legs of a chair bear a real distinction to each other. Independence of existence is the key here.

Second, Suarez identified the *distinction of reason*. If two things differ by means of a distinction of reason, then they are identical. For Suarez there are two kinds of distinctions of reason. One is the *distinction of reasoning reason,* which arises solely because we use the same word twice in sentences like "Peter is Peter." Here, there is no distinction that exists in reality, and merely the process of thought or language gives rise to a distinction in which the same, identical thing is named (or thought of) twice.

Another distinction of reason is the *distinction of reasoned reason*. An example would be "the red object is the sweet object" said of a red, sweet apple or "the evening star is the morning star" where each description refers to the planet Venus. When the distinction of reasoned reason is present, the objects referred to are identical (the apple or Venus), but the concepts or terms used to refer to the object (the red versus the sweet object, the evening versus the morning star) do not exhaust the object in question, and they express different nonidentical aspects (intrinsic properties of the object or relations it sustains to other things) of the same, identical object.

A third type of distinction for Suarez is the *modal distinction*. If *a* is modally distinct from *b*, then *a* could exist without *b*, but not vice versa; *b* is a mode of *a*, *b* is an inseparable aspect of *a*, and *b* is dependent upon *a*. For instance, consider the property of redness. When redness is exemplified by or had by an apple, then at least these three entities are involved: the property of redness, the apple and the having of redness by the apple. This latter entity is an instance of redness. Redness is modified by its being exemplified by the apple. Redness could exist without its being possessed by this apple, but the exemplification of redness by the apple—that is, this specific instance of redness in this specific apple—could not exist without redness. This instance of redness is not identical to but is modally distinct from redness. In chapter six, we will argue that *the body is modally distinct from the soul.*

Identity statements. The identity relation itself is independent of language users. The sun would be identical to itself if no language user would have existed. Nevertheless, we *use* identity statements to express claims of identity, so it is important to *mention* identity statements to see whether we can learn something about them and about identity itself.

The ancients noticed that one star in the evening sky was brighter than the other stars, and they called this star the "evening star," or Hesperus. They also noticed that one star in the morning sky was brighter than the other stars, and they called this star the "morning star," or Phosphorus. However, an empirical discovery was made that the "two" stars were identical and that "they" were, in fact, the planet Venus. This discovery was contingent; that is, it was dependent on what the facts turned out to be. It could have turned out that the evening star and the morning star were two different heavenly bodies. Now consider the following two statements:

(p) Hesperus is identical to Hesperus.
(q) Hesperus is identical to Phosphorus.

There are a number of ways to understand identity statements like these, but two accounts are very prominent in philosophy. The first is called the *traditional* or *objectual account*. On this view, an identity statement asserts that the thing referred to by the first term has a certain characteristic true of it, namely, that it is identical to itself.

Now, this certainly does account for much of what we say when we use identity statements. However, the philosopher Gottlob Frege (1848-1925) raised a problem with the traditional account and offered a different understanding of identity statements. Frege argued that on the traditional view, statements (p) and (q) assert the same thing—that the thing referred to by the first term (i.e., the planet Venus) is identical to itself. But this cannot be right because (p) and (q) do *not* assert the same thing. How do we know this? Statement (p) is not very informative. It tells us very little and seems to be necessarily true by definition. We know (p) is true before we make any empirical study of the heavens. However, (q) is very informative; the truth of (q) was an empirical discovery, and thus it is a contingent truth (it could have been false and its truth depended on the discovery of certain empirical facts). It is not true by definition.

Frege offered a different view of identity statements called the *metalinguistic account* (*meta* here means "about," and *metalinguistic* means "about language"). On this view, an identity statement like (p) or (q) does not merely say something about the entity Venus referred to by using the words *Hesperus* and *Phosphorus;* more importantly, it mentions the words themselves: it says something about the words *Hesperus* and *Phosphorus.* Identity statements are statements about language, and they assert that a certain relation holds between the two referring expressions used in the statement—namely, they are co-referring expressions (i.e., they each refer to the same thing).

Each account has something to be said for it, and it is beyond our purpose to weigh the strengths and weaknesses of each. However, one thing is of real importance. The identity relation itself is fairly straightforward and clear, but identity statements themselves are more ambiguous. And whenever one looks at an identity statement itself, one should try to understand just exactly what the person using that statement is trying to say. For example, when someone says, "Thank God that Beckwith is himself today," we shouldn't take this to mean that Beckwith literally was not identical to himself yesterday but that he was acting out of character yesterday.

We have looked at two different theories of identity statements. Here now is a list of three kinds of identity statements.

Meaning identity statements. These occur when the two referring expressions are synonyms. "A bachelor is an unmarried male" is an example. These can be found in the dictionary or discovered by conceptual analysis, and they are made true by our use of words. To refute one of these, you must show that one term doesn't mean or cannot be analyzed entirely into the other term.

Referential/name identity statements. These occur when two proper names (names of individuals, like *Hesperus*) or two natural kind terms (terms that name naturally occurring kinds of things like H_2O or *the lion*) stand on either side of an "is" of identity (e.g., "Hesperus is Phosphorus"). Each functions merely to tag or refer to its object of reference in every possible circumstance or world in which it could exist. Such terms are called *rigid designators.* If "Ben Franklin" is a rigid designator, it refers to the man who was Ben Franklin in every possible world in which he exists—for example, worlds where he was named "Thomas Jefferson" or where he did not invent bifocals.

Terms like *the inventor of bifocals* (called a *definite description*) refer to whatever it is that satisfies or is described by the term. Thus in our world "the inventor of bifocals" refers to Franklin; but if Jefferson and not Franklin had invented bifocals, the term would refer in that possible world to Jefferson. Nonrigid designators do not stay with the same object throughout possible worlds but refer to whatever object it is that satisfies the description.

In "blue is the color of the sky," *blue* is rigid and designates the same color in all worlds, including those with pink skies. *The color of the sky* refers to whatever color it is that is the color of the sky (blue in our world, pink in a world where God made the sky pink).

Contingent identity statements. These usually occur when an object referred to by a proper name (e.g., Ben Franklin) happens to satisfy the description expressed by the other term in the identity statement (e.g., the inventor of bifocals) or when two descriptions of something happen to be fulfilled by the same thing but could have been fulfilled by different things. Suppose Aunt Sally's favorite color is blue. Then "the color of the sky is Aunt Sally's favorite color" expresses an identity. But this identity statement, though true, is contingent. God could have made the sky green, and Aunt Sally could still favor blue; or the sky could be blue, but Aunt Sally could have preferred pink. Either way, "the color of the sky is Aunt Sally's favorite color" would be false. These kinds of identity statements can be understood as saying this: "Whatever turned out to be the color of the sky is identical to whatever turned out to be Aunt Sally's favorite color." Identity statements can be contingent, but the fact that something is identical to itself is necessary.

Before we leave the topic of identity statements, three further remarks will allow us to fill out our account of them.

1. *De re* (pronounced "day ray") means "concerning the thing"; *de dicto* (pronounced "day dictoe") means "concerning the proposition (dictum)." *Modality* expresses one of these four notions: *(i)* necessary, *(ii)* possible and actual, *(iii)* possible but not actual and *(iv)* impossible.

Modality de re refers to the way a thing possess a property (e.g., Franklin possesses humanness necessarily in the de re sense); *modality de dicto* refers to the manner or mode in which an entire proposition is true ("2 + 2 = 4" is necessary de dicto). Is "the tallest spy is a spy" a necessary truth (true in all possible worlds) or a contingent truth (true in some worlds, false in others)? If the statement is taken in the de re sense, then the subject term is referring to that thing there, Smith (who happens to be the tallest spy) and is saying of him that he necessarily has the property of being a spy. In this case, "the tallest spy is necessarily a spy" amounts to this claim: "that man there, Smith, who happens to be the tallest spy, is necessarily a spy." But this is false since Smith could have become a grocer instead of a spy, so the statement is not necessarily true; it is only contingently true. If the statement is taken in a de dicto sense, then it means "whatever turns out to be the tallest spy is a spy," and it is necessarily true.

2. True meaning-identity statements are necessary de dicto; true name-identity statements (statements with two rigid designators) are necessary de re. As we have already noted, assuming both terms refer to the same entity, contingent identity statements include cases when an object referred to by a proper name (e.g., Ben Franklin) happens to satisfy the description expressed by the other term in the identity statement (e.g., the inventor of bifocals) or when two descriptions of something happen to be fulfilled by the same thing but could have been fulfilled by different things ("the color of the sky is Aunt Sally's favorite color"). Sometimes, the main sense of contingency in these identity statements is epistemological: "Although Aunt Sally's favorite color is indeed blue, for all we know, the sky may just appear blue to us but actually be a different color, say, pink. So it is epistemologically contingent—we might be mistaken in thinking—that Aunt Sally's favorite color, blue, is the color of the sky, since for all we can tell, the latter may actually be pink."

3. There are four grades (types) of necessity. *Strict logical necessity* is a de dicto necessity and refers to the fact that some entire propositions are true necessarily (in all possible worlds) either in virtue of the form of the proposition $(p \lor \sim p)$ or the meanings of its terms (as in meaning-identity statements). *Metaphysical* or *Kripkean necessity* is a de re necessity, and it refers to the way a property is possessed by a thing (water is necessarily H_2O or has H_2O as its essence). *Physical necessity* expresses the fact that given the (contingent) physical laws of nature, certain things must happen in accordance with those laws. For example, given the law of gravity,

objects must fall to the ground, but there are possible worlds with different laws of nature where this is not the case. *Epistemological necessity* expresses the fact that it is impossible to be wrong about some judgment; *epistemological possibility* means that for all we know we could be mistaken in some judgment.

Types of Reduction

Reductionism is the view that what we take to be two individuals, properties, concepts, laws, theories, explanations and so on actually turn out to be only one. Unfortunately, *reduction* is an ambiguous term in philosophy because there are several forms of reduction, and one must be careful to use the term with enough clarity to indicate which form is in view.[14] Here is a very brief list of important varieties of reduction.

Individual ontological reduction. Individual objects of a certain type (macro-objects) are reduced to objects of another type (micro-objects). For instance, some claim that macro-objects (e.g., chairs) are nothing but swarms of atoms and molecules or that genes are identical to segments of DNA molecules. There are two versions of individual ontological reduction: strong and weak. The strong version claims that the macroparticular is strictly *identical to* a group of microentities. On this view, the macro-object is depicted as containing various constituents—separable parts, various relations among its parts and properties characterizing those constituents—that can be completely described in terms applicable to the micro level. For example, human beings would be regarded as complex physical wholes that are totally physical with no emergent mental properties.

On the weak view, the macro-object is not identical to a collection of microparts and the various microrelations among them; rather, the macro-object is entirely *constituted by* or completely *consists in* concrete particulars at the micro level. Many philosophers hold that an "is" of constitution is different from an "is" of identity. For example, a vase is constituted by clay bits but is not identical to them because if the vase is shattered, the vase ceases to exist while the collection of clay bits continue to exist. In this case, there is something true of the collection of bits that is not true of the vase (the former but not the latter continues to exist after the shattering event) therefore, the vase is not identical to but rather is constituted by the bits. On the weak view, entities at the macro level are composed entirely of micro level parts; no new particular appears at the higher level (e.g., a substantial mind) that is not simply an aggregate of lower-level entities.

For example, some claim that the only concrete particulars in the space-time world are material particles and their aggregates, but that macro-objects may have emergent or supervenient structural relations or properties that cannot be described adequately in microlevel terms. The weak version of individual ontological reduction is consistent with a rejection of property reduction; but it, along with the strong version, is usually combined with and justified by causal or theoretical reduction discussed below.

Property ontological reduction. A certain property is claimed to be identical to another property. For instance, it is allegedly the case that heat (of a gas), color and pain are identical to the mean kinetic energy of molecular movements, a wavelength and a certain type of brain state, respectively. For reasons we cannot go into here, we disagree with each of the claimed reductions just listed, but nevertheless they are the ones usually cited as examples of property ontological reduction.[15] This form of reduction is usually justified by causal or theoretical reduction.

Linguistic or definitional reduction. This is a form of reduction that relates words or concepts to other words or concepts. Here a certain word or concept is defined as or analyzed in terms of another word or concept such that statements containing the former can be translated without remainder into statements containing the latter. For example, the statement "the average family has 2.5 children" can be replaced by "take the total number of children, divide by the number of families, and you get 2.5." Some claim that "red is a color" can be reduced to "red things are colored things." This form of reduction plays a diminished role in current debates about reduction compared to its role in discussions in the first half of the twentieth century.

Causal reduction. The existence and causal activity of a reduced entity is entirely explainable in terms of the existence and causal activity of a reducing entity. For example, some claim that the solidity of macrosolids can be totally explained in terms of the vibratory movements and lattice structures of molecules at the micro level. Often a causal reduction has been used to justify individual ontological reductions in both forms and property reductions. For instance, some think that because a brain state causes a pain or a certain wavelength of light causes a specific color to be exemplified, then the brain state is identical to the pain and the light is identical to the wavelength. In general, if *a* (heat, hereditary traits) can be shown to be regularly caused by *b* (molecular agitation, DNA instead of genes on older models), then in certain circumstances, this has been taken to justify an ontological reduction of some form (heat *is* molecular motion; genes *are* or *consist in* segments of DNA).

Theoretical or explanatory reductions. This is a form of reduction in which a theory, law or concept at the macro level is reduced to and explained by a theory, law or concept at the micro level. Thus theoretical reduction is a relation between theories, laws and concepts, not primarily the entities to which those theories, laws or concepts refer. Sometimes these types of reductions are called "Nagel-type" reductions after Ernest Nagel, who clarified and made popular a certain form of theoretical reduction.[16]

To illustrate this, suppose we are interested in reducing some macrolevel theory (T_2) to a microlevel theory (T_1). With certain exceptions, this means that the laws of T_2 must be derived from those of T_1 in some way or another. Such a derivation is accomplished with the help of what are called *bridge principles*. Suppose the following is a law of T_2:

(1) $(x)(Fx \rightarrow Gx)$

Law (1) says that for any entity x, if x is F, then x is G. Now suppose we have these two bridge laws (where F and G are terms used in the macro-theory T_2, and F^* and G^* are the associated terms in microtheory T_1):

(2a) $Fx \leftrightarrow F^* x$
(2b) $Gx \leftrightarrow G^* x$

Bridge principles are materially equivalent, coordinating principles that relate terms in the two theories. They claim that whenever F or G applies to something, then F^* and G^* also apply, respectively, and vice versa.

Given (2a) and (2b) and our law (1) of T_2, we can reduce (1) to (3):

(3) $(x)(F^* \, x \rightarrow G^* \, x)$

Note that (3) is a law of our microtheory T_1. Note also that the two bridge laws only coordinate the relevant T_2 and T_1 terms F and F^*, G and G^*. They do not identify the properties expressed by, say, F and F^*, nor do they say that something with F causes something to have F^*. But if terms in the two theories can be given one-to-one bridge coordinations, then some reductionists claim that this justifies the reduction of the macrotheory to the microtheory. On this view, we can explain macrophenomena by microphenomena, and this in turn justifies an ontological reduction of the entities referred to by F and G to the entities referred to by F^* and G^*.

However, it seems false that explanatory reductions of this sort can be used by themselves to justify ontological reductions. Why? Because in cases like these, the reduced theory or law (e.g., $[x][Fx \rightarrow Gx]$) is replaced by the reducing theory (e.g., $[x][F^* \, x \rightarrow G^* \, x]$) *plus* bridge laws (e.g., $Fx \leftrightarrow F^* \, x$ and $Gx \leftrightarrow G^* \, x$). No advance in ontological reduction has been made because the bridge laws still contain terms *(F* and *G)* that refer to the undesired entities, and the bridge laws themselves do not justify identifying those entities *(F* and *G)* with the so-called reducing ones *(F** and *G*).*

The classic example of this sort of reduction is the reduction of classic thermodynamics to statistical mechanics. Consider ideal gas theory. Classically, thermodynamics deals with temperature, heat and entropy and their relations to various macrolevel gas phenomena such as temperature, volume and pressure. For example, if P, V and T refer to the pressure, volume and temperature of a gas, Boyles's law says that at constant temperature, PV = a constant; Charles's law says that at constant pressure, V/T = a constant; and the ideal gas equation for one mole of a gas says that PV = RT (where R is a constant). Note that these laws are part of a macrolevel theory of thermodynamics because they focus on large-scale, observable features of a gas.

Mechanics deals with energy and forces and their effects on bodies. If we assume that a gas is a swarm of point particles that engage in elastic collisions, then both sciences (thermodynamics and mechanics) use some of the same concepts (pressure, volume, mass), but thermodynamics uses certain terms (temperature, entropy, heat) not employed in mechanics. If we assume a certain bridge principle that relates the macrophenomenon of pressure, P, in thermodynamics to the number of times per second that gas particles strike some surface area of the container walls, and if the frequency of striking the walls is a function of the velocity of the gas particles, then we have a bridge principle that coordinates the macrofeature pressure with a microfeature of individual gas molecules (velocity, or more exactly, kinetic energy, $\frac{1}{2}mv^2$, where m is mass and v is velocity).

The details of the derivation need not concern us here, but suffice it to say that if we properly replace pressure with mean kinetic energy in the gas equations above, we can derive another bridge principle relating temperature (a macrolevel phenomenon) to mean kinetic energy (a microphenomenon), and we can reduce the thermodynamic theory with its laws employing temperature to a mechanical theory with laws employing mean kinetic theory. Note carefully, that *all this proves is that every time a gas is in such and such a temperature state, its molecules or atoms will have thus and so mean kinetic energy coordinated with that temperature*. But some reductionists take the theoretical reduction to justify an ontological property reduction in which we *identify* temperature with mean kinetic energy.

Parts and Wholes

Mereology is the study of parts, wholes and part-whole relations.[17] The term is derived from the Greek word *meros,* which means "part." Consider a pot made of clay pieces. If the pot were annihilated, its properties—being brown, round and so on—would continue to exist, but its parts would pass out of existence along with the pot. Properties are universals; parts are particulars that are constituents of wholes. There are various types of parts and part-whole relations. For example, a pot has physical parts that are spatially located at different places. A long event (say, a baseball game) has a series of temporal parts (e.g., each inning) that are temporally located at different moments. A major subcategorical division among parts is the distinction between separable and inseparable parts. A separable part is one that can exist when separated from the whole of which it is a part. An inseparable part is one that cannot exist independently of the whole of which it is a part. An entity is simple just in case it has no internal differentiation within it.

In order to illustrate and apply this distinction, consider the following. A simple entity is fundamental and basic. It is not composed of more basic properties or parts. It does not contain further divisions within it. In our view, the soul is a substance (a category to be discussed below). However, the soul is not simple but complex. To be sure, the soul's complexity is not like that of a material object—say, a table. A table is a complex unity that is extended in space and whose parts (the left leg, the right leg) occupy different spatial locations. Further, one can destroy the table by breaking it up, and its parts can still survive. They are separable parts, capable of existing on their own independently of the whole table itself or of the other parts of the table. For example, if the table is disassembled, each leg will still exist and can be put by itself in different places in the garage.

The soul has a different type of complexity. The soul is a primitive (nonemergent) unity of parts, properties and capacities. The soul is diffused throughout the body and can enter into complex cause-effect interactions with that body. Our vast array of intellectual, emotional and volitional capacities differ from each other, and the soul is a primitive unity of this complex array of internal differentiations. Of course, the soul is not a mere heap of separable parts. One's sensory abilities cannot survive the soul's destruction, nor can they be separated from one's intellectual abilities and put in different places in the garage. The various faculties of the soul are inseparable parts of the soul. So while the soul's unity is different and, in fact, deeper than that of a table, the soul is still a complex unity and not a simple entity.

Mereological essentialism is the notion that a whole has each of its parts necessarily: that is, a whole cannot lose parts or gain new ones and still be the very same object. More generally, no object could have parts other than the ones it actually has. Mereological essentialism is most plausible for mere chunks of matter or artifacts, but it is most likely false when applied to living organisms. Accounting for this difference is one of the benefits of drawing a distinction between substances and property-things to which we now turn.

Substances and property-things. The English term *substance* has many different meanings associated with it.[18] Likewise, there have been different uses of the term in the history of philosophy. However, the most central idea of substance in the history of metaphysics is one that takes living organisms as the paradigm cases. In this section we will examine the traditional notion of substance and compare a substance with a property-thing. In order to understand what follows, let us consider an individual brown adult dog, Fido. A doctrine of substance should explain what appear to be things we know about Fido, and the traditional notion of substance does just that.

The Traditional View of Substance

The traditional view of substance is the one held by Aristotle and Thomas Aquinas.[19] There are seven things apparently true of Fido, and these seven features form the core of the traditional position.[20]

Basic ownership of properties.[21] Properties do not show up in the world all by themselves. You do not, for example, find brownness sitting on a bookshelf all by itself. Properties have owners, and a substance owns properties. Substances have properties that are "in" them; properties are had by the substances that possess them. Fido has brownness, a certain shape, the property of weighing twenty-five pounds and so on. These properties are present in Fido. In this sense substances are more basic than properties. It makes sense to ask of a property, What has that property? But it does not make sense to ask of a substance (e.g., Fido), What has that substance? Properties are *in* or *predicated of* substances, but substances are *basic* in that they are not in or had by things more basic than they. Substances do the having; properties are had. The etymology of the word *substance* (*sub* means "under," *stance* means "stand," *substance* means "to stand under") brings out this aspect of substance as that which stands under (accidental) properties as their owner.

Unity and wholeness at a time.[22] A substance like Fido is a whole and, as such, is a primitive (nonemergent) unity of properties, parts and capacities. First, a substance is a primitive unity of properties. Properties come together in groups, not individually: for instance, brownness, weighing twenty-five pounds and having a certain shape are three different properties that form a unity in Fido. Moreover, the brownness is united to the shape of Fido in a way that the redness of a nearby apple is not united to Fido's shape. This would be true even if the apple were inside Fido's mouth and, thus, if the redness of the apple were spatially closer to parts of Fido—for example, his nose—than was the brownness of his tail. Finally, Fido is a deeper unity of properties than, say, a heap of salt is. Such a heap would be a unity of whiteness and the heap's shape. But such a whole, though a true unity of these properties, is not as deep a unity as is Fido. In fact, the heap's unity is derived from or emergent upon a collection of previously existing parts brought together in certain ways. Fido's properties are much more intimately related to each other than are the properties in lesser unities like heaps of parts. The unity of properties (parts, capacities) found in Fido is primitive—that is, it is an unanalyzable or irreducible fact about Fido and the kind of thing he is.

These facts about the unity of properties are called the *adherence* of properties. Properties adhere together in substances: they are united together. What explains this fact? The traditional view says that adherence is explained by *inherence*. All of Fido's properties are united because they all are owned by (or inhere in) the same substance that stands under them.

A substance is also a primitive unity of inseparable parts. Fido's nose, eyes, heart and legs are parts that form a unified whole. The parts of a substance are united in such a way that the whole is ontologically prior to its parts in this sense: the unity of a substance is basic and primitive, it is not derived after its parts come together, and the parts of a substance are what they are in virtue of the role they play in the substance as a whole. Thus, the identity of a substance's parts presupposes the substance as a whole, and those parts are internally related to that whole. The chamber of a heart is what it is in virtue of the role it plays in the heart as a whole; a heart is what it is in virtue of the role it plays in the circulation system as a whole; the circulation system is what it is in virtue of the role it plays in the organism as a whole. Moreover, when the parts of a substance are removed, they change. As Aristotle said, a severed human hand is no longer human because it is no longer a part of the substance that gave it its identity. The severed hand is merely a heap of atoms and other parts, which will become evident in a few weeks. It has lost its unity and identity.

Finally, a substance is a primitive unity of capacities (potentialities, dispositions, tendencies). There is a distinction between *(a)* some *x* is *F* but can be *G* and *(b)* some *x* is *F* but cannot be *G*. For example, salt is solid but can be dissolved in water; a diamond is solid but cannot be dissolved in water. Counterfactual statements are true of substances. A counterfactual statement is a claim that says what would be the case if, contrary to fact, such and such were to happen. For example, if an acorn were to be put in the soil (even though it is now in a jar), then it would sprout a root. Such counterfactuals are explained by saying that a substance has a set of capacities that are real even though they are not actualized. These real capacities serve as metaphysical grounds for true counterfactual statements. They also place limitations on what counterfactuals can be truly ascribed to a substance. The acorn has the capacity to sprout a root even though it is in a jar. But if the acorn were placed in soil, it would not grow a tail and start barking because no such capacities are embedded in the essence of the acorn.

Capacities come in natural groupings and in hierarchies. For instance, a human has various capacities to believe and think certain things, various capacities to feel certain things and various capacities to choose certain things. These different capacities form natural groupings in an individual substance (e.g., a particular human being) that can be called intellectual, emotional and volitional faculties. Psychologists, doctors, biologists and others study the groupings and interconnections among the capacities of various types of substances—of birds, plants and so on.

Capacities also come in hierarchies. There are first-order capacities, second-order capacities to have these first-order capacities and so on, until ultimate capacities are reached. For example, if Sue can speak English but not Russian, then she has the first-order capacity for English as well as the second-order capacity to have this first-order capacity (which she has already developed). Sue also has the second-order capacity to have the capacity to speak Russian, but she lacks the first-order capacity to do so.

Higher-order capacities are realized by the development of lower-order capacities under them. An acorn has the ultimate capacity to draw nourishment from the soil, but this can be actualized and unfolded only by developing the lower capacity to have a root system, then by developing the still lower capacities *of* the root system, and so on. When a substance has a defect (e.g., a child is colorblind), it does not lose its ultimate capacities. Rather, it lacks some lower-order capacity it needs for the ultimate capacity to be developed.

A substance's capacities culminate in a set of its ultimate capacities that are possessed by it solely in virtue of the substance belonging to its natural kind: for example, Smith's ultimate capacities are his because he belongs to the *natural kind* "being human." A substance's *inner nature* or *essence* includes its ordered structural unity of ultimate capacities. A substance cannot change in its ultimate capacities; that is, it cannot lose its nature and continue to exist. Smith may replace his skin color from exposure to the sun and still exist, but if he loses his humanness— his inner nature of ultimate capacities that constitutes being human—then Smith ceases to exist.

In sum, a substance is a primitive unity of properties, parts and capacities. Moreover, the type of unity in a substance is to be explained by seeing the substance as a whole that is metaphysically prior to its parts in that the parts get their identity by the role they play in the substance as a whole.

Identity and absolute sameness through change.[23] A substance is a continuant that remains the same through change. Change presupposes sameness. If some x (a dog) goes from being F (being brown) to being G (being yellow), then the very same x (the dog itself) must be present at the beginning, during and at the end of the change. *It* changes. A substance regularly loses old parts, properties and lower-order capacities and gains new ones. But the substance itself underlies this change and remains the same through it. A substance like a living organism can undergo mereological change (loss of old parts, part replacement, gain of new parts) because it is not simply a system of physical parts that stand to each other in various external, physical (e.g., causal) relations. Rather, a living organism has an internal, immaterial entity—in our view, its individual essence or soul—that is fully "present" at each part, that has those parts, that underlies change and that controls and regulates the types of and limitations upon part substitution and replacement according to the potentialities immanent within that individual essence.

A long event like a baseball game has temporal parts and, in fact, is the sum of its temporal parts. A baseball game is a sum or totality of nine innings, and each inning is a temporal part of the game. Because the game is a temporally extended entity with temporal parts, the game does not move *through* time—for instance, the whole game does not exist in the first inning. Each inning is a temporal slice or stage of the game. By contrast, substances do not have temporal parts. Substances move *through* their histories: for example, Fido is fully present at every moment of his life. Fido is not a sum of individual "dog stages" like a baseball game is a sum of "game stages" (innings).

Law and lawlike change.[24] As a substance like an acorn grows, it changes through time. These changes are lawlike; that is, each new stage of development and growth comes to be and replaces older stages in repeatable, nonrandom, lawlike ways. These lawlike changes are grounded in a substance's inner nature which in this context can be understood as a dynamic principle of activity or change immanent within the individual substance. Change involves the actualization of potentialities contained in the essence of the substance. The acorn changes in specific ways because of the dynamic inherent tendencies latent within its nature as an oak. Each natural kind of thing will have its own type of lawlike changes that are normative for members of that kind. These changes are grounded in the nature of the substances of that kind, and they are irreducible to the laws of chemistry and physics, though they employ chemical or physical processes as means for the realization of their own species-specific order of development according to the functional specifications contained in the substance's essence.

Moreover, this inner nature sets limits to change. If a substance breaks these limits, we say that the substance no longer exists. For instance, as a caterpillar changes into an adult butterfly, the organism's inner nature specifies the precise sequence of stages the organism can undergo in the process of growth. If the organism goes beyond the boundaries of such a change—say if the caterpillar turned into a fish—we would not say that the caterpillar still exists as a fish; rather, we would say that the caterpillar ceased to be and a fish came to be. Thus, the lawlike changes that make up a substance's nature (1) specify the ordered sequence of change that will occur in the process of maturation and (2) set limits to the kind of change a thing can undergo and still exist and be counted as an example of its kind.

The unity of the natural kind itself.[25] The unity of a natural class of things, say the class of red objects, is best explained by saying that each member (and only members) of the class has the very same property in it—in this case, redness. This property explains the unity of the class, why certain objects (a fire truck) belong in the class and why other objects (a banana) do not.

The same point can be make regarding substances. Substances fall into natural classes called natural kinds (e.g., the class of dogs, humans and so forth). This can be explained by saying that each member of a natural kind has the very same essence in it.[26] All humans have humanness, and that explains the unity of the class of humans, why certain things (Smith) belong in that class and why other things (Fido) do not. In this sense, a thing's membership in its natural kind is grounded in its essence (nature, "whatness," secondary substance). The essence is the set of properties the thing possesses such that it must have this set to be a member of the kind and that if it loses any of its essential properties, it ceases to exist.

Final causality.[27] The traditional doctrine of substance contrasts efficient, material, formal and final causes. An efficient cause is that by means of which an effect takes place. The efficient cause brings the effect about. For example, when one ball hits and moves another, the first ball is an efficient cause. A material cause is the matter or "stuff" of which something is made. A formal cause is the essence or whatness of a thing (the humanness of Smith). A final cause is that for the sake of which an effect or change is produced.

Many advocates of the traditional view hold that an individual substance has, within its nature (formal cause), an innate, immanent tendency (final cause) to realize fully that nature. An acorn changes "in order to" realize a mature oak nature; a fetus grows with the end in view of actualizing its human nature. When a part or process of a living thing functions naturally, it functions the way it *ought* to function, that is, in the way appropriately specified by its nature.

Today, the doctrine of final causality is often rejected because it does not harmonize with evolutionary naturalism. For example, Joshua Hoffman and Gary S. Rosenkrantz claim that

> Aristotle's account [of natural function and teleology] does *not* provide a
> naturalistic reduction of natural function in terms of efficient causation.

Nor do characterizations of natural function in terms of an irreducibly emergent purposive principle, or an unanalyzable emergent property associated with the biological phenomenon of life, provide such a reduction. Theistic and vitalistic approaches that try to explicate natural function in terms of the intentions of an intelligent purposive agent or principle are also nonnaturalistic. Another form of nonnaturalism attempts to explicate natural function in terms of nonnatural evaluative attributes such as intrinsic goodness. . . . We do not accept the anti-reductionist and anti-naturalistic theories about natural function listed above. Without entering into a detailed critique of these ideas, one can see that they either posit immaterial entities whose existence is in doubt, or make it utterly mysterious how it can be true that a part of an organic living thing manifests a natural function. . . . The theoretical unity of biology would be better served if the natural functions of the parts of organic life-forms could be given a reductive account completely in terms of nonpurposive or nonfunctional naturalistic processes or conditions.[28]

Accordingly, modern scientific descriptions of living organisms and their development offer reductive accounts of teleology and natural function that usually go something like this:

(1) The function of x is z.
(2) x does a in order to z.

So stated, (1) and (2) make reference to teleology and natural function, and this is as it should be according to the substance position. On the substance view we embrace, the function of the heart is to pump blood. The heart moves in such and such way *in order to* pump blood. Note that a heart is internally related to the other parts of the circulation system (a heart is whatever functions to pump blood in this system), and thus the whole system (and, eventually, the whole organism) grounds and defines the heart. Further, the heart does what it does in order to reach some end. Now a popular natural reductive account reduces (1) and (2) to something like this:

(3) x was a cause of z in the past, and its having been a cause of z in the past causes x to be there now.
(3′) x has the function of doing z if and only if item x is now present as a result of causing z.

(3) and (3′) say the same thing, and they are examples of what is called the *aetiological account* of teleological notions like design, purpose and function. For example, the heart *(x)* was a cause of pumping blood *(z)* in the past, and its having been a cause of pumping blood *(z)* in the past causes the heart *(x)* to be there now. This account gets rid of genuine function and teleology and replaces them with an evolutionary account of the existence of body parts and activities along with a reduction of final causality (that for the sake of which something happens) to efficient causality (that because of which something happens).

The problem of individuation. There is a final issue regarding substances called the problem of individuation: given that two things have exactly the same properties, how is it that the two are not the same thing? What differentiates them and makes them two individuals? Consider two spots that share all their properties in common: for instance, both have the same color, size and shape.[29] If properties are universals (a universal is something that can literally be present in more than one thing at the same time or in the same thing at more than one time), what then is it that makes them two spots instead of just one? You may be tempted to say that the spots are different because of their different spatial locations on a sheet of paper. But clearly, this won't do. Why? Because two spots cannot be *at* different locations if, metaphysically speaking, they are not already different spots. Difference of spatial location presupposes individuation and, thus, cannot constitute individuation.

The same problem of individuation arises with individual substances. If Smith and Jones have the very same human nature, then how are they different? What makes them two humans instead of one? Several answers have been offered to this question, and we cannot survey them here. Suffice it to say that there must be something in an individual substance besides its nature that individuates it. What ever that something is, it can be called a substance's "thisness." Thus, an individual substance like Smith is sometimes called a "this-such." By claiming that Smith is a "such," a philosopher means that Smith possesses a universal nature, shared by all members of Smith's natural kind "being human," and that this nature answers the deep question, what kind of thing must Smith be to exist at all? By claiming that Smith is a "this," a philosopher means that Smith is also an individual different from other members of his kind. Thus an individual substance is a this-such; it is a combination of two metaphysical entities: a universal nature related by predication to an individuating component.[30]

Substances Versus Property-Things

In chapter three we will look at a number of reasons why almost all philosophical naturalists and Christian complementarians deny that living things are substances. The clear trend is to depict living organisms as property-things—ordered aggregates or systems of externally related parts.

The world around us contains a number of different kinds of wholes with parts. Different types of wholes manifest different kinds and degrees of unity. Here are three examples that go from lesser to greater unity: a heap of salt, a car, a living organism. A heap is a weak kind of unity. It contains parts that are merely united in that those parts are spatially close to each other. A heap can have either homogeneous or heterogenous parts. A pile of salt is a heap with homogeneous parts: all the parts (e.g., the grains of salt) are the same as each other. A pile of junk could be a heap with heterogeneous parts.

An artifact is a classic example of a deeper type of unity found in wholes called *property-things, ordered aggregates* or *structured stuff*. For example, the parts of a car are not merely united by spatial proximity; they also have a mechanical unity. Their parts move and causally interact with each other according to a design in the mind of the designer of the car. Strictly speaking, the parts of a property-thing do not really act functionally or teleologically, since there is no source of functional motion within the property-thing. Rather, a property-thing is a passive medium through which energy passes and whose parts enter into efficient causal chains. The parts move to accomplish a function that stays in the designer's mind and that, strictly speaking, is not part of the being of the property-thing. While property-things have a deeper type of unity than a mere heap, property-things have different, lesser kinds of unities than true substances. The following chart brings out the difference between property-things and substances.

Area of comparison	Property-thing	Substance
Basic ownership of properties	Wholes have no new properties not in parts except new utility for human purpose and new shape, dimension and spatial order.	Wholes are independent, basic owners or unifiers of distinctive properties grounded in the essence of the substance as a whole unit.
Unity at a time	(1) Derives its unity from an external principle in mind of designer artificially imposed from the outside on a set of parts to form the object (2) Parts are metaphysically prior to whole, are related by external relations and sustain identity inside or outside whole. Composed of separable parts	(1) Derives its unity from its own internal essence that serves as a principle of unity from within (2) Whole is metaphysically prior to parts. Parts are internally related to whole and lose identity when severed from the whole. Creates inseparable parts according to its essence
Sameness through change	A perduring mereological compound: no absolute sameness and strict identity through part replacement, loss, gain	An enduring continuant: maintains absolute sameness and strict identity through accidental change
Lawlike change	Bottom-up development determined by/complementarity to laws of chemistry and physics	Species-specific, irreducible, top-down process of change controlled by essence and employing chemical and physical processes as means
Unity of class membership	Artificial unity that resides in surface features of the whole or in functional intentions of designer totally outside the whole	Natural unity that resides in identical essence in each whole that grounds membership in natural kind
Teleology and function	Nonteleological efficient causality, (1) "functions" solely in designer's mind (artifacts) or (2) statistical averages or whatever contributes to evolutionary survival (organisms)	Irreducible teleology and normative functioning grounded in the essence of the substance
Individuation	Grounded in separable parts	Grounded in metaphysical individuator linked by predication to an essence to form the individual substance

In order to understand the main differences between a substance and a property-thing, a few comments should be made on the points contained in the chart as they apply to examples of each category.

Basic ownership of properties. Those property-things that are artifacts have no new kinds of properties not already resident in their parts. An artifactual property-thing merely provides a structure through which an already existing natural agency can channel energy to produce an effect that can be interpreted in a new way. For example, a clock has no new *kinds* of properties not resident in its parts. It does have a different set of spatial properties—a new shape and dimension—but these are not new *kinds* of properties not already in the parts of the clock. Instead, they are different spatial properties due to a new arrangement of the spatial properties already resident within the clock's parts prior to assembly.

Further, the wound spring of the clock serves as a natural agency, a natural source of energy, that the structure of the clock (its gears and so on) can channel in a new way not possible if the spring did not have the clock's structure to serve as a medium for directing that energy. This allows an effect to be produced—the moving of the clock's hands—that is new. But the newness of this effect is not due to the clock's possessing a new kind of property not present in the parts of the clock prior to assembly. Rather, this new effect can be understood as (1) a new geometrical motion (e.g., circular motion of the hands), which is the same kind of property possible for a wound spring without being in a clock (i.e., it could produce a different noncircular geometrical motion, but the motion would still be geometrical) and (2) an effect that can be externally interpreted in a new way according to an artificial convention (e.g., we interpret this circular motion as "telling time," yet this is not really a property of the clock's hands but rather a conventional way of viewing the motion of the hands from a system outside the clock).

By contrast, a substance has new properties true of it as a whole not true of its parts prior to their incorporation into their substances. These new properties are founded in the nature of the substance (doghood for Fido). For living organisms these new properties would include things like specific kinds of reproduction, assimilation, growth and so forth. These new properties cannot be accounted for solely by the laws of chemistry and physics, and they are due, in part, to the new nature governing the substance taken as a whole.

In the next chapter we will look at the topic of emergent or super-venient properties. For now, we should point out that many advocates of a property-thing view of living organisms claim that they have new emergent properties. Clearly, living organisms do have new, distinctive properties not exemplified by mere chemical or physical entities taken in isolation from those organisms. The real question is this: *Does the property-thing view have the intellectual resources to explain (a) the fact of such emergence and (b) the precise type of internal unity of parts, properties and capacities characteristic of living organisms?* We believe the answer to this question is no, and we will try to support our answer in the next few chapters.

Unity at a time. Property-things are not natural, primitive unities but are, rather, accidental (nonessential) combinations of an ordering relational property (e.g., the structure of the table) artificially and externally imposed upon preexistent materials (e.g., the wood). The unity of a property-thing does not spring from or reside within its own being; instead, it resides in the plan contained in the mind of the designer of the property-thing. Here, a designer assembles an arrangement of parts and uses a principle of unity in her mind to impose externally a structural order from the outside onto a set of parts to form the object in question. The unity of a watch does not spring from within the parts of the watch or from within the watch taken as a whole; it resides merely in the designer's mind.

By contrast, the unity of a substance springs from and resides within the substance and is due to the internal essence or nature of the substance that serves as its principle of unification. The parts and properties of a dog or human are due to the essence within it.

Further, for a property-thing the parts exist prior to the whole, not only temporally (i.e., the clock's parts were on the desk before the clock was assembled) but metaphysically. The parts of a clock exist and are what they are independently of their incorporation into the clock as a whole. A table leg, watch spring and automobile tire are what they are prior to their incorporation into their wholes. These parts are identified by the stuff that composes them—structured wood for a table leg, wound iron for a clock spring. In fact, the wholes depend upon those parts for their overall structure.

For substances, however, the order is reversed. The substance as a whole is prior to its parts in this sense: its parts are gathered and formed by the direction of the substance and its essence taken as a whole, and those parts receive their identity by virtue of their incorporation into the substance as a whole. For example, a specific chamber of the heart is what it is not by virtue of the stuff that composes it (as with parts of a property-thing) but due to the role the chamber plays in the heart taken as a whole (e.g., a chamber is that which functions to open and close in a precise way due to the nature of the heart as a whole). And a heart is what it is in virtue of the functional role it plays in the circulation system taken as a whole. Finally, the circulation system (and other systems) gains its identity by the role it plays in the organism as a whole. Thus the whole organism is prior to its parts in that the whole has a principle of unity within it that gives identity to its parts.

These insights lead to a crucial distinction between the structures of a substance and a property-thing: *the internal structure of a substance is a set of internal relations, and the structure of a property-thing is a set of external relations.* The parts of a property-thing are related to each other by means of external relations. This means that the relations do not enter into the very nature of those parts and that the parts are "indifferent" to the relations. For instance, the spring and gears of a clock are related to each other by various mechanical and spatial relations. But these relations do not make the parts what they are. In fact, the spring is "indifferent" to the other parts of the clock or to the clock taken as a whole. That is, the spring is the same as itself whether inside or outside the clock. Again, a table leg can change its relations with other parts of a table, by being removed and placed in another room, but this does not affect the identity of the leg.

By contrast, the parts of a substance are related to each other or to the whole by means of internal relations. This means that the parts are what they are by virtue of the relations they sustain to other parts or, perhaps, to the substance as a whole. If the parts drop out of those relations, the parts lose their identity. If a heart or a hand is severed from an individual human, it ceases to be a heart or a hand: it loses its principle of unity (which will become evident over time as it decays), and it becomes a property-thing. The parts of a substance are not "indifferent" to their incorporation in a substance. They gain their identity from the substance of which they are parts, and they lose their identity when outside those substances.

Sameness through change. Because of space considerations we can only assert, without much defense or detail, that when a property-thing undergoes a change by losing old parts and gaining new ones, it does not really remain the same entity. If the parts of a clock were gradually replaced by a new set of parts, the clock would literally be a different clock. Property-things are mereological compounds, systems constituted by separable parts standing in external relations. Mereological essentialism would seem to be true of property-things: the separable parts of a property-thing are essential to its identity, and if it gains new parts, loses old ones or undergoes part replacement, then, strictly speaking, there is a new whole that exists.

Lawlike change. The developmental changes of a growing substance are grounded in the nature of the substances of that kind, and they are irreducible to the laws of chemistry and physics, though they employ chemical or physical processes as means for the realization of their own species-specific order of development according to the functional specifications contained in the substance's essence. Because living organisms construed as property-things are systems of separable chemical and physical parts, the most natural way to understand their growth and development is in terms of bottom-up causation, that is, solely in terms of the chemical and physical laws and interactions of the separable parts. Indeed, some evolutionary advocates of this view of living things claim that genes make bodies during morphogenesis in order to give them a competitive edge in the struggle for survival: a chicken is a gene's way of making another gene. We will look more deeply into this issue in the next chapter, but many advocates of the property-thing position allow for top-down causal feedback from the whole back to its parts. The question is not whether this does, in fact, occur, because it surely does. *The real question is whether a consistent property-thing view, especially as that view is employed by complementarians (see chapter three) has the resources to allow for top-down causal feedback, especially in comparison with the substance position as a rival viewpoint.*

Unity of class membership. Property-things require two metaphysical categories to classify them. For example, a table is structured wood. Wood is included in the category of "stuff" and is a kind of material.[31] The structure of the table is a set of ordering relations, in this case spatial relations of shape, size and volume. When it comes to artifacts, the unity of a class is most likely the function or use of the artifacts in question: for instance, tables are all and only items upon which we eat and so forth. The function or use is not part of the being of the artifact in question but, rather, is in the minds of the people who use the artifacts in the required way.

If living things are property-things, the unity of such classes is constituted by similarities in structure and compositional materials: for example, dogs are all and only things with such and such parts placed in thus and so structural arrangements. As Richard H. Bube puts it, "To be alive [e.g., to be a dog] is a systems property of a particular type of material system composed of suitable parts arranged in a suitable pattern of interactions. To be human is a systems property of a particular type of living material system composed of suitable parts arranged in a suitable pattern of interactions."[32] Thus the category of relation and the category of stuff are required to classify a property-thing, and they have a derived, emergent unity. By contrast, a substance is a deep, primitive unity and only requires one category—that of substance—to classify it. As Aristotle noted in *Metaphysics* 1052a.22-25: "That which is a whole and has a certain shape and form is one in a still higher degree; and especially if a thing is of this sort by nature, and not by force like the things which are unified by glue or nails or by being tied together, i.e., if it has in itself the cause of its continuity."

Teleology and function. A property-thing is a passive medium through which chains of events run. The internal structure of a property-thing does direct the flow of events, but a property-thing does not contain the source of change or motion within it: it is not a first mover. And as we saw in our discussion of substances earlier in the chapter, if living things are property-things, we must reduce their apparent teleology to efficient causes and the notion of function for various organs to statistical averages or the demands of the struggle for reproductive advantage. On this view, the heart doesn't function *in order to* pump blood, nor is this the way hearts *ought by nature* to function. Rather, hearts do, in fact, pump blood because such passive happenings contributed to survival; and, statistically speaking, most hearts do, in fact, pump blood. This is what we mean by saying the "normal," that is, the "usual," heart pumps blood.

Individuation. In our discussion of substance above we saw that an individual substance is a this-such; it is a combination of three metaphysical entities: a universal nature, an individuating component and the relation of predication. Focusing on living organisms as substances (e.g., Fido), this individuated essence is ontologically prior to its body, which is composed largely of inseparable parts. The substance, Fido, stands under his body, develops it according to his essence and is individuated without reference to his body parts. Fido *is identical to* doghood, the relation of predication and an individuator, and he *has* a body. By contrast, if Fido is taken to be a property-thing, he is a mereological compound, a system composed of separable parts standing in an "appropriate" set of external relations. As such, two exactly resembling dogs are individuated from one another by having different separable physical parts.

In this chapter we have looked at a number of important metaphysical distinctions, and we have examined the differences between a substance and a property-thing. Equipped with these insights we now turn to a deeper examination of the depiction of human persons by strict naturalists and Christian complementarians.

Particles . . . are organized into larger systems.
It would be tricky to try to define the notion of a system,
but the simple intuitive idea is that systems are collections of particles
where the spatio-temporal boundaries of the system
are set by causal relations.[1]

JOHN SEARLE

The natural sciences have been giving us a picture of the world as consisting
of a complex hierarchy—a series of levels of organization of matter
in which each successive member of the series is a "whole" constituted of "parts"
preceding it in the series. . . . These "wholes" are organized systems of parts
that are dynamically and spatially interrelated.
Such a sequence is particularly well illustrated in the various levels
of organization of living systems.[2]

ARTHUR R. PEACOCKE

If species evolve in anything like the way Darwin thought they did,
then they cannot possibly have the sort of natures that traditional philosophers
claimed they did. . . . Because so many moral, ethical, and political theories
depend on some notion or other of human nature,
Darwin's theory brought into question all these theories.
The implications are not entailments. One can always dissociate "Homo Sapiens"
from "human being," but the result is a much less plausible position.[3]

DAVID HULL

CHAPTER 3

Human Persons in Naturalist & Complementarian Perspectives

. . . .

*D*URING THE LAST DECADE THERE HAS BEEN A GROWING BODY of literature about the ethics of abortion, infanticide, euthanasia and suicide. In spite of the claims of philosophers like John Rawls and Kai Nielsen, who assert that ethics can and ought to be done without metaphysics, the central issues emerging in this body of literature involve, crucially and essentially, a treatment of metaphysical themes—the nature of being human, personhood and personal identity.[4] Ultimately, one's views on these matters will merely elaborate the more basic metaphysical question, Are human persons substances or property-things? Unfortunately, among ethicists who treat end-of-life issues there is a widespread trend of avoiding serious metaphysical analysis in conjunction with these issues. Often, what follows are not conclusions purged of metaphysics but rather conclusions guided by an inadequate metaphysical perspective implicit (or supposedly implicit) in natural science.

The thesis of this chapter is that strict philosophical naturalists and Christian complementarians are united by the inner logic of their views in depicting human persons as property-things and that this depiction has serious, troublesome implications for the ethical issues mentioned in the

last half of this book. To justify this thesis we will do three things:
☐ describe strict philosophical naturalism and the view of human persons implied by it
☐ describe Christian complementarianism and the view of human persons implied by it
☐ present a brief description of a representative example of a Christian complementarian view of human persons developed explicitly in light of ethical issues

Philosophical (Scientific) Naturalism and the Human Person

Throughout much of contemporary intellectual culture, the world-view of naturalism is the accepted creed. David Papineau boldly proclaims that "nearly everybody nowadays wants to be a 'naturalist.'"[5] Along similar lines, naturalist Jaegwon Kim states that most philosophers today have accepted naturalism—and more specifically, physicalism, as the best contemporary version of naturalism—as a basic commitment. Such a commitment, says Kim, involves recognizing that naturalism "is imperialistic; it demands 'full coverage' . . . and exacts a terribly high ontological price."[6]

Thus, when philosophical naturalist John Bishop approaches questions about human actions, freedom and moral responsibility, his goal is to reconcile the ethical and scientific naturalist perspectives regarding human beings because "it is *better* for reconciliatory naturalism to be true than for it to turn out either that our belief in agency is mistaken or that, as agents, we belong mysteriously beyond the natural universe that is open to scientific inquiry."[7]

In a similar vein and despite of his protestations against physicalist treatments of consciousness, philosopher John Searle's own study of the mind leads him to treat it as an irreducible feature of the world. But Searle is quick to distance himself from substance or even property dualism and to label mental properties as just natural, biological features of natural organisms because he wants to identify himself with what he calls "the 'scientific' world view," which constitutes the modern worldview for reasonably well-educated persons.[8]

A Sketch of Philosophical (Scientific) Naturalism

Just exactly what are the central features of philosophical (scientific) naturalism (hereafter, simply referred to as *naturalism*)?[9] Roughly, naturalism is the view that the spatiotemporal universe of entities studied by the physical sciences is all there is. Scientific naturalism includes:

1. different aspects of a naturalist epistemic attitude; that is, a naturalist theory of the nature and limits of knowledge and justified belief (e.g., a rejection of the autonomy or foundational authority of philosophy with respect to science, an acceptance of either weak or strong scientism)

2. an etiological account of how all entities whatsoever have come to be, constituted by an event causal story (especially the atomic theory of matter and evolutionary biology) described in natural scientific terms

3. a general ontology in which the only entities allowed are those that bear a relevant similarity to those thought to characterize a completed form of physics.

The ordering of these three ingredients is important. Frequently, the naturalist epistemic attitude serves as justification for the naturalist etiology, which, in turn, helps to justify the naturalist's ontological commitment. As naturalist John F. Post notes:

> According to a number of influential philosophers, the sciences cumulatively tell us, in effect, that everything can be accounted for in purely natural terms [the naturalist epistemic attitude]. The ability of the sciences to explain matters within their scope is already very great, and it is increasing all the time [an etiological account]. The world view this entails, according to many, is *naturalism:* Everything is a collection of entities of the sort the sciences are about, and all truth is determined ultimately by the truths about these basic scientific entities [an ontological commitment].[10]

Moreover, naturalism seems to require a coherence among what is postulated in these three different areas of the naturalistic turn. For example, there should be a coherence among third-person scientific ways of knowing; a physical, evolutionary account of how our sensory and cognitive faculties came to be; and an ontological analysis of those faculties themselves. Any entities that are taken to exist should bear a relevant similarity to entities that characterize our best physical theories, their "coming to be" should be intelligible in light of the naturalist causal story, and they should be knowable by scientific means.

Most naturalists embrace strict physicalism (all particulars, properties, relations and so on are strictly physical entities capable of description by the hard sciences) because it seems to be implied by the constraints placed on philosophy of mind by the coherence of these three aspects of naturalism. Philosopher William Lyons's statement is representative of most naturalists on this point: "[Physicalism] seem[s] to be in tune with the scientific materialism of the twentieth century because it [is] a harmonic of the general theme that all there is in the universe is matter and energy and motion and that humans are a product of the evolution of species just as much as buffaloes and beavers are. Evolution is a seamless garment with no holes wherein souls might be inserted from above."[11] However, some naturalists allow for the emergence or supervenience of irreducible mental states.

Curiously, Christian complementarians share much in common with strict naturalists. For example, Christian scholar Malcom A. Jeeves says, "The way to an integrated understanding of man is not to hunt for gaps in any particular scientific picture so that we can fit in other entities, whether it be the soul or whatever, but to explore how the accounts at the different levels are related."[12] The soul and, more generally, a substance view of the human person are out of fashion for strict naturalists and Christian complementarians. Let us probe more deeply the three main aspects of naturalism.

The naturalist epistemic attitude. As is the case with much of modern philosophy, naturalism first and foremost is an expression of an epistemic posture, specifically, a posture called *scientism*. In the early 1960s Wilfred Sellars expressed this posture when he said that "in the dimension of describing and explaining the world, science is the measure of all things, of what is that it is, and of what is not that it is not."[13] Steven J. Wagner and Richard Warner claim that naturalism is "the view that only natural science deserves full and unqualified credence."[14] Contemporary naturalists embrace either weak or strong scientism. According to the former, nonscientific fields are not worthless, nor do they offer no intellectual results, but they are vastly inferior to science in their epistemic standing and do not merit full credence. According to the latter, unqualified cognitive value resides in science and in nothing else. Either way, naturalists are extremely skeptical of any claims about reality that are not justified by scientific methodology, explanation and the like.

For the naturalist the preeminence and exhaustive nature of scientific knowledge entail that the only explanations of value are scientific explanations. Whatever exists or takes place in the world either is a brute fact or is susceptible to explanation by natural scientific methods, and there is nothing that lies (in principle) beyond the scope of scientific explanation.

At least four implications follow from the naturalist commitment to scientism. First, there is no such thing as first philosophy—philosophical knowledge about what is real that is independent of and, in fact, fundamental to scientific knowledge. According to David Papineau there is a continuity between philosophy and natural science:

> The task of the philosophers is to bring coherence and order to the total set of assumptions we use to explain the natural world. The question at issue is whether *all* philosophical theorizing is of this kind. Naturalists will say that it is. Those with a more traditional attitude to philosophy will disagree. These traditionalists will allow, of course, that some philosophical problems, problems in *applied* philosophy, as it were, will fit the above account. But they will insist that when we turn to "first philosophy," to the investigation of such fundamental categories as thought and knowledge, then philosophy must proceed independently of science. Naturalists will respond that there is no reason to place first philosophy outside of science.[15]

Among other things, this means that there is no philosophical or theological contribution to the study of the ontology of living organisms.

A second and closely related thesis is that "the philosopher who wants to regard human beings and mental phenomena as part of the natural order [must] explain intentional relations in naturalistic terms."[16] For the naturalist, "A scientific or naturalistic account of [human beings and their mental states] must be a causal account."[17] Human beings, along with their organic life and mental states, are mere property-things that engage in physical cause-effect relations with their environment and through which run causal chains of events according to the set of externally related chemical and physical parts that constitute humans.

Third, naturalists typically eliminate the first-person point of view or else reduce it to the third-person perspective. The basic reason is that the methods of natural science employ an objective, third-person description of the entities in its domain of study, and those entities are thought to be totally describable in third-person language. We will say more about the first-person perspective later in this chapter.

Finally, the naturalist will be extremely skeptical of introspection, of beliefs that receive their justification from common sense (especially if they are not beliefs that can also be justified from science) and of philosophically justified entities that are not "at home" in the naturalist worldview. In this vein D. M. Armstrong wrote the following: "I suppose that if the principles involved [in analyzing the single all-embracing spatiotemporal system that is reality] were completely different from the current principles of physics, in particular if they involved appeal to mental entities, such as purposes, we might then count the analysis as a falsification of Naturalism."[18]

We have looked at several philosophical expressions of different aspects of the epistemic attitude that constitutes naturalism. Let us now turn to an overview of the naturalist's view of how things came to be.

The naturalist Grand Story. The naturalist has an account of how all things whatever came to be. We can call this account the Grand Story. The details of the Grand Story need not concern us here. Suffice it to say that some version of the big bang is the most reasonable view currently available regarding the origin of the cosmos. On this view, all of reality—space, time and matter—came from the original "creation" event, and the various galaxies, stars and other heavenly bodies eventually developed as the expanding universe went through various stages. On at least one of those heavenly bodies—Earth—some sort of prebiotic-soup scenario explains how living things came into being from nonliving chemicals. The processes of evolution, understood in either neo-Darwinian or punctuated-equilibrium terms, gave rise to all the life forms we see, including human beings. Thus all organisms and their parts exist and are what they are because they contributed to (or at least did not hinder) the struggle for reproductive advantage—more specifically, because they contributed to the tasks of competing for food, fighting, running away from enemies and reproducing.

There are several important things to note about the Grand Story. First, it is an expression of a naturalist version of philosophical monism according to which everything that exists or happens in the world is susceptible to explanations by natural scientific methods. This means that whatever exists or happens in the world is natural in this sense. Prima facie, the most consistent way to understand naturalism in this regard is to see it as entailing some version of strict physicalism: everything that exists is fundamentally matter—most likely, elementary particles (whether taken as points of potentiality, as centers of mass or energy or as units of spatially extended stuff or waves)—organized in various ways according to the laws of nature. By keeping track of these particles and their physical traits, we are keeping track of everything that exists. No nonphysical entities exist, including emergent ones (and, for some, including abstract objects). This constitutes a strict sense of physicalism.[19]

Further, the naturalist notion of matter is passive is this sense: A chunk of matter is inert; it cannot exert its own causal powers and act as a first, unmoved mover or either choose or refrain from choosing to do something. Rather, a material entity does what it has to do given the laws of nature (either deterministic or probabilistic) and prior causal conditions. This is true irrespective of what we decide about the "ultimate" nature of matter, for instance, as a corpuscle of stuff, as a point field of force or as whatever. It is also true regardless of whether we take a chunk of matter to "act" on another chunk of matter merely by means of mechanical pushes and pulls or whether we attribute various forces to a chunk of matter. One's decisions about these scientific issues are irrelevant to the question about whether or not matter is passive in a naturalist construal because of what it means to say that matter is passive. Something is active only if it has power it can exert and refrain from exerting as a self-mover, if it is the absolute originator of its own change.[20] Among other things, this means that active agents exercise spontaneous agency, such as agent causation. For the naturalist matter is not like that. A unit of matter only acts because it has been acted upon, and in this sense, matter is passive. As Papineau says:

> I take it that physics, unlike the other special sciences, is *complete,* in the sense that all physical events are determined, or have their chances determined, by prior *physical* events according to *physical* laws. In other words, we never need to look beyond the realm of the physical in order to identify a set of antecedents which fixes the chances of subsequent physical occurrence. A purely physical specification, plus physical laws, will always suffice to tell us what is physically going to happen, insofar as that can be foretold at all.[21]

Thus event causation is the view of causality for the naturalist: all events are a result of prior events combined with either deterministic or probabilistic law. In general, event x is a cause of event y only if there is some (deterministic or probabilistic) law of nature under which x and y can be subsumed. Suppose a brick breaks a glass. Event causation can be defined in this way: an event of kind k (the moving of the brick and its touching of the surface of the glass) in circumstances of kind c (the glass's being in a solid and not liquid state) occurring to an entity of kind e (the glass object itself) causes an event of kind q (the breaking of the glass) to occur. If we say that the wind caused the brick to break the glass, strictly speaking this is not correct. Rather, we should say that the moving of the wind caused a moving of the brick which, in turn, caused a breaking of the glass. Here, all causes and effects in the chain are events.

When naturalists apply event causation to human "free" acts, they offer what is called a *causal theory of action:* an act is free if and only if the chain of events leading up to the action from outside the agent passes through its "own" mental states and if these mental states, in turn, are followed by a chain of events that eventually cause the action in the right sort of way. On the causal theory of action, if Jones desires to vote and believes that raising her arm will satisfy that desire, strictly speaking, it is not Jones herself who raises her arm in order to vote as a teleological goal of her own action. Rather, a belief/desire event within Jones (her desiring to vote plus her believing that raising her hand will satisfy that desire) event-caused a raising of the arm inside of Jones.

There is another way to clarify the naturalist commitment to causation that is relevant to the nature of human freedom. It would seem that a naturalist would accept the following principle, which we may call the *principle of spatiotemporal fixation* (STF), as one that characterizes physical systems[22]: For any sphere of radius r centered at point $p,$ and for any smaller sphere of radius $(r - \Delta r)$ also centered at $p,$ there is a time interval (Δt) such that the state of the larger sphere at t fully determines or fixes the chances of all the details of the state of the smaller sphere at $t + \Delta t.$

STF expresses the naturalist idea that the state of the universe over any region determines or fixes the chances of the state of a smaller region within the larger region at a slightly later time. It also captures the idea that organisms are aggregates of microphysical entities standing to other entities in the aggregate and standing individually or collectively to other entities in the organisms' environment in physical causal relations (see below). On this view, organisms are passive aggregate media through which energy runs. Applied to libertarian agency the notion of an unmoved first-mover—an active originator of causal power—conflicts with STF. It is precisely because libertarians locate the source of control and, thus, responsibility for such actions with the agent itself that STF cannot be applied to libertarian actions.

Furthermore, the most consistent naturalist view is to hold that the physical realm is causally closed and that there are no "gaps" in the causal fabric to be filled by causes at so-called higher, emergent levels of description. In this regard Kim says, "a physicalist must, it seems, accept some form of the principle that the physical domain is causally closed—that if a physical phenomenon is causally explainable, it must have an explanation within the physical domain."[23] But to the degree that a naturalist allows for such higher-level causality, it will be viewed along the lines of feedback mechanisms, and such cases will still conform to event causation. It would seem, then, that the most reasonable view for naturalists to take is to commit themselves at least to what is called *causal reduction:* the existence and causal powers of "reduced" macroentities are entirely explainable in terms of the causal powers of the "reducing" microentities (e.g., the resistance to penetration for solid objects is entirely explainable in terms of the structure and movements of molecules or atoms).

Second, a machine metaphor is used by naturalists to explain living organisms. This follows from the two key elements of the Grand Story: the atomic theory of matter (and the rejection of any form of vitalism) and evolutionary biology (where macrofeatures, phenotypes, are explained by causal mechanisms at the microlevel, genotypes, and in terms of so-called functional explanations given in light of the constraints of reproductive advantage). This implies two things about living creatures.

To begin with, living creatures are property-things and not genuine substances. John Searle's statement is typical of naturalists when he says that living organisms are systems (i.e., property-things) and that "systems are collections of particles where the spatio-temporal boundaries of the system are set by causal relations. . . . Babies, elephants, and mountain ranges are examples of systems."[24]

Charles Darwin's theory of evolution has made belief in, say, human substances with human natures quite implausible, though logically possible. As E. Mayr said, "the concepts of unchanging essences and of complete discontinuities between every *eidos* (type) and all others make genuine evolutionary thinking impossible. I agree with those who claim that the essentialist philosophies of Aristotle and Plato are incompatible with evolutionary thinking."[25]

This belief has, in turn, led thinkers like David Hull to make the following observation:

> The implications of moving species from the metaphysical category that can appropriately be characterized in terms of "natures" to a category for which such characterizations are inappropriate are extensive and fundamental. If species evolve in anything like the way that Darwin thought they did, then they cannot possibly have the sort of natures that traditional philosophers claimed they did. If species in general lack natures, then so does *Homo Sapiens* as a biological species. If *Homo Sapiens* lacks a nature, then no reference to biology can be made to support one's claims about "human nature." Perhaps all people are "persons," share the same "personhood," etc., but such claims must be explicated and defended *with no reference to biology*. Because so many moral, ethical, and political theories depend on some notion or other of human nature, Darwin's theory brought into question all these theories. The implications are not entailments. One can always dissociate *"Homo sapiens"* from "human being," but the result is a much less plausible position.[26]

As Mayr and Hull acknowledge, evolutionary theory is not logically incompatible with a view of living organisms as substances constituted by natures. But in light of our comparison of substances with property-things in chapter two, it should be clear why the latter is more at home with evolutionary accounts of the origin of species. Those accounts provide an etiology of living things told in terms of physical processes, bottom-up causation and the rearrangement of chemical and physical entities to form more and more complicated aggregates. On this view, living things are most likely systems of chemical and physical parts, properties and relations shaped by the demands of reproductive advantage.

The machine metaphor implies a second feature of living organisms mentioned in chapter two: the functional explanations mentioned above are such that teleology is abandoned in a literal sense and that efficient and material causes are used to explain different aspects of living creatures (as well as all other entities).

A third and final point about the naturalist Grand Story is this: while some naturalists eschew questions about the nature of existence itself, other naturalists have formulated a definition of existence based on naturalism and consistent with the Grand Story. Bruce Aune defines *a exists* as "*a* belongs to the space-time-causal system that is our world. Our world is, again, that system of (roughly) causally related objects."[27] Along similar lines Armstrong says that for any entities the following question settles the issue of whether or not those entities can be said to exist: "Are these entities, or are they not, capable of action upon the spatio-temporal system? Do these entities, or do they not, act in nature?"[28]

The naturalist ontology. We shall not go into detail about the general view of reality that constitutes naturalism, since our focus is specifically on the naturalist view of human persons. As we have already stated, naturalism implies that any entities that are taken to exist should bear a relevant similarity to entities that characterize our best physical theories, that the entities' coming to be should be intelligible in light of the naturalist causal story and that they should be knowable by scientific means. Most naturalists have taken this to mean that all entities whatever (e.g., properties, relations, events, processes, states, individuals) are identical to something that is only and completely physical. Some naturalists allow for emergent entities that are nonphysical; but while it is clear that nonphysical entities exist (e.g., universals, mental states), what is not so clear is whether the naturalist can justify belief in their existence in light of his or her commitment to the naturalist epistemology and Grand Story detailed above.

Human Persons in Naturalist Perspective

It is widely agreed among philosophers that the following are not easy to justify given a naturalist property-thing depiction of human beings: property and substance dualism; the absolute unity of a person at a time; the irreducibility of the first-person perspective; the absolute sameness of a person through change; the organic unity of the human body and the distinctive, irreducible, lawlike ways it changes through time; the irreducibility or uneliminability of literal biological function or, more generally, teleology; the metaphysical possibility (let alone the reality) of disembodied existence; libertarian freedom; and the existence of human nature as that which constitutes the unity of the class of all humans. In light of our discussions in this and the previous chapter, it should be obvious why most of the items on this list (e.g., irreducible teleology, the existence of natures) are eschewed by self-reflective naturalists. We believe that all these features of human persons are real and are best justified by adopting a Thomistic dualist view of human persons, or so we will argue in chapters four through six. For now, we want to focus on three items on the list and show why most naturalists have abandoned them: property-substance dualism, absolute personal identity at and through time and libertarian agency.

Strict physicalism and the unacceptability of property or substance dualism. So far as we know, there are no important naturalist thinkers who accept substance dualism in any form. Kim's statement is representative in this regard:

> The idea of minds as souls or spirits . . . has never gained a foothold in a serious scientific study of the mind and has also gradually disappeared from philosophical discussions of mentality. . . . The idea that our mentality consists in the possession by each of us of some immaterial mental substance is fraught with difficulties. In the first place, there seems no compelling reason to think that there are wholly immaterial things in the world. Second, even if there were such things, it is dubious that they could do the job for which they were intended. . . . In addition, the idea of an immaterial and immortal soul usually carries with it various, often conflicting, religious and theological associations that are best avoided.[29]

We disagree with Kim and will say why in the next three chapters. For now we simply note that most contemporary philosophers and scientists dismiss substance dualism without much serious consideration of the notion and with very little argumentation against it. Most such dismissals rest on vague generalizations about souls as being out of step with science and about problems of mental and physical causation.[30] But this last difficulty will not be an issue for Christian theists or even for those who find conceivable the notion that God, an immaterial substance, could create and interact with a physical world. For if such a notion is at least intelligible in God's case—even if he does not exist—then there is in principle no reason why causal interaction should be taken as conceptually problematic for finite immaterial substances.

What about property dualism? Should a naturalist be a property dualist, a certain sort of supervenient physicalist?[31] An example may help to clarify what is meant here by supervenience. Wetness is a supervenient property that arises when water molecules are structured in a certain way. If we boil water, then although we still have water molecules themselves in the form of a gas, we can no longer have wetness because this property supervenes upon a specific structured arrangement of water molecules sufficient for its supervenience.

Supervenient physicalists accept these three theses about the mind-body problem[32]:

1. Mind-body supervenience: The mental (e.g., a pain state) supervenes on the physical (e.g., a brain state) in that two things (e.g., events, organisms) exactly alike in all physical properties cannot differ in respect to mental properties.

2. The anti-Cartesian principle: There can be no purely mental beings (e.g., substantial souls) because nothing can have a mental property without having a physical property as well.

3. Mind-body dependence: What mental properties an entity has depends on and are determined by its physical properties.

Until now, we have been using *emergent* and *supervenient* synonymously, but this is not quite right. Now is a good time to draw a distinction between two forms of supervenience—emergent supervenience and structural supervenience—since the distinction is crucial to our question about naturalism and property dualism.[33]

To get at this distinction, consider two different ways of characterizing a pain. First, we may analyze the essence of a pain in a commonsense sort of way in terms of its intrinsic nature—namely, a private, subjective, felt, sentient state of hurtfulness of which we are aware from first-person introspection. In our view, this is the correct analysis of a pain-type state.

But there is a second (and in our opinion, inaccurate) way that many naturalists analyze pain—as a state consisting entirely of the functional role the state plays in an organism's (or even a computer's) behavior. On this view, a mental state in general, and a pain in particular, is whatever brain state is caused by the right inputs (e.g., being stuck with a pin), causes the right behavioral outputs (e.g., grimacing and shouting, "Ouch!") and causes the right other "mental" states (e.g., self-pity) that, in turn, are reduced to further behavioral outputs (e.g., saying, "Leave me alone!"). According to this functional analysis, being in pain is having some brain state or other—which state does not matter insofar as the internal features of the brain state in question are totally describable in physical language—that stands in the correct causal relations to inputs and outputs. A completely unconscious computer could be in pain if it realized the correct functional role!

In this case, we may say that the brain state "realizes" pain: the brain state plays the proper role in the system of causes and effects. "Mental" states are entirely physical causal intermediaries between certain inputs and outputs, and something is in pain in virtue of being in some brain state that plays the "right" functional, causal role. On the functional analysis one may say the functional role that constitutes what it is to be a pain supervenes on a certain brain state just in case that brain state "realizes" the functional role—it is caused by the correct inputs and causes the proper outputs. The functional role supervenes on the brain state because the functional role is identical to the structural pattern of physical happenings of which the realizing brain state is a part.

To further clarify the contrast between these two analyses of pain, imagine a possible world in which a Vulcan who is stuck with a pin experiences the taste of a banana—not a felt hurtfulness—and shouts, "Ouch!" The first analysis implies that the Vulcan is not in pain (he weirdly is caused to experience the taste of a banana), and the second analysis implies the Vulcan is in pain because he is in the correct functional state.

Second, given these two ways of analyzing pain we see that on the first view (pain is characterized by its intrinsic, subjective feel), painfulness is a completely *new kind* of property that is different from any physical property, especially from the physical properties attributed to brains and bodies. Here, pain is a simple, nonstructural property unique to the "emergent" level of reality; and in no way is it captureable in terms of the spatiotemporal, physical, causal relations among the states and parts of the lower-level reality of the brain. Let us call this the emergent supervenient view: the view that the supervenient property is a simple, intrinsically characterizeable, new kind of property different from and not composed of the parts, properties, relations and events at the subvenient level.

By contrast, the functional analysis of pain treats it as a structural supervenient property of the brain itself.[34] A structural property is one that is constituted by the parts, properties, relations and events at the subvenient level. A structural property is identical to a configurational pattern among the subvenient entities. It is not a *new kind* of property; it is a new pattern, a new configuration of subvenient entities. A structural property may require a new concept in order to describe or refer to it; that is, the functional concept of a pain is the concept of an entire pattern of causal relations among subvenient entities (bodily inputs, brain states, and behavioral and "mental" outputs). But this new concept does not express any new entity "over and above" those at the subvenient level. Given this difference between emergent supervenience and structural supervenience, our question is this: *Should a naturalist hold to an emergent supervenient view of mental states and properties?*

Prominent naturalists have offered at least five reasons why emergent supervenient physicalism is not an option for someone who has taken the naturalist turn. The first two can be gleaned from this statement from Paul M. Churchland: "The important point about the standard evolutionary story is that the human species and all of its features are the wholly physical outcome of a purely physical process. . . . If this is the correct account of our origins, then there seems neither need, nor room, to fit any nonphysical substances or properties into our theoretical account of ourselves. We are creatures of matter. And we should learn to live with that fact."[35]

Churchland puts his finger on two reasons why the naturalist should opt for strong physicalism: there is neither need nor room for anything else. Regarding need, we take it he means that everything we need to explain with respect to the origin and workings of human beings can be supplied by physicalist causal explanations. Regarding room, entities do not come into existence ex nihilo, nor do radically different kinds of entities emerge from purely physical components placed in some sort of complex arrangement. What comes from the physical by means of physical processes will also be physical. As Arthur R. Peacocke puts it, "I find it very hard to see why that functional property [consciousness] coded in a certain complex physical structure requires a new entity to be invoked, of an entirely different kind, to appear on the scene to ensure its emergence. How could something substantial, some substance or some other entity different in kind from that which has been evolved so far, suddenly come in to the evolutionary, temporal sequence?"[36]

A third and related point is the unity of science and, more specifically, the completeness of physics. According to Papineau, physicalists cannot allow for mental properties (and, presumably, any other mental entities) distinct from physical ones because this would threaten the completeness of physics.[37] For Papineau physicalism is a doctrine that constrains properties as well as particulars.

Fourth, Kim, Papineau and others use a reductio for strict physicalism that can be put briefly as follows[38]: Given that physicalism is committed to the physical being causally closed, supervenience physicalism[39] implies epiphenomenalism (the view that mental entities exist, are caused by physical states and do not in turn cause anything); and epiphenomenalism must be rejected because (1) it is intrinsically implausible and (2) it is inconsistent with other aspects of naturalism mentioned above (the naturalist epistemology, etiology and ontology).[40]

A fifth reason for strong physicalism is the naturalist aversion to anything that smacks of vitalism or that opens the door for theology. As Howard Robinson writes, "If science cannot encompass the subjective, then subjectivity becomes a door through which mystical, irrational and religious notions can enter and reassert themselves against the modern metaphysic of scientific realism."[41] Emergent supervenient physicalism comes perilously close to being a version of vitalism, and it opens the door for a theological, personal explanation for the emergence of the mental.

To elaborate, a number of Christian theists like Robert Adams and Richard Swinburne have offered what is called the argument from consciousness for the existence of God based on the existence of mental properties.[42] The general form of the argument goes like this:

1. Mental events are genuine nonphysical mental entities that exist.

2. Specific types of mental events are regularly correlated with specific types of physical events.

3. There is an explanation for these correlations.

4. Personal explanation is different from natural scientific explanation.

5. The explanation for these correlations is either a personal or a natural scientific explanation.

6. The explanation is not a natural scientific one.

7. Therefore, the explanation is a personal one.

8. If the explanation is personal, then it is theistic.

9. Therefore, the explanation is theistic.

Our purpose here is not to defend the argument but merely to show that the existence of mental events or properties is not at home in a naturalist worldview and, in fact, may even provide the resources for a theistic argument.

Naturalism and absolute personal identity at and through time. Virtually all naturalists reject absolute personal identity, by which we mean an interrelated triplet of notions regarding the self: (1) the irreducible existence of the first-person point of view, along with a substantial self as its ground; (2) fundamental, underived, absolute unity (not to be identified with simplicity) of the self at a time; and (3) fundamental, underived, absolute sameness of the self through change. The basic reason for this denial can be put in this way: *The naturalist epistemic attitude, etiology and ontology are too impoverished to have room for a deep enough notion of unity—one that lies between simplicity, on the one hand, and ordered aggregates (with or without emergent properties) constituted by external relations, on the other hand—to serve as grounds for absolute personal identity.* This claim can be expanded into two separate points.

First, Swinburne has persuasively argued that the best way to justify absolute personal identity is to adopt substance dualism[43] (more on this in chapter five). Naturalists depict living organisms as property-things, and as we saw in chapter two, according to philosophical naturalists property-things are mereological compounds that (1) can be fully described in objective, third-person language, (2) are systems of externally related separable parts and, as such, possess a loose, derived unity, and (3) do not sustain absolute identity through change of properties or parts.

Second, the naturalist conception of objective, physical reality does not set easily with the first-person perspective or a substantial self as its ground. Thomas Nagel observes that if "one starts from the objective side, the problem is how to accommodate, in a world that simply exists and has no perspectival center, any of the following things: (a) oneself; (b) one's point of view; (c) the point of view of other selves, similar and dissimilar; and (d) the objects of various types of judgments that seem to emanate from these perspectives."[44] Robinson put his finger on the problem of the first-person perspective for the naturalist when he noted that "the idea that science captures everything, except the centre of everyone's universe, his own consciousness, makes a laughing-stock of its claim to present a plausible world view. If science cannot encompass the subjective, then subjectivity becomes a door through which mystical, irrational and religious notions can enter and reassert themselves against the modern metaphysic of scientific realism."[45]

Because reality is objective, says the naturalist, the best way to study the mind is to adopt a third-person perspective. Science is objective (in this third-person sense) because, for the naturalist, reality itself is objective. Moreover, a complete physical description of the world will need to use only third-person descriptions. This is because physical facts are able to be captured entirely from a third-person point of view without reference to any first-person perspective.

Naturalism and libertarian agency. Friends and foes alike are agreed that libertarian freedom and the theory of agency it entails are difficult to countenance in light of a consistent naturalist perspective. Thus Roderick Chisholm claims that "in one very strict sense of the terms, there can be no science of man."[46] Along similar lines Searle says that "our conception of physical reality simply does not allow for radical freedom."[47] And if moral (and intellectual) responsibility has such freedom as a necessary condition, then reconciling the natural and ethical perspectives is impossible. In what may be the best naturalist attempt to accomplish such a reconciliation, Bishop frankly admits that "the idea of a responsible agent, with the 'originative' ability to initiate events in the natural world, does not sit easily with the idea of [an agent as] a natural organism. . . . Our scientific understanding of human behavior seems to be in tension with a presupposition of the ethical stance we adopt toward it."[48]

Let us use the term *libertarian agency* to stand for the type of agency that constitutes a necessary condition for libertarian freedom. In chapter four we clarify and defend libertarian freedom and agency, but for now we merely state the basic ideas contained in a theory of libertarian agency.

Person p exercises libertarian agency and freely and intentionally does some act e (e.g., raises a hand to vote) just in case

1. person p is a substance that has the active power to bring about e

2. person p exerts power as a first-mover (an "originator") to bring about e

3. person p has the ability to refrain from exerting power to bring about e

4. person p acts for the sake of reasons that serve as the final cause or teleological goal for which p acts

There are at least five reasons why libertarian agency is not compatible with naturalism. First, for those naturalists who are determinists about the world of macro-objects, libertarian agency is not possible because determinism is sufficient (but not necessary) to disallow such agency. The issue of quantum indeterminacy is irrelevant here for four reasons: (1) We are addressing this problem to those naturalists that are determinists. (2) Quantum indeterminacy may be merely epistemological and not ontological if some sort of hidden variable theory is correct. (3) Even if quantum indeterminacy is ontological at the micro level, determinism could still rule at the macro level, and there would be no guarantee that the statistical indeterminacy of micro-events could be directed by a mental act of willing down a specific pathway. (4) Indeterminacy still does not allow the type of control thought necessary by libertarians to ground freedom (see point 3 below).

Second, it has been argued that libertarian agency has a traditional substance dualist view of the self as a necessary condition or at least as the most reasonable metaphysical depiction of a libertarian agent in light of the nature of libertarian agency. The traditional doctrine of substance includes the notions of absolute identity through change (the same self exists as the initiator of an action and as the teleological guide of the various stages of complex acts until the end is reached), of active causal capacities and of organisms as self-movers. But we have already seen that naturalism most plausibly denies the substance view of human beings.[49] As naturalist William Provine admits, "Free will as it is traditionally conceived . . . simply does not exist. . . . There is no way that the evolutionary process as it is currently conceived can produce a being that is truly free to make choices."[50]

Searle is another naturalist who is sensitive to this problem, and indeed he admits that it is decisive against a reconciliation of naturalism and libertarian agency:

> In order for us to have radical [libertarian] freedom, it looks as if we would have to postulate that inside each of us [our physical bodies] was a self that was capable of interfering with the causal order of nature. That is, it looks as if we would have to contain some entity that was capable of making molecules swerve from their paths. I don't know if such a view is even intelligible, but it's certainly not consistent with what we know about how the world works from physics.[51]

Third, the notion of a substance that is acting as an unmoved mover by exerting active power for teleological ends while retaining the ability to refrain from so acting is simply not something a naturalist can countenance. In this regard, Bishop says that

> the problem of natural agency is an ontological problem—a problem about whether the existence of actions can be admitted within a natural scientific perspective. . . . Agent causal-relations do not belong to the ontology of the natural perspective. Naturalism does not essentially employ the concept of a causal relation whose first member is in the category of person or agent (or even, for that matter, in the broader category of continuant or "substance"). All natural causal relations have first members in the category of event or state of affairs.[52]

Further, most naturalists hold that event x is the cause of event y only if there is some (deterministic or probabilistic) law of nature under which x and y can be subsumed. Libertarian acts are not subsumable under laws in this way because such acts involve spontaneous, first-moving exercises of power by an agent who retains the ability to refrain from acting, and in this sense libertarian acts transcend the laws of nature.

Bishop's point reminds us that the real problem of agency for the naturalist is not the problem of determinism. Determinism is sufficient but not necessary to generate a problem of agency. The real problem is that naturalism cannot allow for the existence of libertarian agency irrespective of the determinism question. Among other things, this means that the existence of so-called top-down feedback causation may be irrelevant to the problem of agency. We will have more to say about agency and top-down feedback in the next section.

Another way to get at this problem is by way of our earlier principle of spatiotemporal fixation (STF): For any sphere of radius r centered at point p and for any smaller sphere of radius $(r - \Delta r)$ also centered at p, there is a time interval Δt such that the state of the larger sphere at t fully determines or fixes the chances of all the details of the state of the smaller sphere at $t + \Delta t$.

Applied to libertarian agency the notion of a unmoved or first-mover —an active originator of causal power—conflicts with STF. Because libertarians locate the source of control and, thus, responsibility for libertarian actions within the agent himself, STF conflicts with libertarian actions.

Fourth, the view of reasons in libertarian agency is incompatible with naturalism. For one thing, most libertarians accept the view that a reason is an intrinsic and irreducible mental content. That is, a reason has propositional content that, in turn, has a number of features problematic for the naturalist: it is not located in space or time, nor is the way in which it is "in" the mind a spatiotemporal, physical sense of "in": it is not an entity with causal powers, it is not identical to anything (e.g., a sentence) that can be sensuously perceived, it need not be grasped by the mind of any person at all to exist, it is intrinsically intentional, and it can stand to other propositions in various logical and epistemic relations.[53] Bishop says that the naturalist theory of agency requires as a necessary condition a physicalist theory of mind, and it is easy to see why thoughts or reasons would have to be part of that physicalist theory. Further, reasons play an irreducibly teleological role in the version of libertarian agency we are presenting; and, as we have seen, irreducible teleology is eschewed by strict naturalists.

Fifth, as Nancey Murphy acknowledges, a main difficulty with mind-body interaction (of which libertarian agency is the most egregious in a naturalist framework) "has to do with the law of conservation of matter and energy."[54] Libertarian acts most likely violate the principle of the conservation of matter and energy because such actions imply that if we set aside the possibility of causal over determination, then there is a gap between the state of the brain (or body) prior to or at the time of the action and the brain (or body) state after the action is done.[55] This is because on the libertarian view, no physical description (or mental description for that matter) of the person at time t_1, just prior to the person's freely raising his arm to vote, is sufficient for the arm's raising. The state of affairs obtaining at t_2 (the arm's being raised) is not smoothly continuous with the state of affairs at t_1 (there is a causal gap between them) because the agent's own spontaneous exercise of active power is one of the necessary causal conditions for the arm's being raised. Microphysical causal connections and the laws describing them are disrupted by the "downward" active causal power that originates with the agent himself. As Searle acknowledges, libertarian freedom seems to require the existence of a self that is "capable of interfering with the causal order of nature . . . [and] of making molecules swerve from their paths."[56]

This violation of the principle of conservation is not a cheerful prospect for the naturalist, and many have abandoned libertarian agency to avoid this situation. But the libertarian has another way out. He or she can distinguish a strong and weak form of the principle. The former states that energy can be neither created nor destroyed; the latter says that energy can be neither created nor destroyed *in a closed system*. The libertarian can go on to assert that in free acts, the "system" is open to the "intervention" or causal contribution of an agent that transcends the system, but, obviously, such a move is not open to the naturalist.

Some have attempted to avoid this problem by appealing to quantum indeterminacy. The idea is that quantum indeterminacy at the micro level is somehow amplified to allow for quantum indeterminacy at the macro level; and thus in a libertarian act, one probabilistic brain state is realized over another in such a way that no "violation" of natural law obtains. But this response misses the point. For the libertarian the essence of causality is power, not relata (in this case, events), standing in a causal relation, probabilistic or otherwise. Thus, in libertarian acts originative power is exercised irrespective of whether or not such an exercise brings about a brain state that is in some way or another only probabilified by a physical description of the agent's brain prior to the exercise of power. Since power is defined in terms of the doing of work and since energy is the capacity to do work, an exercise of power involves a release of energy; a first-moving originative exercise of power involves a creation of energy.

With this understanding of strict naturalism in mind, we turn to an examination of Christian complementarian approaches to science and theology in general and to the human person in particular.

Christian Complementarity and the Human Person

Metaphysically speaking, either a strict or supervenience naturalist and a Christian complementarian view of human persons are virtually identical in their ontological depiction of human persons. Naturalist Kim says, "Suppose we were called upon to construct a system with mentality. It seems that the only way to proceed is to try to build a physical/biological structure; if we should succeed in constructing an appropriately complex physical system . . . a mental life would emerge in that system."[57] Similarly, naturalist Papineau proclaims that "to be alive is just to be a physical system of a certain general kind."[58]

Christian complementarian Richard H. Bube asserts that consistent with modern science and biblical revelation

> is the possibility of "emergent properties" that arise from the appropriate dynamically patterned interaction of physical parts in consistence with the creating and sustaining activity of God. . . . To be alive is a systems property of a particular type of material system composed of suitable parts arranged in a suitable pattern of interactions. To be human is a systems property of a particular type of living material system composed of suitable parts arranged in a suitable pattern of interactions.[59]

In the rest of the chapter we will offer a general sketch of complementarity, followed by a specific example of a complementarian depiction of human persons that is particularly concerned with ethical issues related to human personhood.

A General Sketch of the Complementarity View

A number of Christian thinkers advocate the complementarity perspective, including Bube,[60] Peacocke,[61] Jeeves,[62] Murphy,[63] D. M. Mackay[64] and David G. Myers.[65] In the sketch to follow we are not suggesting that all complementarians agree in every detail, but still there is wide agreement about the main features of complementarity, and we shall state those features, along with important differences among complementarians when they are relevant to our purposes.

1. Reality is a hierarchy of systems. According to complementarians, when we seek to understand the structure of the world around us, we should look first and foremost to physical science to see what it tells us, and then we should find room for other disciplines like philosophy, psychology or theology to offer complementary descriptions of the picture science presents.

a. The hierarchy itself. When we do this we discover that science offers a picture of the world as a hierarchy of physical systems, a series of levels of matter in which the wholes at any given level are material aggregates of the separable parts that exist at the lower levels. Going from the lowest level to the top, this series of levels looks something like this: subatomic particles, atoms, molecules, organelles, cells, tissues, organs, organ systems, organisms (including human beings), populations, species, biological communities, ecosystems. At each level (above the bottom one) the wholes are physical property-things—systems of aggregated physical parts that are dynamically interrelated in certain ways. This is the description of the world's structure that science gives us: a system of levels of reality containing systems of interacting parts with increasing complexity of interaction.

b. The relationship between entities at different levels in the hierarchy. There are three important, related entities in this hierarchy: the concrete, physical, individual wholes themselves; the properties of the different wholes at each level; and the descriptions used to characterize the wholes, properties and events/processes at each level.

First, let us look at the relationship between wholes at various levels, for example, living organisms and the chain of part-whole relations down to the fundamental, physical level. The various wholes in the hierarchy are constituted by the parts occupying lower levels. Thus a living organism is a property-thing, a spatiotemporal physical system or aggregate composed entirely of physical, separable parts that stand to each other in various chemical or physical external relations. The parts in the hierarchy are (1) strictly physical individuals all the way up (though they may have various "irreducible" properties) and (2) separable (the same whether in or out of the aggregates at the higher levels). Though not all complementarians would agree with him, Bube claims that "wholes at a higher level depend upon and yet transcend the parts at a lower level (e.g., biological life and physical 'particles') in such a way that the unique properties of the wholes are not present even implicitly in the parts but emerge when the parts participate in a particular, suitable pattern of interactions. It is the pattern of interaction that is responsible for the real properties of the whole."[66]

There are no individual particulars constituting a living organism that is not physical—for instance no substantial soul, no entelechy, no vital entity of any kind. Living organisms qua wholes are more than the "sum" of their separable parts in that they possess irreducible properties (or are described by irreducible concepts or laws) not characteristic of the wholes at lower levels. Thus complementarians accept at least the weak version of individual ontological reduction mentioned in chapter two.

How are we to characterize the complexity of wholes at higher levels of organization? According to Peacocke the answer lies in the concept of organization and complexity.[67] Roughly, organization is the opposite of thermodynamic disorder and amounts to the number of possible arrangements of matter or available energy states associated with those arrangements. Peacocke also characterizes organization as a system of dynamically and spatially related parts. Complexity is a function of the number of connections among parts that facilitate the functions of the whole and of the number of different kinds of parts. Complexity is a necessary but not sufficient condition for organization. Putting this together we see that a living whole is a mere aggregate of heterogeneous separable parts in which each part stands to other parts in various external, especially spatial, relations.

What is the relationship between properties of the different wholes at each level and the descriptions used to characterize the wholes, properties and events or processes at each level? Here complementarians differ.

According to Bube, when the appropriate parts are arranged in an appropriate pattern, genuinely new properties emerge. The whole has properties not exhibited by its parts. In this sense, wholes are more than the sum of their parts. These properties are not something added from outside to the material system, nor are they implicit in the parts themselves as panpsychism (roughly, the view that a mental element is present in everything that exists) implies regarding mental emergents. The parts are purely chemical and physical with no potentiality for the emergent property. Rather, emergent properties arise from the specific pattern of interaction of parts at the lower level. And while the structure itself among the parts does not indicate the origin of novel emergents, still, it is the structure itself or, perhaps, the structured whole that is the possessor of emergent properties. At each level of reality the whole with its emergent properties depends on the parts and their structural arrangement at lower levels. Each level of reality is totally complete at its own level without gaps, unless God acts in the system by way of a direct, miraculous intervention. From what we have seen, it is clear that Bube is an advocate of emergent supervenience: at each level in the hierarchy, wholes have new kinds of supervenient properties.

The relationship between descriptions at different levels is nonreductive and additive. Just as the description of an apple's shape and color are noninteracting—complementarity descriptions that, taken together, give a fuller account of the apple—so are the different concepts and descriptive laws employed at different levels in the hierarchy. Each level requires terms that describe a different range of phenomena. Each description is exhaustive at its own level with no gaps to be filled in by other levels; and since each level gives only a partial insight, the whole truth about, say, a human person is the additive sum of descriptions at each level.

Peacocke's views are quite similar to Bube's. At each level of reality new properties, functions, capacities and behaviors supervene or are superimposed on the dynamic, interlocking pattern of complexity that constitutes the system of separable parts at the lower level. Moreover, at each level nonreducible concepts are required to capture the emergent entities that are seen only at that level. The various descriptions at the different levels are noninteracting, but they are additive in that together they capture all the features of the material system in focus.

What about the relations among the levels of wholes, properties and descriptions? Peacocke claims that higher-level descriptions express theory autonomy but not process autonomy. According to Peacocke, at each level the wholes are nothing but the sum of their parts in one sense but not another. Wholes are the sum of their parts in that the laws of chemistry and physics apply to all processes at all levels and in that there are no vital processes autonomous from chemical or physical ones. Peacocke explicitly rejects strong organicism, the view that living things are substances with immaterial essences that ground their own, species-specific causal powers and laws of development autonomous from chemical or physical processes. For Peacocke the laws of higher-level processes are fully determined (or have their chances fully fixed) by chemical or physical processes. The sense in which wholes are more than the sum of their parts is that there is more to be said about, say, a human person than can be expressed at the level of chemistry and physics. Higher-level concepts cannot be defined as or reduced to lower-level concepts, but theory autonomy does not justify belief in process autonomy for higher levels.

Upon reflection it is not entirely clear whether Peacocke embraces emergent or structural supervenience. Sometimes he seems to hold to the former when he says that the wholes at each level have new properties. This can be taken to mean new kinds of properties. However, more frequently, he seems to affirm that a whole at a given level will exhibit a new structural property with a functional complexity that can be expressed by nonreducible concepts. For example, Peacocke says that a mental event (e.g., a pain) is an internal description of a total state of the brain and not an event in a mind that interacts with the brain.[68] The "experience" of being an "I" at a point in time is a supervenient set of integrative activities.[69] Indeed, for Peacocke, consciousness, mind and life are special organized activities.[70] The most consistent reading of Peacocke is a structural supervenience position, but we leave the matter open.

Murphy seems to be an advocate of structural supervenience, especially with regard to supervenient "mental" entities. She claims that the concepts used to describe the wholes at a given level of reality are not reducible to those employed at subvenient levels. But she defines *supervenience* in this way: Property *b* supervenes on property *a* just in case being *a* in certain circumstances *constitutes* its being *b* (e.g., an act of religious sacrifice supervenes on a basic act of killing an animal if and only if the former is constituted by the latter). She goes on to characterize mental states as functional states that are capable of being realized by a variety of different kinds of subvenient states. Thus Murphy holds to a version of nonreductive physicalism: mental concepts cannot be defined or analyzed into physical concepts employed at subvenient levels, but mental properties are not genuinely new *kinds* of nonphysical entities that causally interact with the brain, rather, they are functional states, structural properties that are realized by brain states.[71]

Before moving on we wish to raise a serious difficulty for Murphy's analysis of mental events. Consider any particular pain event. That specific event is a token of the class of events called *pain-type events*. This particular pain event is necessarily such that it has the property of being a pain. There is no possible world in which this very pain event is not a pain. Now consider Murphy's nonreductive physicalist analysis of an individual pain event[72]: This pain event is identical to some specific brain event that happens to be in the right circumstances to "realize" the proper functional role. However, in this case, this very pain event—that is, this very brain event—is only contingently a pain, since there are possible worlds in which this very brain event obtains but does not "realize" the proper functional role. But since no individual pain event contingently exemplifies the property of being a pain, and since, on Murphy's view, all individual pain (brain) events do contingently realize being a pain, then Murphy's view is incorrect: "pain" events in Murphy's analysis turn out not to be identical to genuine pain events because they lack something (necessarily exemplifying the property of being a pain) that real pain events have. Moreover, on this view one would not be able to tell whether one was in pain by simple introspective awareness of the pain state itself since it is not the state's intrinsic properties that make it a pain. But this seems absurd.[73]

2. Top-down causation. Most complementarians allow for what is called *top-down feedback and causation.* We will not spend time here looking at whether or not top-down causation is an easy thing to accept given the overall complementarian view of human persons. Here we simply note that for emergent supervenient complementarians, when genuinely new kinds of properties supervene on some whole, these properties may, in some way or another, have a causal impact through feedback on lower levels of reality, though those lower levels will constrain that feedback by determining which causal pathways are allowed.

Advocates of structural supervenience hold that a living organism taken as a whole interacts with an environmental system of causes and effects that impact the parts of that whole at lower levels of reality in ways that would not obtain if those parts were in isolation from the whole organism. For example, the struggle for survival selects certain organ structures over against others in a way that requires reference to the whole organism and its environmental interactions. Whichever organ structure is selected must be possible given the laws of chemistry and physics, but those laws by themselves do not adequately explain why some particular configuration of chemical or physical parts composes an organism's structure as opposed to other configurations allowed by chemistry and physics. To describe and explain this sort of causal feedback, one must employ concepts (e.g., the organism as a whole, its environment, evolutionary concepts) that resist reduction to subvenient levels of reality. Seen in this light it may be better to characterize structural supervenient views of causation as "outside-in" (taking account of broader contexts) instead of top-down (genuinely new kinds of properties contributing to lower-level effects).

3. Human persons. From what we have seen, it becomes clear that on a complementarian construal, human persons are property-things and not substances. Human persons do not have a substantial soul/self that grounds an absolute, primitive unity of consciousness at a time, that sustains absolute sameness through (accidental) change, that possesses the powers of libertarian freedom and that both forms the body and grounds genuinely teleological, organic functioning.[74]

Peacocke cites approvingly Nagel's claim that "the self is not a substance."[75] He also says that the I is nothing but a sense of inwardness, that a person is a human-brain-in-a-human-body and that consciousness is the I-at-a-time and amounts to a set of functional activities integrated into a system, a set of dispositional powers in the brain. The I-through-time is a series of discrete events. For Peacocke the human agent is the brain in the body, and human freedom is to be understood in terms of an event-causal theory of action such that freedom is compatible with determinism. The self as a substance does not produce its own actions for the sake of reasons as final causes. Rather, a "mental" state in the brain event-causes other events that terminate in a body movement, and as long as one's "own" prior mental states are part of a chain of events leading to the body movement in the proper chain of events, this is all that is needed to secure free will.

For Bube the human person is a property-thing characterized by the relevant systems property.[76] Humans have no vital essence. The I-at-a-time is a property or set of properties of the whole system. The I-through-time is a constantly changing set of properties, and memory is what constitutes personal identity through change. "Consider, for example," says Bube, "what is meant when we speak of 'I' as though the 'I' of today were the same as the 'I' of a decade ago or of a decade in the future. The 'I' of today is bound to the 'I' of yesterday by only a single influence, only by memory. Take away the tie of memory, and what identity is left between the man and the boy? . . . Any other criterion we attempt to develop to establish continuity fails."[77]

Finally, Bube holds that human freedom is to be understood in terms of an event-causal theory of action compatible with determinism. He claims that a scientific description is deterministic if it can predict a future state from a present one and is chance if it can only predict the probability of a future state. Moreover, such descriptions must be one or the other. Now Bube thinks that these observations raise a paradox about human responsibility. Such responsibility is hard to square with determinism (how can I be responsible if determined), yet it also seems to require determinism (how can a responsible choice exist without its being described in a definite cause [the basis of the choice] and effect [the result of the choice] sequence). On the other hand, responsibility is hard to harmonize with chance, which seems to be required for responsible action; yet chance is utterly random. Bube's solution to the problem is simply to assert, without adequate justification, that scientific descriptions of determinism or chance do not entail determinism or meaninglessness as worldviews and that the two types of descriptions can be complementary. Thus freedom is compatible with determinism.

Finally, Murphy holds that a human person is a physical system that realizes various functional states. Murphy's version of nonreductive physicalism treats human persons as property-things. Regarding free will Murphy claims that it is a necessary condition of moral responsibility and that it is compatible with a deterministic view of the subvenient bodily and brain processes within a human being. Murphy develops a theory of free will as self-determination in the sense that one's actions are produced by one's prior mental states, especially the state of balancing the various mental states relevant to the various options available to the chooser. Consider the decision to continue working or not:

> Suppose that there is in fact no unconscious motive that determines the outcome, and no socially engendered presiding conviction that quantity of

work is better than quality, or vice versa. Our phenomenal experience does seem to present us with such cases: opportunities to choose one of several lines of reasoning with no overriding reason to choose one rather than the other. In this case, there is a hierarchy of mental states. There are the mental states that constitute the two lines of reasoning; there is the state of feeling a need to choose; and there is the higher-order, complex state that incorporates all of these, and precedes the final state, the choice to do one or the other. The sense that I am an "I" who chooses seems to amount simply to the fact that I associate myself with the global, transcendent state, rather than with any of its various components.[78]

In the final analysis it is the state itself—the global, transcendent state (composed of the two lines of reasoning and the feeling of a need to choose)—that event-causes the state of choosing which event will cause the relevant body movement that constitutes the "action," and this is an event-causal theory of action and not a libertarian one.

Because the complementarian view of human persons is so central to the issues in this book, we shall close this chapter by presenting another complementarian analysis of human persons.

A Complementarian View of the Human Person in Ethical Perspective

We select the views of Robert N. Wennberg as our paradigm case of a Christian complementarian view of human persons because he has developed his anthropology with a specific focus on the key ethical issues we treat in the second half of this book.[79]

Among other things, Wennberg is concerned with ethical issues involved in terminal choices regarding permanently unconscious patients. He summarizes his own view in this way:

> I argued that what is of special value about human life is personal consciousness, which makes it possible for the individual to participate in God's creative and redemptive purposes for human beings; biological human life is valuable because it sustains and makes possible personal consciousness, but where there is only biological or somatic human life, that special value no longer attaches to the individual, and biological or somatic death may be allowed to proceed unimpeded.[80]

We can break this thesis down into three important subtheses.

Personal identity. Though Wennberg does not explicitly say so, it seems his view of personal identity is an echo of the view of John Locke.[81] For one thing, Wennberg takes a substance to be a propertyless substratum, and that was Locke's view.[82] Further, Wennberg says that "when an individual becomes permanently unconscious, the *person* has passed out of existence, even if biological life continues. There cannot be a person where there is neither the capacity for having mental states nor even the potentiality for developing that capacity."[83] Elsewhere he says that "psychic life is what is essentially significant about human beings."[84]

It becomes clear that personal identity is constituted by continuity of consciousness or the developed capacity of consciousness—of personality, agency, memory, purposeful action, social interaction, sentience, thought, will and emotional states. This leads Wennberg to define the image of God as the actual or potential capability of "engaging in acts of intellect, emotion, and will" and of participating "in God's creative and redemptive purposes for human life."[85] To be in the image of God is to be a human person, and that image is conferred on those with the capacity for personhood.[86] On this view, death is the total and irreversible loss of these capacities. When these are gone, personhood itself is gone and the person has ceased to exist.

Finally, when it comes to the unity of a person at a time, Wennberg approvingly cited Churchland's claim that "it is the maturing of the nervous system that more than anything else renders the fetal organism a unity and not a collection of cells."[87] Wennberg's statements clearly entail a rejection of absolute personal identity through change and unity at a time, and persons turn out to be physical and biological property-things with sufficient parts and structure to sustain mental functioning.

Humanness. Humanness itself is merely a biological notion. To be a human is simply to have "human organic life" or "biological human life" and be a "human biological organism."[88] Wennberg explicitly claims that to be a human is merely to fall under a biological classification, namely, *Homo sapiens.*[89] Thus biology (and perhaps chemistry and physics) exhaust what it is to be human. Humans are physical, biological property-things.

Personhood itself. For Wennberg the paradigm case of a person is an adult human being: a creature with the developed capacities to think, will, feel and have agency.[90] Both the soul and personhood are properties (or sets of properties and the capacities for them) that supervene upon human biological life. It is possible to be a human nonperson when psychic death occurs and when there is irreversible loss of the capacities of consciousness cited above. In cases like this, there is a human present because human biological life continues, but the person has ceased to be. In general, being human is neither necessary nor sufficient for personhood.[91]

In sum, the Christian complementarian approach as advocated by Wennberg views human beings as property-things, and it treats the relationship between personhood and humanness as a supervenience relation. The result is that there are such things as potential persons, and certain dysfunctional or underdeveloped beings are human nonpersons.

Our substance view of human persons disallows the possibility of potential persons and human nonpersons. Regarding potential persons, as a substance matures it does not become more of its kind; rather, it matures as a member of its kind, which guides that maturity. Thus puppies are immature dogs and not potential dogs; human fetuses are immature human persons and not potential persons.

Regarding human nonpersons, note, first, that sometimes properties relate to each other as a genus does to a species. Here are some genus-species relationships: being a color/being red, being a shape/being square, and according to the traditional view, being a person/being a human. The species is a *way* by which the genus exists. Being red, square or human are ways that being colored, being shaped or being a person exist in individual things.

There can be colored things that are not red things, but there cannot be red things that are not colored things. Similarly, there can be persons that are not humans (Martians, angels), but there are no humans that are not persons. In fact, there is no such thing as a colored thing or person plain and simply. There are only *kinds* of colored things (e.g., red things) and *kinds* of persons (e.g., divine, human, angelic). Thus, in the classic doctrine of substance there are no such things as human nonpersons.[92]

In this chapter we have looked at the nature of philosophical naturalism and at the depiction of human persons in naturalist and complementarian perspectives. The naturalist and complementarian views of human persons reduces persons to property-things and contrast with a substance dualist view that we believe to be both biblical and superior on rational grounds. In the next three chapters we shall offer some arguments for substance dualism and clarify the version of substance dualism we take to be most adequate.

In one very strict sense of the terms, there can be no science of man.[1]

RODERICK CHISHOLM

*The idea of a responsible agent, with the "originative" ability to initiate events
in the natural world, does not sit easily with the idea of [an agent as]
a natural organism. . . . Our scientific understanding of human behavior
seems to be in tension with a presupposition of the ethical stance
we adopt toward it.*[2]

JOHN BISHOP

*Something peculiar happens when we view action from an objective
or external standpoint. Some of its most important features seem to vanish
under the objective gaze. Actions seem no longer assignable to individual agents
as sources, but become instead components of the flux of events in the world
of which the agent is a part. . . . The essential source of the problem
is a view of persons and their actions as part of the order of nature.*[3]

THOMAS NAGEL

CHAPTER 4

Substance Dualism
& the Human Person

FREE AGENCY

. . . .

*I*N CHAPTER ONE WE SAW THAT THE FOLLOWING IS THE BEST WAY
to understand the biblical model of a human person: A human
person is a unity of two distinct entities—body and soul. The soul,
while not by nature immortal, is, nevertheless, capable of entering an
intermediate disembodied state upon death and, eventually, of being
reunited with a resurrected body. Throughout history most philosophers
and theologians have understood the biblical model in terms of some
form of substance dualism. In chapter two we surveyed a number of
metaphysical distinctions of crucial importance for developing a defensible position about the constitution of human persons, and we compared
substances and property-things. In chapter three we noted that both strict
naturalists and Christian complementarians embrace a property-thing
model of human persons.

The purpose of this and the next chapter is to defend a substance-dualist construal of human persons. We will argue that human persons are
identical to immaterial substances, namely, to souls. In chapter six we will
explain the soul's relationship to the development and functioning of its
body. However, in chapters four and five we will limit our investigation of

human persons to those considerations supporting the claim that human persons are essentially immaterial substances. We shall direct our attention to three important areas:

☐ human agency and freedom

☐ the nature of our conscious, mental lives and what this tells us about the types of things we are

☐ a set of critical considerations about personal identity

In each of these areas of investigation our argument will be this:

1. There are certain features about ourselves that we know or at least about which we have a right to be sure (i.e., to take ourselves to be justified in believing). There are adequate grounds for believing these features to be real, and naturalist or complementarian attempts to provide alternative depictions of these features fail to be convincing.

2. The features mentioned above support the claim that human persons are essentially immaterial substances for at least two reasons: *(a)* When these features are accurately described and reported to others, these descriptions and reports express facts that are best captured by a substance-dualist model of human persons, and *(b)* the best explanation for the reality of these features is a substance-dualist model of human persons.

Each area requires a book-length treatment to deal adequately with it. However, we believe that the discussion to follow in the next two chapters, though necessarily brief, gives a sufficient account of the main issues and arguments to indicate why we take substance dualism to be true. In this chapter we will limit our investigation to freedom and agency and postpone until chapter five an examination of topics central to personal identity. In this chapter, we shall clarify the nature of freedom and agency, consider the main philosophical arguments for and against libertarian agency, and explain why substance dualism is the best explanation for its reality.[4]

The Nature of Freedom and Agency

We begin our investigation of human persons by clarifying the nature of freedom and agency in order to see what we can learn about ourselves from this topic.

Clarifying the issues and options. All Christians agree that we have free will, but there are major differences among Christians about what free will is. We can define *determinism* as the view that for every event that happens, there are conditions such that, given them, nothing else could have happened: for every event that happens, its happening was caused or necessitated by prior factors such that, given these prior factors, the event in question had to occur. Libertarians affirm free will and hold that determinism is incompatible with it. Compatibilists claim that freedom and determinism are compatible, thus determinism does not eliminate freedom. As we will see, compatibilists' understanding of free will is different from the one embraced by libertarians.

General comparison. Event causation is a model of efficient causality widely employed in science.[5] All causes and effects are events that constitute causal chains construed either deterministically (causal conditions are sufficient for an effect to obtain) or probabilistically (causal conditions are sufficient to fix the chances for an effect to obtain). Associated with event causation is a covering law model of explanation according to which some event (the explanandum) is explained by giving a correct deductive or inductive argument for that event. Such an argument contains two features in its explanans: a (universal or statistical) law of nature, and initial causal conditions.

The initial idea behind compatibilism is this: If determinism is true, then every human action is causally necessitated by events that obtained prior to the action, including events that existed before the agent's birth. That is, human actions are mere *happenings;* they are parts of causal chains of events that lead up to them in a deterministic fashion. But freedom, properly understood, is compatible with determinism. Some compatibilists deny that determinism is true of the physical world and embrace a form of quantum indeterminacy. However, these thinkers still hold that event causation is the type of efficient causality exhibited by agents. Thus the essence of compatibilism is an acceptance of event causation and not an acceptance of determinism and its consistency with freedom.

In sum, compatibilists describe human actions in terms of event causality and employ a covering law model to explain such actions. Since both strict and Christian complementarian naturalists depict human persons as physical systems of parts, both groups agree that human action is to be understood (1) as law-governed happenings subsumable under either deterministic or probabilistic law and (2) in terms of event causation and a causal theory of action.

Advocates of libertarian freedom demur, and they have developed different versions of an alternative model of human action. In our view, the core component of intentional action is intentional endeavoring—exercising an active power as a first or originating mover in trying to bring about some effect for a reason.[6] We may incorporate this characterization of intentional action in the following depiction of libertarian agency: Person *p* exercises libertarian agency and freely does some intentional act *e* (raising a hand to vote) just in case

(i) *p* is a substance that has the active power to bring about *e*

(ii) *p* exerts active power as a first-mover (an "originator") to bring about *e*

(iii) *p* has the categorical ability to refrain from exerting active power to bring about *e*

(iv) *p* acts for the sake of a reason, which serves as the final cause or teleological goal for which *p* acts

Taken alone, *(i)* through *(iii)* state necessary and sufficient conditions for a pure voluntary act. A *pure voluntary act* is one freely done by an agent for no reason. Examples would be choosing simply and freely to think about one thing and then another or directing one's attention at one part of the room and then another. Propositions *(i)* through *(iv)* state necessary and sufficient conditions for an intentional act. An *intentional act* is a voluntary act done for a reason. When we cite the reason for the act—for example, Jones raised his hand *to vote*—the reason, the intention to vote, is not the efficient cause of the act; rather, it is the teleological goal or reason for the sake of which Jones raised her hand.

We have already developed the meaning of *substance* in chapter two. *Active power* is a primitive notion with a sense that is ultimately understood ostensively in acts of first-person introspective awareness of one's own initiation of change. A characteristic mark of active power is the ability to initiate motion, to bring something about. Active power is a dual ability to exert or refrain from exerting one's power. So understood, it is impossible for an exercise of active power to be causally necessitated by prior events. A first-mover is a substance that has active power. The notion of *categorical ability* in *(iii)* has two important aspects to it. First, it expresses the type of ability possessed by a first-mover that can exercise active power, and as such it contrasts with the conditional ability employed by compatibilists. Second, categorical ability is a dual ability: if one has the ability to exert his power to do (or will to do) *a*, then one also has the ability to refrain from exerting his power to do (or to will to do) *a*. Finally, *(iv)* expresses a view of reasons as irreducible, teleological goals for the sake of which a person acts. In general, we may characterize this by saying that person *s e*'d (e.g., went to the kitchen) in order to *r* (e.g., get coffee or satisfy *s*'s desire for coffee). This characterization of action, according to *(iv)*, cannot be reduced to a causal theory of action that uses belief or desire event causation (see below).

Three things should be mentioned about this definition of libertarian agency. First, there are two basic schools of thought regarding libertarian agency. Advocates of the first school hold to agent causation and, thus, believe that the first-mover in *(ii)* causes his actions. Advocates of the second school accept a noncausal view of agency in which the actions of unmoved movers are uncaused events done for reasons as final causes. Either way, an unmoved mover is an agent that can act without sufficient causal conditions necessitating that the agent act—the agent is the absolute source of his own actions. Second, libertarian agency theorists are divided about the role of reasons in an over-all theory of agency. Noncausal theorists are clear in seeing reasons as final causes. Either advocates of agent causation accept this view of reasons or else they hold reasons to be necessary (efficient) causal conditions that, together with the agent's own active exercise of power (and, perhaps, other conditions), cause the action. Therefore, some agent causationists would adjust *(iv)* accordingly. Third, it is broadly logically impossible for a person to be caused to agent-cause something. Libertarian acts are spontaneous in the sense that there are no causal antecedents sufficient to determine that an agent act with libertarian freedom.

Four areas of comparison between compatibilism and libertarianism. We can clarify the differences between compatibilism and libertarianism by briefly comparing them in four different areas.

1. The ability condition. Most philosophers agree that in order to have the freedom necessary for responsible agency, one must have the ability to choose differently from the way the agent actually does. A free choice, then, is one where a person *can* will to do otherwise. Most compatibilists and libertarians agree about this. They differ, however, about what it means to say that a free act is one in which a person *can* act other than how she does act.[7]

According to compatibilists the ability necessary for freedom should be expressed as a hypothetical ability. Roughly, this means that the agent would have done otherwise had some other condition obtained, for example, had the agent desired to do so. We are free to will whatever we desire even though our desires are themselves determined or outside our control. Freedom is one's willing to act on one's strongest preference.

Libertarians claim that this notion of ability is really a sleight of hand and not sufficient for the freedom needed for responsible agency. For libertarians the real issue is not whether we are free to do what we want but whether we are free to want in the first place. A free act is one in which the agent is the ultimate originating source of the act. Freedom requires that we have the categorical ability to act or, at least, to will to act. This means that if Smith freely does (or wills to do) action *a*, then he could have refrained from doing (or willing to do) *a* or he could have done (or willed to have done) *b* without any conditions whatever being different. No description of Smith's desires, beliefs, character or other things in his make-up and no description of the universe prior to and at the moment of his choice to do *b* is sufficient to entail that he did *a*. It was not necessary that anything be different for Smith to do *b* instead. This means that there will be a gap in the universe just prior to and after a free act due to the causal activity of the agent as first-mover.

The libertarian notion of categorical ability includes a dual ability: if one has the ability to exert his power to do (or will to do) *a*, one also has the ability to refrain from exerting his power to do (or will to do) *a*. By contrast, the compatibilist notion of hypothetical ability is not a dual ability. Given a description of a person's circumstances and internal states at time *t*, only one choice could obtain, and the ability to refrain is not there; its presence depends on the hypothetical condition that the person had a desire (namely, to refrain from acting) that was not actually present. There is no causal gap just prior to and after the act of a substantial agent's contributing causal power as a first-mover into the natural causal chain of events because this view of agency is rejected by compatibilists.

2. The control condition. Suppose Jones raises her hand to vote. Compatibilists and libertarians agree that a necessary condition for the freedom of this act is that Jones must be in control of the act itself. But they differ radically as to what control is.

In order to understand compatibilist views of the control condition, recall that most compatibilists agree determinism is true and that all compatibilists hold that cause and effect is to be characterized as a series of events making up causal chains with earlier events together with the laws of nature (either deterministic or probabilistic) causing later events. The universe is what it is at the present moment because of the state of the universe at the moment before the present together with the correct causal laws describing the universe. A crude example of such a causal chain would be a series of one hundred dominoes falling in sequence from the first domino on, until the one-hundredth domino falls. Suppose all the dominoes are black except numbers forty through fifty, which are green. Here we have a causal chain of events that progresses from dominoes one through one hundred and that "runs through" the green dominoes.

Now, according to compatibilism an act is free only if it is under the agent's own control. And it is under the agent's own control only if the causal chain of events—which extends back in time to events realized before the agent was even born—that caused the act (Jones's hand being raised) "runs through" the agent herself in the correct way. But what does it mean to say that the causal chain "runs through the agent in the correct way"? Here compatibilists' views differ from each other. But the basic idea is that an agent is in control of an act just in case the agent's body movement (e.g., the hand going up) that is part of the act (the agent's raising her hand to vote) is caused in the right way by prior states of the agent herself (e.g., by the agent's own character, beliefs, desires and values). This idea is sometimes called a *causal theory of action*.

Libertarians reject the causal theory of action and the compatibilist notion of control, and they claim that a different sense of control is needed for freedom to exist. Consider a case where a staff moves a stone but is itself moved by a hand that is moved by a man. In *Summa contra Gentiles* 1.8, Thomas Aquinas states a principle about causal chains that is relevant to this example and, more generally, to the type of control necessary for freedom according to libertarians:

> In an ordered series of movers and things moved [to move is to change in some way], it is necessarily the fact that, when the first mover is removed or

ceases to move, no other mover will move [another] or be [itself] moved. For the first mover is the cause of motion for all the others. But, if there are movers and things moved following an order to infinity, there will be no first mover, but all would be as *intermediate movers*. . . . [Now] that which moves [another] as an instrumental cause cannot [so] move unless there be a principal moving cause [a first cause, an unmoved mover].

Suppose we have nine stationary cars lined up bumper-to-bumper, and a tenth car runs into the first car, causing each to move the next vehicle until car number one on the other end is moved. Suppose further that all the cars are black except cars five through eight, which are green. What caused the ninth car or car number one to move? According to Aquinas, cars two to nine are not the real cause of motion for car nine. Why? Because they are only *instrumental causes;* each of these cars passively receives motion and transfers that motion to the next car in the series. Car number ten is the real cause since it is the first-mover of the series.[8] It is the source of motion for all the others. Only first-movers are the sources of action, not instrumental movers that merely receive motion passively and pass that on to the next member in a causal chain.

In our earlier example neither the staff nor the hand is the controlling cause of the stone's motion since each is an intermediate cause. Rather, the man himself is the first, unmoved mover and, as such, is the cause of action. For libertarians it is only if agents are first causes or unmoved movers that agents have the control necessary for freedom. An agent must be the absolute, originating source of her own actions to be in control. If, as compatibilists picture it, an agent is just a theater through which a chain of instrumental causes passes, then there is no real control. Further, the control that an unmoved mover exercises in free action is a dual control—it is the power to exercise her own ability to act or to refrain from exercising her own ability to act.

3. The rationality condition. The rationality condition requires that an agent have a personal reason for acting before an intentional act counts as free. Consider again the case of Jones's raising her hand to vote. In order to understand the difference between the two schools about how to handle this case in light of the rationality condition, we need to draw a distinction between an *efficient* and a *final cause.* An efficient cause is *that by means of which* an effect is produced. One ball's moving another is an example of efficient causality. By contrast, a final cause is *that for the sake of which* an effect is produced. Final causes are teleological goals, ends or purposes for which an event is done; the event is a means to the end that is the final cause.

Now a compatibilist will explain Jones's voting in terms of efficient and not final causes. Jones had a desire to vote and a belief that raising her hand would satisfy this desire, and this state of affairs in her (the *belief/ desire set* composed of the two items just mentioned) caused the state of affairs of her hand's going up. In general, whenever some person *s* does *a* (raises her hand) in order to *b* (vote), we can restate this as *s* does *a* (raises her hand) because she desires to *b* (vote) and believes that by *a*-ing (raising her hand), she will satisfy desire *b*. On this view, a reason for acting turns out to be a certain type of state in the agent, a belief/desire state, that is the real efficient cause of the action taking place. Persons as substances do not act; rather, states within persons cause latter states to occur. The compatibilist, in possession of a clear way to explain cases where *s* does *a* in order to *b*, challenges the libertarian to come up with an alternative explanation.

Many libertarians respond by saying that our reasons for acting are final and not efficient causes. Jones raises her hand *in order to* vote or, perhaps, in order to satisfy her desire to vote. Here the person acts as an unmoved mover simply by exercising her powers in raising her arm spontaneously. Her beliefs and desires do not cause the arm to go up; she herself does. But various reasons serve as final causes for the sake of which actions are done. Thus, compatibilists embrace a belief/desire psychology (states of beliefs and desires in the agent that cause the action to take place), while most libertarians reject it and see a different role for beliefs and desires in free acts.

4. Causation. As noted earlier, for the compatibilist the only type of causation is event-event causation: If we say that a desire to vote caused Jones to raise her arm, we are wrong. Strictly speaking, a desiring to vote caused a raising of the arm inside of Jones.

Libertarians agree that event-event causation is the correct account of normal events in the natural world, like bricks' breaking glass. But when it comes to the free acts of persons, the person himself as a substantial agent directly produces the effect.[9] Persons are agents and, as such, are first-movers, unmoved movers who simply have the power to act as the ultimate originators of their actions. It is the self that acts, not a state in the self that causes a moving of some kind. Libertarians claim that their view makes sense of the difference between actions (expressed by the active voice, e.g., "Jones raised her hand to vote") and mere happenings (expressed by the passive voice, e.g., "A raising of the hand was caused by a desiring to vote, which was caused by x . . .").

Before we turn to another issue of clarification, we should reiterate something we have already mentioned about the relationship between determinism, free agency and strict or complementarian naturalism. First, for those naturalists who are determinists about the world of macro-objects, libertarian agency is not possible because determinism is sufficient but not necessary to disallow such agency. This is due to the categorical ability, the type of dual control and the self-moving active power that are components of libertarian agent theory.

Moreover, it is crucial to see that the issue of quantum indeterminacy is not the central issue about the reality of free agency for three reasons. Roughly, quantum indeterminacy may be understood to mean that certain quantum events—for instance, the precise location of an electron hitting an x-ray plate after passing through a slit or the precise time at which a specific uranium atom decays into lead—have no necessitating causes sufficient to produce them and, instead, are only probabilistically related to the relevant prior circumstances. First, even if quantum indeterminacy is ontological at the micro level, determinism could still rule at the macro level.[10] Second, in our view, it is likely that quantum indeterminacy should be understood epistemologically and not ontologically. That is, we should take it that our ability to know, predict or measure quantum phenomena is undetermined, but the phenomena themselves are governed by strict deterministic, necessitating dispositions. Finally, indeterminacy is neither necessary nor sufficient for the type of control thought necessary by libertarians to ground freedom. It is not necessary because even if the physical world is strictly deterministic, libertarian freedom could still be true if human agents are immaterial souls and not physical aggregates.

Nor is indeterminacy sufficient to ground freedom. In this regard Bishop says that the problem of natural agency is an ontological problem—a problem about whether the existence of actions can be admitted within a natural scientific perspective. . . . Agent causal-relations do not belong to the ontology of the natural perspective. Naturalism does not essentially employ the concept of a causal relation whose first member is in the category of person or agent (or even, for that matter, in the broader category of continuant or "substance"). All natural causal relations have first members in the category of event or state of affairs.[11]

Bishop's point reminds us that the real problem of agency for the naturalist is not the problem of determinism. The real problem is that a consistent form of either strict or complementarian naturalism embraces only event causation and, thus, cannot allow for the existence of libertarian agency irrespective of the determinism question (see chapter three).[12] Among other things, this means that the existence of so-called top-down feedback causation is irrelevant to the fundamental problem of agency, namely, the debate between libertarian and event-causal accounts.

In our view, Thomas Nagel's analysis of the relevance of determinism to the debate about free agency is correct:

From an external [naturalistic] perspective, then, the agent and everything about him seems to be swallowed up by the circumstances of action, nothing of him is left to intervene in those circumstances. This happens whether or not the relation between action and its antecedent conditions is conceived as deterministic. In either case we cease to face the world and instead become parts of it; we and our lives are seen as products and manifestations of the world as a whole. Everything I do or that someone else does is part of a larger course of events that no one "does," but that happens.[13]

Basic and nonbasic actions. Finally, human persons engage in basic and nonbasic actions. To grasp the difference between a basic and nonbasic action, note first that often more than one thing is accomplished in a single exercise of agency. Some actions are done by doing others: for example, you perform the act of going to the store to get bread by getting into your car and by driving to the store. Basic actions are fundamental to the performance of all others but are not done by doing something else. In general, s's e-ing is basic if and only if there is no other nonequivalent action description "s's y-ing" such that it is true that s e-ed by y-ing. Your endeavoring to move your arm to get your keys is a basic action. Your choosing to think about *x* instead of *y* is a basic action. In general, basic actions involve moving one's body or altering one's own mental events.

A nonbasic action contains basic actions as parts of and means to the ultimate intention for the sake of which the nonbasic action is done. To fulfill a nonbasic intention, one must form an action plan: a certain ordered set of basic actions that one take to be an effective means of accomplishing one's nonbasic intention. The action plan that constitutes going to the store to get bread includes the acts of getting your keys and walking to your car. In general, when an agent performs a nonbasic action, she

☐ conceives of an ultimate, teleological end she intends to accomplish

☐ conceives of various sub-acts she takes as means to accomplishing the ultimate, intended end

☐ freely performs each sub-act in order to accomplish the ultimate, intended end

In our view, an action is something contained wholly within the boundaries of the agent. Thus, strictly speaking the results of an action are not proper parts of that action. A basic result of an action is an intended effect brought about immediately by the action. If one successfully endeavors to move one's finger, the basic result is the moving of the finger. Nonbasic results are more remote intended effects caused by basic results or chains of basic results plus more remote intended effects. The firing of the gun or the killing of Lincoln are respective illustrations of these types of nonbasic results.

Assessing the Key Philosophical Arguments

In this section we will advance four arguments for libertarian agency and freedom and respond to one key objection raised against it.

Fundamental awareness of and belief about ourselves and our actions. There are certain things about ourselves and our actions of which we are aware and that we seem to know or that we at least justifiably believe. These things provide grounds for preferring libertarian agency to compatibilism. At the very least they offer prima facie justification for believing in libertarian agency, and they shift the burden of proof onto those who deny such agency. To begin with we all seem to be aware of the fact that we are the absolute originators of our actions. Indeed, we often are aware of the distinction between cases where our actions are coerced by drives outside our control and cases where they result freely from our own exercise of originative, active power. We express this distinction by recognizing the difference between coercion, which necessitates a behavior, and influence, which stops short of coercion. For example, we all know the difference between a passive and an active thought. A passive thought is one that is produced in us by something else and over which we have no control. An active thought is one that we have freely and directly chosen to entertain.

We also experience ourselves engaging in pure voluntary acts, acts that are not caused or determined by any of our own reasons or motives. For example, we sometimes experience *akrasia*—weak-willed actions we freely do even though these actions are actually *contrary to* our overall strongest, most preferred beliefs, desires and values (more on this below). Another example is cases where we have no preference for choosing one alternative over another. You may have two quarters before you and voluntarily choose to flip one and not the other for no reason at all. In weak-willed actions we act contrary to or fail to act consistently with our strongest overall preference where "preference" can be spelled out in various ways—as a set of first- or second-order desires, as a judgment of the rational thing to do, as a view of an action as expressing one's values.

Finally, in processes of deliberation or in nonbasic actions where we carry out a plan, we are directly aware of the fact that we are enduring agents who continue to posses and exercise the active power of control throughout these processes, all the while reserving the power to refrain from so acting as we teleologically guide our deliberative processes or sub-acts toward our intended goals. When we deliberate about what we shall do, we are aware that an action is "up to us." When we drive to the store to carry out our plan to get groceries, we are aware that at any moment, we have the active power to drive somewhere else or to continue on our journey to the store. Deliberative processes and cases where plans are carried out are not experienced as instances where we passively have a stream of events run through us on the way to an output—a body movement.

Some have claimed that all libertarians are claiming here is that in free acts all we are aware of is the absence of a cause for those acts and it is always possible that there are causes for those acts we have simply overlooked. In response, we point out that in the cases listed above, we are, in fact, not aware of any causes for those acts and that this surely counts for something. Even though there *could* be a cause for the act that one has overlooked, the absence of awareness of such a cause is still evidence for the fact that there is no cause even if this evidence were not conclusive. Further, we are not claiming that, in the cases just cited, we merely lack an awareness of a cause for our actions. In all these cases we have a positive awareness of something. We are aware of acting as originative, first-movers who exercise active power and who could have refrained at any moment from exercising this power. We experience the fact that in these cases, our actions are "up to us" in precisely this sense. We are not merely aware of the absence of causes for our acts in these cases, though this is part of that of which we are aware.

Critics of this argument can respond in at least two ways. First, they can claim that we do, indeed, seem to be aware of what the libertarian affirms, but these awarenesses must be wrong because the naturalist view (in either sense) of human persons is correct and cannot allow for this sort of freedom. This is John Searle's response. Searle admits that even though we seem unable to abandon the libertarian concept of freedom, since naturalism is true, the libertarian view must be false because "our conception of physical reality simply does not allow for radical [libertarian] freedom."[14]

This claim is clearly question-begging against the libertarian. Moreover, the authority of science cannot be employed to strengthen the critics' claim because, taken alone, science is incompetent to judge which view of freedom is correct. It is science combined with certain philosophical claims as exhibited by strict or complementarian naturalists that lie behind the critics' assertion. But again this broader philosophical assertion assumes its conclusion before it makes the argument; it goes against our basic self-awareness and self-knowledge, and since science is silent on the question, science cannot be used to justify the critics' assertion.

A second response by the critic is to say that we are aware of hypothetical ability and compatibilist control as opposed to the libertarian alternatives in the cases listed above. In our view, this response is simply mistaken. We ourselves have taught dozens of classes on the nature of freedom to laypersons and college students. In our experience, when students have no prior ideological ax to grind, they almost universally accept libertarianism as the view most in keeping with their intuitions about their own actions. Moreover, a number of scholars—libertarians and compatibilists alike—have admitted the same thing and have agreed that the libertarian view is the commonsense position adopted by the majority of people. Philosopher John Foster is typical when he says that in adopting libertarianism, we "are simply endorsing the common-sense view—the view which we all accept prior to philosophical reflection."[15] Along similar lines, J. A. Cover and John O'Leary-Hawthorne claim that

> when ordinary people come to consciously recognize and understand that some action is contingent upon circumstances in an agent's past that are beyond that agent's control, they quickly lose a propensity to impute moral responsibility to the agent for that action. We can readily explain this fact by supposing that ordinary people have a conception of freedom [i.e., the libertarian conception], agency, and moral responsibility according to which an action by an agent is free and accountable only if that action is not fully determined by circumstances, past or present, that are beyond the agent's control. Similarly, we believe that the best explanation for why so many philosophy students find compatibilism *prima facie* implausible is that they carry with them the workaday conception of freedom that cannot be done full justice by the compatibilist account.[16]

Philosopher Stewart Goetz has offered a second argument related to knowledge of our own actions—specifically, to knowledge of the intrinsically active, originative nature of our exercises of power in free choice as depicted by libertarians.[17] Goetz points out that when we make choices, we know we are doing so *while* we are choosing. The libertarian has a natural way of explaining this fact: we know while we are choosing that we are choosing by simply being aware of the choice, the exercise of power itself. If this is so, there must be something about the act of choosing itself that allows us to be aware of its intrinsic active nature and that allows us to recognize the difference between an intrinsically active choice and the occurrence of a mere happening within us.

On a causal theory of action (CTA) an agent who knows he is choosing cannot possess this knowledge by being aware of the choice itself. Why? Because on the causal theory there is no intrinsic difference between a mere passive happening and an active choice. The only difference is that the latter has the agent's own mental state in the causal ancestry of the "choice" and that the former does not. Thus the CTA implies that before we can know we are currently exercising a choice, we must direct our attention away from the choice itself and to some other event— the relevant prior mental state—and to the appropriateness of the chain of events running from the mental state to the choice itself.

An advocate of the CTA may simply insist that this is exactly what we do to become aware of the freedom of our choices. We leave it to the reader to judge which account more accurately depicts his or her own self-awareness of choices. Moreover, in some actions, we are aware of choosing freely while we do so even though we have forgotten the reason why we are acting. This would seem to present a real problem for advocates of the CTA.

Finally, the mere fact that we have a concept of certain parts of libertarian theory provides evidence for the truth of libertarianism. It seems reasonable to believe that we can have a concept of something only if we have had, at some time, an experience of the relevant items the concept is about. For example, one can have a concept of redness only if one has experienced redness. People blind from birth have no concept of redness itself.

Two qualifications are in order here. First, we can obviously have a complex concept—for example, of a unicorn—without experiencing a unicorn, as long as we have previously experienced the relevant elements of the concept (being a horse, a horn). We can also extrapolate to a concept of, say, a shade of blue never before experienced as long as we have experienced enough shades of blue to allow for the extrapolation. But we do not form concepts of totally new kinds of things that (or whose elements) we have never experienced. Second, we are not limiting experience to sense experience. In the history of philosophy there is a rationalist tradition that embraces other forms of awareness and insight besides sensory awareness: for instance, rational intuition of abstract objects, laws of logic and so on, first-person introspective awareness of one's own self and its states, axiological awareness of value (e.g., moral or aesthetic) properties or propositions, religious awareness of God and angels. We side with this tradition and expand the notion of experience accordingly.

Now if the CTA is true, there are no intrinsically active events (volitional exercises of power), nor are there real, intrinsically teleological ends, goals or means done *for the sake of* those goals. For the causal theorist all events whatever (including "choices") are mere passive happenings caused by prior passive happenings according to natural law. Moreover, there is no genuine, irreducible teleology that makes a causal difference to sequences of events within causal processes. Cosmic history, including the biographies of individual humans, is just one event after another. And if there are no intrinsically teleological ends, there are no means, since means are events done for the sake of ends. Given these facts, it is hard to see how we could even form the relevant parts of our concept of libertarian agency. The libertarian has no such problem because she claims that the relevant concepts are ultimately formed by direct awareness of our own acts.

Causal theorists could respond by denying that we must have an experience of the relevant entity before we can formulate the associated concept. We invite them to provide examples and suspect that none will be forthcoming. Others, like Daniel Dennett, explain how we have the libertarian concept of freedom by telling a just-so evolutionary story about the survival value of taking ourselves to be free in the libertarian sense.[18] But just-so stories miss the point. Even if they succeed in describing the survival value of having a concept of libertarian agency and of believing in it, these stories offer no account whatever as to how we could formulate the concept in the first place. We conclude, therefore, that the very concept of libertarian freedom is a problem for the CTA.

"Akrasia" or weak-willed action. It seems evident that, occasionally, we exhibit *akrasia* or weakness of will. Either we fail to act on our overall strongest beliefs and desires or we act contrary to our strongest preferences. Now, genuine *akrasia* presents a problem for the CTA in this way: On the CTA an action is one caused in the right way by one's own prior mental states related to the act. The body movement of one's arm going up counts as a free act if and only if it is caused in the correct way by a chain of events that go back through the "agent's" own reasons for acting. Thus, according to the CTA, since reasons are causes, one's strongest reasons are one's strongest causes. In intentional acts we always act because of our strongest overall preferences. Thus *akrasia* is a problem because it apparently shows that satisfying the CTA is not a necessary condition for acting freely. It would seem then that on the CTA there are no weak-willed actions, and the causal theorist must either admit this, which seems implausible, or else develop a theory that allows for them while remaining faithful to the CTA.

The libertarian has no such problem. On his view, even after one has deliberated about an action and formed his strongest overall preference, he retains, as a free agent, the active power to refrain from acting or to act contrary to his strongest preferences. What can the causal theorist say about the problem of *akrasia?*

Philosopher Donald Davidson has offered the following solution.[19] In *akratic* acts, agents form and act on unconditional judgments that are at odds with their summing-up conditional judgments. So intentional acts are rational relative to (i.e., is caused by) the unconditional judgment even if they are not rational (and thus *akratic*) relative to the summing-up judgment. To understand Davidson's solution, consider the following chart of the process of deliberating about what to do in cases of action:

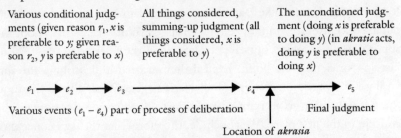

Various conditional judgments (given reason r_1, x is preferable to y; given reason r_2, y is preferable to x)	All things considered, summing-up judgment (all things considered, x is preferable to y)	The unconditioned judgment (doing x is preferable to doing y) (in *akratic* acts, doing y is preferable to doing x)

$$e_1 \longrightarrow e_2 \longrightarrow e_3 \longrightarrow e_4 \longrightarrow e_5$$

Various events ($e_1 - e_4$) part of process of deliberation   Final judgment

Location of *akrasia*

Suppose one is deliberating about going to the polls to vote *(x)* versus going home to watch football *(y)*. The events $e_1 - e_3$ represent various conditional judgments like this: "Given that I have been gone from home lately, I should go home and watch football with my family; given my duty to my country, I should go and vote." Event e_4 is one's summing-up judgment: "Given all the relevant factors I can think of, voting is preferable to going home to watch football." Now, says Davidson, in normal acts, we form a final judgment (the unconditional judgment without "given all the relevant factors I can think of"), e_5—for example, "voting is preferable to going home." This causes the event (or series of events) of going to the polls and voting. However, in *akratic* acts the unconditional judgment (in this case, "watching football is preferable to voting") that actually causes the act doesn't match and is, therefore, *akratic* with respect to the summing-up judgment. Note that Davidson's account is a CTA analysis because it depicts free actions as chains of passive events ($e_1 - e_5$) that cause body movements. It also leaves room for *akrasia*—or so it seems.

Unfortunately, Davidson's solution is unpersuasive for a number of reasons. We mention only one here. As fellow naturalist and causal advocate Bishop admits, Davidson's employment of an "all out unconditional judgment" (e_5) is ad hoc and psychologically implausible.[20] It is ad hoc, says Bishop, because the only reason for believing in such judgments is that if we do, it saves the CTA from falsification in light of *akrasia*. It is psychologically implausible, Bishop continues, because we simply are unaware of forming such judgments in our deliberative processes and intentional actions, *akratic* ones included.

Bishop offers a different solution to the problem of *akrasia,* one that involves accepting Davidson's analysis except for changing one thing. Bishop replaces Davidson's unconditional judgment with another candidate for e_5, namely, a pure intention expressed in the imperative mood. Instead of Davidson's "doing x is preferable to doing y" (a mental *judgment*), Bishop proposes a completely unique type of mental state—a pure intention, such as "let x be the case over y." Such a state is a pure, self-directed command with no evaluative component. In *akratic* acts the act (doing y not x) is not rational with respect to (i.e., is not caused by) the summing-up judgment, but it is rational with respect to (i.e., is caused by) the pure intention ("let y be the case, not x"), which is contrary to the summing-up judgment.

What should we make of Bishop's solution? For at least two reasons it must be rejected. First, if Bishop tries to give content to the idea of a pure intention, then it collapses into the libertarian notion of an exercise of active power or at least a resolve to perform such an exercise. The state "let y be the case over x" is most clearly understood as "I currently possess and shall exercise my power to do y, and I shall refrain from exercising my power to do x." Bishop admits that pure intentions are totally unique mental states. The libertarian makes the same claim about active exercises of power, and Bishop's "pure intentions" look strangely like active exercises of power or the resolve to so act. It may be that Bishop gives no content whatever to his notion of a pure intention, preferring instead to characterize it formally as "whatever mental state is needed to insert between the summing-up judgment and the body movement to save the CTA from falsification due to *akrasia*." If so, Bishop's own solution is as ad hoc and psychologically implausible as Davidson's.

Here is a second problem with Bishop's solution: Granting the existence of his pure intentions, it seems plausible that one could form such an intention and still fail to carry it out (or act contrary to it) due to final-stage (last-minute) *akrasia*. If so, Bishop's "solution" does not effectively solve the problem of *akrasia;* it only postpones the location of purely voluntary libertarian *akratic* acts. Bishop is sensitive to this objection and responds by simply digging in his heels and denying that final-stage *akrasia* is possible.[21] Unfortunately, Bishop's claim is merely an assertion that begs the question, and it is implausible in light of what we know about ourselves. In our view, Davidson and Bishop have offered the most promising CTA responses to *akrasia*. In light of what we have seen, it seems that *akrasia* provides strong evidence for preferring libertarianism over against compatibilist causal theories of action.

Causal deviancy. A third argument for preferring libertarianism to the CTA is one we can only mention briefly: the problem of causal deviancy. Suppose an advocate of CTA says that a free act takes place if and only if the relevant body movement is caused by one's own prior mental states and leaves it at that. It is easy to come up with a counterexample that shows that such an analysis can be satisfied and yet the act not be done freely—that satisfying the CTA is not a sufficient condition for free action.

Consider a case in which a spy has agreed to send a signal to his compatriots if the enemy is going to attack tomorrow. He knows his friends will be using a telescope to look through the window of a room where he will be having a meeting with the enemy that afternoon. If the attack will come, he will signal this by knocking over his cup of coffee. The meeting occurs, the attack is planned for the following day, and the spy intends to signal his compatriots in the agreed upon way. However, his desire to signal them combined with his belief that by knocking over his cup he can send the signal causes him to be so nervous that he accidentally knocks over the cup, and the event is observed by those viewing through the telescope. Here the CTA is satisfied. The body movement is caused by the spy's own prior mental state. But the act is not freely intended.

Advocates respond by claiming that a correct CTA requires that the body movement be caused by the agent's prior mental state *in the correct way* and not merely that it only be caused by the mental state. Thus, in the spy case, the body movement was not caused in the correct way, and the CTA can explain why the act was not free within the constraints of the causal theory.

The trick here is for the CTA advocate to clarify what "in the correct way" means without implicitly or explicitly appealing to libertarian exercises of power. It would not do, for example, to say that the spy's belief/desire state causes the body movement in the correct way just in case the spy deliberately raises his own arm in light of the belief/desire state. A CTA analysis is an attempt to analyze the notion of deliberately doing something in purely event-causal terms, and thus the analysis itself cannot employ the concept of deliberate action on pain of circularity.

Moreover, for each CTA analysis of "in the correct way," a new counterexample can be set up to show that it is not sufficient for free action. For example, to solve the spy case a CTA advocate may say that the spy's belief/desire state must run through the agent's own pure intention (in Bishop's sense) on the way to the body movement, and this does not happen in the spy case. But a counterexample easily shows this not to be sufficient. Suppose a mad scientist places a device in the spy's brain; sees that his belief/desire state will, if left alone, cause the relevant body movement; and intervenes after the formation of the belief/desire state by hitting a button and causing the pure intention himself, which then leads to the spy's body movement. The spy is not in control of the production of the pure intention and, thus, is not acting freely.

A new qualification of "in the correct way" can be given to solve this counterexample, but another one would then surface against the new analysis. Now just exactly what conception of freedom is operating in this dialogue? How is it that we can tell that each CTA analysis is not sufficient, that a new counterexample counts against it and that a new analysis meets the old counterexample? Bishop admits that it is the commonsense conception of libertarian agency that guides the process of deliberation in the debate about causal deviancy between libertarians and advocates of a CTA, even though he feels forced to reject libertarianism as a naturalist.[22] We believe that the libertarian conception of freedom is, indeed, behind the problem of causal deviancy as well as of the various CTA responses to it and that this is evidence for the truth of libertarian agency and against CTA theories.

At the end of the day the problem of causal deviance raises the issue of an enduring agent's continued possession of active power throughout the duration of an action. The CTA depicts us as smart bombs. If we distinguish guidance control (e.g., a robot's actual and continual guidance of a car) from regulative control (e.g., a driver's having guidance control and also possessing the continual power to direct the car in a different direction), causal theorists disallow regulative control and only permit guidance control. However, it becomes clear that this depicts us as complicated smart bombs that passively process feedback loops and chains of events merely running through us and over which we have no control. The libertarian accepts regulative control, and we believe the problem of causal deviance shows that the libertarian is correct.

The transitivity of causality or control. Our final argument focuses on the transitivity of causality, or control (hereafter, merely causality). Recall that if a relation R is transitive, then if a stands in R to b and b stands in R to c, then a stands in R to c. "Larger than" is transitive; "father of" is not. Causality is transitive. If a is the cause of b and b is the cause of c, then a is the cause of c. Consider a train with three cars. If the middle car causes the caboose to move and the engine causes the middle car to move, then it is actually the engine that causes—controls—the movement of the third car. The middle car is merely an instrumental car and is not in control of the next event. If Anderson pushes a stick that moves a rock, Anderson, not the stick, is responsible for and in control of the rock's motion.

Now if the strict or complementarian naturalist CTA is true, humans are mere passive systems of physical parts through which chains of events run. Recall our earlier discussion of a series of black dominos, each knocking the next one down, from domino one to domino one hundred. Suppose dominoes forty through fifty are green and are contained in a cardboard box such that an opening exists at each end. When black domino thirty-nine (outside the box) strikes green domino forty (inside the box), dominoes forty through fifty fall down inside the box, and domino fifty falls through the opening, knocking down domino fifty-one and so on to one hundred. It should be clear that the cardboard box is not in control of dominoes fifty-one through one hundred's falling down. The box is just a passive medium that is neither in control of its input (domino thirty-nine falling through its opening) or its internal structure (the specific arrangement of internal dominoes). Thus the cardboard box is not in control of its outputs. It changes nothing if we choose to label domino thirty-nine a "mental state" domino and if we characterize the chain of dominoes from forty through fifty-one as the correct path from the "mental state" to the output. No control is present.

Now this example is admittedly crude, but it is an accurate depiction of the control characteristic of the CTA. We are the cardboard boxes who are in control of neither the causal inputs that produce our mental states nor the internal structures that process the causal path of passive happenings from our mental states to bodily outputs. Since causality (control) is transitive, the CTA implies that "agents" are not in control of their outputs any more than the cardboard box is, however more complicated our insides are and however different the "dominoes" inside agents are.

Causal theorists have offered at least two responses to this argument. First, they simply reassert that the CTA depiction of control is adequate to capture what is needed for a robust theory of action. In response, we think that once the CTA view of control is clear, it becomes apparent that it is inadequate. We also believe that the arguments already presented in this chapter, though brief, are sufficient to show that the CTA does not offer an adequate view of control to capture what is required to make sense of free agency.

Second, Nancy Holmstrom has argued that because the argument from the transitivity of control forces us to trace causal chains to events outside or in back of the agent, the argument "leave[s] the person behind."[23] According to Holmstrom a theory of agency requires that we specify factors within the agent that are responsible for his or her actions. It is not required of a theory of action that it go outside the agent since this leaves the agent herself behind and since it is the agent and her internal states that are of interest to action theory.

To see what is wrong with Holmstrom's argument, consider our example of the cardboard box and dominoes. The dominoes inside the box clearly differ from those outside the box in, say, color (green inside, black outside) or spatial location. Unfortunately, neither of these factors are relevant to the issue of control, which focuses on causal power and production. Since control is transitive, we are forced to leave the box and look to causal inputs if we are to trace adequately the relevant factors that bring about the falling of domino fifty-one. Now it is precisely the CTA analysis of action, coupled with the transitivity of control, that makes the inside-outside distinction irrelevant when it comes to agent control. The distinction is arbitrary as far as control is concerned. For an act to be free and under an agent's control, the agent must be the source of her actions and not a mere passive structure through which chains of passive happenings run on their way to outputs. Since libertarians depict agent control as a first, originative moving exercise of power, the libertarian can justify limiting the search for control to things within the agent. The causal theorist is correct to recognize the need for such a limitation, but unfortunately, on the CTA, any such limitation is arbitrary, given transitivity. Since the CTA itself requires that we leave the person behind, so much the worse for the CTA. The central core of agency must be the absolute origination of action within the agent, and this is precisely what libertarians affirm and compatibilists deny.

A problem: Libertarian freedom is unintelligible. We believe that the main issues relevant to adjudicating theories of agency are the ones already mentioned. However, there is one main argument most frequently raised against libertarian agency that we wish to consider here.[24] For the purpose of brevity, let us assume for now, without argument, a volitional theory of action according to which normal actions like raising one's arm are to be parsed this way: the bodily movement is caused by a specific sort of event—a volition (an endeavoring)—which, in turn, is brought about in some way or another by the agent herself.

Now there is a certain difficulty for the libertarian theory of agency if we grant that whatever has a beginning has a cause. The raising of one's arm is an event with a beginning, and it is caused by another event—a volition. But the volition is an event with a beginning, and it has a cause as well, namely, the agent. What does the agent *do* to cause her volition? If the agent does something, is what she does itself an event? And if so, does it need a cause? Let us side with the majority of philosophers and grant that this solution to the difficulty is inadequate: the agent causes an infinite hierarchy of events in causing her volition. What other solutions are available that do not make libertarianism vulnerable to the charge of unintelligibility? Here are descriptions of the three most widely recognized solutions.[25]

AC I: The agent does not do anything to cause her volition. The volition is a basic act produced directly by the agent without exercising any power to produce it. The agent is simply the first *relatum* that stands in a primitive causal relation to the second *relatum,* the volitional event. This objection has been raised against AC I: if the volition occurs at a particular time t_1 and the cause is an enduring substance that existed for some time prior to t_1, then why did the volition occur when it did? One reason this problem arises is that in cases of libertarian agency, no set of conditions within an agent is sufficient to produce a volition. There may be necessary conditions (e.g., motives, beliefs and desires), but these may exist in an agent over a protracted time period with no volition brought about. If the agent does not do something to produce the volition, why does it happen at t_1? So far as we can see, short of abandoning AC I, the best solution to the problem is to work with the second *relatum.* An agent does not just produce a volition simpliciter, say a "volition to *f.*" The agent produces a "volition to *f* at t_1" (or now).

AC II: The agent does do something to cause her volition; namely, she exercises a power. According to this view the causal relation between an agent and her volition is not primitive; it is grounded in an active exercise of power. In AC II we should revise the causal principle and recognize that an exercise of power is not an event in the sense relevant to this revised principle. The causal principle should read "every substance that begins to exist or every change that a substance undergoes has a cause."

Now an exercise of power is simply the exertion of a self-moving power or principle of self-determination that is not itself a change undergone by the agent. In libertarian acts agents are unmoved movers or first-movers. They do not first undergo a change (an exercise of power) before they can produce a change (a volition). Rather, agents qua substances directly produce their volitions by virtue of possessing and exercising their power to do so. Since an exercise of power is not a change undergone by an agent (nor a "coming to be" of a substance), it is not an event with a beginning in the sense relevant to the causal principle, even though there was a time before and after which the agent produced her volitions. Besides coming into existence, only changes (internal or relational) need a cause.

AC III: The agent simply brings about but does not cause her volition for the sake of a reason. Here is a third response to the problem. The correct causal principle is "every event that can broadly logically have a cause does have a cause." It is broadly logically impossible for someone to be caused to agent-cause something else, say, a volition. So if we grant that an exercise of power is an event (i.e., a change within the agent), then when we recognize that such an exercise is the event of an agent's directly agent-causing her volition (the exercise of power is not an event caused by the agent that, in turn, event-causes the volition), it becomes clear that it does not have an efficient cause because it cannot (though it may have a reason that serves as the final cause of the exercise of power). In this case there is an explanation for the action—the reason for the sake of which the act was done—even if there is no cause of the action.[26]

In conclusion, we agree with Nagel that compatibilist, causal accounts of action "fail to allay the feeling that, looked at from far enough outside, agents are helpless and not responsible. Compatibilist accounts of freedom tend to be even less plausible than libertarian ones."[27]

Substance Dualism and Free Agency

What metaphysical account of agents does the best job of providing for the possibility and actuality of libertarian freedom? We have already listed reasons why the overwhelming majority of strict naturalists reject libertarianism (cf. chapters two and three), and we will not rehearse those objections here. And while we have not read every Christian complementarian in sight, we know of no complementarian who accepts libertarian freedom. Clearly, the best known complementarians—for example, Arthur R. Peacocke, Richard Bube, D. M. Mackay and Nancey Murphy—are not libertarians. It would seem, then, that the truth of libertarian agency counts against strict or complementarian naturalists.

The main problem for naturalists of both kinds is their construal of the agent in physical, naturalist terms, as we have already indicated. A number of points we have made in chapters one through three indicate serious problems for trying to embrace libertarianism within the constraints of naturalism, especially physicalist aspects of naturalism. Recently, University of California at Berkeley philosopher Barry Stroud defined *supernaturalism* as "the invocation of an agent or force which somehow stands outside the familiar natural world and so whose doings cannot be understood as part of it. . . . A naturalistic conception of the world would be opposed to [the existence of such agents]."[28]

Libertarian agents and actions are supernatural in Stroud's sense. Given that the nature and "actions" of physical property-things are natural and not supernatural in Stroud's sense, it follows that that libertarian agents are not physical property-things nor are their actions merely physical events. Moreover, substance dualism provides an excellent model of libertarian agents that makes sense out of how such acts can be possible by depicting the agent as a supernatural entity as Stroud defines that notion (e.g., mental substances "stand outside the familiar natural world").

However, there is a tension in the academy relevant to the thesis of this chapter. Currently, substance dualism is sociologically unpopular, and libertarianism is quite popular among many intellectuals, so there are sociological reasons, if not good intellectual ones, for trying to embrace libertarian agency while eschewing substance dualism.

At least two strategies have been adopted by those who wish to avoid substance dualism while accepting libertarian freedom. First, some philosophers, like Randolf Clarke, defend libertarianism and simply leave ontological questions about the agent aside, except for assuring us, as does Clarke, that "only a very minimal commitment as to the nature of a person is implied here. All that is implied is a denial of the bundle view, the view that a person is simply a collection of qualities or events. It is certainly *not* implied here that a person is a Cartesian ego . . . or any sort of nonphysical thing. . . . On the contrary, on the [libertarian] view sketched here, an agent's causal powers depend on her attributes."[29]

In response to Clarke it simply will not do to set aside crucial questions relevant to the development of a positive account of the nature of the agent that exercises libertarian agency. And as we shall see below, Clarke's point that "an agent's causal powers depend on her attributes" is not only correct, it also supports substance dualism.

The second strategy goes like this.[30] All sorts of novel, emergent properties arise when matter is placed in various configurations, and some of these emergent properties endow the objects possessing them with nonreducible, new causal powers. There is no a priori way to place limitations on what sorts of emergent properties are or are not potential in matter. We just don't know enough about matter to set these limits. Given reasons to think we are simply material objects (e.g., brains), it may just be a brute fact that matter in the right configuration gives rise to the types of properties and causal powers required by libertarian agency theory. To be sure, these types of properties and causal powers would be utterly unique throughout the physical world, but this is not sufficient to justify the conclusion that the underlying possessor is a nonphysical object.

As a first response let us assume that when an agent exercises active power, the agent exemplifies the intrinsically characterized mental property of being an active power.[31] Now, presumably, this is the property that is supposed to supervene on a properly structured brain at the time the agent exercises libertarian agency. Let us call this property AP. If this is so, then given the nature of supervenience, the appropriate brain state of the agent—call it B—is sufficient for the supervenience of AP. Two agents cannot differ in respect to AP without differing in respect to B. We may state the situation as follows[32]:

> Principle S: At time t, property AP—the property of an agent's exercising active power—supervenes on B.

In this case, we must understand supervenience as emergent supervenience and not as structural supervenience because, according to libertarian agency theory, AP is *sui generis*—it is a unique kind of property and not a structural microphysical property.[33] Property AP is one of the "joints of nature" and is a genuinely distinct kind of entity on this view.

Now suppose we accept a widely embraced principle N, often used to motivate libertarian agency:

> N: Np and N (if p, then q) entails Nq

where Np means "p and no one has libertarian freedom with respect to p."

Principle N expresses the transitivity of control and causality. For example, N may read as follows: no one has libertarian freedom regarding the existence of laws of nature and the history of the cosmos up to the time one is going to act; and if the laws of nature and the actual history of the cosmos up to the time one is going to act are sufficient to entail that one "does" a certain thing, then one does not have libertarian freedom with respect to "doing" this certain thing.

But now a problem arises for the view under consideration. It is part of the nature of libertarian acts that there are no sufficient conditions for such acts to occur or for the chances to be fixed for such acts to occur. Conrad could be in brain state B and not act freely, not exemplify AP; Moore could be in B and exemplify AP. At the very least the intrinsic properties that are exemplified as the essences of libertarian acts do not supervene on the intrinsic properties that constitute the brain states at the time such actions take place. So the supervenient strategy would seem to be ruled out given the nature of libertarian action.

Instead of focusing our objection on the lack of sufficient conditions required by the very nature of libertarian acts, we may focus our objection a bit differently by combining principles S and N above with two further, plausible principles[34]:

> Principle M: Agents do not have libertarian power over their microphysical states or the brain states that supervene upon them.

> Principle C: No state of affairs x can metaphysically necessitate some state of affairs y if y is causally relevant to the obtaining of x.

Principle S is the view that libertarian exercises of power emergently supervene on the relevant brain states, and S is the view espoused by the naturalists currently under consideration. Principle N tells us that if our microphysical and brain states are not under our libertarian control—and if the fact that given those states, the relevant libertarian state supervenes is not under our libertarian control—then it is not under our control that the relevant libertarian state obtains. Principle M seems to be the fairly reasonable naturalist view that microphysical entities are at bottom the real causal entities in the Grand Story (see chapter three). Principle M also captures the causal closure of the physical, which is widely accepted by naturalists. It also expresses the fact that because naturalists use the supervenience relation as an expression of the ontological priority of the physical level and the dependency of higher level states on the physical, the supervenience relation is asymmetric in character.

Now given principles S, N and M, we seem to run into a problem. Principle M tells us we are not in control of our micro or brain states; principle N tells us that if this is the case, we are not in control of the relevant emergent libertarian states; yet principle S tells us that these states do, in fact, supervene on appropriate physical states. But now we seem to be in a position of denying principle C, and C seems to be intuitively correct. Principle C amounts to something akin to the notion that something cannot cause itself. Moreover, when applied to libertarian actions, principles S, N and M imply that we are not in control of the fact that libertarian states obtain, yet it is of the very nature of such states that we are in control of their obtaining. As far as we can see, the most reasonable way for a naturalist to avoid this problem is to deny M, and this seems to be a pretty high price for reconciling naturalism and libertarian agency. Naturalists like Searle agree that although libertarian agency seems to be the intuitively correct account, given naturalism, we cannot possess libertarian agency precisely because of the considerations just mentioned:

> Why exactly is there no room for the [libertarian] freedom of the will on the contemporary scientific view? Our basic explanatory mechanisms in physics work from the bottom up. That is to say, we explain the behavior of surface features of a phenomenon, such as the transparency of glass or the liquidity of water, in terms of the behavior of microparticles such as molecules. And the relation of the mind to the brain is an example of such a relation. Mental features are caused by, and realized in, neurophysiological phenomena.[35]

Further, we note first that libertarian agency seems to require the agent to be a substance. This strong view of substance may not be a necessary condition for libertarian agency, but it seems to be the most reasonable metaphysical analysis of libertarian agents, especially when compared to the main naturalist rivals, since the former depicts human beings in such a way as to affirm three features crucial to what it is to be a libertarian agent:

1. Libertarian agency is possible only if there is a distinction between the capacity to act or refrain from acting and the agent that possesses those capacities, and this is precisely what the classic doctrine of substance implies.

2. The type of unity present among the various capacities possessed by an agent is the type of unity (i.e., a diversity of capacities within an ontologically prior whole) that is entailed by the classic notion of substance.

3. Typical free acts take time and include sub-acts as parts, and an enduring agent is what gives unity to such acts by being the same self who

is present at the beginning of the action as the intentional agent who originates motion, who is present during the act as the teleological guider of means to ends and who is present at the end as the responsible actor— all the while retaining the power of regulative control.

The main naturalist rivals to the classic substance view of organic wholes like human beings are three: the Lockean bare substratum view, some form of bundle theory and the property-thing position. The bare substratum view pictures agents as simple, bare "I's" to which various properties are externally related. This view does allow for a distinction between the agent and its various properties, the former being a bare particular. But since bare substrata are simples with no internal capacities or powers, it is hard to see how bare agents can have the capacity to act or refrain from acting.

As we are using the term, the "bundle theory" eschews mereology (i.e., an analysis of wholes in terms of separable parts) in favor of an analysis of substances as a combination of properties and the bundling relation. Moreover, when it comes to change, such bundles become series of events, especially on a property exemplification account of events, in which the bundles contain different combinations at different moments. It is widely recognized that bundle theories do not allow for absolute sameness through change. Further, a human being construed as a bundle is just a combination of properties and not an ontologically prior whole that predicatively has properties. Thus, a bundle of properties does not have the metaphysical grounding necessary to exercise or refrain from exercising a capacity.

Finally, by far the most popular naturalist view of living things is the property-thing position. As we have seen, a property-thing is a system of parts standing in external relations and possessing supervenient properties. Microparts are ontologically prior to the whole they constitute. In such a view either macroproperties, like those mental features necessary for agency, are epiphenomenal or else they (or more accurately, the events that contain them) can exhibit top-down, event-causal feedback to subvenient states. Either way, libertarian agency is denied. Further, property-things do not sustain absolute sameness through change, nor do they exhibit genuine, irreducible teleology. Thus if a necessary condition for libertarian agency is that the agent be a substance in the sense just described—and the vast majority of naturalists are correct in claiming that our best scientific account of living things (including human persons) is a physicalist account that does not depict them as substance in the relevant sense—then our scientific, physicalist account of human persons is at odds with a necessary condition of libertarian agency.

The point is so crucial we reiterate it: due to the treatment of the agent as a system of parts, the Christian complementarian view that embraces emergent, "higher-level" mental properties still does not have an ontology that makes room for libertarian agency. As Nagel notes, the problem of free agency in a third-person naturalist description of the world arises "because [on this view] my *doing* of an act . . . seems to disappear. . . . There seems no room for agency in a world of neural impulses, chemical reactions, and bone and muscle movements. Even if we add sensations, perceptions, and feelings we don't get action, or doing—there is only what happens."[36]

A second point to note is that there is no adequate scientific evidence to show we are physical objects. As substance dualists, we wish to have pointed out just exactly what scientific findings we must reject to sustain our substance dualism. It is scientism, not science, that opposes substance dualism. Moreover, it does not follow that libertarian freedom is a power of a physical object—the brain—just because someone cannot exercise such agency in an embodied state without the brain functioning in a certain way. In chapter six, we will argue that the brain itself is an organized structure that is rooted in the soul. We will claim that both the body (including the brain) and the powers of agency are features of the soul and that the soul forms a suitably structured body in order to express libertarian agency. If this is correct, then even if the exercise of libertarian agency is dependent on a certain development of the brain, the power of agency itself could be a feature of the soul and not an emergent property of the brain, even though its exercise depends in certain ways on the brain.

It is important to point out that a thing is the kind of thing it is in virtue of the properties and powers that characterize it. Now while there may be many new features to matter yet undiscovered, we have studied matter long enough to be justified in claiming to know what *kinds* of features characterize a physical object. One cannot simply both assert that material structures have the power to give rise to active power and also claim to be operating with a naturalistic depiction of matter. As David Papineau has correctly pointed out, matter with emergent features typically associated with conscious beings is not the sort of matter countenanced by naturalists. This is why, when Papineau attempts to characterize the physical in terms of a future, ideal physics, he places clear boundaries on the types of changes allowed by naturalism for developments in physical theory. According to Papineau the naturalist will admit that future physics may change some features of what we believe about matter, but in light of a naturalist commitment and the past few hundred years of development in physics, future physics will not need to be supplemented by psychological categories, of which active power is one.[37]

If it claimed that it is just a brute fact that libertarian agency emerges, then this is a totally unique, brute fact unlike all other features of matter. To restate Nagel's point, "There seems no room for agency in a world of neural impulses, chemical reactions, and bone and muscle movements. Even if we add sensations, perceptions, and feelings we don't get action, or doing—there is only what happens."[38] Elsewhere Nagel adds that "the only solution [to the problem of agency] is to regard action as a basic mental or more accurately psychophysical category—reducible neither to physical nor to other mental terms."[39] We take Nagel to be claiming that even if we allow that the naturalist standpoint leaves room for certain emergent mental properties, the features necessary for agency are so utterly unique that it is hard to see how they can be classified in a category countenanced by naturalism. In this regard naturalist Terence Horgan seems correct: "In any metaphysical framework that deserves labels like 'materialism,' 'naturalism,' or 'physicalism,' supervenience facts must be explainable rather than being *sui generis*."[40]

There are several features of matter, as it is understood throughout virtually all of the hard sciences, that unite to justify the notion that libertarian agency is not a feature of a physical object. Among these are the facts that matter is passive and engages in event causation, that material systems are rule governed (i.e., their behavior can be subsumed under natural law), that matter does not exhibit genuine teleology and that the causal behavior of a physical entity does not violate the first law of the conservation of energy, which arguably is involved in exercises of active power. This is why virtually all naturalists reject libertarianism. If someone wishes simply to assert that the properties or powers involved in libertarian agency are emergent physical properties, then the substance dualist can point out that we then have two very different types of matter: those "physical" objects with the relevant libertarian features and all other physical objects. But now, we have a new dualism between "libertarian physical" objects and "normal physical" objects. It should be clear that this is just a verbal difference from the more traditional labels for the dichotomy. If an object contains the properties and powers of libertarian agency, it is not simply a physical object, no matter what we choose to call it.

Finally, not only are there inadequate reasons to think that mere physical objects can possess libertarian agency, there are good reasons to think that a spiritual substance is the proper way to characterize a libertarian agent. Note that in all cases where an entity exhibits libertarian agency, it is a conscious personal being of some sort. Clearly, God, angels and disembodied souls in the intermediate state possess libertarian agency even though they do not have brains or bodies. Even if there is no intermediate state, such a state is conceptually possible. Now it seems clear that libertarian agency is a feature of immaterial, spiritual substances in these cases. In fact, part of what we mean by calling something a "spiritual" being is that it possesses the ultimate capacities for thought, feeling, consciousness and active volitional power. If libertarian agency is possessed by purely immaterial substances and, in fact, partly constitutes what it means to call them "spiritual," it is not clear in what sense libertarian agency is a physical set of powers and properties.

It could be remarked that all we mean by a "spirit" such as God, angels or disembodied souls is an immaterial substance. So the notion of active volitional power is not part of what it means to be a spirit. Unfortunately, this approach suffers from what plagues all attempts to characterize entities solely by way of negation. It is not enough to say that a diamond is not a golf ball. World War II, President Clinton and the inside of your finger are not golf balls either. But they are not diamonds, nor is the negative characterization alone sufficient to give content to *diamond*. Likewise, "immaterial substance" is inadequate to characterize a spirit. If someone says a spirit is an unextended immaterial substance, this suffers from the same problem. Some have argued that numbers are immaterial substances. Even if this is false, the view is still not asserting that numbers are spirits. A positive characterization of "spirit" is needed to give content to notions that God, angels and disembodied persons are spirits. And this can be done by saying that spirits are the kinds of substances that possess the ultimate capacities for thought, feeling, consciousness and active volitional power.

Over twenty years ago Christian philosopher Bruce Reichenbach wrote an excellent book on human persons and life after death. In the book Reichenbach advances a form of Christian physicalism. However, to his credit, he admits that the most reasonable form of freedom is the libertarian one and that if such freedom is real, the physicalist construal of human persons is in trouble. Says Reichenbach, "In conclusion, if we are to hold that man is governed by moral oughts, and that human performance or failure of performance of these yields moral responsibility, it would seem that we must reject the monistic [i.e., physicalist] view of man, for on this view both of these appear to be impossible because man is not free. This, I believe, constitutes a most serious objection to this view of the nature of man."[41]

Along similar lines, philosopher John Foster argues that the notion of libertarian agency requires a "suitable ontology of entities to serve as the relevant agents (nonphysical mental subjects to exercise nonphysical mental agency)."[42] In our view, Reichenbach and Foster are correct, and in this chapter we have tried to say why.

My personal identity, therefore, implies the continued existence
of that indivisible thing which I call myself. Whatever this self may be,
it is something which thinks, and deliberates, and resolves, and acts,
and suffers. I am not thought, I am not action, I am not feeling;
I am something that thinks, and acts, and suffers.
My thoughts, and actions, and feelings change every moment—
they have no continued, but a successive existence; but that self or I,
to which they belong, is permanent, and has the same relation
to all the succeeding thoughts, actions, and feelings, which I call mine.[1]

THOMAS REID

My conclusion—that truths about persons are other than truths
about their bodies and parts thereof—is, I suggest, forced upon anyone
who reflects seriously on the fact of the unity of consciousness over time
and at a time. A framework of thought which makes sense of this fact
is provided if we think of a person as body plus soul,
such that the continuing of the soul alone guarantees
the continuing of the person.[2]

RICHARD SWINBURNE

The idea that science captures everything, except the centre of everyone's universe,
his own consciousness, makes a laughing-stock of its claim to present a plausible
world view. If science cannot encompass the subjective then subjectivity
becomes a door through which mystical, irrational and religious notions
can enter and reassert themselves against
the modern metaphysic of scientific realism.[3]

HOWARD ROBINSON

CHAPTER 5

Substance Dualism & the Human Person

PERSONAL IDENTITY

....

*J*OHN CALVIN WROTE THAT *"NO MAN CAN SURVEY HIMSELF WITH-*
out forthwith turning his thoughts towards the God in whom he
lives and moves."[4] Calvin's remarks should come as no surprise to
anyone who thinks that human persons are made in God's image. There is
something about the way God is that is like the way we are. In our view,
some of these similarities are to be expressed as various facts about God
and human persons, facts that capture what it means for both of us to be
persons—immaterial substances with a rational nature as Boethius (c.
480-524) put it. In chapter four we claimed that libertarian agency is one
of those facts. In this chapter we will look at others, especially at the
nature of mental properties and states and various features of personal
identity.

Mental Properties and States and What They Say About Us
Our first argument can be put in this way: The various properties and
states that constitute the conscious lives of human persons are immaterial
mental properties and states. Moreover, these mental properties are
kind-identifying properties; they tell us about the kind of thing that has

them. Therefore, human persons are at least immaterial, mental kinds of things.

Before we develop the argument, recall something we said about identity in chapter two. Let *x* and *y* stand for any entity whatsoever. If *x* is identical to *y*, then whatever is true of *x* is true of *y* and vice versa. Moreover, if *x* is identical to *y*, then, necessarily, *x* is identical to *y;* it is not possible for *x* not to be *y*. We shall argue that mental states are not identical to anything physical. As substance dualists we cheerfully embrace mental and physical causal interaction and functional dependence. If something happens to the brain, memory loss occurs; if a person persists in anxious thoughts, brain chemistry changes. But none of this says anything at all about *what mental states themselves are.* Something is what it is in virtue of its intrinsic constituents—its properties, potentialities and parts—and not in virtue of what caused it or what must be present for it to function.

Mental states are characterized by their intrinsic, subjective, inner, private, qualitative feel or texture made present to us by first-person introspection. For example, a pain is a certain felt hurtfulness. In no way can mental states be intrinsically described accurately by physical language (e.g., the language of physics, chemistry or commonsense physical descriptions), even if we can study the brain and find out the causal and functional relations between mental and brain states.

There are at least five different kinds of mental states: sensation, thought, belief, desire and act of will. A *sensation* is a state of awareness or sentience, a mode of consciousness: for instance, a conscious awareness of sound, color or pain. A visual sensation like an experience of a tree is a state of the soul, not a state of the eyeballs. The eyes do not see. You (your soul) sees with or by means of the eyes. The eyes, and the body in general, are instruments, tools the soul uses to experience the external world. Some sensations are experiences of things outside you, like a tree or table. Others are awarenesses of other states within you, like pains or itches. Emotions are a subclass of sensations, and, as such, they are forms of awareness of things. You can be aware of something angrily or lovingly or fearfully.

A *thought* is a mental content that can be expressed in an entire sentence and that only exists while it is being thought.[5] Thoughts can be true or false, and they are about things: the thought that Kansas City is a great place to live is about Kansas City. Some thoughts logically imply other thoughts. For example, "all dogs are mammals" entails "some dogs are mammals." If the former is true, the latter must be true. Some thoughts don't entail; they merely provide justification for other thoughts. For example, certain thoughts about evidence in a court case provide justification for the thought that a person is guilty. A thought is not the same thing as the sentence used to express it. "Es regnet" and "it is raining" are very different sentences, but they both express the same thought. Further, a person can think without using language. If this were not so, a maturing infant would never be able to learn language itself since the infant would not be able to think until a language mysteriously arose within the infant. Finally, sentences are sense perceptible and publicly accessible realities. Oral sentences have sound characteristics, and written ones have shape, color and so on. But the thought expressed by the sentence is invisible and in the mind of the speaker.

A *belief* is a person's view, accepted to varying degrees of strength, of how things really are. If a person has a belief (e.g., that it is raining), then that belief serves as the basis for the person's tendency or readiness to act as if the thing believed were really so (e.g., one gets an umbrella). Thus beliefs are not dispositions to behave but are the grounds for such dispositions. At any given time one can have many beliefs that are not currently being contemplated. Beliefs are not the same thing as thoughts. A person has many thoughts he or she does not believe and many beliefs that are not currently being thought. Thoughts exist only while they are being thought, but we have many beliefs not currently being contemplated.

A *desire* is a certain felt inclination to do, have, avoid or experience certain things. Desires are either conscious or such that they can be made conscious through certain activities, for example, through therapy. An *act of will* is a volition or free choice, an active exercise of power, an endeavoring to do a certain thing. We looked at free acts of will in the last chapter.

In general, mental states have some or all of the following features, none of which is a physical feature of anything: Mental states, like pains, have an intrinsic, raw conscious feel. There is a "what it is like" to a pain. Most if not all mental states have intentionality; they are of or about things. Mental states are inner, private and known by first-person, direct introspection. Any way you have of knowing about a physical entity is available to everyone else, including ways of knowing about your brain. But you have a way of knowing about your mental states that is not available to others—through introspection.

Mental states are constituted by self-presenting properties. You can only be aware of the external, physical world by means of your mental states, but you need not be aware of your mental states by means of anything else. For example, it is by way of a sensation of red that you are aware of an apple, but you are not aware of the sensation of red by way of another sensation. The red sensation makes the apple present to you by virtue of your having the sensation, but the sensation also presents itself directly to you without another intermediary. Mental states are necessarily owned, and, in fact, your mental states are necessarily such that there is no possible world where, for example, this very pain of yours could have been owned by anyone else. Someone else could have a pain just like this one, but he could not have had this very pain itself. However, no physical state is necessarily owned by anyone, much less necessarily owned by you.

Some sensations are vague—a sensation of a distant object may be fuzzy and vague—but no physical state is vague.[6] Some sensations have the property of being pleasurable or unpleasurable, but nothing physical has these properties. A cut in the knee is, strictly speaking, not unpleasurable. It is the pain event caused by the cut that is unpleasurable. Mental states can have the property of familiarity (e.g., when a desk looks familiar to you), but familiarity is not a physical property of something physical.

Since mental states have these features and physical states do not, we conclude that mental states are not identical to physical states. But the matter need not be left here. We wish to elaborate two further arguments for the irreducible mental nature of mental states. First, we will focus on sensations and present what is called the *knowledge argument*. Second, we will look at thoughts and beliefs and examine the nature of intentionality.

The knowledge argument.[7] Before it can be appreciated, we need to note two preliminaries. To begin with, there are at least three kinds of knowledge.

1. Knowledge by acquaintance. This happens when we are directly aware of something: for example, when you see an apple directly before you, you know it by acquaintance. One does not need a concept of an apple or a knowledge of how to use the word *apple* in English to have knowledge by acquaintance of an apple. A baby can see an apple without having the relevant concept or linguistic skills.

2. Propositional knowledge. This is knowing that an entire proposition is true. For example, knowledge that "the object there is an apple" requires having a concept of an apple and knowing that the object under consideration satisfies the concept.

3. Know-how. This is the ability to do certain things—for instance, to use apples for certain purposes. Generally, knowledge by acquaintance provides grounds for propositional knowledge, which, in turn, provides what is necessary to have genuine know-how. It is because you see the apple that you know that it is an apple, and it is in virtue of your knowledge of apples that you know how to do things to or with them.

In addition, let us recall what was mentioned above about self-presenting properties like sensations. Such properties present other things to us intermediately by means of them, and they present themselves to us directly simply in virtue of the fact that we have them. A person sees red by means of the sensation of red and is made directly aware of (but does not actually see in the same way he sees the red on the apple) the sensation itself by having that sensation.

When a person has a self-presenting property, she is modified in some way. We may put this by saying that when a person has a red sensation, the person is in the state of being appeared to redly. Suppose the light is such that an orange jar looks red to Lee. If Lee says the object is red, her statement is about the jar and is false. If Lee says, "I seem to see something red" or "the jar appears red to me," what she says is true because she is reporting a description of her own sensation. She is not talking about the jar. Lee's statements employ what is called a *phenomenological use* of *seems* or *appears*. When we use *seems* or *appears* phenomenologically, we use them to report our own description of our self-presenting properties, that is, to report the private, directly accessed mental sensations going on inside us.

We are now in a position to offer a version of what is known as the knowledge argument for the nonphysical, mental nature of our sensations. Suppose Sullivan is a neuroscientist who lives thousands of years in the future. She knows all there is to know about the physics and neurophysiology of seeing. She can describe in complete detail what happens when light reflects off an object, interacts with the eye, optic nerve, brain and so on. However, suppose that Sullivan was born blind and, suddenly, gains sight for the first time and sees a red object. There will be some totally new facts Sullivan learns for the first time that were left out of her exhaustive knowledge of all the relevant physical facts prior to gaining vision. Since Sullivan knew all the physical facts before gaining sight and since she now has knowledge of new facts, these facts are not physical facts; at least some are mental facts, facts involved in what it is like to see.

To expand the argument a bit, Sullivan comes to exemplify the self-presenting mental property of being appeared to redly. In this way Sullivan gains six new kinds of knowledge—she gains knowledge by acquaintance, propositional knowledge and know-how regarding the color red, and she gains these three types of knowledge about the phenomenological aspects of her own red sensation. Sullivan now knows by acquaintance what redness is. Upon further reflection and experience, she can now know things like (1) necessarily, red is a color, (2) necessarily, something cannot be red and green all over at the same time, and (3) necessarily, red is darker than yellow. She also gains know-how about comparing or sorting objects on the basis of their color, about how to arrange color patterns that are most beautiful or natural to the eyes and so on.

She also gains knowledge about her red sensation. She is now aware of having a red sensation for the first time and can be aware of a specific red sensation being dim, vague and so on. For example, at the eye doctor, when you report a letter on the eye chart as appearing vague, you are accurately describing your sensation of the letter, not the letter itself. Indeed, the doctor can see that the letter on the chart has clear borders; however, he needs you to tell him how it appears to you since he has no access to your inner mental sensation. Sullivan could now report things like this about her red sensations. She also has propositional knowledge about her sensations. She could know that a red sensation is more like a green sensation than it is like a sour taste. She can know that the way the apple appears to her now is vivid, pleasant or like the way the orange appeared to her (namely, redly) yesterday in poor lighting. She also has know-how about her sensations. She can recall them to memory, reimage things in her mind or adjust her glasses until her sensations of color are vivid. Sullivan had none of this knowledge prior to gaining color vision, and among the things she now knows are nonphysical facts.

Physicalists David Papineau and Paul M. Churchland have offered slightly different versions of the most prominent physicalist rejoinder to this argument[8]: When Sullivan gains the ability to see red, she gains no new knowledge of any new facts. Rather, she gains new abilities, new behavioral dispositions, new know-how, new ways to access the facts she already knew before gaining the ability to see. Before the experience, Sullivan knew all there was to know about the facts involved in what it is like to experience red. She could imagine in the third-person what it would be like for some other person to experience red. She could know what it is like to have an experience of red due to the fact that this is simply a physical state of the brain and she had mastered the relevant physical theory before gaining sight. But now she has a *"prelinguistic representation of redness,"* a *first-person* ability to *image* redness or *re-create* the *experience* of redness in her memory. She can *re-identify* her *experience* of red and *classify* it according to the type of experience it is by a new *"inner" power of introspection.* Prior to the experience, she could merely recognize when someone else was experiencing red "from the outside," from observing the behaviors of others. Thus the physicalist admits a duality of types of knowledge but not a duality of facts that are known.

For two reasons we think this response is inadequate. First, is it simply not true that Sullivan gains a new way of knowing what she already knew instead of gaining knowledge of a new set of facts. Above, we have listed what we think some of Sullivan's new factual knowledge (both by acquaintance and propositional knowledge) is, and we deny that Sullivan has this factual knowledge prior to gaining the ability to see. We leave it to the reader to judge which is the most accurate way to understand what happens to Sullivan. When making your judgment about this matter, we remind you of a simple fact. We all know the difference between two different ways of knowing the same thing and having two different sets of knowledge about two different sets of facts. An example of the former is your knowledge that a ball is moving by holding it or by seeing it. This is quite different from having knowledge of the ball's shape and then gaining knowledge of its color.

Second, when Churchland and Papineau describe the new know-how that accrues to Sullivan, they help themselves to a number of notions that seem clearly to be dualist ones, which are listed in italics above: prelinguistic representation, image, first-person introspection and so forth. Speaking of Churchland, Geoffrey Madell notes that "Churchland simply helps himself to a whole range of states which are *ineffable,* states like *acquaintance, awareness, the subjective qualitative nature of sensations, introspection,* and the idea of what an experience *feels like.* None of these is a term known in physical science, nor can any of them be given a place within the framework of materialism."[9] In our view, these dualist notions are the real intuition pumps for the physicalist rejoinder; they do rhetorical work in making the physicalist view even remotely plausible. Remove the dualist language and replace it with notions that can be captured in physicalist language, and the physicalist response becomes even more implausible than it already is in light of our first rejoinder above. We conclude, then, that the knowledge argument is successful.

Intentionality. In addition to the knowledge argument, intentionality has been used in arguments for the nonphysical nature of mental states. The argument goes like this: Some (perhaps all) mental states—thoughts, beliefs—have intentionality. No physical state has intentionality. Therefore, (at least) those mental states with intentionality are not physical. Intentionality is the of-ness or about-ness of various mental states. Consider the following points about intentionality:

1. When we represent a mental act to ourselves (e.g., an act of thinking about something), there are no sense data associated with it; this is not so with physical states and their relations.

2. Intentionality is completely unrestricted with regard to the kind of object it can hold as a term—anything whatever can have a mental act directed upon it, but physical relations only obtain for a narrow range of objects (e.g., magnetic fields only attract certain things).

3. To grasp a mental act, one must engage in a reflexive act of self-awareness (e.g., to grasp one's awareness of a tree, one must be aware of an awareness), but no such reflexivity is required to grasp a physical relation.

4. For ordinary physical relations (e.g., x is to the left of y), x and y are identifiable objects irrespective of whether or not they have entered into that relation (ordinary physical relations are external); this is not so for

intentional contents (e.g., one and the same belief cannot be about a frog and later about a house—the belief is what it is, at least partly, in virtue of what the belief is *of*).

5. For ordinary relations, each of the participants must exist before the relation obtains (*x* and *y* must exist before one can be on top of the other); but intentionality can be of nonexistent things (e.g., one can think of Zeus).[10]

6. Intentional states are *intensional:* equals cannot be substituted for equals with the guarantee that the same truth value will be preserved. For instance, if Piper knows that Clinton is president but doesn't know that Clinton is from Arkansas, he won't know that a man from Arkansas is president even though Clinton is identical to a man from Arkansas. But physical states are *extensional:* if a billiard ball is on the table and the only round object in the room is identical to the billiard ball, then the only round object in the room is on the table.

Physicalists try to reduce intentionality to physical causal relations of input and output. For example, to have a thought of a dog is to have certain inputs come into you (say, you scan the room and "see" a dog). These inputs, in turn, produce a disposition to behave in certain ways, and the behavior is produced (you run in the opposite direction while shouting "Dog!" in English). Thus the intentionality of thoughts is reduced to or is replaced by artificial intelligence and computational models of inputs, internal states and outputs all standing in causal relations to each other.

Philosopher John Searle has offered a famous counterargument to this reduction and elimination of intentionality in favor of causal inputs and outputs. The argument is known as the Chinese Room argument. In it, Searle depicts a situation where the artificial inputs and outputs are present and where there is no semantic meaning, no thought with intentionality; so intentionality cannot be identical to causal inputs and outputs because you can have the latter without the former. Here is the argument[11]:

> Imagine that you are locked in a room, and in this room are several baskets full of Chinese symbols. Imagine that you (like me) do not understand a word of Chinese, but that you are given a rule book in English for manipulating the Chinese symbols. The rules specify the manipulations of symbols

purely formally, in terms of their syntax, not their semantics. So the rule might say: "Take a squiggle-squiggle out of basket number one and put it next to a squoggle-squoggle sign from basket number two." Now suppose that some other Chinese symbols are passed into the room, and that you are given further rules for passing back Chinese symbols out of the room. Suppose that unknown to you the symbols passed into the room are called "questions" by the people outside the room, and the symbols you pass back out of the room are called "answers to the questions." Suppose, furthermore, that the programmers are so good at designing the programs and that you are so good at manipulating the symbols, that very soon your answers are indistinguishable from those of a native Chinese speaker. There you are locked in your room shuffling your Chinese symbols and passing out Chinese symbols in response to incoming Chinese symbols.

Now the point of the story is simply this: By virtue of implementing a formal computer program from the point of view of an outside observer, you behave exactly as if you understood Chinese, but all the same you don't understand a word of Chinese.

The Chinese room with the person inside would simulate a computer to an outside person. For a person outside, the room receives input and gives output in a way that makes it appear that the room understands Chinese. But of course, all the room does is *imitate* mental understanding, it does not *possess* it. Computers are just like the Chinese room. They imitate mental operations, but they do not really exemplify them. Computers and their programs are not minds because they fail to have consciousness, intentionality and understanding of real semantic contents. We believe that Searle's argument and the six points listed above are sufficient to show that intentionality is not a physical property or relation and that those states necessarily characterized by intentionality are not physical states. Indeed, it is not even clear what it would mean to say literally that one system of particles is of or about something.[12]

The knowledge argument and the nature of intentionality justify the belief that our mental states and properties are genuinely immaterial and not physical. Now, what does the nature of our mental properties tell us about what kind of thing we ourselves are? Are you a suitably structured brain that causes mental properties to emerge or supervene upon yourself? Or are your mental properties kind-defining; that is, do they tell you what kind of thing you are, namely, an immaterial kind of thing? Remember, if a property is kind-defining, it is not possible for a member of that kind to exist without that property (or at least the ultimate capacity for it). And if a member of a kind can exist without some property, the property is not kind-defining. For at least two reasons we believe mental properties are kind-defining.

First, your mental states are necessarily such that there is no possible world in which they could exist and (1) be ownerless and (2) belong to someone else. Mental states don't just float around by themselves; they are necessarily someone's mental states. Moreover, this very pain you are now having could not possibly have belonged to someone else, though another could have had a pain exactly resembling yours. Your pain is necessarily hurtful, but it is also necessarily owned and owned by you. To generalize, this means that your mental states are modes of your self; they are intrinsic to your very being, and they are part of what characterizes the properties and states that make you the kind of thing I am. Your mental states are not somehow outside your being and externally, causally related to or emergent upon you. In general, when a causes b or a emerges upon b, b does not compose, is not contained within the being of, a. If you are identical to your brain and your mental states emerge and are externally related to your brain (i.e., to you), then there is a possible world where they could exist without you. But this is just false. Your mental states are modes of your self, and, as such, they give information about the type of thing they modify; they are clues to the nature of the self of which they are inner modifications.

Second, if some entity x changes so as to exemplify some property F, then prior to x's exemplifying F, x must be the type of thing that has the property of being potentially F. An acorn does not have the actual property of being shaped like an oak; but even while it is an acorn, it already has the property of being potentially shaped that way. Now a thing is characterized by both its actual and potential properties. In the next chapter we will argue that consciousness does not emerge from the brain even if certain states of consciousness depend on a properly structured, functioning brain. There we will argue that consciousness is ultimately grounded in the soul and that the soul forms the body, in this case the brain, in order to realize some of its conscious potentialities. But even if we grant that a person is identical to a brain with the ultimate capacity for consciousness, it would not follow that a person is a physical object. For on this view the brain would be accurately characterized by both its physical and mental (actual and potential) properties, and this would require that the self be a mental-physical entity of some kind. This is not our view. We believe a person is identical to an immaterial soul that has the potentialities for producing its body (more on this in the next chapter). We merely point out here that the immaterial nature of conscious states indicates that the self is at least immaterial, even if we grant that it is not only immaterial.

Before we move to the next argument for substance dualism, it is important to pause and reflect about the implications of our first argument for methodology in developing an adequate view of the human person. Nancey Murphy is typical of physicalists—Christian or otherwise—who admit that while advances in science do not prove that substance dualism is false, they do show that it is a position with incredibly weak epistemic justification. Roughly, according to Murphy, this is because, say, nonreductive physicalism is not primarily a philosophical thesis but is instead the hard core of a scientific research program for which there is ample evidence. This evidence consists in the fact that "biology, neuroscience, and cognitive science have provided accounts of the dependence on physical processes of *specific* faculties once attributed to the soul."[13] Dualism cannot be *proven* false—a dualist can always appeal to correlations or functional relations between soul and brain or body—but advances in science make it a view with little justification.

Now this approach to the mind-body problem seems to be an expression of the low epistemic value usually attributed to theology by advocates of the complementarity approach, at least in areas other than ethical or so-called spiritual matters of meaning. If someone disagrees with this assessment, then we invite him or her to explain just when it would be appropriate for theology to provide external conceptual problems that would require science to revise its views in areas of direct interaction and that are legitimate areas of scientific investigation. By contrast, our approach (see chapter one) to the nature of human persons places greater weight on philosophy and theology than on science. We are now in a position to see why we believe our methodology is preferable to the complementarian approach within our purview.

Recall what we have said about a faculty and capacities and what they tell us about the things that have them. A faculty of some particular thing is a natural grouping of resembling capacities or potentialities possessed by that thing. Moreover, a capacity gets its identity and proper metaphysical categorization from the type of property it actualizes. The nature of a "capacity to exemplify *F*" is properly characterized by *F* itself. Thus the capacity to reflect light is properly considered a physical, optical capacity. And as we have seen, the capacities for various mental states are mental and not physical capacities. Thus the faculties that are constituted by those capacities are mental and not physical capacities.

Now something is the kind of thing it is in virtue of the actual and potential properties or faculties essential and intrinsic to it. Thus a description of the faculties of a thing provides accurate information about the particular that has those faculties. Note carefully that a description of a particular's capacities and faculties is a more accurate source of information about what kind of thing that particular is than is an analysis of the causal or functional conditions relevant for the particular to act in various ways. This is because the causal-functional conditions relevant to a particular's actions can either be clues to the intrinsic nature of that particular or else information about some other entity that the particular relates to in exhibiting a particular causal action. For example, if Jones needs to use a magnet to pick up certain unreachable iron filings, information about the precise nature of the magnet and its role in Jones's action does not tell us much about the nature of Jones (except that she is dependent in her functional abilities on other things, e.g., the magnet). We surely would not conclude that the actual and potential properties of a magnet are clues to Jones's inner nature.

In the same way, functional dependence on the brain and causal relations to the brain are of much less value in telling us what we are than is a careful description of the kind-defining mental capacities described above. In this case, nonreductive physicalism and dualism are empirically equivalent theses, and, in fact, there is no nonquestion-begging theoretical virtue (e.g., simplicity, fruitfulness) that can settle the debate if it is limited to being a scientific debate.

Thus it is not simply that science cannot *prove* dualism to be false.

Rather, science provides little evidence at all for settling the issue. This is especially true in light of our insights about the relative merits of descriptions of faculties of a particular versus analyses of causal-functional dependencies related to that particular. Read any book in philosophy of mind, look at the issues and arguments relevant to the truth of the matter regarding the nature of human persons, and ask just how it would be that science could even formulate, much less resolve, the issue at hand. Science is a wonderful tool for explicating various relationships between mind and body (and it needs to be said that the mind/soul affects the brain/body and not just vice versa). But, in our view, it is a poor guide for resolving the main ontological questions of the mind-body problem, questions that are distinctively and primarily philosophical and even theological in nature.

Substance Dualism and Absolute Personal Identity

Traditional Christian theology, common sense and various philosophical arguments unite to affirm that persons sustain a primitive, absolute unity of the self at a time and absolute, real sameness through various kinds of change. This position is called the *absolute view* of personal identity, and it is most often grounded in a substance-dualist view of the self. As we saw in chapter three, those strict or complementarian physicalist naturalists who depict human persons as property-things render absolute sameness through change impossible. Richard Bube's remarks are fairly typical in this regard: "Consider, for example, what is meant when we speak of 'I' as though the 'I' of today were the same as the 'I' of a decade ago or of a decade in the future. The 'I' of today is bound to the 'I' of yesterday by only a single influence, only by memory. Take away the tie of memory, and what identity is left between the man and the boy? . . . Any other criterion we attempt to develop to establish continuity fails."[14]

Property-thing advocates have offered various *empiricist views* of personal identity as alternatives to the absolute view. In this section we will, first, look at conceivability as a test for possibility; second, investigate the identity of physical artifacts through change; third, spell out the absolute view and two empiricist views of personal identity (the body position and the memory view); and fourth, assess the arguments for and against these three positions.

Before we press on, a few preliminary distinctions should be made. First, we must distinguish an *absolute, strict sense of identity* from a *loose, popular sense of identity.* If an entity x at time t_1 maintains absolute, strict identity with entity y at time t_2 (say x is Smith at twelve years old and y is Smith at forty-three years old), then x and y stand in the identity relation to each other such that Leibniz's law of the indiscernibility of identicals (see chapter two) holds for x and y (something is true of x if and only if it is true of y). Everything true of Smith at twelve years old is true of Smith at forty-three years old because the very same person who was twelve is now forty-three. In absolute sameness, a person moves through time and exists fully at each moment of his life. Persons have no temporal parts or stages; thus, tenses and dates are not parts of persons. Smith at twelve was four feet tall and was to be six feet tall at forty-three. Smith at forty-three is six feet tall but was four feet tall.

We will look at the loose, popular sense of identity when we look at the identity of physical objects. But for now we should point out that if something sustains loose, popular identity through change, then our judgment of sameness is to some extent arbitrary and not to be understood in a strict way. For example, the Kansas City Royals baseball team could change all of its players, managers and owners and even its stadium and uniforms and still be judged the same team in a loose and popular sense, even if, strictly speaking, the team is different. One issue we will look at is whether or not persons sustain strict, absolute sameness through change or merely loose, popular "sameness."

Second, the metaphysical aspects of personal identity must be kept distinct from the epistemological ones. The former focuses on what *constitutes* personal identity—what *is* personal identity and what makes it *real.* What is it to say that person x at time t_1 is the same person as y at t_2? The latter focuses on *criteria* for personal identity: how it is possible to know or justifiably believe that a person at time t_2 is the same person as someone at t_1.

Conceivability, Possibility and the Modal Argument

The central metaphysical issues in personal identity are these: (1) what is essential to being a human person? and (2) to what is an individual human person identical? To answer these questions we have to try to discover what can or cannot happen to a human person for us to still maintain the person exists. Issue (1) focuses on what is essential to human persons. If something F is essential to human persons, there is no possible world where human persons exist and fail to have *F*. Issue (2) focuses on identity. An entity's identity to itself is necessary. There is no possible world where an entity is not identical to itself and does not share all its properties in common with itself.

Thought experiments have rightly been central to debates about personal identity. For example, we are often invited to consider a situation in which two persons switch bodies, brains or personality traits, or in which a person exists disembodied. In these thought experiments someone argues in the following way: Because a certain state of affairs *s* (e.g., Norris's existing disembodied) is conceivable, this provides justification for thinking that *s* is metaphysically possible. Now if *s* is possible, then certain implications follow about what is and is not essential to personal identity (e.g., Norris is not essentially a body).

Some have criticized the use of conceivability as a test for possibility on the grounds that the notion of conceiving is vague and is used in a variety of different ways.[15] We agree that "to conceive" does not mean "to image" (we can conceive of things, e.g., God, without imaging them) or "to understand" (we can understand impossible states of affairs, e.g., that there are square circles). What exactly do we mean by "to conceive"? In our view, what is conceived is "what seems to be coherently supposed." Note carefully that conceiving is a form of intuition, specifically, an intuition of possibility or impossibility. An intuition is not a belief, much less an uncritically accepted belief. As we are using the term, an *intuition* is the way something seems to you upon careful reflection and attention. We sometimes express an intuition by saying that we can just "see" that something is the case. For example, *modus ponens* is this famous principle of logic:

1. If *P*, then *Q*.
2. *P*.
3. Therefore, *Q*.

When this is put on the board in an introductory logic class and the students are asked if *modus ponens* is a correct law of logic, students correctly answer that it is. When asked how they know it is a correct law of logic, they usually say that one can simply "see" that it is correct. In our sense, they have an intuition that modus ponens is correct. In general, if *a* is an intuition for person *s*, then it seems to *s* that *a* is the case.

There are two forms of conceiving relevant to personal identity: weak and strong conceiving.[16] Something is *weakly conceivable* for a person when she reflects on it and sees no reason to believe it to be impossible. Something is *strongly conceivable* for a person when she judges that it is possible on the basis of a more positive grasp of the properties involved and of the compatibility of what she is conceiving with what she already knows. If something is weakly conceivable, one sees no reason for thinking it is impossible. If something is strongly conceivable, one sees good reason for thinking it is possible.

We all use conceiving as a test for possibility and impossibility throughout our lives.[17] You know that life on other planets is possible because you can conceive it to be so. You are aware of what it is to be living and to be on Earth, and you conceive no necessary connections between these two properties. You know square circles are impossible because it is inconceivable given your knowledge of being square and being circular. To be sure, judgments that a state of affairs is possible or impossible grounded in conceivability are not infallible. They can be wrong. Still, they provide strong evidence for genuine possibility or impossibility. In light of this, we offer the following criterion: For any entities *m* and *n*, if one has grounds for believing one can conceive of *m* as existing without *n* or vice versa, then one has good grounds for believing *m* is not essential or identical to *n* or vice versa.

Let us apply these insights about conceivability and possibility to the modal argument for substance dualism. The argument comes in many forms, but it may be fairly stated as follows[18]:

(1) The law of identity: If *m* is identical to *n*, then whatever is true of *m* is true of *n* and vice versa.

(2) I can strongly conceive of myself as existing disembodied.

(3) If I can strongly conceive of some state of affairs *s* such that *s* possibly obtains, then I have good grounds for believing of *s* that *s* is possible.

(4) Therefore, I have good grounds for believing of myself that it is possible for me to exist and be disembodied.

(5) If some entity *m* is such that it is possible for *m* to exist without *n*, then *(a)* *m* is not identical to *n* and *(b)* *n* is not essential to *m*.

(6) My body is not such that it is possible to exist disembodied; that is, my body is essentially a body.

(7) Therefore, I have good grounds for believing of myself that I am not identical to my body and that my physical body is not essential to me.

A parallel argument can be advanced in which the notions of a body and of disembodiment are replaced with the notions of physical objects. So understood, the argument would imply the conclusion that I have good grounds for thinking I am not identical to a physical particular nor is any physical particular essential to me.[19] A parallel argument can also be developed to show that possessing the ultimate capacities of sensation, thought, belief, desire and volition are essential to me. The two key premises of the argument are (2) and (3).[20] We cannot treat here all the objections to them, but we do want to respond to the most serious criticisms raised against (2) and (3).

Regarding (2), there are a number of things about ourselves and our bodies of which we are aware that ground the strong conceivability expressed in (2). One is aware that one is unextended (one is "fully present" at each location in one's body as Augustine claimed); that one is neither a complex aggregate of separable parts nor the sort of thing that can be composed of physical parts but rather that one is a basic unity of inseparable faculties that sustains absolute sameness through change (one is an entity per se); and that one is not capable of gradation (one cannot become two-thirds a person).[21]

In near-death experiences, people report themselves to have been disembodied. They are not aware of having had bodies in any sense. Rather, they are aware of themselves as unified egos that exemplify sensations, thoughts and so forth. Moreover, Christians who understand the biblical teaching that God and angels are bodiless spirits also understand by direct introspection that persons are like God and angels in the sense *(a)* that persons are spirits with the same sorts of powers God and angels have but that persons also have bodies and *(b)* that the New Testament teaching on the "intermediate state" is intelligible in light of what they know about themselves and that it implies we will—and, therefore, can—exist temporarily without our bodies. Recall that in 2 Corinthians 12:1-4 Paul asserts that he may actually have been disembodied. Surely part of the grounds for Paul's willingness to consider this a real possibility was his own awareness of his nature through introspection, his recognition of his similarity to God and angels in this respect and his knowledge of biblical teaching (see chapter one). The property-thing depiction of one's body, and of regular physical objects generally, is the opposite of each of these.[22]

Two key objections have been raised against (2). First, physicalists claim that one can just as easily conceive of one's self as one's body or one's brain and that this cancels out the dualist conceivability assertion. We offer this response[23]: the physicalist confuses conceiving himself to be identical to his body (or his body as being metaphysically essential to him) with conceiving himself to be integrally embodied, that is, to be deeply interrelated to his body. In the next chapter we will clarify our view of the nature of the "integrated relationship." But we believe we can explain physicalist thought experiments (e.g., conceiving cases where the demise of the brain brings about mental dysfunctioning) along the lines of a deep integration between person and body without asserting that person's identity. So physicalist intuitions do not cancel out the dualist conceivability claim.

Here is the second objection: Your natural kind is essential to you. Now, being an animal with a body, which science has accurately characterized, is part of your natural kind. So having such a body is essential to you, and thus it is not possible for you to exist without a body. We offer the following response to this argument: your natural kind is "human person," and it is essential to you that you belong to that kind. However, it is not essential to being a human person that you be embodied. Rather, it is essential to being a human person that you have the natural capacities for informing and developing a body. When science studies your body, it studies the actualization of capacities for embodiment within the soul. It is necessary for a human person that it have these capacities, but it is not necessary that these capacities are actualized.

Regarding (3), it is pointed out that we can be mistaken in thinking that what is conceivable is, in fact, possible. I may conceive that it is possible for Muhammad Ali to be in a room while Cassius Clay is not, even though Ali is identical to Clay. In response, we have already admitted that conceivability is not an infallible test for possibility. But this does not show that it does not provide good evidence for possibility. Moreover, in the Ali/Clay case, it is easy to see how one could be ignorant of important facts that misdirect conceivability (e.g., one may not know that Muhammad Ali used to be named Cassius Clay). But it is not so easy to see where the source of error is in the dualist modal argument. You know quite a lot about physical objects and about your body. And through self-awareness you know a number of things about yourself as listed above. Where is the source of error here?

Finally, the vast majority of human beings through history have believed in the possibility of disembodied survival, if not in its reality. And almost everyone takes the reports of out-of-body experiences (OBEs) in, say, near-death cases, to be intelligible. Even if people think OBE claims are false, they still take them to be possibly true. In such cases no one thinks a brain is on the ceiling of the operating-room, staring down at a body. Based on knowledge from self-awareness, people know themselves to be centers of consciousness with the features that ground the modal argument, and that is why they can conceive of OBEs and of a disembodied afterlife. Surely the burden of proof is on the physicalist to show why these cases are not possible, and, in our view, that burden has not been met.[24] We conclude, then, that the modal argument is successful in providing good grounds for believing substance dualism.

The Identity of Physical Artifacts Through Change

The world contains living entities, like humans and dogs, and physical artifacts, like tables and ships. However, the world also contains entities called *processes* (e.g., the boiling of water) and events (e.g., a birthday party or a baseball game). Consider an event that takes some time, such as a baseball game. An event of this sort is extended through time and, thus, is composed of temporal parts; for instance, the game is a sum of nine temporal parts, or innings.

Next, consider an artifact, like a ship. Such an entity is extended throughout space and, thus, has spatial parts (e.g., the sides, deck, sails of the ship). Do such physical artifacts maintain strict sameness through change? Do they have temporal parts in addition to physical parts? Such questions have been part of philosophy since its inception, and they have often been focused on the ship of Theseus, an ancient Greek sailor and warrior who was a king of Athens. Over the years the ship of Theseus had all its parts replaced—plank by plank, nail by nail and so on—so that the ship that continued to sail had all new parts and none of its original parts. Was this ship replaced or repaired? Was it literally the same ship as the original ship of Theseus, or was it a new ship that merely resembled the original one and continued to function as a vessel of war?

To embellish the story, suppose that each time an original wooden part of the ship was replaced, a plank of frozen green Jell-O and not wood was used. Suppose further that all the original parts, which were removed piece by piece over the years, were saved in a warehouse and that years later they were reassembled into a ship composed of all and only the original ship's parts in the very same structural arrangement. Now, assuming for the sake of argument that one of the ships is the original, which ship would be identical to the original ship of Theseus—the frozen green Jell-O ship or the one with all and only the original parts in the very same structure?[25] Commonsense intuitions (and most philosophers) agree that the original ship is the one with the same parts and structure and not the frozen green Jell-O one.

Let us assume what seems reasonable, namely, that this answer is the correct one. Four lessons can be drawn from the ship of Theseus example and from our conclusion to the puzzle. First, physical artifacts do not maintain absolute, strict identity through change. An artifact cannot gain new parts and lose old ones (or have the parts structurally rearranged) and still be the very same ship. Physical artifacts are merely structured parts (property-things), and when the parts or the structure changes, the ship loses its identity. For physical artifacts, strict sameness through change is a fiction.

Second, the best we can hope for is loose, popular identity for artifacts. Such objects become a series of spatiotemporal parts and are sometimes called *space-time worms,* or paths:

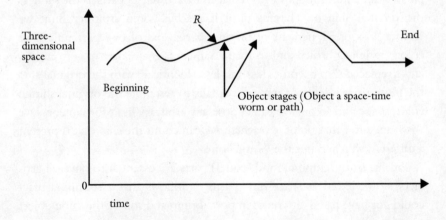

If we claim that a ship is the "same" over time, we mean that the ship is a sum of its spatial and temporal parts. The temporal parts are called *object stages,* or time slices, of the object. Two implications follow from this:

1. The ship does not exist at each moment from its beginning to its destruction; rather, a ship stage exists at each moment. The ship does not exist *through* time; it is like a baseball game. The whole ship is a sum of each temporal (and spatial) part (ship stage). This view is a version of what is called *mereological essentialism* from the Greek word *meros,* which means "part." Mereological essentialism means that the parts of a thing are essential to it as a whole; if the object gains or loses parts, it is a different object.

2. If we ask what it is that unites all the various stages of the ship of Theseus into the "same" ship (the same space-time path), the answer will be that all the ship stages stand to each other in some relationship R and that no other ship stages (say, the various time slices of a second ship owned by Ulysses) stand in that relation R to any of the stages of the ship of Theseus. Various accounts have been given to what R must be: earlier stages must cause the existence of later stages; each stage must be continuous in space and time with its neighboring stages (no *Star Trek* beam-up here!); each stage must closely resemble its neighbors in appearance, or the entire ship cannot lose some arbitrary amount of parts (e.g., not over 50 percent); and part replacement must be slow and gradual. Whatever R turns out to be, it is something that relates the various successive stages of the ship into "one" ship, and R is a weaker relation than identity. Sometimes it is called *genidentity*.

Third, identity is somewhat arbitrary and comes in degrees. For example, we can count the ship with replaced frozen Jell-O parts as the same as the original ship of Theseus until it reaches some arbitrary limit we choose: loss of 51 percent of original parts, loss of one part unless we color the Jell-O brown and so forth. Sameness is a matter of convention, and a replaced ship becomes less and less "identical" with the original ship the more parts it loses or the more it fails to resemble the original ship in color, shape and so on. We can choose any arbitrary limit for sameness we wish, and after that point is reached, we can count the ship that is present a different ship and not the "same" one.

Finally, since temporal (and spatial) parts are essential to physical artifacts, now viewed as space-time paths, it follows that a specific artifact could not have had a different temporal origin and still be the same object (nor could it have lasted longer or traced a different path through space and still have been the same object). If the ship of Theseus had been made a week later from the day it was actually made, then it would have a different set of temporal parts, and thus it would be a different ship. As we will see later, it is not clear that the same could be said of persons.

It is time, now, to turn to a clarification of the different views of the identity of persons through time. The absolute view holds that persons maintain strict sameness through change. Two different types of empiricist views deny this and treat persons like physical artifacts.

Three Views of Personal Identity

Statement of the views. First, there is the commonsense view, advocated by philosophers such as Bishop Joseph Butler (1692-1752) and Thomas Reid (1710-1796), which is known as the absolute view of personal identity. According to this position, persons differ from physical artifacts in that persons maintain strict, absolute sameness through change. Leibniz's law of the indiscernibility of identicals holds between all the moments a person exists except for tenses because persons do not have temporal parts. A six-foot-tall adult is strictly identical to the three-foot-tall person who was he as a child. The child *was to have* the property of being six feet tall, and the adult *currently has* that property; the adult *used to have* the property of being three feet tall, a property the child currently had, say, twenty years ago.

Personal identity is absolute; it is not a matter to be settled by convention, it does not come in degrees, and it is not partial. If we ask of a person at time t_2 whether he is the same person as one existing at t_1 earlier than t_2, the question will have a yes or no answer. Contrast this with material objects taken as property-things. Suppose half of a table is taken away and replaced with new table parts. Is the new table the same as the old one? Strictly speaking, the answer is no. But we could say that the new table is partially the same as the old one (50 percent in this case), and we may arbitrarily choose to draw a line at 50 percent and say that the table is still the "same" if it loses 50 percent of its original parts or less and is not the same if it loses more than 50 percent of its original parts. But we could draw the line at any point that suits our purposes. If we valued table legs, we might wish to say that the table was the "same" if it still had three original legs even if it had lost more than 50 percent of its original parts.

Personal identity is not like that. It is an all-or-nothing affair, and it is not a matter of convention on the absolutist view.

Next, the absolutist holds that personal identity is unanalyzable and primitive. It cannot be broken down into a more basic something else that could be taken to constitute personal identity. The identity of any property-thing, such as a table, can be so analyzed. We can say that the "sameness" through change of a table is to be broken down into a position about the stability of the parts of the table. But personal identity cannot be defined in terms of something more basic than itself. Sometimes this is put by saying that the entity that grounds the first-person point of view, the "I," is illusive and cannot be fully captured by a third-person point of view. The I is ultimate and serves as the unifier of persons in two senses. First, a person is a *unity at a given time*. Right now, you may be having several different but simultaneous experiences: an itch on your foot, a thought about personal identity, an awareness of music in the background, a desire for coffee and a feeling of the chair on which you sit. These different experiences are united as experiences of the same person, namely you, because they are all owned or had by the very same center of consciousness, the same I. Second, a person is a *unity throughout a period of time*. Over the years your body parts come and go, and your various mental states (e.g., memories, personality traits, etc.) come and go. But they are all aspects of the same person because they all belong to the same enduring I, according to the absolutist view.

Finally, most though not all advocates of the absolutist view hold that substance dualism is the best way to understand the I, or the ego, that accounts for personal identity.[26] You are essentially your soul—same soul, same person; different soul, different person. And it is because your soul exists, owns your mental life, diffuses your body and endures through change that personal identity has a foundation. Personal identity is grounded in the soul for many advocates of the absolutist view.

Two radically different positions about personal identity are both called *empiricist views*, and each of them expresses a property-thing depiction of human persons. The two main empiricist views are the *body view* and the *memory view*. Before we look at these, there are three things they share in common, and these center around the rejection of the absolutist position. First, empiricists start with a view of identity through change that is derived from physical artifacts, and they extend this to the identity of persons. They do this because they depict both artifacts and human persons as property-things. This means that personal identity through change—just like that of nations and tables—comes in degrees, is partial and is to some extent a matter of convention.

Second, empiricists hold that personal identity is not unanalyzable; it should be defined in terms of something else. For the body view, "sameness" of person is constituted by "sameness" of body. For the memory view, it will be the continuity of various psychological factors (memories, personality traits, interests and goals and, perhaps, continuity of the brain as the necessary "carrier" of those psychological factors) that constitutes personal identity. Either way, a person is like a process—a person is a series of person-stages related to each other in an appropriate relationship. The main point of a theory of personal identity is to spell out what the relationship or connection is between various person-stages that makes them all stages of the "same" person. This means that the first-person perspective, expressed with the word *I,* can be exhaustively replaced without loss of any information by a third-person description of the person in question.

Finally, empiricists assert that there is no substantive soul or ego. According to empiricist advocates, such an entity is a prescientific, unobservable, useless postulate. As we saw in chapter three, both strict and complementarian naturalists view the human person as a system of parts and functional activities.

The bodily version of empiricism holds that the connection between various person-stages—the connection that united them as stages of the "same" person—is that all the mental states of the person are connected to the "same" body. The reason that you now are the "same" as the person who read the first sentence of this paragraph is that the experience of reading this sentence is tied to a specific body, the experience of reading the first sentence was connected to a specific body, and the body is the "same" in both cases. Since "sameness" of person is analyzed in terms of "sameness" of body, advocates of this view must tell us what it means for the body to be the same (in a loose, nonabsolute sense) through change. Various answers have been given to this: new body stages must have a certain percentage of parts in common with neighboring stages just before and after it; new stages must be spatiotemporally continuous with neighboring stages; new body stages must resemble neighboring stages in appearance. In each case, the body view often allows for significant replacement of parts, change in spatial or temporal location and alteration in appearance by latter body stages compared to earlier ones. But, generally speaking, such changes must be gradual and continuous and not drastic and abrupt.

The memory view holds it is continuity of psychological characteristics that constitutes personal identity. The internal connections between experiences themselves is all that is needed to make sense of the idea of a series of experiences through time as being experiences of the "same" person. Chief among these psychological traits is memory. The reason that you are the "same" person as the person who got up this morning is that you currently have most of the "same" memories as the person who got up (except, of course, you now have memories of the day not possessed by your prior stage upon waking). Note that memories are not seen as epistemological criteria for determining "sameness" of person; memories constitute "sameness" of person.

Often, the memory criterion is supplemented with the "continuity" of other psychological factors—"continuity" of likes and dislikes, goals and interests, character traits, feelings of warmth, and ownership of earlier person-stages. Some add that since the brain is what carries and contains these psychological traits, then "continuity" of brain is a necessary condition for "continuity" of psychological traits and, thus, for personal identity.

Arguments for the Absolutist View

1. Basic experience of the self. Suppose you are approaching a brown table and in three different moments of introspection you attend to your own awarenesses. At time t_1, you are five feet from the table, and you experience a slight pain in your foot (n_1), a certain light-brown table sensation from a specific place in the room (s_1) and a specific thought that the table seems old (l_1). A moment later, at t_2, when you are three feet from the table, you experience a feeling of warmth (f_1) from a heater, a different table sensation (s_2)—with a different shape and slightly different shade of brown than that of s_1—and a new thought that the table reminds you of your childhood desk (l_2). Finally, a few seconds later (at t_3), you feel a desire to have the table (d_1), a new table sensation from one foot away (s_3) and a new thought that you could buy it for less than twenty-five dollars (l_3).

In this series of experiences you are aware of different things at different moments. However, at each moment of time you are also aware that there is a self at that time which is having those experiences and unites them into one field of consciousness. Moreover, you are also aware that the very same self had the experiences at l_1, l_2 and l_3. Finally, you are aware that the self that had all the experiences is none other than you yourself. This can be pictured as follows:

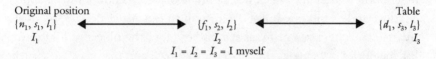

Original position   Table

$\{n_1, s_1, l_1\}$ ⟷ $\{f_1, s_2, l_2\}$ ⟷ $\{d_1, s_3, l_3\}$

I_1 I_2 I_3

$I_1 = I_2 = I_3$ = I myself

Through introspection, you are simply aware that you are not your body or a group of experiences. Rather, you are aware that you are the self that owns and unifies your experiences at each moment of time and that you are the same self that endures through time. In short, you are aware of being a mental subject that is in your body, that owns and unites your experience and that maintains sameness through change.

It can be argued that such awarenesses are either misleading or nonexistent.[27] For example, David Hume claimed never to have an awareness of his own "I" but only of this or that experience or group of experiences. However, two things seem wrong with this claim. First, how did Hume know which stream of consciousness to focus on in order to look for his own I? Wasn't he already aware in some sense of his own self *before* he could identity which experiences were his? We will return to this point below.

Second, it may be true that we never have an experience of our own I if we allow only sensations (e.g., of color, taste, smell, sound, texture, pain, pleasure) to count as experiences. But it can be argued that the I itself is not the sort of thing that *could* be sensed in that way, and the conclusion to draw from this is not that we are not aware of our own selves, but that there are other kinds of awarenesses besides sensory awarenesses and that our awareness of our own selves is by means of a different kind of awareness. It is hard to conceive of something we could be aware of with more certainty than this: while you listen to a song, you are the one having your experiences and that continues to endure during the whole performance.

2. First person irreducible to third person.[28] No account of the world in terms of third-person descriptions will be able to capture without remainder the information captured in my own *first-person* point of view, nor can it tell me which object in that world is I myself. No description of my body or my psychological traits will entail that the entity being described is I. A complete physicalist description of the entire material world, including all the bodies in it, could be given in *third-person* terms (e.g., there is an object at location *k* that is six feet tall, white, etc.). This would suffice to identity all the physical objects in space and time. But no such description will tell me which body is mine or which entity I myself am.

If we add to this physicalist description an exhaustive description of all the mental states present in all the bodies (e.g., the object at location *k* has memories of being at the 1979 Super Bowl, and that object has such and such character traits, desires and so forth), the problem is still present: such an account will not tell which entity so described is I myself. The I and the first-person standpoint cannot be eliminated or reduced to a third-person point of view. My own I—my own first-person point of view, my knowledge of myself by direct acquaintance—would be left out of such third-person descriptions.

Certain words are called *indexicals (I, here, there, now, then, this, that)*. These words are *token reflexive:* they necessarily refer to the situation in which they are used. The most basic indexical word is *I*.[29] *Here* refers to where I am, *there* to where I am not. A complete third-person account of the world will not capture the information expressed by indexicals. This fact can be explained if I am a first-person center of consciousness, a mental substance different from my body and mental states, capable of immediate self-awareness and of referring directly to myself. If my identity consisted in simply being my body or in being a certain bundle of mental states, a third-person account of the world would be exhaustive and would clearly identify which object I am. Thus the irreducibility of the first-person point of view supports the absolutist position.

These basic intuitions about the unity and singularity of my self and the first-person point of view can be illustrated with a thought experiment.[30] Suppose it becomes possible someday to perform a brain operation upon a person in such a way that exactly half of her brain, along with half of her body, is transplanted and joined to two different half bodies without brains awaiting the transplanted parts. We might diagram the situation like this:

Suppose further that upon recovery each of the two persons, p_2 and p_3, manifest the same character traits and have the same memories as did p_1. Note first, that the transplant would have created two new persons, but p_1 cannot be identical to both p_2 and p_3 for the very simple reason that one thing cannot be the same as two things. On the memory view, sameness of person obtains if and only if sameness of character traits and memories obtain. Thus the memory view would imply that p_1 is identical to p_2 and p_3, which is absurd if taken literally. However, advocates of the memory view hold that p_2 and p_3 are each p_1 in that they both exactly resemble p_1 in psychological traits. We will return to this option later.

Since p_1 cannot literally be both p_2 and p_3, what are our other options? It may be that p_1 ceased to exist that and p_2 and p_3 are two totally new people. Or it may be that p_1 survived and is identical to p_2 (or p_3) and that one new person, p_3 (or p_2), came into being as a result of the operation.

Either way, we learn two things from the example. First, a person is not identical to her body or her memories and character traits. (Remember that persons *have* these things; they are not *identical* to them or to a collection of them.) Why? Because p_2 and p_3 each have p_1's memories and character traits and an equal share of p_1's brain and body, but they cannot both *be* p_1. Therefore, the fact that p_1 is a person must amount to a person's being more than just a brain with memories and character traits or being just a body. There is a second lesson: persons are not capable of partial identity and survival as are physical objects. If you break a table in half and use each half to build two new tables, then it makes sense to say that the original table partially survives and is partly present in each of the new tables. But as we have seen in our brain-operation example, the following four options are possible ways to understand what happened[31]:

☐ p_1 ceases to be and two new persons, p_2 and p_3, come to be
☐ p_1 survives and is identical to p_2, and a new person, p_3, comes to be
☐ p_1 survives and is identical to p_3, and a new person, p_2, comes to be
☐ p_1 partially survives in p_2 and p_3

The last option may make sense of physical objects like tables, but it is not a reasonable option with regard to persons.

To see why this last option is not a good one, consider a second thought experiment. Suppose a mad surgeon captures you and announces that he is going to transplant the left hemisphere of your brain and the left half of your body into one half-body and transplant the right hemisphere of your brain and the right half of your body into another half-body. After the surgery, he is going to torture one of the resultant persons and reward the other one with a gift of a million dollars. You can choose which of the two persons, *q* or *r*, will be tortured and which will be rewarded. It is clear that whichever way you choose, your choice would be a risk. Perhaps you will cease to exist and be neither *q* nor *r*. But it is also possible that you will be either *q* or *r*. However, one thing does not seem possible—your being partially *q* and partially *r*. For in that case you would have reason to approach the surgery with both a feeling of joyous expectation and horrified dread! But it is hard to make sense of such a mixed anticipation because there will be no person after the surgery who will experience such a mixed fate. Partial survival, at least when it comes to persons, does not seem to make sense. Persons are unities, not collections or combinations of things that admit of partial survival like physical objects. Substance dualism captures this fact; the property-thing view does not.

3. Fear of future pain and punishment for the past. Fear of some painful event in the future or blame and punishment for some deed in the past appear to make sense only if we implicitly assume that it is literally you yourself that will experience the pain or that was the doer of the past deed. Future pain or past deeds are not yours by convention, and if real identity is a fiction, it is hard to make sense of these cases of fear and punishment. We would not have such fear or merit such punishment if the person in the future or past merely resembled your current self in having similar memories, psychological traits or a body spatiotemporally continuous with yours or that had many of the same parts as your current body.

Empiricist theorists have responded to this argument in different ways. Regarding future pain, some have pointed out that empiricist views give a way of grounding altruism—that in future pain we are really concerned for someone else, and that is good. Others claim that fear of future pain rests solely on the "continuity" of "our" desires, goals and memories. If a person twenty-five years from now were to face pain but had no memories or other psychological traits in common with you now, you simply would not worry about him or her.

Regarding past deeds, some philosophers grant that retribution is hard to justify on an empiricist view of personal identity. But they go on to point out that other aspects of punishment can be justified (deterrence of others, rehabilitation, protection of society due to incarceration), and those aspects are all that matter in justifying the punishment of a present person-stage for a past deed. We leave to the reader to judge whether these responses are adequate.

4. Rationality and thought processes. Some have argued that to realize the truth of any proposition or to even entertain it as meaningful, the very same self must be aware of its different parts (e.g., subject, verb, predicate). If one person-stage contemplated the subject, another stage the verb and still another the predicate, literally no self would persist to think through and grasp the proposition as a whole.[32]

The same point applies to thinking through the premises of an argument and drawing a conclusion. The same self must be present to unite and compare the premises, to see they entail a conclusion and to draw that conclusion. If nothing can occupy our attention for a while—since we do not endure through time—then we could only have momentary contents and these processes would be impossible. To attend to a proposition or argument, we must continue to be. If this argument is sound, then it means that empiricist views are self-refuting if they are asserted as rational by using supporting arguments, because such theories render this type of rationality impossible.

A major response to this argument is that as each person-stage emerges or ceases to be in a series of "thinkings," that stage passes on to the next one its content and a feeling of ownership ("this thought was mine"). Thus at the time a conclusion of an argument is thought, there are simultaneously a thought of the conclusion and a thought from memory of the premises of the argument. You will have to decide for yourself whether a momentary person-stage could simultaneously combine all these different thoughts at once and if, in fact, this is what is going on when we think.

5. Switch cases. Certain situations seem to be metaphysically possible. For example, it is possible that you could wake up in an entirely different body or with a totally different set of memories and psychological traits. If he so desired, God could put you in my body and vice versa, and he could give me memories exactly like yours and vice versa. In short, alternative biographies are possible: the same person could have had a different body and memories. If this is possible, then this shows that "sameness" of body or memories is not a necessary condition for personal identity. You can continue to exist without psychological or bodily continuity.

Similarly, your current body could come to be occupied by a new person in a switch or in cases of demon possession, or your body could be occupied by more than one person. In the same way, God could create a double of you and give that person the very "same" memories and psychological traits you have while you yourself retain qualitatively identical memories and traits. In short, distinct but qualitatively identical biographies are possible: the same body or qualitatively identical set of memories could be possessed by different persons. If this is possible, then this shows that sameness of body or sameness of memories is not a sufficient condition for personal identity.

Advocates of empiricist views can simply deny that such cases are, in fact, possible. Or they can grant that they are possible or not possible depending on your conception of personal identity, and all this shows is how arbitrary and conventional our concept of persons is.

6. Specific problems in empiricist positions. Finally, absolutists point out certain problems that plague empiricist views but, they claim, not absolutist positions of personal identity. Consider first the body view. For one thing, you can wake up in the morning and know who you are without opening up your eyes. In fact, though it may sound strange, at the moment you awake, you could simultaneously know who you are and that you are an enduring self and doubt that you even have a body (suppose you have been reading Hal Lindsey and think for a moment that the rapture happened during the night). The body view has difficulty accounting for this.

Second, as we have already pointed out, surely demon possession is logically possible, and, in fact, there is good evidence that it actually occurs. But in this case the bodily principle of "same body, then same person" is false because two persons "occupy" the same body. Finally, your knowledge of yourself is incorrigible; that is, you cannot be mistaken about which self you are. It does not seem to make sense that you could misidentify yourself at the present moment. But, if self-knowledge requires you to first know facts about a certain body and then ascribe that body to you, then (1) such self-knowledge presupposes direct acquaintance with your own I before you can ascribe a given body to yourself (for knowledge of your body presupposes and cannot, therefore, constitute self-knowledge); and (2) you could always make a mistake in ascribing some body to yourself. Since first-person identification is incorrigible and since it could not be incorrigible if self-knowledge is acquired according to the picture given us by the body view, then that view must be false.

Regarding the memory view, the problem of circularity arises just as it does for the body view. From the time of Butler and Reid it has been argued that memories presuppose and, therefore, cannot constitute personal identity. The thing that now makes you the same person as an individual in the past cannot be that you now have that past person's memories. In order for you to have those memories, you would already have to be that person. In other words, the thing that distinguishes real past memories of an event (where you were the one who did that past event) from qualitatively indistinguishable but only apparent memories is that in the real case you were there but in the apparent case you were not. Thus memory is only an epistemological test for personal identity, but it does not give us the nature of such identity.

Besides the problem of circularity, there is an additional problem with the memory view. Consider the brain-operation thought experiment mentioned earlier. It is surely possible that a person could undergo a transplant and that two persons could come to have all and only the very same set of memories and psychological traits as had the original person before the transplant. Some memory advocates assert that in this situation we should simply claim that the original person is the "same" as both new persons. Now it is obvious that they cannot mean by "same" here literal identity, because one thing (in this case a person) cannot be literally identical to two things (or persons). What they mean is that sameness is just resemblance. In other words, both new persons are exactly similar in traits to the person who existed before the operation, so it is arbitrary which one to count as that person.

But does this really make sense? Can your own identity really be so arbitrary? From a first-person perspective it is easy to imagine your waking up after the operation in one body and looking at the person next to you who has your exact traits and memories. It would not be an arbitrary matter from your first-person perspective as to which person you were, though from a third-person point of view, someone else may not be able to tell which new person is the pre-operation self.

Some memory advocates respond to a case like this by adding a condition to the memory criterion. Person y at time t_2 is the "same" as person x at an earlier time t_1 if and only if (1) there is continuity of memory and other psychological traits and (2) there is no other person z at time t_2 that resembles x as much as does y. The problem with this view is that the case above is simply easy to imagine: an operation could be performed, you could survive as one of the two psychologically indistinguishable people, you could know from your own point of view that you yourself are the pre-operation person—and all of this is quite independent of whether that other new person exists. How can a person's identity or nonidentity with a person at an earlier time depend on the existence or nonexistence of another person?

A final problem seems to plague both empiricist views. Since they depict persons as series of stages with temporal parts, then if parts are essential to their wholes (different parts, different wholes), no person could have been born at a time different from his or her actual birth. However, if such a thing is possible, as would seem to be the case, then empiricist views may be inadequate.

Arguments Against the Absolutist View

Among the arguments raised against the absolute view, three stand out. First, Hume and a number of others claim that we are never aware of our I; we are only aware of our bodies and, through introspection, of our current mental states (e.g., our current sensations of pain and color, thoughts, willings). Thus, the I is a fiction.

Absolutists respond in two ways. They point out that we are, in fact, aware of our own selves but that such acts of awareness are not like sensations of pain and color. The empiricist limits the types of awareness we can have to the latter, but we do, in fact, have the former in cases where we are aware of ourselves as the enduring owners and unifiers of our mental lives and bodies. Further, if we were not already aware of ourselves, how would you know which stream of consciousness or which body to investigate in order to confirm or rule out an awareness of your I? Introspection and knowledge of your body and mental life presupposes awareness of the I.

Second, empiricists claim that if the I is some immaterial entity, say, a soul, that is in the body and underlies our mental states, then we could never know who someone else is because we only have their bodies, memories and character traits to go on. We have no direct acquaintance with this other person's bare self. This is a version of the problem of other minds, and it states that the absolutist view leads to skepticism about our knowledge of other selves.

Some absolutists respond in this way. They admit that it is always logically possible that when confronted with a body or set of memories, a different person than we normally know is present. But skepticism need not be refuted by showing that skepticism is logically impossible and that there is no chance whatever for error or doubt in some area of belief. This same problem of skepticism is present about the existence of the external world (i.e., it is logically possible we are having sensations of a world when no world exists). To rebut the skeptic it is enough to point out that, in your own first-person case, you know who you are and that you are an enduring self by direct introspective awareness; you also can correlate your own enduring self with the continuity of your body and psychological traits. From this you learn that a good inductive correlation exists between these, and you can then use this correlation to justify the use of bodily continuity and memory as evidence of personal identity in the case of others even though such continuity does not constitute personal identity and even though it is logically possible that such judgments are wrong.[33]

Finally, some empiricists have argued that postulating an enduring soul to ground an enduring self solves nothing. How do we know that an immaterial soul is not just a collection or bundle of experiences at a time and a series of discrete souls through time? Moreover, how would you know which soul was yours? The same problem of identification regarding bodies and psychological traits occurs regarding immaterial souls.

Absolutists respond by claiming that, in the first-person case, you do not "postulate" that you are an immaterial substance that owns your experiences and body and endures through time. You are directly aware of it, and you simply report it to others. There is a major tradition in philosophy that claims our knowledge of our own selves is among the very best knowledge we have; for example, the clearest and most obvious case of a substance we are presented with is in our own self-acquaintance. And in acts of introspection we are simply aware of ourselves as enduring, immaterial centers of feelings, thoughts, beliefs, desires and willings. As a matter of ultimate fact, your own self simply is such an enduring entity, and your awareness of this is basic and fundamental.

A Final Option: The Material Composition Position

There is a different view of human persons currently gaining momentum among Christian thinkers that we shall call the *material-constitution view* (MC).[34] For two reasons, our discussion of MC will be brief. First, though it bears certain, important similarities with the property-thing position, MC is a distinct standpoint currently in the minority compared to the property-thing position, which is widely accepted among Christian intellectuals. Thus we have chosen to give our main attention to the latter. Some, though not all, of our critique of the property-thing view applies with equal force to MC. Second, the MC analysis of human persons is too sophisticated to treat adequately at the level of exposition at which this book aims. Still, we believe a brief treatment of MC will be helpful. Advocates of an MC view of human persons are by no means in agreement with all details of their views, but a fair summary of many MC proponents may be offered as follows:

1. The "is" of composition is not the "is" of identity. Suppose we have a vase composed of bits of clay. These bits of clay are, in turn, composed of smaller separable parts. Now suppose we reach a set of all and only nonoverlapping ultimate, simple, separable physical parts that compose the vase. Taken collectively, we may call these parts "the p's." When we say, "The vase is the p's," we do not mean that the vase is identical to the p's. Why? Because if we destroy the vase and scatter its parts, the vase ceases to exist but the p's still exist.[35] In this case, something is true of the vase that is not true of the p's, so they cannot be identical. When we say, "The vase is the p's," we mean that the vase is composed of or constituted by the p's. Moreover, if we consider the p's, taken collectively, to be an object and if we recall that the p's compose and are not identical to the vase, then it follows that we have two different objects—the p's and the vase—that occupy the same place at the same time.

2. The main concern for a Christian view of human persons according to MC is to make intelligible the resurrection of the dead such that the human person who dies is numerically identical to the human person raised on the last day.

3. We can make sense out of the resurrection of the dead while avoiding an undesirable substance dualism if we adopt a form of nonreductive

physicalism regarding human persons. On this view, mental states involve the exemplification of genuinely mental properties by the human person, and the human person is identical to his body taken as a physical organism. Now the body (and thus the human person identical to the body) is an enduring mereological compound (a whole composed of its ultimate physical simples). That is, it is composed of the p's (its ultimate, nonoverlapping, simple, separable parts) in such a way that it can gain new p's and lose old ones and still be the very same body. This is one of the differences, if not the most important difference, between MC and the property-thing position. The former treats human persons (bodies) as enduring mereological compounds, the latter as perduring ones.

4. Just as a watch goes out of existence when dissembled but the very same watch comes back into existence when reassembled, so a human person—a body—can cease to exist at death and come back into existence at the future resurrection.[36] Many advocates of MC adopt an extinction/re-creation view of life after death. However, they differ on what is required for the resurrection body to be identical to the body at death.

In our view, MC is preferable to the property-thing view for at least two reasons. First, it purports to offer an account of human persons as enduring and not perduring entities. Second, it is motivated by an important biblical concern, namely, to render intelligible how the resurrection body can be identical to the person's mortal body at death. However, for at least three reasons we believe that MC is less preferable to the sort of substance dualism advocated in this book.

First, the resurrection of the dead is not the only or even the primary biblical teaching that a theologically informed Christian anthropology must include. In chapter one we delineated the biblical evidence against any form of Christian physicalism—teaching about a disembodied intermediate state and teaching that seems to rule out an extinction/re-creation view. We believe that this biblical evidence is formidable.

Second, it is strongly conceivable that we can survive in a disembodied state; and, therefore, we are justified in believing that this is possible and that we are not identical to our bodies. Now some advocates of MC simply deny that disembodied existence is conceivable. But Paul claimed that to be "absent from the body" is to be present with Christ (2 Cor 5:8 KJV), that he did not wish to be found "naked" (i.e., disembodied, in 2 Cor 5:3-4) and that he actually thought he may have been out of his body during a time when revelation was given to him (2 Cor 12:1-4). Apparently, disembodied existence was conceivable, possible and actual in Paul's view. Moreover, the widespread belief in disembodied existence throughout many cultures in history, in the history of the church and as reported in intelligible near-death experiences (which are surely conceivable and may well be actual) combine with Pauline teaching to place a severe burden of proof on those who deny the very conceivability or the possibility of disembodiment.

Third, if the body is not identical to the p's that compose it, then it is up to an advocate of MC to give an ontological assay of the body so as to exhibit its ontological constituents that go beyond the p's. An ontological assay is a list of the various constituents (e.g., properties, property-instances, relations, relation-instances, separable and inseparable parts) that comprise some entity's being. For example, on a bundle theory of substance, a substance like a ball is just a bundle of properties. A bundle theoretical assay of an individual ball may look something like this:

{redness, roundness, smoothness, weighing two ounces, the bundling relation}

We offer this assay merely for the purpose of illustration.

Now at the very least, advocates of MC need to offer an assay of the body, especially its constituents beyond the p's. We believe that such an assay should render intelligible three things:

1. how the mereological compound can be taken as an enduring and not a perduring whole

2. how the various parts of the body can be taken to form a primitive, nonemergent, unanalyzable unity

3. how the various parts of the body can be functionally interdependent to allow for a genuine, unified teleological development of the whole body in the process of morphogenesis

We will develop our own view of these matters in chapter six, especially our view of the body in light of points two and three. There we hope to clarify more fully what we mean by these propositions. However, we believe that the teleology and special sort of unity of (inseparable) parts possessed by living organisms have throughout the history of philosophy been among the factors that have caused many to accept a substance account of living things and to reject the idea that separable part-whole relations and constitution are adequate to deal with living substances.[37]

Regarding point one, which is about endurance, an MC advocate may claim that the endurance of a body composed of the p's is simply primitive and, thus, that no analysis of it can be given. We think this is unlikely for the following reason: a scientific description of the types of parts and individuated relations (e.g., spatiotemporal, causal relations) that constitute bodies (or their lives) seems to justify the property-thing description of living things as identical to aggregates of separable parts standing in various external individuated relations (with or without supervenient properties). Remember, it is not simply separable parts that present a collection of multiplicities at a time and nonidentical, successive collections at different times for philosophical analysis; the various activities and individuated relations among the parts are multiplicities as well. What is needed is an account of the unity of these multiplicities that allows for the possibility of endurance. Otherwise, the claim that organisms (bodies) endure appears to be nothing but an assertion.

Now it would seem that if the aggregate (e.g., the body) gains or loses parts, activities or individuated relations among parts—since the aggregate seems to be identical to a compound of parts and individuated relations (this allows for bodies to be constituted by but not identical to the p's because bodies are also composed of the various individuated relations among its parts) and since scientific descriptions of these parts and relations treat them as aggregates—then it is hard to see what the primitive ontological ground for endurance would be. It doesn't seem to be the aggregate itself because it, considered as a multiplicity of separable parts and individuated relations, is not the same from one moment to another.

There must be some other entity over and above the aggregate that grounds endurance. But what exactly is the additional entity "in" the aggregate that does this? To the degree that MC is motivated by a desire to depict living organisms as closely to a scientific account as possible and in a way that is minimally offensive to physicalist intuitions, whatever metaphysical account of endurance is given, it will go beyond the scientific description of living organisms; and it is not clear that the metaphysical account of this additional entity will be preferable to Thomistic substance dualism on scientific grounds or to physicalist intuitions. We believe this is one reason why most advocates of the complementarity view simply identify the organism with the property-thing and draw the correct implication that qua aggregate, it perdures and does not endure.

Alternatively, an MC advocate may give an analysis of a body taken as an enduring mereological compound so as to assay the entities that account for endurance. Now we suspect that any such account will be relational. We think that it will appeal to some sort of structure that together with the p's give the assay of the body. We wish to close our discussion of MC with two problems and, therefore, two suggestions for further clarification for those taking this alternative.

First, a structure is an abstract object, so it will not be sufficient to ground the endurance of an individual body. What is needed is an individuated structure. An account of what individuates a given body's structure so as to allow for the same individuated body to exist through time and part replacement is essential for a complete assay.

Second, the structure among parts of living bodies is not a single, unified entity. Rather, it is a bundle or collection of distinct individuated relations that stand among various parts and combinations of parts. At any given time a living body is constituted by a collection of parts and a collection of individuated relations. Now if relational structure is appealed to in order to ground endurance through gain and loss of separable parts, this does not advance us toward a solution for this reason: the relational structure itself is an aggregate that gains and loses individuated relations. This, we believe, is a problem for anyone who appeals to structured or causal relations that constitute the body (or the life) of a living organism as the ground for endurance.

Though we cannot prove it, we also suspect that if a relational account of structure is given that avoids these problems, it will be virtually indistinguishable from the notion of an essence that, according to the substance view, grounds a living being's membership in its natural kind. In the next chapter we will look more at the relationship between an essence—more accurately, an individuated essence—and a human person's body.

In this chapter we have provided evidence for substance dualism from the nature of mental properties or states and from various features of personal identity. In the next chapter we will clarify more fully the type of substance dualism we advocate by looking at the relationship between the soul and the body.

The human form or "soul" shapes the human bodily organism,
gives it the purposes of biological, psychological, rational, social, cultural,
and moral existence, and provides the biological, psychological, rational,
and volitional powers to function in all the ways proper to human nature.[1]

JOHN COOPER

We have now recovered organisms as the irreducible entities that are engaged
in the process of generating forms and transforming them by means
of their particular qualities of action and agency, or their causal powers. . . .
Species of organisms are therefore natural kinds,
not the historical individuals of Darwinism.
The members of a species express a particular nature.[2]

BRIAN C. GOODWIN

The reality is that genes do not code for traits.
What the genes do is mediate the production of proteins,
or influence when the production of proteins begins or is terminated.[3]

RICHARD LEVINS

CHAPTER 6

Substance Dualism
& the Body

HEREDITY, DNA & THE SOUL

. . . .

*I*F ALL WE HAD WERE THE ARGUMENTS OF CHAPTERS FOUR AND
five, we would be left with a form of substance dualism wherein
the substantial mind would be viewed as an entity essentially characterized by the ultimate capacities for sensation, thought, free action,
belief and desire. Among other things, what would be left out of such a
view would be the nature of the human body and its relationship to the
mind. It is to this and related topics we turn in the present chapter. We
will argue for a form of Thomistic substance dualism over against Cartesian substance dualism. Before we take up the details of the argument, a
few preliminary remarks are in order.

First, in the same way that John Calvin may not have been a Calvinist,
René Descartes may not have consistently been a Cartesian dualist and
Thomas Aquinas may not have accepted all aspects of our version of Thomistic substance dualism.[4] The thought of Descartes or Aquinas is
extremely sophisticated, and it is beyond our present concerns to sort out
the various details of their respective philosophical anthropologies. Still,
there are certain broad features that have come to be associated with Cartesian substance dualism as advocated, for example, by Richard Swin-

burne and John Foster, and the same may be said about Thomistic substance dualism for contemporary Thomistic substance dualists like John Cooper, Peter Kreeft and Ron Tacelli.[5]

As we use the labels of Cartesian substance dualism and Thomistic substance dualism from now on, we will employ them in widely accepted ways; we make no claim to be accurately representing Descartes or Aquinas in every detail of these theories. Still, we do believe our use of these labels accurately captures the spirit—and often the letter—of each thinker. It also needs to be said that due to the current loathing for substance dualism, there is a widespread revisionist tendency among philosophers to show that, after all, Aristotle and Aquinas were not really dualists.[6] We do not wish to enter that debate here.

Second, by opting for Thomistic as opposed to Cartesian substance dualism, we have no desire to join the chorus of scorn often heaped on Descartes. In our view, he got a lot of things correct in his version of dualism, among which are a number of points advocated in the last two chapters. For example, Swinburne is a contemporary Cartesian dualist, and we agree with virtually all of Swinburne's version of dualism. We part company with his understanding of the body and of the soul's relationship to it. But we emphasize that this debate is an intramural one among advocates of two forms of substance dualism—forms that have far more in common with each other than they have with alternative views of human persons currently in vogue.

Third, one burden of this chapter will be to develop a claim we merely indicate here, namely, that there are two key mistakes in Descartes's substance dualism (as we are interpreting it) that we believe are corrected in Thomistic substance dualism. For one thing, Descartes reduced the soul to the mind, and we now have a mind-body problem instead of the more preferable soul-body problem. For the Thomist the mind is a faculty (a natural grouping of capacities) of the soul that may require certain physical states of affairs to obtain in the brain and central nervous system before it can function. But for the Thomist the soul itself does not require these states of affairs to obtain before it is present; in fact, it is the soul that is responsible for the development of the brain and nervous system and, more generally, the body. Descartes's reduction of the soul to the mind brought about an identification of the person with a purely conscious substance or at least a substance with the ultimate capacities for consciousness. For the Thomist, the soul is broader than the capacities for consciousness and is responsible for organic functioning and the activities of life.

Descartes's second mistake was his view of the body as a physical machine with the result that he could not explain just what it is that makes the body human. His substance dualism involved a dualism of two separable substances—mind and body. For modern Cartesians the mind is a substance and the body is a property-thing. Either way, the body is merely a physical object totally describable in physical terms. The Cartesian notion of the body includes the idea that the sole relationship between the mind and the body is an external causal relationship. In this way, while Cartesian substance dualists do, indeed, treat the mind as a substance, they nevertheless depict the body-soul unity as a property-thing in which the substantial soul is externally related to an ordered aggregate, the body.

By contrast, the Thomist who adopts our view will admit that the body is a physical structure of (both separable and inseparable) parts, but she will want to insist that it is also a *human* body due to the diffusion of the soul as the essence of the body fully present in every body part. In keeping with this view the Thomist will insist on a more deep, intimate relationship between soul and body than the mere causal connection between a Cartesian mind and a solely physical body. For the Thomist there is a modal distinction between soul and body: the soul could exist without the body but not vice versa. Thus our version of Thomistic substance dualism is not a dualism of two separable substances. There is only one substance, though we do not identify it with the body-soul composite. In our view, the one substance is the soul, and the body is an ensouled biological and physical structure that depends on the soul for its existence.

These two issues—the soul versus mind and the humanness of the body along with its relationship to the immaterial soul or mind—are major factors that distinguish Thomist and Cartesian dualism.

In this chapter we will do the following:

☐ explain our version of Thomistic dualism more fully and indicate the sorts of evidence that support it

☐ consider a set of objections to Thomistic dualism

☐ apply our model of Thomistic dualism to questions about the origin of the soul in normal and abnormal cases

☐ briefly indicate certain ethical implications that follow from our form of Thomistic dualism

Clarification and Defense of Thomistic Dualism

According to Thomistic dualism the soul is an individuated essence that makes the body a human body and that diffuses, informs, animates, develops, unifies and grounds the biological functions of its body. The various chemical processes and parts (e.g., DNA) involved in morphogenesis are tools, means or instrumental causes employed by the soul as it teleologically unfolds its capacities toward the formation of a mature human body that functions as it ought to function by nature. In a way to be clarified shortly, in different senses, *the body is in the soul and the soul is in the body.*

States and faculties of the soul. The soul is a very complicated substance with an intricate internal structure. In order to understand that structure, we need to grasp two important issues: *the different types of states within the soul* and the notion of a *faculty of the soul.* The soul is a substantial, unified reality that informs its body. At a minimum, in some ways the soul is to the body like God is to space—it is fully "present" at each point. The soul occupies the body, but it is not spatially located within it, just as God occupies space but is not spatially located within it. Further, the soul stands under, unifies, informs and makes human the body.

When we say that the soul *occupies* the body we mean at least that (1) it has *direct, immediate* conscious awareness throughout the body, though not necessarily of each and every part of the body, and (2) it can *directly* and *immediately* will to move the various parts of the body. Now it is true that when you will to move your finger, there may be a series of brain and central nervous system events that are necessary conditions before your willing can be made effective. But these brain and central-nervous-system events are not parts of the act of your soul's intentionally and effectively willing for your arm to go up, nor are these physical events spatially located between you and your arm. Rather they are necessary factors that must happen before your soul can directly and immediately raise your arm by an act of volition.

While it is true that you "occupy" your body, you (your soul) are not a spatially extended thing that is located within the geometrical boundaries of your body. You can search in vain throughout all of your body parts, and you will never find your thoughts, feelings, sensations or your self. Moreover, if your arm is cut off, you do not lose, say, ten percent of your soul. Clearly, the soul and body relate to each other in a cause-and-effect way. For example, if you worry in your soul, your brain chemistry will change; if you will to raise your arm in your soul, the arm goes up. If you experience brain damage, this can cause you to lose the ability to remember certain things in your soul. And so forth.

The soul contains various mental states within it—for example, sensations, thoughts, beliefs, desires and acts of will. This is not as complicated as it sounds, and we have already looked at the nature of some of these states in chapter five. Water can be in a cold or a hot state. Likewise, the soul can be in a feeling or thinking state.

In addition to its states, at any given time the soul has a number of capacities that are not currently being actualized or used. To understand this, consider an acorn. The acorn has certain actual characteristics or states—a specific size, shape or color. But it also has a number of capacities or potentialities that could become actual if certain things happen. For example, the acorn has the capacity to grow a root system or to change into the shape of a tree. Likewise, the soul has capacities. You have the ability to see color, think about math or desire ice cream even when you are asleep and not in the actual states just mentioned.

Now, capacities come in hierarchies. There are first-order capacities, second-order capacities to have these first-order capacities and so on, until ultimate capacities are reached. For example, if you can speak English but not Russian, then you have the first-order capacity for English as well as the second-order capacity to have this first-order capacity (which you have already developed). You also have the second-order capacity to have the capacity to speak Russian, but you lack the first-order capacity to do so. Higher-order capacities are realized by the development of lower-order capacities under them. An acorn has the ultimate capacity to draw nourishment from the soil, but this can be actualized and unfolded only by developing the lower capacity to have a root system and then developing the still lower capacities *of* the root system and so on. When something has a defect (e.g., a child is colorblind), it does not lose its ultimate capacities. Rather, is lacks some lower-order capacity it needs for the ultimate capacity to be developed.

The adult human soul has literally thousands of capacities within its structure. But the soul is not just a collection of isolated, discrete, randomly related internal capacities. Rather, the various capacities within the soul fall into natural groupings called *faculties* of the soul. In order to get hold of this idea, think for a moment about this list of capacities: the ability to see red, see orange, hear a dog bark, hear a tune, think about math, think about God, desire lunch, desire a family. Now it should be obvious that the ability to see red is more closely related to the ability to see orange than it is to the ability to think about math. We express this insight by saying that the abilities to see red or orange are parts of the same faculty—the faculty of sight. The ability to think about math is a capacity within the thinking faculty (the mind). In general, *a faculty is a compartment of the soul that contains a natural family of related capacities.* Among other things, the soul contains five sensory faculties; and the mind, will and, arguably, the spirit are among the faculties of the soul.

The soul and the body. The soul is a substance with an essence or inner nature, for instance, human personhood. This inner nature contains, as a primitive unity, a complicated, structural arrangement of capacities and dispositions for developing a body. Taken collectively this entire ordered structure can be called the substance's *principle of activity* and will be that which governs the precise, ordered sequence of changes that the substance will go through in the process of growth and development. This sequence of changes may be called the *law* or the *information* in the essence.

The essence conceived as a law or information sets the limits of what types of changes the substance can undergo and still exist, and it contains the set of capacities that determine the appropriate type of developmental sequence the substance should undergo as it develops. This development is a process of maturation in which the soul's essence guides the development of its body teleologically so as to realize the necessary bodily structure for the organism's functions to be actualized. The law is a teleological structure, a principle of unity, an orderly sequence of activities whose unfolding forms body parts in order to realize bodily functions.

When the soul comes into existence, it begins to direct the development of a body. As morphogenesis takes place, the soul begins to take parts within itself through nourishment; it informs these parts with its own essence; and it develops a spatial order or extended structure of heterogeneous parts in order to realize other properties, functions or activities through that order. The parts, at least macrolevel organs (e.g., the heart) and systems (e.g., the circulation system), are internally related to the whole substantial soul. They are the external realization of the internal structure within the soul's essence. To reiterate, this complex spatial extension is the body of the organism, and it is an external realization of a nonextended internal structure of capacities within the soul's essence.

On this view, function determines form and not vice versa. The various teleological functions latent within the soul are what guide the development of and ground the spatially extended structure of inseparable parts (the body). Thus the substantial soul is a whole that is ontologically prior to the body and its various inseparable parts. The various physical and chemical parts and processes (including DNA) are tools—instrumental causes employed by higher-order biological activities in order to sustain the various functions grounded in the soul. Thus the soul is the first efficient cause of the body's development as well as the final cause of its functions and structure internally related to the soul's essence. The functional demands of the soul's essence determine the character of the tools, but they, in turn, constrain and direct the various chemical and physical processes that take place in the body.

Regarding the way the soul is in the body and vice versa, the soul is "in" the body as the individuated essence that stands under, informs, animates, develops and unifies all the body's parts and functions and makes the body human. And the body is "in" the soul in that the body is a spatially extended set of internally related heterogeneous parts that is an external expression of the soul's "exigency" for a body, that is, of the nonextended law (structural set of capacities) for forming a body to realize certain functions latent within the soul itself.

Because this view may sound foreign to many people, we wish to recap in different words what we have been claiming. For the Christian theist who accepts the Thomistic substance view, the human person is identical to its soul, and the soul comes into existence at the point of conception either by a direct act of God (creationism) or by transmission from parents (traducianism, see below). Now the individual soul is constituted by a human essence and consists in a very complicated and hierarchically ordered, internal structure of capacities. As the organism is nourished, the soul develops the body as a physically extended structure of parts, which are internally related to each other and to the soul's essence and through which the various biological functions of the human organism (respiration, digestion and so on) can be realized.

On this view, the organism or soul is a whole that is ontologically prior to its parts—in this case, its body. The function of those parts reflects the internal structure of capacities in the essence of the soul. Moreover, the function of those parts is what determines the form in which they are placed to make the body (function determines form). The body develops and matures as a teleological development in which the soul's internal structure for a body is progressively realized in a lawlike way, grounded in the human essence in the soul, toward the end of realizing a mature, human body. The various biological operations of the body have their roots in the internal structure of the soul, which forms a body to facilitate those operations.[7] And the internal structure of the soul is what it is because God conceived, intended and designed it to be that way.

In sum, the Thomistic substance view of the human organism has these implications:

☐ The organism as a whole (the soul) is ontologically prior to its parts.

☐ The parts of the organism's body stand in internal relations to other parts and to the soul's essence; they are literally functional entities (the heart functions literally to pump blood).

☐ The operational functions of the body are rooted in the internal structure of the soul.

☐ The body is developed and grows in a teleological way as a series of developmental events that occur in a lawlike way, rooted in the internal essence of the human soul.

☐ The efficient cause of the characteristics of the human body is the soul; and various body parts, including DNA and genes, are important instrumental causes the soul uses to produce the traits that arise.

Assessing the view. With this background in mind, we can turn to the two arguments for the superiority of the Thomistic substance view, especially as it is understood by Christian theists, over either the Cartesian or complementarity property-thing view of the body-soul unity. The first argument centers on the notion of proper function and the internal relatedness of inseparable macrolevel body parts (e.g., the heart) to the organism taken as a whole.[8] For the Christian theist the Thomistic substance view explains our intuitions that when, say, a hand is severed from the body, it is no longer, strictly speaking, a human hand (a fact that will become evident in a few days). This view also has a very clear way to explain what it means for some biological part to function properly. A part functions properly just in case it functions the way it ought to according to how its internal essence was conceived, intended and designed to function by God.[9]

This may become clearer if we somewhat crudely picture the human essence, humanness, as a blueprint. In creating human beings, God first conceived of humanness as a blueprint. Then, when he created Adam and Eve, he literally placed the blueprint in them as an internal organizing principle. When we say that *the* heart functions to pump blood, we are not talking about any particular heart or any statistical collection of hearts. We are talking about *the ideal heart*. How is it ideal? We are talking about the ideal heart that is a part of ideal human nature as it was conceived and designed by God.

On this picture, statements about proper function (*the* heart functions to pump blood) have two features true of them. First, they are normative. A heart that pumps blood functions the way it *ought* to function according to the role in human nature it was intended to play. Second, the functional language about the heart is literal. The blueprint of what a heart is supposed to do is within the being of each human being, and the heart is a literal functional entity internally related to other parts of the body, an entity that works with them in a real, teleological way.

Contrast this view with the one embraced by most scientific naturalists. The scientific naturalist will do away with this notion of proper function. In its place, proper function will be understood as a function that is usual, common and statistically most prevalent or that confers advantage in the struggle for survival. The heart ought to pump blood in the sense that this is what most hearts, in fact, do (or what reproductively advantageous hearts do). The Thomistic dualist takes this naturalistic understanding of proper function to be neither necessary nor sufficient for real proper function. To show this, all we need to do is list counterexamples to the naturalistic understanding that are merely logically possible even if they are scientifically bizarre. This is because (1) if *p* is necessary for *q*, there is no possible world in which *q* obtains without *p*, and (2) if *p* is sufficient for *q*, there is no possible world in which *p* obtains without *q*.

First, the naturalistic understanding of proper function is not necessary. Suppose the Earth were bombarded with radiation from outer space such that 80 percent of human beings did not need blood to be pumped in order for them to survive and such that their hearts mutated to be a part of the system that facilitates hearing. Suppose, further, this arrangement were reproductively advantageous. In this case, it would be statistically common (or reproductively advantageous) for hearts to aid in hearing and not in pumping blood, but it would still be true that the heart *ought* to function to pump blood. The 20 percent of human hearts that pumped blood would be functioning properly, even though they would be statistically uncommon and even though their pumping blood would be no longer reproductively advantageous.

Second, the naturalistic understanding of proper function is not sufficient. In our example of radiation from outer space, 80 percent of the hearts would fit the naturalistic definition of proper functioning (e.g., they would be statistically common), but they would still be functioning improperly even if, by accident, they contributed to survival.

The naturalist may simply reject these arguments and insist that there is no such thing as irreducibly normative, proper function. We admit that we cannot conclusively refute this assertion, but we think that the considerations above are more intuitively plausible than is the naturalist position. At the very least, the naturalist property-thing view is not clearly superior to our position, and in fact we think it is more in keeping with our basic intuitions if we judge the naturalist property-thing position to be inadequate in its treatment of proper functioning as compared to the theist Thomistic substance view of human beings.

Unfortunately, things are not this straightforward when it comes to comparing the theist Thomistic substance view with the theist property-thing treatment of proper function. The difference between them lies in two key points. First, the Thomistic advocate will view the macroparts of the body as inseparable parts; property-thing advocates will depict them as separable parts. Second, the Thomistic substance theist views the human essence as a blueprint that is literally designed and *placed within* the individual human being as the internal, metaphysical ground of genuine internal relations, real functional entities and actual teleology within human bodily development. The property-thing theist will depict the human person's body as an artifact only. The blueprint of a car in a designer's mind causes him to assemble certain parts in a certain way, but those parts (e.g., a carburetor) are really only mechanical devices that are externally related to other parts and that engage in efficient causality only. Strictly speaking, there are no internal relations, no teleology, no functional movement *within* the car itself. The car's parts behave *as if* they were real functional entities. Still, there is a real sense in which the proper-versus-improper function is genuine and normative. A carburetor functions properly if its movements are isomorphic with and "realize" the concept of a carburetor in the mind of the car's designer.

For Thomistic substance theists and property-thing theists, then, the issue comes down to this: both can allow for true, normative statements about the proper functioning of the parts of the human body. The Thomistic substance theist will claim that the human essence is a blueprint designed by God and placed within the individual human being such that the parts of the human being are themselves literally constituted by internal relations to other parts and that these parts play a functional, teleological role metaphysically contained in the organism itself. The property-thing theist will admit that the human essence is a blueprint designed by God and will admit that it serves as the standard for proper versus improper functioning. But he will insist that, metaphysically speaking, the individual human body is still a property-thing composed of separable parts with no internal relations, irreducible functional roles or teleology literally within the body of the individual human.

We cannot argue in detail the relative merits of the two positions here, and we admit that this is a limitation of our exposition. But we hope we have made the issue clear enough to foster further dialogue about these issues. At the very least, we point out that it has been almost impossible for biologists to avoid functional, teleological language, and the Thomistic view explains why. Moreover, in what follows, we hope to show that at least in the case of DNA, the Thomistic substance theist's view has the

upper hand regarding internal relations and the like over the property-thing view, whether theist or not.

There are two different views about DNA, living organisms and the
process of morphogenesis—the process in which a zygote is transformed
into an adult through a series of well-defined steps. The first view
expresses the contemporary dogma of the "primacy of DNA" and is
sometimes called the *genocentric view:* the genes, which are lengths of
DNA with a specific function, are the fundamental units of life; they provide all that is needed to produce the organism in that those organisms
are built up according to instructions encoded in their DNA. Genes contain all the instructions needed to construct the organism, and they control morphogenesis. The adult organism is just the vehicle for passing on
genes from one generation to the next. In fact, organisms are mere
molecular machines, ordered aggregates assembled piecemeal by the
activity of an all embracing part, DNA, which is itself an ordered aggregate. The genocentric view is an expression of a property-thing depiction
of living organisms.

Why is this view so popular? At least three main reasons (all of which
we take to be erroneous in certain ways) for its popularity can be given:

1. DNA can replicate itself and is, in fact, passed on from one generation to the next, so it must be that which plays the causal role in specifying and controlling the development of organisms.

2. Because a change in a single gene can cause a change in an organism's structure, genes must contain all the information for making that
structure.

3. Since evolutionary theory explains how all life came to be, then bottom-up causation must constitute the correct etiological account of origins, and DNA is the best candidate for the correct causal entity. At the
very least, it has been argued, given evolutionary theory, DNA is a better
candidate than the cell taken as a whole. As Jonathan Wells puts it, "The
evolutionary story cannot start with a complete, fully functional cell. . . .
The *de novo* formation of such a cell from non-living materials would be
nothing short of a miracle."[10]

There is a second view currently gaining ground in the scientific literature, which Brian C. Goodwin calls the *organocentric view*[11]: Living
organisms qua irreducible wholes are the fundamental units or primary

loci of morphogenesis, the autonomous centers of action and creativity. The organism as a whole (not DNA, which actually presupposes the organism as a unity before it can function) is the fundamental unit of control and information.

On this view, what is the role of DNA and genes? In answering this question it will be helpful to consider an analogy such as the construction of a house. Consider three things needed to construct a house. First, one needs to specify the building materials that will be used. Second, one needs a complete floor plan or blueprint for the house. Third, one needs a specification of the order in which things are to be assembled. Now, in terms of this analogy, DNA plays the role of specifying the patterns for making the materials (proteins) to be used in assembling the organism. Genes play a role in stabilizing certain aspects of the spatial and temporal order of growth and development, but they does not generate that order. Genes produce cell materials but not the overall plan or internally related organization among the organism's parts. According to organocentrism, living organisms are substances that are irreducible to and ontologically prior to their parts.

There is considerable evidence that the organocentric view is correct. First, the two main functions of DNA (being copied in the process of cell division and serving as a template for protein synthesis) require the coordinated activity of numerous complex molecules, and it can occur only within the context of an entire cell. The feedback process between DNA and the rest of the cell is species specific: it is unique to each species, and it depends on the nature of the specific organism for its distinct activity.

Second, DNA is not the only thing passed on in reproduction. A single-celled zygote contains an intricate machinery without which the DNA is biologically inert. This extra material is copresent with DNA, and DNA requires the former for its specific functioning. Experiments have shown that "if a nucleus [which contains DNA] of one species is transplanted to the enucleated egg (an egg from which the nucleus has been removed) of an unrelated species, the egg may continue to develop for a while, following the pattern characteristic of its own species, rather than the injected nucleus—but the end result is premature death."[12] There are limits to this sort of thing (nuclear transplants must involve species that would normally hybridize anyway), but the point still stands.

In the movie *Jurassic Park* DNA from a dinosaur is inserted into a frog egg from which the DNA has been removed. This idea trades on the popular misconception that the egg is a neutral medium that receives all of its instructions from the DNA. Embryologists know, however, that much of the information in a fertilized egg is independent of the egg's DNA. As we noted above, in many species early development proceeds quite well even if the DNA is removed, until the embryo dies for lack of proper ingredients. If the embryo's own DNA is replaced by that of another species (as in the movie), the embryo will behave (at best) as though it had no DNA at all. So a *Jurassic Park*-style operation would yield nothing more than a dead frog embryo.

If organocentrism is correct, what about the three arguments advanced for the genocentric position? We have already addressed argument one (that DNA replicates itself and is passed on in reproduction), and the organocentric position seems to be the clear winner here. We shall set aside argument three (the argument from evolution) because we find it begs the question, and in any case it is not clear that the formation of DNA is not a fairly substantial miracle in its own right.[13]

That leaves argument two: changing a gene can alter characteristics. In our opinion, the organocentric view has an easy solution to this problem. Consider an artist who is using a fine paintbrush to produce a painting. Now if you alter the brush—say by giving the painter either a large brush used to paint houses or an ice pick—then you will alter the product produced. But this does not prove that the brush (or ice pick) produces the product or that there is no artist. The brush is a tool used by the artist, and if something happens to either, the result will change. Similarly, the genes that compose DNA are tools or instruments, and that is all. As H. F. Nijhout notes, certain genes produce (via interaction with other parts of the cell) certain materials that, in turn, play a role in determining which of various possible developmental pathways is actualized. According to Nijhout, "Such genes can thus be said to control alternative developmental pathways, just as the steering wheel of a car controls the direction of travel. However, this is far from equating the steering wheel with the driver."[14]

What is it then that plays the role of driver? Goodwin says it is the organism as an autonomous, irreducible center of activity; a whole with its own internal nature; its own species-specific principle of development in which the various parts are genuine functional entities that exist for and by means of each other and the whole of which they are parts.[15] It should be clear that this language is expressing the fact that organisms are substances and not ordered aggregates.[16] If by *soul* we mean an individuated nature, then every living organism is identical to its soul, and it is plausible to take the soul to be what Goodwin is getting at when he talks about the organism as a whole.

Two Further Objections to Thomistic Substance Dualism

Before we turn to some applications and implications of Thomistic substance dualism, we want to respond to two further objections that are sometimes raised against it. The first objection is the claim that if Thomistic substance dualism is true, then animals, in addition to humans, have souls. But, the objection continues, animal souls are not taught in Scripture, nor do animals survive into an afterlife. So the view should be rejected.

By way of response, it is sometimes a surprise to people to learn that the Scriptures teach that animals, no less than humans, have souls. In the Old Testament, *nephesh* (soul) and *ruach* (spirit) are used of animals in Genesis 1:30 and Ecclesiastes 3:21, respectively. In the New Testament, *psychē* (soul) is used of animals in Revelation 8:9.[17] Moreover, it is a matter of common sense that animals are not merely unconscious machines. Rather, they are conscious living beings with sensations, emotions (like fear), desires and, at least for some animals, thoughts and beliefs. The history of Christian teaching is widely united in affirming the existence of the "souls of men and beasts" as it has sometimes been put. But what is the animal soul like? Can it survive the death of the animal? Let us consider these two questions in the order in which they were just raised.

How do we decide what an animal's soul is like and what its faculties and internal states are? Obviously, we cannot inspect them directly. We cannot get inside an animal's conscious life and just look at its internal states. The best approach seems to be this: based on our direct awareness of our own inner lives, we should attribute to animals by analogy those states that are necessary to account for the animal's behavior, nothing more and nothing less.[18] For example, if a dog is stuck with a pin and a short time later howls and holds up its paw, we are justified in attributing to the dog the same sort of state that happens in us just after such a stick and just prior to our own form of grimacing. The dog feels pain. Now the dog may also be having thoughts about the morality of sticking animals with pins, but there is no adequate evidence for this if we stick to what we observe about the dog's behavior. Such an attribution would be unjustified.

One interesting implication of this method of approach is this: As we move down the animal chain to creatures that are increasingly unlike humans—for instance, from primates to earthworms—we are increasingly unjustified in ascribing a mental life to those animals. Now an organism either does or does not have a conscious life (e.g., a worm either does or does not feel pain). But we have more grounds for ascribing painful conscious sensations to primates than to worms according to the methodology we are employing here. Now all living animals have souls if they have organic life, regardless of the degree to which they are conscious, but we are justified in attributing less and less to the animal soul as the animal in question bears a weaker analogy to us.

In light of this methodology, what can we say about animal souls? Obviously, our answer will vary depending on the animal in question. But it seems reasonable to say that virtually all animals have certain sorts of sensations: experiences of taste, color, sound, pain and the like. Many, if not most, animals seem to have desires as well, such as a desire for food and so forth. Many animals appear to engage in thinking and have certain sorts of beliefs. For example, a dog seems to be able to engage in means-to-ends reasoning. If she wants to go through a specific door to get food and if the door is closed, she can select an alternative means to achieve the desired end. Many animals also engage in willings; that is, they will to do certain things, though there is no adequate evidence to suggest that they have libertarian freedom. It is more likely that the animal will is determined by its beliefs, desires, sensations and bodily states.

There are several capacities that animals do not seem to have. We have already mentioned libertarian freedom of the will. Animals also do not seem to have moral awareness. Animals do not seem to grasp key notions central to morality, such as the notion of a virtue, of a duty, of another thing's having intrinsic value and rights, of universalizing a moral judgment and so on. They cannot distinguish between what they desire most and what is most desirable intrinsically. Alleged altruistic behavior can be explained on the basis of animal desire without attributing a sense of awareness of intrinsic duty to the animal. Animals, therefore, do not seem to be capable of having a conflict between desire and duty, though they can experience a conflict between desires (e.g., a desire to bite the chair and a desire to avoid being spanked). Animals do not seem to be able to entertain various sorts of abstract thoughts, for example, thoughts about matter in general or about love in general or even about food in general. Moreover, animals do not seem to be able to distinguish between true universal judgments (all alligators are dangerous) and mere statistical generalizations (most alligators are dangerous), nor do they have a concept of truth itself.

While this is controversial and while we may be wrong in this judgment, animals do not seem to possess language.[19] One problem that keeps people from getting clear about this is the presence of certain ambiguities about what language is. More specifically, the question of animal language cannot be adequately discussed without drawing a distinction between a sign and a symbol. A sign is a sense-perceptible object, usually a shaped thing like BANANA or a sound (the utterance of *banana*). Now if an animal (or human infant for that matter) comes to experience repeatedly the simultaneous presence of a sign (the visual presentation of BANANA) and the presence of a real banana, a habitual association will be set up such that the animal will anticipate the sense perception of a real banana shortly after seeing this shape: BANANA. In this case, BANANA does not represent or mean a banana, so it is not a symbol. Rather, BANANA is merely a certain geometrically perceived shape that comes to be associated with a banana in such a way that the latter is anticipated when the former is observed.

By contrast, real language requires symbols and not mere signs. When language users use the word *banana,* it is used to represent, mean and refer to actual bananas. Now the evidence suggests that animals have certain abilities to manipulate and behaviorally respond to signs, but it is far from clear that they have a concept of symbols. One reason for this claim is the lack in animals of grammatical creativity and logical thought about language itself, which are present in real language users.

Finally, Augustine once noted that animals have desires but that they do not have desires to have desires. They may have beliefs, volitions, thoughts and sensations, but they do not seem to have beliefs about their beliefs, they do not choose to work on their choices, they don't think about their thinking, and they are not aware of their awarenesses. Nor do they seem to be aware of themselves as selves. In short, they do not seem to be able to transcend their own states and engage in reflection about their own selves and the states within them.

Animals are precious creatures of God and ought to be respected as such. But the animal soul is not as richly structured as the human soul, and it is far more dependent on the animal's body and its sense organs than is the human soul. Animal souls, no less than human ones, could not evolve from the simple rearrangement of matter. Since naturalistic evolution is a story that only involves explaining how physical events (mutations, etc.) affect physical systems (DNA, other body parts), it is in principle incapable of explaining the emergence of conscious souls in the animal kingdom.[20]

Our second question focuses on whether or not animals survive death. The best answer appears to be that we cannot be sure either way. There are no compelling reasons against the idea, but there are no clear biblical statements that favor animals being in heaven either.[21] Certain texts, such as the four horses mentioned in Revelation 6, simply employ figures of speech involved in visions. Other texts, for example, the wolf's dwelling with the lamb in peace (Is 11:6), refer to life in the millennial kingdom and not the future state. And even if some of these texts are taken to refer to the new heaven and earth, they only justify the belief that animals will be there; they do not justify the idea that those animals are the same ones who lived with us, died and continued into the afterlife.

If animals do not live forever, is that unfair? The answer seems to be no. It would be unfair only if animals were made to live forever, if that were the purpose for which they were made and if they had a desire for eternal life within them. But neither of these seem to be true of animals, though we cannot be sure. It seems best to be skeptical about animal survival after death, but the case cannot be considered a closed one.

Here is the second objection: the Thomistic substance view is just a form of biological vitalism, and vitalism has been uniformly and justifiably rejected by modern biologists. Since vitalism has rightly been rejected and since the Thomistic substance view is a form of vitalism, it should be rejected as well. There have been several different forms of vitalism, but relevant to our purposes, it amounts the view that in addition to physically interacting parts, living things also have a vital force or fluid that interacts mechanistically with the physical parts of living things.

The short answer to these problems is this: the Thomistic substance view is an intellectual response to a set of distinctively metaphysical issues that are relatively independent of (and arguably conceptually prior to) and not in competition with most of the more empirical, scientific issues associated with living organisms.

To elaborate, the debate about vitalism has been misunderstood frequently since the concepts of that debate have been used in many different ways. For example, during its zenith as a scientific research program, there were several distinct forms of vitalism.[22] The more crude forms of vitalism have rightly been rejected because of their tendency to depict the individuated essence as either a spatially located vital entity, a force or a fluid (like caloric or phlogiston) that was viewed as a mechanistic entity alongside other mechanical parts. The effect of this strategy was actually to reduce the living organism to a special sort of property-thing, and it was used as a quick and easy solution that closed inquiry.

A more adequate vitalism—if we wish to use this term of the Thomistic substance view (and we prefer the term *organicism*)—grounds the doctrine of substance in factors like the irreducible organic, holistic relation among parts to parts and parts to whole, the species-specific immanent law of organization and development, and the internal structural form and normative functioning found in living things. Such a position does not eschew the methodological use of a machine metaphor as a means of answering "how" questions about organisms (e.g., how does digestion take place) as long as this is not taken to reduce those organisms to mere heaps or property-things. Moreover, it seems to capture adequately the two features cited above (irreducible function and the internal relatedness of inseparable body parts to the organism taken as a whole, the role of DNA in morphogenesis) in its favor.[23]

In this regard it is interesting to read those who reject "vital forces" and claim that life can be entirely captured in physical terms such as the relevant powers and activities of *self*-boundedness, *self*-generation and *self*-perpetuation. Aside from the fact that a vital entity need not be taken as a force or field and that physical characterizations of life may reasonably be taken as operational definitions only, the terms *self-boundedness, self-generation* and *self-perpetuation* are clearly consistent with (though it may not require) the substance view we are advocating. As these terms seem to indicate, the activities of life presuppose an ontologically prior whole within which they take place and in reference to which those activities are characterized as living activities. This is consistent with the view that life is a set of activities grounded in an individuated essence.

Implications and applications of Thomistic substance dualism. In this final section of the chapter, it remains to tease out some of the implications and applications of the Thomistic substance-dualist position. We shall do this, first, by considering issues that arise in trying to understand the origin of the soul and, second, by listing briefly some ethical implications of the position.

The Origin of the Soul in Normal and Abnormal Cases
Questions about the origin of the soul are of interest for two reasons. First, a developed version of substance dualism should include a treatment of the origin of the soul. Second, certain metaphysically and morally relevant phenomena—twinning, cloning and frozen embryos—have been presented as evidence against substance dualism.[24] Thus, we shall offer a rebuttal to those who would use these phenomena as defeaters of substance dualism.

Before we dive into the issues, however, two preliminary points should be made. For one thing, justification for believing in substance dualism does not depend on developing a view about the origin of the soul. Why? Because the main issues that justify belief in substance dualism are those presented in the last three chapters. If our justification for believing in substance dualism is solid, then one could have adequate grounds for believing that, say, Dolly the cloned sheep has a soul even in the absence of a view of the soul's origin. This often happens in our intellectual lives; that is, we are often justified in believing something exists even if we have no idea how the thing came about. Further, we believe that the defeating force of twinning, cloning or frozen-embryo cases is not sufficient to overturn all the evidence for substance dualism.

For another thing, what exactly are we looking for when it comes to an answer to questions about the origin of the soul? Clearly, our answer should not contradict established scientific facts (though we should be sure that certain pieces of evidence are established scientific facts and not what naturalists tell us the facts have to be for philosophical or complementarian naturalism to be true). In this sense our answer should be consistent with science. But the nature of the question is not basically a scientific one. As we mentioned in chapter one, certain issues cannot be resolved by science because they are (1) primarily philosophical and theological issues and (2) different solutions are, strictly speaking, consistent with the scientific data, and thus adjudication among those solutions is not a matter of the scientific data themselves. What we should be after is an answer that makes theological and philosophical sense while remaining consistent with genuine scientific facts. This is what we will attempt to do in the remainder of this section.

Cases of twinning, cloning and frozen embryos have been raised as defeaters of substance dualism. In twinning, a single zygote splits to form identical twins during the early stages of development, while each cell is still totipotent—capable of making an entire new organism. The conclusion is sometimes drawn that during these early days of development, there is not a single human person present. Nor is there a soul, because a soul (if it exists at all) is not the sort of thing that splits, which one apparently would have to believe if one is committed to the idea that a soul comes into existence at the point of conception and that each zygote after twinning has its own soul.

In what is called *nuclear transplant cloning,* an individual organism is created from a single somatic (body) cell without sexual reproduction. In this case, the genetic material from a body cell is transplanted into an egg from which the nucleus (and thus the genetic materials) has been removed.

In cases where frozen embryos exist, some have wondered what to make of the soul's reality when it is not functioning. What is a substance dualist to make of the soul's existence and origin in light of these three phenomena?

In response to these questions, let us begin by focusing on normal cases in which a human soul is generated. In the history of the church there have been two different positions about the origin of the human soul: creationism (not to be confused with the use of this term in the creation-evolution dialogue) and traducianism.[25] Each has had its fair share of advocates. Briefly put, creationists hold that at some point God creates a new soul ex nihilo, and traducians affirm that the soul is in some way generated by way of the act of reproduction and comes to be at the time of conception. For creationists God is the primary cause of the soul's coming to be; for traducians he is a secondary cause. In order to understand these views more clearly, let us call all the strictly physical conditions involved in reproduction (e.g., the chemical and physical aspects of sperm, egg and their union) the "PR conditions." PR conditions are fully describable in the language of physical science.

There are two different versions of creationism: Cartesian dualist creationism and Thomistic dualist creationism. According to Cartesian creationism, egg and sperm are merely physical-chemical entities, and the PR conditions are sufficient for the generation of a human's body, which, you will recall, is merely a physical object. On the Cartesian creationist view, at some point between conception and birth, God creates a soul and connects it to a body that results entirely from PR conditions. For reasons mentioned earlier, we do not accept Cartesian creationism.

By contrast, according to at least one form of Thomistic creationism, PR conditions are not sufficient for the formation of a human body, which requires ensoulment (and thus the instancing of human nature to form an individuated soul) to be human.[26] On this view, when PR conditions obtain, God directly instantiates the abstract property of being human and creates an individual human soul. When the individual soul comes into existence, it is not then externally linked to a strictly physical body. Rather, the physical entities that constitute the PR conditions undergo substantial change and are incorporated into and subsumed under the new individuated essence to form one single substance.

There have been different versions of traducianism, and some of them must be rejected. For example, one form of traducianism found in Tertullian asserts that the soul of the child is a separated fragment of the father's soul. As one theologian put it, in this case, we are all literally a chip off the old block![27] While souls may certainly fragment in the sense of containing poorly integrated functioning (e.g., in multiple-personality or split-brain cases), souls are not the sorts of things from which pieces can be taken because they do not have separable parts.

A more sophisticated form of traducianism asserts that PR conditions are not merely physical. In addition to physical and chemical properties and parts, egg and sperm have soulish potentialities that, on the occasion of fertilization, become actualized. Here the union of sperm and egg amount to a form of substantial change in which two different entities come together, and this gives rise to the emergence of a new substantial whole—a soul that informs the zygote body and begins to direct the process of morphogenesis. This traducian view has much in common with the Thomistic creationist position, especially when it comes to describing (1) the incorporation of PR entities under the new essence to form a unified substance and (2) the subsequent role of the soul in the development of the body. The main difference between them is whether the soul is created on the occasion when PR conditions obtain or whether those conditions are sufficient for the soulish potentialities within sperm and egg to give rise to a new soul by way of God's secondary causality.

What resources do these three views have for dealing with the abnormal cases mentioned earlier? First, all three views accept various forms of relationship (e.g., causal interaction) between soul and matter. God, angels and demons are not physical, but they can actually interact with matter.[28] Even if one does not believe in their reality, it is strongly conceivable that if they existed, they could interact with matter. Moreover, your intending to raise your arm brings the latter about, and if you get stuck with a pin, you feel pain, so soul-matter interaction is perfectly intelligible and actually takes place.

Second, Christian theists have developed different models for God's relationship to the laws of nature and to natural causal processes. The main views of the world's causal activity in relationship to God are

1. *The full secondary causality view:* God sustains the world in existence; but in the normal course of things, the entities of the world exert their own causal powers, and such exertions are sufficient to produce changes in the world

2. *Occasionalism:* there are no autonomous, distinct causal powers possessed by created objects; God is the only true cause and no effect in

nature is brought about by natural entities

3. *Concurrentism:* every event cause has God collaborating with the natural causal entity, cooperating with its causal activity by ratifying that activity, which alone would not be sufficient to produce the effect

In all three views the regularity of natural law and causal processes is due to God's faithfulness in regularly sustaining, causing or ratifying certain effects when certain causal conditions obtain in the world.

In light of causal interaction and of God's relationship to natural causal processes, let us think through these cases beginning with the Cartesian creationist view. For the Cartesian creationist God desires for a human soul to have a body through which it interacts with the world. The body is something God makes for a purpose: to be causally connected to a soul and to be its primary means of effecting the natural world. On this view, God regularly and faithfully creates a soul when the PR conditions for body formation obtain because that's why PR conditions were created in the first place. Now just as God continues to cooperate regularly and faithfully with laws of nature in general, so God continues faithfully and regularly to create souls when the normal PR conditions obtain *regardless of the pathway used to reach PR conditions.* Thus, if PR conditions obtain via cloning or twinning, God still honors his commitment to why he created those conditions in the first place, namely, to be the body of a soul.

In frozen-embryo cases, the Cartesian creationist has two options: she can deny that the soul has been created yet or, more likely, she can argue that the soul follows a pattern throughout reality, that something can exist without functioning. Just as the life principle in an acorn can exist even though its capacities are dormant and unrealized, so the soul can exist even if its capacities for organic functioning and consciousness are not actualized.

As we are representing the view, the Thomistic creationist will adopt the same line of approach except for two differences. First, he will say that when PR conditions obtain in cloning or twinning cases, God uses this as the occasion for creating a soul that incorporates the physical PR constituents into one substance rather than creating a soul and causally connecting it to a body developing out of PR constituents. Here the Thomistic creationist adopts a form of miraculous concurrence as a model of God's activity in generating the body and its unity with the soul to form a substance: PR conditions are not sufficient for such a unity to appear, and God must exercise causal power and create a soul that then forms a body. Second, the Thomistic creationist will say that in cases of frozen embryos, since the PR conditions have obtained, there is a soul present with latent powers, which, under the right circumstances, will begin to function.

The traducian will agree that in frozen-embryo cases, the soul exists with dormant potentialities. But the traducian will take a different approach to cloning and twinning cases. For the traducian there is no a priori way to read off from the abstract notion of a soul's containing an essence the precise nature of the immanent laws that constitute that essence. We cannot specify what the boundaries are regarding what physical conditions can or cannot lead to the generation of a new soul.

For example, if we assume that a necessary condition for something's being physical is that it is extended and if we assume, for the sake of argument, that chemical elements and compounds are substances, then those elements and compounds have unextended, immaterial (though not soulish) essences (e.g., goldness, being salt). Moreover, on our assumption, chemical change is substantial change.[29] This means, for example, then when sodium and chlorine are brought together to form salt, purely physical processes of attraction, rearrangement of electrons and such cause two immaterial essences to cease to be exemplified (being sodium, being chlorine), and a new immaterial essence to obtain (being salt). Note carefully that even if this is the wrong read of chemical change, this understanding is certainly conceivable, and thus the idea that purely physical conditions can affect the presence or absence of an immaterial essence is at least intelligible.

On this view, it would be wrong to say that either sodium or chlorine is potentially salt. Something either is or is not sodium, chlorine or salt, and sodium and chlorine taken as individual substances are not salt. If we wish, we could say that sodium and chlorine are *possibly* salt. This simply means that under the right circumstances, sodium and chlorine are the right sorts of things that can undergo substantial change and form a completely new individual substance (salt) with a new nature.

In Genesis 1 we are told that animals (and plants) reproduce after their kind, and this has frequently been taken to imply a traducian view of the generation of animal souls. Now in this case it should be clear that the genetic materials of animals contain soulish potentialities and, thus, are not merely physical-chemical entities. In the case of chemical change and animal generation, physical changes, in some way or another, give rise to changes in which immaterial essences are exemplified (chemical change) or to the generation of an immaterial soul. There was no way a priori to decide the precise nature of these causal connections, and empirical research was necessary for their discovery.

As for the issue of twinning or cloning, we simply discover as a brute fact that certain substances—once they have developed a structure adequate to provide a framework for part replacement or for generating new substances—have the capacities in question. Nothing whatsoever in the notion of substantial soul provides a bar to these realities. Because starfish are living, we take them to have souls. But a piece of a starfish can be split off and used to grow a new starfish. In this case the soul of the original starfish is not losing a piece of itself. Rather, as a brute fact we discover that certain organic body parts of the starfish have totipotentiality, soulish potentials to develop a new organism.

Why should this seem odd if we grant the intelligibility of viewing chemical change as substantial change or if we grant that sperm and egg have these potentialities? In twinning or in cloning, certain organic entities (cells) simply have the relevant potentialities, and nothing whatsoever about belief in a substantial soul can place a priori limits on what physical conditions can or cannot give rise to a new soul. We must look to empirical study or revelation for help in that way.

Ethical Implications of Thomistic Substance Dualism

The debate about the Thomistic substance view of human persons is not a dialogue of pure academic interest alone. It also has significant ethical implications. Since the second half of this book offers a detailed analysis of many of these, here we shall only mention briefly three different areas in which ethical implications of the Thomistic view are crucial. The first area focuses on the possibility of potential persons and human nonpersons. For the Thomist, a genus and a species in the category of substance are not degreed properties. That is, either they are fully predicable of an entity or they are absent. They do not come in degrees; they cannot be possessed to a greater or lesser extent. An entity either is or is not a human person or some other type of person. Thus statements like the following one by Lawrence Becker to the effect that the notion of being a potential human (or person) or of becoming more and more of a human (or person) represents a deep metaphysical misunderstanding: "Human fetal development is a process analogous to metamorphosis, and just as it makes good sense to speak of butterfly eggs, larvae, and pupae as distinct from the butterflies they become (to say that they are *not* butterflies) so too it makes sense to say that human eggs, embryos, and fetuses are distinct from the human beings they become—they are not human *beings,* only human becomings."[30]

From the Thomist perspective this line of thought mistakenly identifies a thing's essence or natural kind with an adult member of that kind, and this mistake is rooted in a failure to treat living organisms in general, and humans in particular, as genuine substances with natures constituted by a nondegreed genus and species that define its natural kind. Assuming a substantial change view of chemical change solely for the sake of argument, just as sodium and chlorine are possibly but not potentially salt, so egg and sperm are possibly but not potentially human persons.

By contrast, the property-thing perspective need not treat humanness or personhood as a degreed property, but such a view is allowed by this approach, as is the notion of a potential person, because the standard properties associated with personhood (e.g., self-awareness, ability to use language, etc.) are, in fact, degreed properties.

Moreover, since the Thomist analysis of the personhood-humanness relation treats it as a genus-species relation, then the following implication also arises. Just as there can be colored things that are not red things but not vice versa, so there can be persons that are not humans (e.g., angels, Martians) but not vice versa. For the Thomist it is impossible for there to be a human nonperson. By contrast, the contemporary property-thing viewpoint treats the personhood-humanness relation as a supervenience relation in which the former supervenes on a properly functioning biological human life capable of sustaining psychic functioning. The important thing to note here is that the property-thing appropriation of the supervenience relation makes personhood dependent upon humanness—not vice versa, as is the case in the Thomist view—and this fact makes possible the existence of human nonpersons.

A second implication of the substance versus property-thing debate centers around the notion of a capacity, specifically, the ambiguity in claiming that a human person has lost such and such capacity. Recall that for a substance, capacities come in a hierarchy of lower- to higher-order ones, culminating in the substance's ultimate capacities that constitute its essence or inner nature, which is possessed by it solely in virtue of being a member of its natural kind. Thus the absence of a lower-order capacity says nothing about the absence or presence of a higher-order capacity. In fact, as already pointed out, a higher-order capacity unfolds and develops by a process of realization in which lower-order capacities under it are cultivated in lawlike ways grounded in a thing's inner nature.

Moreover, a defect merely signals the loss of a lower-order capacity, not the absence of a thing's ultimate capacities that make up its nature. A defect is the absence of a lower-order capacity that blocks the development of a higher-order one. When a metal bar is heated, it loses the first-order capacity to reflect certain kinds of light but not the higher-order capacity to have that first-order capacity, as becomes obvious when the metal cools. Note, even if a lower-order capacity is irreversibly lost, that by itself does not mean the higher-order ones are gone. Ultimate capacities are developed through the cultivation of lower-order capacities that realize the ultimate ones, and defects do signal not the nonexistence of ultimate capacities but merely the failure of those capacities to be realizable in the appropriate ways.

Consider again a persistent-vegetative-state (PVS) patient. The absence of certain capacities should be understood as the absence of first-order capacities, not ultimate capacities, even if such loss is irreversible in the bodily state. Why? Because this way of understanding fits the pattern of substances in general, and it implies that in the afterlife God merely restores lower capacities to enduring persons rather than recreating the person ex nihilo.

This distinction between higher- and lower-order capacities serves another purpose as well. There are two things about first-order capacities that are troublesome from a moral point of view. First, we do not have them when we sleep. During sleep, you do not exemplify or have certain first-order capacities of consciousness. You must first awaken (you still have the capacity to be awake while sleeping), and then you can, say, exercise the capacity to make certain volitional choices.

Second, our various capacities to participate in God's creative and redemptive purposes, which some claim constitute our personhood, are degreed properties that can be quantified in greater or smaller degrees and that do not appear to have upper limits. We do not all have the same capacity for thought, volition and so on. Now we do not want to say that a person ceases to exist and has no moral status while sleeping, nor do we want to say that equal rights for all persons is impossible because we do not all have personhood (understood as the possession of degreed properties or capacities without upper limits) to the same degree.

The best way to avoid these implications is to appeal to the continued possession of higher-order capacities in the absence of lower-order ones. But once this is done, two things seem to follow. For one thing, it is recognized that the absence of a first-order capacity, permanent or otherwise, does not signal the loss of higher-order ones. This is why it is intelligible to think that frozen embryos have souls. In addition, such an appeal implicitly uses the notion of the continued possession of human personhood as the inner nature of the individual in question. Thus PVS patients may not have first-order capacities, but they still have higher-order ones in virtue of the continued presence of their inner nature, and this is what makes them human persons.

Property-thing advocate Robert N. Wennberg fails to take this possibility into account, and this failure is curious in light of something he says elsewhere.[31] He claims that personhood grows as a child develops until it is fully a person. But he goes on to say that the person continues to develop beyond this point. Now just what is it that continues to develop? If it is the properties that constitute personhood, how can we say that the child is fully a person? The problem here is that personhood turns out to be a degreed property without an intrinsic maximum, and thus it cannot be exemplified to a complete degree.

On the other hand, Wennberg may be thinking that when the properties of personhood are fully present, then other properties emerge and begin to develop.[32] But this move implicitly uses the notion of higher- and lower-order capacities such that some cannot obtain until others have been developed. If Wennberg uses that move in one case, why can we not use it in the case of PVS patients? The Thomistic substance view, with its notion of an essence or inner nature, can easily accommodate talk about a hierarchy of capacities culminating in ultimate ones possessed throughout an individual's lifetime, but the property-thing position has a more difficult time with such talk. On this view, it is not clear what it is that possesses these ultimate capacities, nor is it easy to see just what it is that continues to endure as the organism changes through time.

The final area of comparison involves criteria for death. If we limit ourselves to the present debate about whole- versus higher-brain criteria, advocates of the Thomistic substance view will tend to prefer the former, and property-thing adherents will prefer the later. This is because substance advocates go beyond mental functioning in their understanding of human personhood and include biological functioning as well. The Thomist will want to know what it is that gives organic unity to the human body and grounds its species-specific principle of individuation, capacities and properties.[33] By contrast, an advocate of the property-thing view will tie personhood into various criteria expressing different aspects of mental life.[34]

In the seventeenth century John Locke once bemoaned the fact that the idea of soul, especially when compared to the idea of matter, was regarded as obscure by many in his day. Locke thought that this judgment followed from people's being preoccupied with the study of material substances compared to the study of immaterial ones: "I know that people whose thoughts are immersed in matter, and have so subjected their minds to their senses that they seldom reflect on anything beyond them."[35]

In this judgment Locke was probably correct. Around two decades before the publication of *An Essay Concerning Human Understanding,* Ralph Cudworth had noted a growing number of thinkers who were "possessed with a certain Kind of Madness, that may be called Pneumatophobia, that makes them have an irrational, but desperate abhorrence from Spirits or incorporeal Substance." According to Cudworth this attitude went along with what he called Hylomania, "whereby they madly dote upon Matter."[36] In the contemporary intellectual climate there is a growing impetus to develop a satisfying version of Christian materialism. In the first part of this book we have tried to show that Christian materialism should be rejected in favor of substance dualism. In part two we will investigate various areas of ethical debate that center on the nature of human persons.

Part Two

Ethical Reflections on Human Personhood

Biological life alone does not endow a being with interests.
Without interests, they cannot have moral status.[1]

BONNIE STEINBOCK

Increasing knowledge is increasing the awe and respect
which we have for the unborn and is causing us to regard
the unborn baby as a real person long before birth.[2]

NAOMI WOLF

CHAPTER 7

The Moral & Metaphysical
Status of the Unborn

ABORTION & FETAL RESEARCH

....

WHAT DIFFERENCE DOES OUR VIEW OF A HUMAN PERSON MAKE? Is our discussion of the metaphysics of a human person simply abstract, philosophical debate that has little to do with things nonphilosophers care about? Or is the notion of human personhood related to and even central to many of the ethical issues with which scientists, philosophers, theologians and public-policy makers are wrestling—the same issues that appear regularly on the front pages of the newspaper?[3] Our goals in this second section of the book are to demonstrate the relevance of our philosophical reflections on human personhood to many of the most intensely debated moral issues of the day and to point out the ethical implications of our theological and philosophical view of a human person.

We have argued for a view of a human person from the perspective of a Thomistic substance dualist, which we hold to be the view that is most consistent with the teaching of Scripture and right reason. That is, a human person is a substance in the Thomistic, not Cartesian, sense and not a property-thing. It is more than simply the material elements that make up the body. It is identical to an immaterial soul, which governs its lawlike development and enables the substance to maintain its essential identity through change. A libertarian view of free will and moral responsibility is most consistent with substance dualism. In fact, some physicalists will admit that the notion of moral responsibility is problematic for them, since their view implies a form of event-causation that rules out an agent's having active power, which seems necessary for genuine moral responsibility.[4] Furthermore, a property-thing view of a human person suggests that as the properties of a person change, so does the person himself or herself, since, from that perspective, there is no essential person that survives the process of change. This would suggest that, for example, the person who committed a crime, the person brought to trial for the crime and the person serving a jail term for that same crime are all different persons. The notions of moral responsibility and criminal justice are both premised on a substance-dualist view of a person; otherwise, it would be conceptually difficult to hold anyone responsible for immoral or criminal actions.

This continuity of personal identity through change seems consistent with biblical teaching. Psalm 139, which is often cited in the abortion debate, strongly suggests that King David is the same essential person from conception to mature adult. In this psalm David is addressing God as both a poet and a worshiper. He is coming to God in deep reverence and prayer, initiating a conversation with God and providing a reflection on that conversation in poetic form. In verses 1 to 6 the psalmist admits that nothing in his life has escaped the penetrating search of the living God. He is the object of God's thorough and ongoing knowledge, known intimately by God. In verses 7 to 12 he attempts, probably hypothetically, to escape from God's knowledge of him. Such knowledge is threatening to him, and he desires to get out from under it, yet he admits that wherever he would flee, God would be there. This section is an eloquent statement of God's omnipresence.

The critical part of the psalm comes in verses 13 to 18, in which the psalmist reflects on the way in which God has intricately created him. He describes the process with vivid figures of speech such as being knit or woven together in the womb. He marvels at the skill of God in fashioning the details of his being in the secret place of the womb. The psalmist describes himself as an "unformed substance" (v. 16 NRSV), translated by the primary lexicon for the Old Testament as "embryo."[5] David sees the person who gives thanks and praise to God (vv. 13-16) as the same person

STATUS OF THE UNBORN

who was skillfully woven together in the womb (v. 13) and as the same person who is known by God inside and out (vv. 1-6). In other words, there is continuity of personal identity from the earliest point of development to a mature adult. That is the significance of Psalm 139 to the discussion of the nature of the embryo. It is not solely that God painstakingly and intricately created David in the womb; it is also that the person who was being created in the womb is the same person who is writing the psalm.

Other passages of Scripture also suggest this continuity of personal identity. For example, in Psalm 51:5 David states, "Surely I was sinful at birth, sinful from the time my mother conceived me." David here is confessing not only his specific sins of adultery with Bathsheba and the arranged murder of her husband, Uriah the Hittite (see 2 Sam 11—12), but also his innate inclination to sin. This is a characteristic shared by all persons, and David's claim is that he possessed it from the point of conception. Thus, an essential attribute of adult persons—an inclination to sin—is attributed to the unborn, underscoring the continuity of identity from conception to adulthood. The same sinful adult began as a sinful embryonic person in the womb.

In Job 10:8-11 the writer uses different figures of speech to describe God's intricate creation of him in the womb, but the point is comparable to that made in Psalm 139: a continuity of personal identity from early embryonic life onward. Similarly, in Job 3:3 the writer uses a poetic form called *synonymous parallelism* to indicate the continuity between conception and birth: "Let the day perish in which I was born, and the night that said, 'A man-child is conceived'" (NRSV). We should be careful about reading too much into the use of poetic parallelism, but the format is used to restate essentially the same point in different language. The use of the parallelism may mean that the writer regarded birth and conception as fundamentally synonymous, simply different language to state the same point. This is strengthened by the use of the term *man-child*, or "boy" in the second half of the verse, which addresses Job's conception. This term (Hebrew *geber*) is also used in other parts of the Old Testament to refer to a man and a husband and, thus, a person. There seems to be a continuity of identity between conception and birth in the case of Job.

The fact that poetic language is used in these passages can make these texts more difficult to interpret, but it does not, per se, disqualify them from making an authoritative contribution to this discussion. It is true that poetry is used in part to create visual images that enable the author to touch the readers' emotions. But it does not follow that therefore poetry bypasses the intellect. Nor does it follow that poetic language is incapable of making a literal point. In fact, that is its purpose. All figurative language is designed to make a literal point about the subject at hand. Figurative language only makes sense when related to a literal point of analogy. Of course, when speaking of God all language has its limits, and poetry is often used to enable the author to write of the surpassing glory of God in a way that prose cannot. But it does not follow from the use of poetry that the writers of Scripture cannot make a literal point about God. In these texts about persons in the womb, poetry is used to try to make sense out of that which was shrouded in secrecy prior to the advent of modern obstetrics. We should be cautious about the details of any passage of poetry. But the poetry in these texts does not obscure the literal overriding point made about the continuity of personal identity. We should be careful but not overly skeptical about poetic texts simply because that genre is used.

One example of the need for interpretive caution is found in Jeremiah 1:5 to indicate a similar point about the continuity of identity. Here the prophet quotes God in saying, "Before I formed you in the womb I knew you, before you were born I set you apart." If taken too far, the synonymous parallelism here would indicate something like preexistence and a separation between biological life and the person. But it may be that the passage points to the significance of what occurred in the womb because of Jeremiah's prophetic calling from before time. One should be careful not to put too much weight on unclear texts such as this one.[6]

A further indication of this continuity of personal identity comes from the narrative of Jacob and Esau (Gen 25:19-34). During Rebakah's pregnancy, God prophesies concerning the twins in her womb, saying, "Two nations are in your womb, and two peoples from within you will be separated; one people will be stronger than the other, and the older will serve the younger" (Gen 25:23). God is speaking figuratively to indicate that the twins in Rebakah's womb are the representative heads of two nations that will emerge from their respective families over time. They will have a relationship different from that which was expected in the ancient world in that the older one, normally the one in a position of prominence, will serve the younger. This text suggests God's election of Jacob over Esau in the womb (Mal 1:2-3) and points out that they are the representative corporate heads of their clan or nation. In other words, they are both subjects of divine election while in the womb, and their roles as heads of their respective peoples was appointed in the womb and realized as adults. God saw them in the womb as the adults they would become and in the roles they would play as adults. This suggests that God saw a continuity of personal identity from the womb through adulthood. The same individuals who would assume headship over their clan or nation are the same individuals who are maturing in the womb.

One passage that appears to suggest a discontinuity between life in the womb and life as an adult is the enigmatic section of the Mosaic law in Exodus 21:22-25. It is a specific law designed to arbitrate a very specific case: "When people who are fighting injure a pregnant woman so that there is a miscarriage, and yet no further harm [to the woman] follows, the one responsible shall be fined what the woman's husband demands, paying as much as the judges determine. If any harm [to the woman] follows, then you shall give life for life, eye for eye, tooth for tooth, hand for hand, foot for foot, burn for burn, wound for wound, stripe for stripe" (NRSV). Some contend that since the penalty for causing the death of the fetus is only a fine but the penalty for causing the death of the mother merits the death penalty, the fetus must not be deserving of the same level of protection as an adult person. It must have a different status, something less than the full personhood that merits taking life for life in this case.

However, there is significant debate over the term translated "miscarriage." At best there is no scholarly consensus on the interpretation. The most likely translation is "she gives birth prematurely" (e.g., NIV), which implies that the birth is successful—that it creates serious discomfort to the pregnant woman but neither she nor her child is killed. The normal Hebrew word for miscarriage is the term *shakal,* which is not used here. Rather the term *yasa'* is used, which is a term normally used in connection with the live birth of one's child. The fact that the normal term for miscarriage is not used here and that a term with connotations to live birth is used suggests the passage means a woman who gives birth prematurely.[7] This would make more sense of the different penalties accruing to the guilty party. And it may be that the phrase "if any harm follows" (v. 23) would apply either to the woman or to the child, so that if the woman actually did have a miscarriage, that would be punishable under the "life for life" scheme. Even if the correct translation was "she had a miscarriage," it would not necessarily follow that the unborn has less of a claim to personhood, since penalty and personhood are not necessarily related.[8] Though the interpretation of this text is debated, it surely does not justify intentionally taking embryonic or fetal life. The most likely interpretation linguistically also makes the best sense theologically, given the Scripture's teaching about personal identity in Psalm 139 and other texts.

Our view of a human person touches virtually every debated issue in biomedical ethics today, from the beginning to the ending edges of life. The moral status of fetuses—and, for some, even newborns[9]—has been central to the ongoing debate over abortion[10] and to the more recent debate over fetal research and the use of fetal tissue from abortions for medical treatment. Not only are fetuses the subject of research, but increasingly embryos are as well. The personhood of embryos and the use of embryos in research are issues now that the U.S. government has removed the moratorium on federal funding for such research. In addition, the standard of practice in infertility treatments such as in vitro fertilization involves cryopreservation of embryos, making the disposition of surplus embryos in these treatments a difficult issue. The notion of personhood is central not only in reproductive technologies but also in genetic technologies. With the Human Genome Project's moving toward completion and bringing an enormous increase in the genetic information available to a person, there is increasing attention given to the notion that human persons are reducible to their genetic content. That is, one's genetic makeup is widely considered in scientific circles to be the basic element of the human person. In genetics and also in cloning, the biomedical breakthrough of the 1990s, questions of human personhood are again at the forefront. What sort of being is a cloned human being? What does cloning suggest about the soul and how it is transmitted? Since the technology is so new, scientists and public-policy makers are asking many of these questions for the first time. Finally, the ongoing debate over physician-assisted suicide (PAS) and euthanasia involve the definition of a human person. Some of the arguments for euthanasia and for the treatment of patients in a persistent vegetative state (PVS) suggest that the patients have lost personhood, thus ending their life does not violate the fifth commandment prohibiting the killing of innocent people. Further, some physicians and bioethicists want to broaden the definition of death from whole-brain death to higher-brain death, making it morally legitimate and legally appropriate to say that PVS patients have died and that anencephalic children were never alive. Even some in the Christian community suggest that PVS patients have lost the image of God, a troubling notion in our view. It seems fair to say that most of the major bioethical issues one reads about regularly in the newspaper involve considerations of what constitutes a human person. We will address these issues in the second half of the book.

In this chapter we will focus our attention on the moral and metaphysical status of fetuses in utero and newborn children. We will show how many abortion-rights advocates assign (or fail to assign) personhood and how their reasoning leads to the logical conclusion (which some are willing to admit) that at the least, certain types of newborns—and in some cases all newborns—are not yet persons because they do not exhibit the characteristics deemed necessary criteria for personhood. We will also address the controversial issue of fetal research, particularly that which has lead to promising treatments for conditions like Parkinson's disease and diabetes. We will turn our attention to extracorporeal embryos and research on embryos in the following chapter.

Legal Status of Fetuses

Since 1973, with the *Roe v. Wade* Supreme Court decision,[11] abortion has been legal throughout the entire nine months of pregnancy. The Court in *Roe* arbitrarily divided up the nine months of pregnancy into trimesters with increasing protections for the unborn in the last trimester. In the first trimester, abortion on demand is legal. In the second trimester, the state can place restrictions on access to abortion in order to safeguard the health of the pregnant woman. These include restricting the availability of abortion to licensed medical facilities and requiring them to be performed by licensed physicians. It is widely perceived in the culture at large that abortion is only legal up until the point of viability or, at the time of the *Roe* decision, roughly at the end of the second trimester.[12] What is not widely known, however, is that on the same day that the Supreme Court handed down the *Roe* decision, it also handed down another abortion decision, *Doe v. Bolton*,[13] which expanded the availability of abortion beyond what *Roe* by itself provides. The *Doe* decision expanded the exception clause in *Roe* that allowed for postviability, or third-trimester, abortions in cases in which the life or health of the mother was in jeopardy. The *Doe* decision expanded the notion of the health of the mother in a way that could be interpreted to justify abortion for virtually any reason. The Court interpreted the health of the mother to include more than simply her physical health. It also included her psychological and emotional health, and it could be construed to include her financial health as well. The Court put it this way:

> That statute [the Georgia law in question] has been construed to bear upon the psychological as well as physical well being [of the mother]. . . . We agree that the medical judgment [of the mother's physician, as to whether continuing the pregnancy constitutes a threat to the mother's health] may be exercised in light of all factors—physical, emotional, psychological, familial and the woman's age—relevant to the well-being of the patient. All these factors may relate to health [of the pregnant woman].[14]

Thus if in the judgment of the mother's physician any of these factors, which include much more than simply medical indications, are present, a postviability abortion would be legal. Not only are the factors broadened well beyond medical indications—aspects of a woman's health that her physician is not trained to assess—but also the judgment is the physician's alone. The physician can authorize a postviability abortion for virtually any reason, ranging from a threat to the life of the mother (which rarely occurs today) to a range of nonmedical reasons that could include the mother's financial ability to raise the child in question (familial factors, as cited by the Court). The well-publicized late-term, partial-birth abortion method is often used in these third-trimester abortions, and though it is widely claimed that these are only performed when the women's life or health is at risk, it is well documented that the majority of partial-birth abortions are performed for birth-control reasons and are not based on the risks of continuing the pregnancy to the mother.[15] The combination of the *Roe* and *Doe* decisions opened the door to abortion on demand at virtually any point in pregnancy.

The precedent established in these two decisions, and upheld in practically every challenge to it,[16] sent a clear message to society about the morality of abortion and the personhood of the unborn. But other aspects of the law appear to view the unborn differently. For example, fetuses have inheritance rights in most states, which would seem to imply that they are persons similar to adults who stand to receive inheritances. Further, some states have laws that allow prosecution of those who cause the death of a fetus for murder or manslaughter.[17] The state supreme courts in Massachusetts and South Carolina ruled that the fetus is a person in some criminal and vehicular homicide cases.[18] The supreme court of Iowa has held that a fetus is a person and a family member under the provisions of its insurance law.[19] The South Carolina Supreme Court recently upheld the conviction of a pregnant woman for cocaine use under the state's child-abuse laws. The court ruled that the state's view of prevention of harm to children should include viable fetuses.[20] In mid-1998 the United States Supreme Court refused to review the case, letting the ruling stand.[21] Other examples of the law's protecting unborn children as though they were adults include the ability to recover damages for prenatal injuries[22] and wrongful death actions after the point of viability.[23] It should be noted that many states do not recognize these measures and do not allow for prosecution of those who intentionally kill a fetus for murder. But the fact that some do and that their views have been allowed to stand by the U.S. Supreme Court reveals an interesting perplexity about the moral status of fetuses in utero.

A further indication of this societal ambivalence is the way that the fetus can be viewed as a patient today as a result of the advances in prenatal medical technology, particularly ultrasound technology, which gives physicians the ability to look into the womb and observe the developing fetus. In addition, prenatal genetic testing puts the fetus in the position of being a patient who is undergoing diagnostic testing. Add to this the newly developing fields of fetal therapy and even surgery on the fetus in utero, which are becoming more available. Combined with the increasing emphasis on preventing prenatal harm to the fetus and even bringing criminal charges against pregnant women for endangering their unborn children, this raises questions about the obligation of the pregnant woman toward her unborn child. It is becoming more difficult to imagine that a fetus in the womb can be a legitimate patient and the subject of medical procedures and, at the same time, not possess the most basic rights to life. These new technologies reveal a cultural schizophrenia about the value of the fetus.[24] The fetus has different value depending on the medical and technological context in which it is found. There is thus a set of medical practices that strongly suggests a high value for the fetus, a value parallel to that attributed to mature adults, which is in conflict with current abortion law.

To be sure, balancing the concerns of pregnant women with the interests of their unborn children can be difficult, as in the case of forced cesarean sections or when forcing a pregnant woman to take the drug AZT (azidothymidine) to prevent the spread of HIV to the fetus. But the fact that the unborn child can be viewed as a patient surely makes it more difficult to deny its rights to life. Simply suggesting that women have responsibilities only toward *wanted* unborn children will not solve this dilemma, since wantedness is much too subjective a criterion for personhood. Wantedness is surely a commentary on the mother and not on the unborn child in utero.

Abortion Rights Arguments and the Assumption of Personhood

Virtually all of the key arguments that justify the morality of abortion make critical assumptions about the personhood of the unborn. These arguments are plausible only if the one advancing the argument assumes that the unborn are something less than fully human persons. As a result, these arguments are guilty of the fallacy of begging the question, of assuming one's conclusion prior to making the argument. It is true that those who oppose abortion often make the assumption that the unborn are full persons, and they can also be guilty of question begging. Both sets of arguments and the assumptions made in advancing them reveal how central the notion of personhood is for the ongoing debate on abortion. However, in this book we laid out a variety of arguments for the full personhood of the unborn that are independent of and prior to our ethical arguments.

However, a number of factors in the discussion have shifted the focus away from the central issue. For example, public policy in general tends to avoid metaphysical questions, particularly ones with religious underpinnings. This is due to a commitment to moral pluralism as the basis for public policy and a desire to formulate such policy in as value neutral a way as possible, using "secular" reasons to undergird policy positions.[25] In some cases, religiously based and philosophical reasons were grouped in the same category of those rationales that are worldview dependent and thus cannot be considered for public policy in a pluralistic culture.[26] Another reason for avoiding metaphysical questions is the implicit and sometimes overt commitment of public-policy makers to scientism as a worldview, one in which only scientifically verifiable things are recognized as facts. On that basis no decision on the personhood of the unborn can be made, since science has not been able to establish consensus on the nature of the unborn. Of course, the concept of personhood is not a scientific one but a philosophical and theological one, and science by definition cannot make any normative claims about the personhood of the unborn. Our view is that public policy on the issues in which personhood is central cannot and should not proceed without metaphysical reflection. Our conclusions about personhood are consistent with but not dependent upon our theological views, and thus they should not be disqualified from the public debate on these issues.[27]

In order to illustrate the assumptions about personhood implicit in the arguments for abortion rights, take the most common argument—that abortion is morally justifiable because a woman has the right to do with her own body whatever she chooses. Because it is her body, it ought to be her choice when it comes to what happens to it, namely, whether or not she should continue a pregnancy that she does not want. One assumption made here is that the fetus is a part of the woman's body, an assumption that is false since the fetus is a unique organic whole (a substance) that has its own unique genetic identity and nervous and circulatory systems and that as it develops will appear even more distinct. This assumption also confuses being dependent on the woman's body with being a part of it. But that's not the critical assumption. This argument based on the woman's right to choose clearly assumes that the fetus is not a person. Otherwise the argument would not be plausible since the one advancing it would be asserting that pregnant women have the right to end the lives of their offspring simply on their decision to do so. Only if the fetus is not a person does the woman have the right to make a choice that would result in the fetus's death, since historically and in the law, when life and liberty (or here, choice) conflict, life virtually always takes precedence. Women cannot choose to kill innocent persons, no matter how dependent those persons are on them.

A second argument for abortion rights that makes a similar assumption is the argument that unwanted children should not be brought into the world. The child may be unwanted due to financial hardship, handicap (genetic or otherwise) or inconvenience.[28] All of these reasons for why a child is unwanted assume that the unwelcome fetus is less than a fully human person. For example, if the child is unwanted due to financial hardship, a justification for abortion clearly assumes that the unborn poor are not persons. Otherwise, the argument would be suggesting that hardship justifies homicide, and there would be no moral difference between abortion for financial hardship and eliminating one or more of the already existing children because of economic reasons. In fact, if applied widely there would be no moral difference between abortion for financial hardship and eliminating the poor because they are a financial burden on society. Of course, the reason society does not condone the latter is precisely because financial hardship and personhood are entirely unrelated. The only way an argument for abortion from financial hardship can be plausible is with the assumption that the unborn poor are somehow less than persons.

The same holds true for the genetically handicapped. Abortion for this reason clearly assumes that genetically anomalous unborn are less than persons. Otherwise, there would be no moral difference between abortion for that reason and killing all the adult handicapped persons. Again the reason society does not condone killing the adult handicapped is precisely because they are full persons meriting protection under the law. Furthermore, no one accepts the rights of parents to kill their handicapped children simply because they are handicapped. The only way to use this justification for abortion is to assume that the unborn handicapped are not full persons. Otherwise, the argument collapses. This argument must rest, then, on the nature of the unborn and not on the handicap with which they are afflicted.

The argument that women should not be forced to bring unwanted children into the world is, in large part, based on the desire to avoid the conditions that might increase the incidence of child abuse. Again this argument assumes that unwanted unborn children are not full persons. Otherwise, permitting abortion could be considered the most serious form of child abuse imaginable. The fact that a child is unwanted is more of a commentary on the mother (and father, if applicable) than on the unborn, and it is unrelated to the essence of the unborn child. Unless one assumes that the unwanted unborn are not persons, this argument for abortion based on unwantedness could be used to justify eliminating the homeless from one's community—simply because they are unwanted. Of course, society would never condone such an action because the homeless are persons, and whether or not they are wanted is irrelevant to their personhood and attendant rights to life. This argument for abortion based on unwantedness hinges on the assumptions about the personhood of the fetus, not on the fact that they are unwanted.

A final argument for abortion rights that perhaps illustrates this assumption most clearly is the argument that denying abortion access to poor women is discriminatory. That is, affluent women can afford to travel to countries where abortion is legal (which they did prior to 1973), and poor women are not able to do this. Thus restrictive abortion laws discriminate against poor women. This argument is the clearest example of begging the question since it assumes that abortion is somehow a good to which women have a right. One cannot be a victim of discrimination unless one is denied something to which one has a right. But whether or not women have the right to abortion is the issue. By assuming that women do have this right, then advancing the argument that denying them this right is discriminatory and concluding that they should have this right, the proponent of this argument has engaged in a clear form of circular reasoning (another term for question begging). This argument also assumes that the unborn are less than persons; otherwise, the proponent of this argument is advancing the absurd notion that a denial of access to medically killing a person is a form of discrimination. Only if one assumes that the unborn are not persons is this argument plausible, and even with that assumption it is still begging the question.

Views of Personhood of the Unborn in the Abortion Debate

It would be quite an understatement to suggest that many commentators on the abortion question have attempted to define human personhood and apply it to the unborn. Space simply does not permit an exposition and critique of the plethora of attempts to establish criteria for the personhood of the fetus.[29] What most of these views have in common is an attempt to define the personhood of the fetus in terms of a set of functions or an attempt to put it in the terms we have used throughout the first section of the book, terms of actualized capacities. We will argue that all of these attempts at establishing personhood on functional grounds fail. Some of the classic analyses of this view include the works of philosopher Mary Ann Warren, bioethicist Joseph Fletcher, philosophers Peter Singer and Helga Kuhse, and philosopher Michael Tooley. Singer, Kuhse and Tooley take their view of personhood beyond simply the fetus and apply their criteria to newborns and infants, producing uncomfortable conclusions for some. More contemporary views of fetuses and embryos are found in the work of philosopher and bioethicist Bonnie Steinbock. We will use these thinkers as representatives of those who explain human personhood in functional rather than essentialist terms.

In the contemporary debate a growing number of proponents of abortion rights either grant the personhood of the fetus or suggest that it is not the central point in the debate. For example, the widely publicized article by feminist leader Naomi Wolf suggested that the abortion rights movement should admit the intuitively obvious—that the fetus is a person. The debate over abortion should shift from the personhood of the fetus to the autonomy of the mother. In other words, granting that the fetus is a person, proponents of this view hold that there may be times in which it is justifiable for a pregnant woman to take the life of the person she is carrying in her womb. This view is reminiscent of the widely read view of philosopher Judith Jarvis Thomson and her well-known analogy of the violinist and the blood transfusion. We will address this shift in the focus of the debate later in this section.

Moral philosopher Warren argues that there is a distinction between "people" as members of the moral community, and human beings. All people, not necessarily all human beings, belong to the moral community and merit protection of the community and the right to life.[30] There is a difference between being human in the genetic sense (a human being) and being human in the moral sense (a person). This separation of a human being from a person is characteristic of virtually all functional definitions of personhood. Having a human genetic code is thus a necessary, but not sufficient, condition for being a person. Defining what constitutes moral personhood is the difficult task, since it involves much more than simply possession of a human genome. Warren suggests the following rough traits are central to the concept of personhood[31]:

1. consciousness (of objects and events external and/or internal to the being) and in particular the capacity to feel pain

2. reasoning (the developed capacity to solve new and relatively complex problems)

3. self-motivated activity (activity that is relatively independent of either genetic or direct external control)

4. the capacity to communicate, by whatever means, messages of an indefinite variety of types: that is, not just with an indefinite number of possible contents but on indefinitely many possible topics

5. the presence of self-concepts and self-awareness, individual and/or racial

Ethicist Fletcher suggests a similar set of tentative criteria for personhood. He outlines the abilities to have self-awareness, self-control, a sense of the future, a sense of the past, the capacity to relate to others, communication and curiosity.[32] These are all functions that are viewed as minimally necessary for it to be said that a being, namely, a fetus, is a person. At what point the person possesses these qualities is not clear, but what seems evident is that at least prior to birth, and likely for a short time after birth, fetuses and newborns do not possess these capabilities.

Warren takes these criteria virtually as givens, without much argument, and then proceeds to apply them to the unborn. She suggests that any being that cannot satisfy any of the five above criteria cannot be a person. She considers "this claim to be so obvious that I think that anyone who denied it and claimed that a being that satisfied none of [criteria] 1-5 was a person all the same, would thereby demonstrate that he had no notion at all of what a person is."[33] One conclusion she draws is that "some human beings are not people, and there may well be people who are not human beings."[34] Examples of human beings who are not persons include the permanently unconscious, human beings with no appreciable mental capacity and fetuses. She also suggests that the coming generation should be prepared to recognize that highly advanced computers (particularly those equipped with artificial intelligence), self-aware robots and even beings from other planets (should they exist and be found) may be non-human persons if they meet her criteria for personhood.[35] She further concludes that, according to these criteria, a third-trimester fetus is not substantially more personlike than an embryo. Rather a fetus, even at late stages of development, meets fewer of the criteria for personhood than the average mature mammal.[36] The resemblance to a mature adult person is irrelevant to the fetus's right to life. So is its potential to become a full person, according to Warren. She equates developing fetuses with future people, or those not yet conceived, and argues that no amount of potential possessed by the fetus gives it the right to life that trumps the mother's right to protect her health, happiness, freedom and even her life (in the rare cases in which her life is threatened by the presence of the fetus in her body). Her rights "will always override whatever right to life may be appropriate to ascribe to a fetus, even a fully developed one."[37]

Warren is clearly troubled by the implications of her personhood criteria for infanticide, since it is not clear at what age a newborn or infant actually meets her criteria for personhood. She argues against the morality of infanticide on the grounds that newborns are *so close* to being persons that killing them requires additional justification, parallel to killing some advanced forms of mammals, such as dolphins and chimpanzees.[38] She further suggests that infanticide is problematic because of the high number of infertile couples seeking children to adopt. This extends to the handicapped or otherwise unadoptable children, for whom Warren suggests that most people would be willing to support through public funding of homes for the handicapped.[39] She anticipates the obvious question of the difference between not allowing for infanticide and allowing for late-term abortions. She justifies late-term abortions on the grounds that after birth the fetus cannot pose any further threat to the mother's life or health and that a pregnant woman has the right to protect her life and health. Yet it is hardly the norm that a fetus threatens the health of the pregnant woman, and extremely rare that the fetus threatens her life. Though one should not underestimate the rigors of late-term pregnancy and childbirth, it is rare that continuing a pregnancy poses a threat to the mother's health from which she cannot recover. Thus any attempt to suggest a morally relevant break in the process of development at birth fails, and it seems that Warren is left with the uncomfortable conclusion that infanticide could be justifiable under her criteria for personhood. She does justify infanticide under conditions of extreme hardship, in which no one is able to care for the child,[40] and when a newborn child has such severe deformities that to care for the child would impose crushing burdens on the parents and little if any benefit to the child.[41] Thus there are social and physical conditions in which infanticide could be justified for Warren, conditions that have nothing to do with the personhood of the newborn child.

Others are not as uncomfortable with the implications for infanticide. Philosopher Tooley, for example, takes many of Warren's criteria for personhood and applies them more consistently. Applying what is called the *particular interests view,* Tooley and others suggest that only beings capable of having interests can have rights, namely, the right to life.[42] Tooley summarizes it in this way:

> 1. An entity cannot have a right to life unless it is capable of having an interest in its own continued existence; 2. an entity is not capable of having an interest in its own continued existence unless it possesses, at some time, the concept of a continuing self, or subject of experiences and other mental states; 3. the fact that an entity will, if not destroyed, come to have properties that would give it the right to life does not in itself make it seriously wrong to destroy it.[43]

These are similar to though a bit less comprehensive than Warren's and Fletcher's criteria.

Tooley admits that such criteria raise the question of at what point a developing human being becomes a person. He takes his criteria consistently and suggests that though the line might be difficult to draw, it surely occurs at some point after birth. He suggests a short time interval, somewhere around one week after birth, in which infanticide would be justified. He is not particularly concerned about where precisely to draw the line and ascribe personhood, since, in his view, the overwhelming majority of cases in which infanticide would be desired occur in cases in which the child is born with a grave deformity. He considers the more troubling issue of whether or not certain species of animals would not also possess the right to life.[44] Like Warren, he too argues that the potential of the fetus to "become" a person is irrelevant to its right to life and cannot be used to defend the rights of the fetus to life.[45] Interestingly, Tooley's criterion that a person must have a sense of a continuing self seems to suggest a substance-dualist view of a person. The notion of a continuity of one's self throughout time and change is characteristic of substance dualism, and it cannot be accounted for on a property-thing or functionalist view of a person.

A similar view to Tooley's is put forth by philosophers Singer and

Kuhse: the critical component of personhood is the ability to experience a continuing self with an interest in a continued life. It is the ability to see oneself as existing over time and to experience a continuity about one's life.[46] They too are not uncomfortable with the implications of their views for infanticide, and they suggest that "when we kill a newborn infant (particularly one that is severely handicapped) there is not person whose life has begun (or will ever begin). It is the beginning of the life of the person, rather than the physical organism, that is crucial so far as the right to life is concerned."[47]

One of the more contemporary and widely cited expressions of the functional view of a human person is the view of Steinbock. Admitting that the moral status of the unborn is the critical issue in the abortion debate, she argues that a being must have interests in order to have rights and that what gives a being interests is sentience, or the ability to experience pain and pleasure.[48] Another way of stating it would be to suggest that conscious awareness is the minimal criterion for personhood and the attendant rights. Possession of interests is both necessary and sufficient for moral status, and the rights that accompany such a status. She specifies this notion of having interests as having it matter what is done to a being as key to its having interests. In other words, "beings that have moral status must be capable of caring about what is done to them."[49] Thus without conscious awareness, it is by definition impossible for a being to have interests.[50] To put it another way, to have interests is to have an interest in having interests.

The criterion of having interests and the sentience, or conscious awareness, necessary to have them are foundational for the other criteria for personhood expressed by Warren, Fletcher, Singer and Kuhse. Steinbock suggests that "conscious awareness is a prerequisite to desires, preferences, hopes, aims and goals (not to mention reasoning, self-motivated activity and communication). Nothing matters to nonsentient, nonconscious beings. Whether they are preserved or destroyed, cherished or neglected, is of no concern to them. . . . We have no obligations to them because it does not matter to them how we treat them."[51] She then applies this view to the issue of abortion and argues that "abortion does not harm or wrong embryos or pre-conscious fetuses. Lacking the capacity for awareness of any kind, early-gestation fetuses do not have interests of their own. Fetuses have only 'contingent' rights and claims—contingent, that is, on future existence as interested beings."[52]

However, Steinbock runs into problems when she attempts to apply her view consistently. For example, she holds that the nonconscious, such as the dead (whom she calls "postmortem persons") can have interests, and she suggests that they can be harmed even though they cannot experience it as such. She comments that "admittedly, dead people cannot know that their wishes were carried out, their families provided for, their reputations intact. . . . But why should their mere lack of knowledge of these events imply that they have not been harmed?"[53] In addition, she admits that one can have "surviving interests" after one's death and that one can be harmed posthumously.[54] In addition, she acknowledges that "future people" can have interests that should be protected, such as interests in inheriting a liveable ecological environment with adequate natural resources. She argues that "because they have interests, future people qualify for moral status."[55] If these categories of persons have interests, it is difficult to see why embryos and fetuses would be excluded from moral status. If persons can be harmed without the capacity to experience it as such, then why cannot fetuses and embryos also be harmed by efforts to destroy them? If a person can have interests after one's death—after sentience and consciousness have permanently been lost—then why cannot embryos and fetuses have interests prior to sentience and consciousness, particularly since they have all the capacities necessary to develop those traits (as opposed to a "postmortem person" for whom those capacities will never again be actualized). If anything, the potential for the fetus or embryo to develop those capacities suggests a higher moral standing than that given to "postmortem persons." In addition, if future people not yet even conceived qualify for moral status, then why cannot fetuses, who already objectively exist in a womb, similarly qualify? "Postmortem persons" and future people do not possess sentience, are not conscious and cannot have an interest in their interests, yet according to this interest view of a human person, they qualify for moral status and have interests that merit protection. Either the possession of consciousness and sentience is not a critical component of human personhood or embryos and fetuses qualify for moral status. In fact, extending moral status to "postmortem persons" suggests a substance view of a human person—a continuity of personal identity that extends beyond one's death.[56]

The interests view runs into further problems when Steinbock attempts to explain why infanticide is wrong. Since newborns have sentience and thus can have interests, killing them is morally wrong, even though babies cannot take an interest in their interests in the period just following their birth. She critiques Tooley's view of a person, in which he denies that there is a causal link between a baby and an adult. Tooley suggests that we err when we attribute a continuity of personal identity from infancy to adulthood, reflecting a clear property-thing view of a person. Yet in her critique of Tooley, Steinbock admits to a substance view of a human person. She puts it this way: "[Tooley] says that we mistakenly attribute to the baby an interest in continued existence because we wrongly identify the baby with the adult person she becomes. We then think that because it is in the adult Mary's [the person used in the example] interest that she was not destroyed when she was a baby, that it must also be in the baby Mary's interest not to be destroyed. After all, *baby Mary just is adult Mary, when she was younger*" (emphasis added).[57] Steinbock objects to Tooley's denial of continuity of identity when she suggests that Tooley's argument "assumes, implausibly, that there are no causal and psychological connections between a baby and the adult person she becomes."[58]

Steinbock cannot make this objection to Tooley without holding a substance-dualist view of a human person, since that is the only view of a person that provides a genuine continuity of personal identity throughout periods of change and development. Further, there is no reason why the fetal stage should not be included in the process of development from baby to mature adult. There is no morally relevant decisive moment at any point during pregnancy that would provide an adequate grounding for human personhood.[59] There is no reason to assume that the continuity between baby and adult should not extend to the fetus and baby. After all, fetus Mary is baby Mary is adult Mary. This line of reasoning suggests that making sentience the ground for personhood is arbitrary and should be rejected in favor of a view that acknowledges what is intuitively obvious—that from fetus to newborn to infant to child to adult, the person is the same, though at difference stages of development. The essence of the person does not change, though the outward form does. The fetus does not become something else as it develops. It simply matures according to its kind and according to a lawlike design, which is a part of its essence and is ultimately directed by the soul. The functions characteristic of a person are grounded in the essence of the person, not the other way around, where functions determine personhood. Advocates of a functional view of a human person have the metaphysical cart before the horse in placing the priority on function in assigning personhood.

All of the above functional views of a human person reflect a property-thing view as opposed to a substance-dualist view. Whatever the function or functions deemed necessary conditions for personhood—be they sentience, consciousness, reasoning, communication or self-awareness—in such a view they represent the addition of a property or properties to the entity such that we can confer personhood on it and give it the protection that personhood brings. According to this view there is no internal essence or nature that guides the process of development. Rather, properties are added and lost in the process of growth and aging. As we have seen in the first half of the book, this kind of property-thing view of a person is fraught with difficulties.

The inadequacy of functional criteria for personhood is evident when one attempts to apply them consistently. Take for example the person under general anesthesia or in a reversible coma. Such a person has none of the fundamental elements of personhood. He or she is not conscious, is not sentient, has no ability to communicate, has no self-awareness and has no ability to respond to his environment. According to the functional criteria for personhood, he does not have the moral status of a person. But this conclusion is absurd. The functionalist counterargument to this illustration is that this state is only temporary and that all these functions will be restored when the effect of the anesthesia wears off or when he awakes from the coma. But the functionalist cannot employ this response without being self-defeating. To say that the person is only temporarily dysfunctional, one needs to be able to appeal to some other higher-order capacities as determinants of personhood. Appealing to such capacities cannot be done without acknowledging that personhood cannot be dependent on lower-order expressed capacities. For the functionalist those capacities are not available to them. Appealing to them forces them to acknowledge that the fetus is in precisely the same place, with personhood not dependent on certain lower-order expressed capacities. Defending the personhood of the person under anesthesia or in a reversible coma is dependent upon unexpressed higher-order capacities that are currently latent as a result of anesthesia or coma. To suggest that this person remains a person while in the dysfunctional state because he at one time expressed those capacities simply begs the question by asserting the functionalist premise as a defense against this objection. This person has the same capability to express these capacities as does the developing fetus. The only difference is that it may take the fetus more time to express those capacities. To use the temporary dysfunctional defense, one must admit that the potential for expression of the capacities necessary for personhood counts for a great deal. Once that admission is made, there is no reason to exclude fetuses from the category of human persons.

Consider an even more pointed scenario. Imagine a newborn child who has been born unconscious. The part of the higher brain that controls consciousness has been damaged, but the rest of the brain functions properly, which means that heartbeat, respiration and digestion are normal, though she needs to be fed through a tube. Imagine further that there is a treatment that will regenerate the damaged brain tissue, restore higher brain function and allow the baby to become conscious and sentient. If the treatment is initiated, the baby will develop normally and will not be any different from any other newborn in the nursery. Of course, this treatment would be in the child's interests, and if she is denied the treatment, she would clearly be harmed and the victim of a tragic wrong. However, under the functional view of a person, this baby would not be a person, would not be entitled to the treatment and would not be wronged if denied it because she lacks the constituent elements of personhood. But that conclusion is absurd, and it won't help to appeal to the fact that she's so close to being a normal baby that it is impossible to treat her as anything else.[60] However, with the fetus, no treatment is necessary. All it takes is time, nutrients and nonintervention for the fetus to develop into a normal infant. No deficiencies need be overcome. The process of development simply needs to run its natural course. In either of these scenarios, functionalists cannot have it both ways. They cannot hold a functional view and then appeal to latent capacities when necessary. It would seem that either sentience, consciousness or some other function is essential for personhood or it is not. If it is, then the functionalist cannot suggest that the patients in these scenarios are persons, a highly counter-intuitive conclusion.[61] If it is not, then the functional view fails and the potential of the fetus to actualize its capacities should carry much more weight.

Most who hold a functional view suggest that a fetus is somehow in the process of becoming a person. For example, philosopher Lawrence Becker compares fetal development to metamorphosis—becoming a person is a process. He writes:

> Human fetal development is a process analogous to metamorphosis. . . . It makes sense to say that human eggs, embryos and fetuses are distinct from the human beings they become—that they are not human beings, only human becomings. When can we say that the fetus is a human being rather than a human becoming? Surely only when its metamorphic-like process is complete—that is, when the relatively undifferentiated mass of the fertilized human ovum has developed into the pattern of differentiated characteristics of the organism it is genetically programmed to become.[62]

It would seem that this would be a logical outgrowth of a property-thing view of a human person, for in that view there cannot be continuity of personal identity. Fetuses must be distinct from the human beings that replace them in the same way that butterfly eggs, larvae and pupae must be distinct from the butterflies that replace them. But that is not the way we view those, and Becker, for example, admits that caterpillars and butterflies are the same insect in different stages of development.[63] Though we make distinctions between fetuses and full-grown adults, it does not follow that they are of two different types.

The reason we don't make such a distinction of types is that to speak of a human becoming is an incoherent notion. To see why this is so, consider the example of someone's entering a room, which is a gradual process.[64] It begins when one foot enters the room, followed by another and then followed by other parts of the body entering the room. When the person is all the way in, he has entered the room. During the process of entering, the man must exist in total in order to be involved in the process. Likewise, in order to enter the class of human beings known as human persons, the man must exist as well. Someone cannot be in the *process* of becoming a human person, since one must first exist in order to enter any process. Thus, we cannot say that any being gradually becomes a person—or ceases to be a person, for that matter.

A further problem with a gradualist view of a human person is that one can never be sure of when the process is complete or of when it begins to work in reverse, when personhood diminishes. Since development of one's fundamental capacities continues well into the teenage years and early adulthood, it is difficult to draw a line at which full personhood has been achieved, not to mention when it begins to diminish. There are clear differences in the actualization of certain capacities among children and even among adults, and there is normally no implication that they are not equals as persons and should be not treated as equals. The reason for this is that we intuitively assume that regardless of abilities or of realization of potentialities, we should be treated equally because we all share a common human nature. We have been arguing in the first half of the book that individual nature—that is, the soul—directs the process of development that has been likened to metamorphosis. These changes do not happen in a human being by accident but by a lawlike design that comes from one's essence as a human person. Again the functions emerge from one's essence and not the other way around. There is ample reason to suggest that the same essence directs the development of the fetus while in the womb.

A further implication of the functional view of personhood is that personhood ends up being a degreed property.[65] Whatever function or functions one suggests as determinative of personhood, virtually all of them are expressed in degrees.[66] One develops the key set of functions and later in life loses them, so by implication one's rights would correspondingly be more or less protected. The right to life would be graded, which is very different from suggesting that a prima facie right to life should be protected for all persons.[67] Just because there are periodic exceptions to the right to life, such as in self-defense, war, possibly capital punishment and the right to end dependence on life-support technology, it does not follow that the right to life can be graded. Such a view of degreed personhood, emerging out of a naturalistic view of the world, is contrary to everything we have developed in the first half of this book. It conflicts with the notion of a human person's having an essence that is independent of one's functions and that actually grounds one's functions. It makes it difficult to draw precise lines at which people's rights, particularly those people at the beginning and ending edges of life, can be drawn, which is no small matter since the rights to life depend on where those lines are drawn. It runs the danger of taking classes of people such as the elderly, the demented and the mentally handicapped as less than full persons and opening the door to their mistreatment. It would mean the erosion of rights of the most vulnerable, who are arguably the most in need and the most worthy of protection.

The Argument That the Fetus's Personhood Is *Not* the Most Important Aspect of the Abortion Debate

In recent discussions, some feminists have attempted to move beyond the centrality of personhood and to locate the crucial issues around a woman's right to choose what happens to her own body rather than around the personhood of the unborn. That is, even if the unborn has the status of a person, it would not necessarily insure that the decision to procure an abortion would be immoral. It would be, by definition, killing a person, but depending on the context in which the abortion took place, would not be an immoral action. In arguing in this way, prochoice advocates are making a startling admission—that the fetus should have the status of a person or, at least, that the fetus so resembles a baby that second- and third-trimester abortions should not be allowed.[68]

A widely read and controversial example of this recent trend in the abortion discussion comes from Naomi Wolf, who stunned her feminist colleagues by calling for a moral context for the abortion, by admitting that ultrasound technology has made it more difficult than ever to discount the personhood of the unborn and by suggesting that women view the abortion decision in the context of the notions of sin and redemption.[69] She puts it this way:

> Since abortion became legal nearly a quarter-century ago, the fields of embryology and perinatology have been revolutionized, but the prochoice view of the contested fetus has been static. This has led to a bizarre bifurcation in the way we who are prochoice tend to think about wanted as opposed to unwanted fetuses. . . . Even while [surgeon general at the time Jocelyn] Elders spoke of our need to "get over" our love affair with the unwelcome fetus, an entire growth industry is devoted to sparking fetal love affairs in other circumstances. . . . The *Well Baby Book,* the kind of whole-grain, holistic guide to pregnancy and birth that would find its audience among the very demographic that is most solidly prochoice, reminds us that 'increasing knowledge is increasing the awe and respect which we have for the unborn and is causing us to regard the unborn baby as a real person long before birth.' . . . So what will it be: Wanted fetuses are charm-

ing, complex, REM-dreaming little beings whose profile on the sonogram looks just like Daddy, but unwanted ones are mere "uterine material"? How can we charge that it is vile and repulsive to brandish vile and repulsive images if the images are real? To insist that the truth is in poor taste is the height of hypocrisy.[70]

Wolf is encouraging her feminist colleagues to face up to what is becoming more obvious to the general public with the advent of technology capable of enabling physicians and parents to peer in to the womb and examine the unborn. In addition, fetal medicine—especially surgery that can now be performed in the womb—is further revealing the bifurcation in how the fetus is viewed to which Wolf refers. Not only can the fetus be the object of the parents' desire, it can also be the patient in medical procedures. Yet at the same developmental point, the fetus can be legally aborted. Wolf correctly points out that feminist abortion-rights advocates cannot ignore the increasing evidence that points to the personhood of the fetus. As a consequence the abortion decision cannot be morally neutral, on par with the removal of organs or tissues. She admits that this increasing knowledge of the fetus demands that the abortion decision be made within a moral context and that it be treated as a moral decision, as opposed to simply a personal choice.

This admission of the personhood of the fetus does not mean that most abortions are now morally problematic. Rather, they become much more difficult decisions. Wolf admits that "abortion should be legal; it is sometimes necessary. Sometimes the mother must be able to decide that the fetus, *in its full humanity,* must die"[71] (emphasis added). Thus it is morally justifiable for Wolf and others who advance this argument to end the lives of unborn, fully human persons. The moral force of the personhood of the fetus is clear from the way in which the decision to end its life is justified. It is justified either by the rights of the mother over her own body, which is employed as the trump card and which overrides the unborn person's right to life,[72] or by invoking the biblical notions of sin and redemption (which are also reflected in other religious traditions).[73] The former notion of the woman's autonomy, which is still widespread in abortion-rights circles, ignores the clear consensus in society and in the law that holds that when the right to life conflicts with rights of liberty and autonomy, the right to life virtually always carries greater weight. In this latter notion of sin and salvation, Wolf suggests that the abortion decision is a matter of conscience and personal responsibility for a morally problematic decision. Employing this notion strongly suggests that women who opt for abortion are committing a sin, one for which redemption is necessary. Yet Wolf and others hold that one can maintain that abortion is an evil and still be pro-choice by seeing the redemptive quality of life.

Of course, the problem with such a view is that it trivializes the concepts of both sin and redemption. In most religious traditions redemption is available for sin, but the availability of forgiveness is never to be used as a pretext for committing an act that one knows is morally wrong. Redemption's being available is never to be used as a justification for committing an evil act. This is tantamount to suggesting that it is easier to obtain forgiveness than permission. In biblical terms God clearly does forgive, yet that is only half of the equation of personal responsibility. Redemption's being available is designed to motivate the believer to avoid those actions that are immoral. If there were no other options for a woman with an unwanted pregnancy and if she were left with a genuinely moral dilemma, then perhaps applying the concept of redemption to such a situation would be appropriate. But the reality is that there are other options, such as adoption, for the majority of women who are contemplating abortion.

If abortion is now being seen correctly in the context of a grave moral decision, then certainly the inconvenience of carrying the child to term cannot compare with the opportunity for life owed to the developing person. In addition, once the personhood of the unborn is admitted, then there is no reason why the prochoice justification of taking the life of a person cannot be applied to neonates, infants and children. It is true that the newborn child no longer is dependent on the mother's body for survival, but as any new parent knows, only the degree of dependence has changed. The way in which newborns are dependent on the parents has only slightly changed, and in many ways the newborn still has a strong claim on the mother's body, not to mention her time, effort and energy. There is no reason why the notion of sin and redemption could not also be applied to one's taking the lives of newborns and infants. The availability of redemption for women who have had abortions is clear, yet that redemption is cheapened if it is used in order to justify a morally objectionable act such as ending the life of an unborn person.

Fetal-Tissue Research and Transplantation

Since the late 1980s there has been significant debate over the morality of using fetal tissue from elective abortions.[74] Though widely considered experimental, this medical technology shows promise for application to a variety of diseases such as Parkinson's disease and diabetes. The ideal gestational age of the tissue depends on the particular disease being treated. There is incentive for maximizing the tissue to tailor the timing and method of the abortion for the specific use of the tissue. Currently, with the number of surgical abortions performed each year, there does seem to be adequate supply of fetal tissue to meet the demand. But with the expanding technology and the potential availability of the RU-486 pill (which would dramatically decrease the number of surgical abortions), it is not difficult to see the day coming in which the demand will overwhelm the available supply.

Proponents of using fetal tissue use insist the decision to donate the tissue can be separated from the decision to procure the abortion. They insist that the morality of abortion can and should be separated from the issues involved in using the tissue from these abortions. Thus, in their view the personhood of the fetal-tissue donor (or donation) is irrelevant to the morality of the use of the tissue. After all, proponents insist, women are continuing to have abortions, and it is immoral to discard usable tissue, particularly when it can help suffering people alleviate their symptoms.[75]

However, if our analysis of a human person is correct, then using the tissue from elective abortions is morally problematic. The use of such fetal tissue is then not analogous to adult organ transplants, which are generally donated when someone is killed in a tragic accident. That parallel fits only miscarriages and ectopic pregnancies, the equivalent of accidental and unplanned deaths. By contrast, the death of the fetus, whose tissue will be donated, is anything but accidental. It is intentionally caused. It makes for an uneasy equivalence between the donor and the donation of the tissue, and it should disqualify the mother of the aborted fetus from being the appropriate person to give consent for the donation of the tissue. LeRoy Walters, chairman of the National Institutes of Health Ethics Panel, argued in conjunction with the debate about experimentation on the fetus, asking:

> Ought one to make experimental use of the products of an abortion system, when one would object on ethical grounds to many or most of the abortions performed within that system? If a particular hospital became the ben-

eficiary of an organized homicide system which provided a fresh supply of cadavers, one would be justified in raising questions about the moral appropriateness of the hospital's continuing cooperation with the suppliers.[76]

If the unborn is a full human person, then the argument from complicity with evil has merit. Consider the scenario in which a banker in the local community regards the drug trade as morally wrong, yet he can use the funds generated from such a trade and deposited in his bank to finance low-income housing or some other morally praiseworthy project in the community. Even though the drug trade will surely continue and someone will benefit from the profit generated by the trade, if the banker accepts those funds, they are morally tainted. He is in complicity with the drug trade. He is an accessory, complicit by an institutional arrangement with the drug industry.[77] Perhaps a better parallel would be with the pornography industry, widely regarded as immoral due to the degradation of women and treatment of them as sexual objects. A banker who takes profits from the pornography industry and uses them to finance projects that would benefit women in the community would also be guilty of complicity and using tainted money to fund those projects.

The complicity argument is often based on an analogy to the Nazi experiments on hypothermia and the resulting use of that information today. During World War II the Nazis performed grisly experiments on Jews and other concentration-camp inmates, one of which involved subjecting them to a lowering of body temperatures—usually by plunging them into vats of ice water—in order to test cold-water-survival equipment and techniques for the Nazi military. The information became accessible in the following decades, and there was great debate over the morality of using the data collected during those tests. The consensus was that one could separate the morality of the testing from the use of the data that resulted. In the same way, proponents of the tissue transplants argue that the morality of abortion can and should be separated from the morality of the use of the tissue. They argue that relieving suffering should be a higher priority than making a symbolic statement about the unborn.

However, unlike the Nazi experiments, abortion is an ongoing immoral practice, though currently protected by the law. If the Nazis were currently involved in the same kinds of barbaric testing, there would be little debate about using their data. There would be a universal outcry against the testing itself, and all efforts would be made to stop such a practice. The use of the information would be considered of relatively little consequence compared to the immorality of such a practice. Surely, anyone who proposed benefiting from such an ongoing evil would be considered in complicity with an evil practice. In our view of a human person, the same can be said of abortion. It is an ongoing evil, one that should be stopped. To claim it is morally permissible to "salvage good out of evil" assumes that the evil in question cannot be stopped, as was the case with the Nazi experiments. Only if nothing can be done to prevent the ongoing evil does the argument from salvaging good have merit. Surely one is not justified in obtaining a benefit from evil while doing nothing to prevent it.[78] Of course, if one does not accept our view of a human person, then fetal-tissue transplants may not be morally problematic. But for the person who holds that the unborn possess full personhood, using their tissue or organs made available from an intentionally caused death is unethical and puts those involved in supplying and using the tissue in a position of complicity with evil.

Conclusion

If one accepts our view of a human person, then intentionally taking the life of the unborn is morally problematic, particularly given the reasons for most abortions today—the failure or lack of birth control. Most of the arguments in favor of liberal abortion rights beg the question by assuming that the unborn is not a person. Attempts to assign personhood according to one or more functional criteria fail because, as we have attempted to show, personhood is a matter of essence, not of function. Attempts to place the issue of personhood on the periphery of the debate either by granting it or by claiming to be agnostic about it also fail, since there is no weightier right that can trump the right to life of the unborn without also heading down a slippery slope that could include newborns and infants. If abortion is morally problematic, then so is using the tissue from induced abortions. Fetal-tissue transplants cannot be seen as attempts to salvage good out of evil, since the practice of abortion is ongoing. In our view, proponents of fetal-tissue transplants are in complicity with an evil parallel to the banker's profiting from the drug trade or the pornography industry.

Looking at embryos in glass dishes on laboratory benches makes it more difficult
to cling to the belief that all human life is equally precious
from the moment of conception.[1]

PETER SINGER

If a fire broke out in a laboratory where the seven embryos were stored,
and a two-month-old child was also in the laboratory,
and only the embryos or the child could be saved, would anyone
hesitate before saving the child? Of course not![2]

GEORGE J. ANNAS

CHAPTER 8

Reproductive Technologies in Substance-Dualist Perspective

S INCE THE MID-1970S TECHNOLOGICALLY ASSISTED REPRODUC-
tion has become a major medical industry. Virtually every major
metropolitan area in the United States, Canada, Australia and
Western Europe has an infertility clinic offering a variety of reproductive
technologies to infertile couples. Many obstetricians and gynecologists
are also specialists in infertility treatments and offer some of the less
sophisticated technologies as part of their general practice. In the United
States alone there are over four hundred assisted-reproduction clinics,
most of which are loosely accountable to nongovernmental professional
societies. Couples who visit these clinics are frequently and understand-
ably bewildered by the vast array of technological options now available to
them.

Consider the hypothetical case of Chuck and Linda. They have been
trying to have a baby naturally for the past four years. They have tried virtually every home remedy for infertility and have recently visited a
well-known infertility clinic in their city. They informed the clinic that
they were interested only in technologies that use the genetic materials of
husband and wife and that they were not interested in things like surro-

gate motherhood.[3] The clinic told them that they were excellent candidates for a number of reproductive interventions, some of which were relatively inexpensive. More expensive, invasive and sophisticated technologies would not be considered until it was determined that such interventions would be necessary.

The clinic explained the variety of technologies that they offered, which included simpler procedures such as intrauterine insemination (IUI) with the husband's sperm in conjunction with fertility drugs to enhance ovulation for the wife. They could also try IUI with donor sperm, should Chuck and Linda so desire, though the clinic did not think it would be necessary.[4] Should the IUI procedure fail, they could try a procedure known as GIFT, or gamete intrafallopian transfer. In this technology the wife is given powerful hormones to stimulate multiple ovulation. The eggs are harvested surgically and four are reinserted, two into each fallopian tube, with sperm, so that fertilization can occur in the best possible environment—the woman's body. The rest of the eggs are fertilized in the lab and stored for future use if necessary.

The clinic explained that they also offer two very similar procedures, known as zygote intrafallopian transfer (ZIFT) and in vitro fertilization (IVF). In these procedures all of the harvested eggs are fertilized in the lab, and normally four embryos are reinserted into the woman's body. The difference between ZIFT and IVF is the place in the wife's body where the embryos are inserted. In ZIFT they are placed in the fallopian tubes, a more invasive and slightly more expensive procedure that has a better chance of achieving a pregnancy. In IVF the embryos are placed in the wife's uterus, usually because there is some sort of blockage or damage to her fallopian tubes. The remaining embryos are frozen for storage in case they are needed for future use. Should the initial attempts—either through GIFT, ZIFT or IVF—fail, the clinic could simply thaw out four more embryos from storage and implant them, rather than start the entire process again.[5] Having embryos available in case they need them will save the couple thousands of dollars, since the expensive part of the procedure is the hormone treatments that stimulate multiple ovulation. Embryos in storage will also enable the wife to avoid the physical wear and tear on her body that comes with the hormone treatments prior to egg harvesting.

The clinic explained to Chuck and Linda that multiple pregnancies are not unusual when couples employ these technologies. Should they become pregnant with more children either than Linda could safely carry or than they desired to have, the clinic could refer them to a specialist who would reduce the number of pregnancies that Linda would be carrying. They were somewhat taken aback by that suggestion, since they both oppose abortion. They wondered why someone would go to such lengths to create these pregnancies and then terminate some of them if they didn't like the results.

The technologies Chuck and Linda were considering were also the ones that raised the most complex moral issues for those who hold to a substance-dualist view of the human person. Technologies that do not involve ex utero embryo creation and preservation may raise other biblical and moral issues. For example, IUI by donor sperm—also known as AID (artificial insemination by donor)—egg donation and surrogate motherhood raise complicated questions about the place of third-party contributors to procreation. Does Scripture allow for such contributors within its model for marriage, family and procreation?[6] In addition, critics of surrogate motherhood have charged that the commercial practice of employing a surrogate constitutes the purchase and sale of children and that it is immoral and should be illegal, since such a practice violates the thirteenth amendment to the Constitution, which prohibits slavery.[7] These methods are beyond the scope of this discussion, but it should be clear that issues surrounding the status of fetuses and embryos as persons are not the only ones that complicate the field of reproductive technologies.

The field of technologically assisted reproduction is dominated by infertility practitioners, who have little interest or training in metaphysical or ethical issues, and by lawyers, who have the responsibility for sorting out the legal complexities that emerge from assisted reproduction when the arrangements go awry. Lawyers are more inclined to discuss the status of embryos and fetuses in the law, and the majority of the academic literature on assisted reproduction comes from law journals and law reviews.[8] However, in the academic discussion of reproductive technologies the major issues are not the status of embryos created in the process. Rather, the issues are primarily legal ones, such as the complicated issues of parental rights when parties other than the infertile couple are involved in the process.[9] Parental rights in the cases of surrogacy and gamete donors have been widely discussed both in popular and academic literature.[10] There has also been substantial discussion of the variety of new and unusual reproductive arrangements that are now possible with these technologies—single women are becoming parents, gay and lesbian couples are having children, and postmenopausal women are bearing children using donor eggs. Here the questions involve who should have access to available reproductive technologies.

Two examples of the legal complexities that emerge from reproductive technologies gone awry include the Rios and Davis cases (the latter of which has been well publicized). Mario and Elsa Rios were a wealthy California couple who traveled to Australia in the early 1980s to undergo IVF using her eggs and donor sperm. Some of the pioneering work in IVF was being done in Australia, and they had the financial means to obtain the best IVF technology available at that time. They had the initial egg harvesting, fertilization and first round of implantation performed, which failed to produce a pregnancy. They left for home, planning to return to Australia for a second round of implants with embryos that were in cryopreservation storage. In the interim between their initial round of IVF and their anticipated second round, they were both killed in a plane crash while vacationing in South America. Since they left a considerable estate and had no heirs, this raised questions of inheritance. Not surprisingly, potential surrogate mothers willing to have the embryos implanted were not difficult to find. A government commission recommended that the embryos be discarded, but a state court disagreed, ordered implantations, which failed and thus removed the issue from further consideration. The outcome of this case appeared to set an interesting precedent, one that seemed to indicate embryos should be implanted when there is no one to handle their disposition. Yet when the "parents" no longer need the embryos they have created for their procreative use, they may be discarded, which is the normal practice in the clinic.

A second and more controversial case occurred in the late 1980s and early 1990s. Junior and Mary Sue Davis, a Tennessee couple, underwent IVF six different times, and at the end of their attempts to achieve a pregnancy, they had seven embryos in storage. Prior to any further efforts to procreate a child through additional implants, the Davises divorced, leaving the embryos created from their respective gametes in legal limbo.

REPRODUCTIVE TECHNOLOGIES ──────────────── 267

Junior Davis wanted the embryos to remain in storage, and Mary Sue Davis's desire was to implant the remaining embryos and attempt to achieve a pregnancy, with or without her ex-husband. In a celebrated lower-court case, the court had to decide first what type of proceeding was most appropriate for embryos. Should they be divided up like property, assuming that they had no moral standing, or should the court decide custody of them, assuming that they were parallel to children? Largely based on the testimony of world-renowned geneticist Jerome Lejune—who argued strongly that embryos were persons from conception onward—the court awarded custody of the embryos to Mary Sue Davis, ruling that implantation was in the best interests of the embryos. However, that ruling was overturned by the Court of Appeals on the grounds that Junior Davis should not be forced to become a parent against his will, a decision that was upheld by the Tennessee Supreme Court.[11]

Both of the above cases illustrate the sense of ambivalence we have about the moral status of extracorporeal embryos. Are they children at a very early stage of development, entitled to a chance at implantation, gestation and birth? Or are they property, to which the rights of disposition belong to the couple whose genetic materials created them? If they are property, may they then be justifiably used for research purposes? Most people intuitively recognize a difference between an extracorporeal embryo and a fetus developing in the womb, not to mention a newborn child. However, most people also intuitively recognize that the potential of the embryo to mature into a newborn baby makes it qualitatively different from other body parts and human tissues. That is, they recognize that the embryo has most of its capacities in latent form; and the potential for expression of these capacities, if given the right environment, makes the embryo fundamentally different from other organs, which have no such latent capacities. What are we to make of these conflicting intuitions? How are we to reasonably sort out the claims made for embryos outside the womb, whether they are used for procreation or for research?

It is widely assumed in the infertility industry (partly based on current abortion law) that extracorporeal embryos, newly implanted embryos and early-gestation fetuses have no moral standing and may be discarded or aborted according to the choice of the infertile couple. It is practically a maxim in the infertility industry that an infertile couple will do whatever is necessary to maximize their chances at a successful pregnancy, and the disposition of leftover embryos is of little consequence when compared to the hopes and dreams of the couple to have a child and to the financial resources it takes to have technology assist them. It is standard practice in the infertility clinic to maximize the number of available embryos for any given couple, implant multiple embryos according to the best statistical probability of achieving a single pregnancy and offer selective termination to couples who achieve more pregnancies than they desire or can safely carry to term.[12]

Some clinics have recently begun to offer a money-back guarantee to infertile couples. This sounds promising—until the couple becomes aware that the clinic may attempt to implant many more embryos than can possibly have a chance at actual implantation in order for the woman to have the best chance at becoming pregnant. Some clinics will implant up to nine embryos, which perhaps minimizes the number of embryos discarded after the process is finished but which increases the risk of the woman's becoming pregnant with more children than is safe either for her or for the developing children. It is too soon to tell whether this will become a well-established trend in the industry, but should the practice of the money-back guarantee and the multiple-embryo implantations become standard, it will have been based on a low view of the value of embryos. That is, they can be implanted in multiples with little regard for their disposition, as long as one or more embryos successfully implants.[13] Ironically, clinics and couples view the embryo as precious and worthless at the same time. They are precious because of their potential to develop into a newborn baby, yet they are worthless because they can be discarded at any time when the couple is finished with their infertility treatments.

Reproductive technologies in substance-dualist perspective raise a number of significant issues that arise from the view of the embryo and fetus as substances with full personhood and full protectability from conception onward.

1. What is the moral status of embryos used in infertility treatments and research? Can the standard practice of discarding unused embryos be justified? How does one account for the difference most people intuitively recognize between a developing fetus and an extracorporeal embryo?

2. What is the status of fetuses that are developing in the womb but that are unwanted? Can the practice of selective termination be justified? Is there ever such a scenario of necessary selective termination in which some fetuses must be aborted for the others to survive and develop normally or to minimize risk to the pregnant woman?

3. What is the moral status of "lifeboat implantations," in which multiple embryos are implanted in the best statistical hope that a pregnancy results?

4. What is the metaphysical status of frozen embryos? How is it conceptually possible to speak of cryogenically preserving a soul? Doesn't this concept of embryo freezing suggest that the naturalist is correct about the human person?[14]

5. How, if at all, can a couple who views the human person from a substance-dualist perspective use assisted-reproductive technology without doing so unethically?

The Moral Status of Extracorporeal Embryos

Throughout the first half of this book we have argued for a substance-dualist view of a human person, suggesting a continuity of personal identity from conception onward. In chapter six we argued for the personhood of fetuses and embryos in utero. We suggested that from conception forward, the embryo or fetus has all the capacities necessary to mature into a newborn baby and eventually into a full-grown adult. Fetuses and embryos are not potential persons who with time and the right environment could become full persons. Rather they are persons with the potential to mature according to their kind. They are not entities that become something other than they already are as they develop. They mature into the fullness of what they already are. Simply because the capacities characteristic of persons are latent within embryos and fetuses (up to a stage of development), it does not follow that these capacities are not present; they simply are not yet actualized.

The debates over abortion and fetal research involve the nature of fetuses and embryos in utero. Embryo research and embryos in the context of reproductive technologies generate discussion of extracorporeal embryos, those created outside the body in the lab. At this point in time it is not technologically feasible for embryos to develop outside the body.

That may change if and when scientists develop artificial wombs, which has been done for some kinds of animals. The fact that embryonic development is possible only when implanted in a human body suggests to some that there is a difference in the moral standing of extracorporeal embryos. For example, popular bioethicist and philosopher Peter Singer and embryologist Karen Dawson put it this way:

> But can the familiar claims about the potential of the embryo in the uterus be applied to the embryo in culture in the laboratory? Or does the new technology lead to an embryo with a different potential from that of embryos made in the old way? Asking this question leads us to probe the meaning of the term "potential." . . . While the notion of potential may be relatively clear in the context of a naturally occurring process such as the development of an embryo inside a female body, this notion becomes far more problematic when it is extended to a laboratory situation, in which everything depends on our knowledge and skills, and on what we decide to do. This line of argument will lead us to the conclusion that there is no coherent notion of potential which allows the argument from potential to be applied to embryos in laboratories in the way in which those who invoke the argument are seeking to apply it.[15]

We argued that the potential for capacity actualization in the fetus and embryo was a significant and persuasive argument for respecting the moral status of in utero fetuses and embryos. But can that notion be extended to embryos outside the human womb? Does the fact that the embryo cannot ever actualize any of its capacities in the lab make a moral difference when it comes to determining the fate of embryos created for alleviating infertility or for research purposes?

Our view is that zygotes, embryos, fetuses, newborns, children and adults are all persons, though each is at a different stage of development and maturity. A clear continuity of personal identity is bound up with the human person's being a substance in the Thomistic sense. In our view, virtually the only difference between embryos in utero and ex utero is location. We do not consider this to be a morally significant difference. Thus extracorporeal embryos should be considered persons in the same way that fetuses should be and that newborns, children and adults are. Such a view of embryos makes nontherapeutic research on embryos morally problematic. Extracorporeal embryos created for the purposes of infertility treatment are no different, and the moral status of such embryos places limits on the normal practice of ZIFT, GIFT and IVF.

One objection to this view is that the difference in location actually does make a morally significant difference. For example, bioethicist Bonnie Steinbock suggests that although the notion of potentiality with regard to embryos in utero and fetuses is persuasive,[16] it cannot be maintained with respect to embryos in the lab. The reason for this is that the embryo in the lab is incapable of developing into a child by itself, as opposed to an embryo in the body, which is capable. She proposes that embryos in the lab have more in common with eggs and sperm than they do with embryos in the body.[17]

This view is echoed by many others,[18] including Singer and Dawson. They too hold that there is no difference between gametes and embryos outside the body and that extracorporeal embryos cannot be considered even potential persons[19] since they cannot develop into newborns without implantation into a uterus. They write that

> whereas the embryo inside the female body has some definite chance of developing into a child unless a deliberate human act interrupts its growth, the egg and sperm can only develop into a child if there is a deliberate human act [to bring them together]. In this respect the embryo in the laboratory is like the egg and sperm, not like the embryo in the human body. This is of fundamental importance for the notion of potential, because lurking in the background of discussions of the embryo's potential is the idea that there is a "natural" course of events, governed by the "inherent" potential of the embryo.[20] (emphasis added)

The two issues raised by both Singer and Dawson's work and Steinbock's work have to do, first, with the potential of the embryo to develop in the lab and, second, with the equation of embryos outside the body to eggs and sperm.

What are we to make of the objection that because an embryo cannot develop on its own in the lab, it has no potential and thus cannot be regarded even as a potential person, not to mention a full person (though at an early developmental stage)? The way we can maintain that the only difference between in utero and ex utero embryos is location—which does not make a morally significant difference—is to distinguish between the possession of higher-order capacities and the development of lower-order capacities.[21] To have one's higher-order capacities actualized or expressed is to see the relevant lower-order capacities develop and become evident. However, if one does not develop a higher-order capacity, it does not follow that one does not possess that capacity. One has many kinds of latent capacities. For example, you have the second-order capacity, though deeply latent, to speak a foreign language, a capacity that may never be realized unless you are in the proper environment to nurture the development of that capacity. But if you never nurture that capacity, it will never be expressed and you will never be able to speak a foreign language. But that is irrelevant to whether or not you possess the second-order capacity to speak a foreign language. Whether the capacity remains latent or whether it is expressed is unrelated to your possession of such a capacity. It appears that Steinbock and Singer and Dawson have confused their metaphysical categories and equated possession with the actualization of capacities.

The environment in which the embryo is placed undeniably makes a crucial difference. But it makes a difference for the actualization, not the possession, of the embryo's higher-order capacities. Being in the wrong environment does not result in loss or nonpossession of these capacities; it results only in their not being in an environment conducive to their development. This confusion of categories is based on a functional view of a human person, a view in which only actualized capacities count as criteria for personhood. This view, as pointed out in the debate over abortion and fetal research, is grounded in a naturalist view of the world, since only the empirically verifiable characteristics of a person count as criteria for personhood. Within such a view of the world there does not seem to be a place for latent capacities that constitute an individual's natural kind (being a human person) or for the possession of higher-order capacities without their actualization.

Steinbock attempts to address the difference that the environment makes. She suggests that

> this lack of potentiality is held by some to distinguish the extracorporeal preimplantation embryo from an implanted embryo or fetus. Others reject this argument, holding that a distinction must be made between what capability the entity has within itself, and what it receives from the environment. Admittedly, the extracorporeal embryo must be put in the right environ-

ment to develop into a person. Nevertheless, it has within itself the capacity to develop into a person in that environment. By contrast, no matter what environment a gamete is put in, it cannot develop into a person all by itself. However, it is not clear that the distinction between internal capacity and environment works to show that fertilized eggs are potential persons but that gametes are not. It could be argued that a sperm *does* have the capacity within itself to develop into a person, so long as it is put in the right environment: a petri dish containing a ripe ovum. At least in the IVF context, embryos are clearly not potential persons any more than gametes are.[22]

Steinbock and others clearly want to say that the argument from potential does not apply to embryos outside the body, and even if we granted that it does, we must then conclude that sperm and eggs are also at least potential persons on the same moral ground as embryos because of their potential. All that is needed is the right environment—namely, an IVF lab with harvested eggs—and sperm could realize their potential and become a person too. The difference that Steinbock neglects to mention is that as a result of interacting with the environment the sperm, when fertilized, actually becomes an entirely different entity with a different genetic code and, in our view, its own soul. Eggs and sperm do not mature by simply realizing their potential when fertilized. They become something entirely different (that is, an individual human substance) when fertilization occurs. Except for extremely rare cases of parthenogenesis (which are anomalies far outside the norm), eggs and sperm do not mature into an adult form of their kind. They become another separate entity, which then matures according to its kind. Thus embryos are qualitatively different from eggs and sperm, and argument from the analogy between them fails. In our view, sperm and egg are possible persons. There are no such things as potential persons; the embryo is a human person with the potential for maturity.

Yet there does seem to be an intuitive and qualitative difference between an embryo in the lab, a developing fetus in the womb and a child who is growing up and maturing toward adulthood. Can we seriously suggest that all three are persons—simply at different stages of development? Consider this pointed suggestion from law professor and bioethicist George J. Annas: "If a fire broke out in a laboratory where seven embryos were stored, and a two-month-old child was also in the laboratory, and only the embryos or the child could be saved, would anyone hesitate before saving the child? Of course not! This shows that no one really does equate embryos with children."[23] Our intuitions suggest that most people would save the child and let the embryos be destroyed in the fire. It is unlikely that anyone would fault most people for such an intuition. But does it follow from that scenario that it is ludicrous to equate embryos with children? How can we explain the intuitive sense that embryos in a petri dish are somehow different from growing, thriving children?

We must make the distinction between the possession and the actualization of one's capacities. The reason we would likely choose to save the child instead of the embryos in the petri dish is because the child has more capacities realized and thus expressed. They are evident to anyone who observes the child. Latent capacities are, by definition, impossible to observe and verify, but they are no less real in a metaphysical sense. Simply because an embryo has not actualized its capacities does not make it any less intrinsically valuable, in the same way that a disabled person, who has not actualized some capacities due to physical or genetic challenges, is no less intrinsically valuable than a fully healthy adult.

In the above scenario the two-month-old child has not developed many of the critical capacities for meeting the criteria for personhood suggested by some in chapter six, such as rationality, self-consciousness and awareness of one's environment. However, one of the key traits that the child has developed is its appearance of humanness. That is, a two-month-old child resembles an adult human person more than a developing fetus does and certainly more than an embryo in the lab does, which gives one an emotional attachment to the child. This is the reason why one would probably choose to save the child instead of the embryos. But the resemblance of the infant to a person (and the expression of other capacities) is an epistemological observation. That is, they are things that we can know from our perception of the child. But what we can know epistemologically about the child and what is true metaphysically about the child are two different things. Annas appears to have confused epistemology and ontology, and he seems to be relying on a far too subjective criteria for personhood—the appearance of humanness—when arguing that an infant and embryos do not have the same moral standing. We cannot use epistemological categories to draw metaphysical conclusions about the essence of embryos, fetuses and infants.

Moreover, these observable surface features may engender emotions of sympathy, identification with another or feelings of responsibility. By contrast, the surface appearance of an embryo seems distant and impersonal. But surface appearances and the emotions they engender are, by themselves, inadequate guides for moral reflection. To a lesser degree, this same sort of "argument" could be used to justify racism, an unjustified preference for individuals who share many of one's own surface features. Since the presence or absence of surface features may be the real basis for the intuitions in this argument, we do not consider it has the force its advocates claim it has.

If the scenario in the infertility clinic were changed slightly, our intuitions might suggest an altogether different decision regarding the embryos. What if the choice were between saving one's own embryos or saving a mass murderer who is caught in the clinic? Or if the choice were between saving one's embryos or a homeless person who had wandered into the lab seeking shelter? We would suggest that most people would save their own embryos over either the mass murderer or the homeless person. But surely that intuition does not suggest that embryos are more intrinsically valuable than these fully mature adult persons. It suggests that there are other factors unrelated to the metaphysical essence of embryos and adults that inform our intuitions about who to save in this situation. Similarly, there are other things informing our intuitions about newborns and embryos that may justify saving newborns over embryos, but these things do not suggest that the embryos are metaphysically on a different continuum or somehow less deserving of moral status as persons.

The argument from one's intuitions cuts both ways, and one can suggest a conclusion from the naturalist view of a person that is equally counterintuitive. For example, Singer and Dawson acknowledge that an eight-cell blastocyst (or early-stage embryo) and a late-stage blastocyst (which consists of perhaps hundreds of cells) have very different potentials to develop when implanted in a uterus. An early-stage embryo can be successfully implanted and develop in the womb, and a late-stage embryo cannot. They suggest that this yields the result that two blastocysts, *to all appearances identical in their internal properties,* may have entirely different potentials. One, because it resulted from natural intercourse and has implanted in the uterus,[24] can be a potential person, while the other one cannot be because it is in a laboratory culture.[25]

For Singer and Dawson this means that while the eight-cell embryo in the laboratory is a potential human being, the embryo loses that status simply by continuing to develop in the laboratory. Singer and Dawson are correct in their assessment that this is a very counterintuitive conclusion, since they admit that the embryos in the lab at different stages of development have the same internal properties. That is the important metaphysical category that determines the ontological essence of the embryo. The fact that the embryo is at a later stage of development that will not permit actualization of its capacities—since it cannot now successfully be implanted—is important for the development of those capacities but not for its internal essence.

Singer and Dawson attempt to find a way out of this counterintuitive scenario by suggesting analogous situations in which a fetus has lost its potential. They cite the example of a risky pregnancy in which the physician concludes at some point that the fetus cannot be delivered even by C-section successfully. In other words the fetus is in a state of eventual demise. They conclude that "at that point the doctor might say that the potential for personhood has been lost."[26] However, one could just as easily and more directly say that the fetus is dying and will not recover, using the same language as we would use for a terminally ill adult. Once a terminal diagnosis is made, the person will not recover. We don't suggest that the potential for personhood is about to be lost. Rather we say that the person is dying. There is no reason why the same cannot be said of a fetus that will not reach viability. It would actually be more accurate to say not that the potential for personhood has been lost with the terminal illness, but that the potential for further actualization of one's capacities will be lost when the person dies. Some of the potential for actualization of capacities may be lost during the demise of the person. We need to be careful that personhood does not depend on the actualization of capacities, keeping epistemological and metaphysical categories separate.

One comes to an even more counterintuitive conclusion when you consider embryos produced by the same couple, using their gametes but ones fertilized in three different ways: one through normal intercourse and implantation, one through GIFT and one in the lab produced through IVF. All three have the same genetic contributors. All three have the same internal properties. All three have the same potential for development if placed in the proper environment. Any differences among the three have to do with things that are external and irrelevant to their essence, principally, their location. It seems counterintuitive to suggest that simply because one of the embryos is still in the lab, it is somehow qualitatively different from the other two embryos, which happen to be located in a womb. All that it needs to have a similar chance at actualizing its capacities is to be placed in a similar environment, with the time and nutrients necessary for it to mature into a newborn child.

What is true for embryos created for infertility treatments would clearly also hold true for embryos used for purposes of research and experimentation. If our substance-dualist view of embryos is correct, then every embryo created in the lab should have the opportunity to mature in the proper environment. If embryos should not be discarded in the process of infertility treatments, then neither should they be used in nontherapeutic research, which will result in their destruction in the process of research or their disposal when their research use is completed.

The current American debate on embryo research began in 1993, when President Clinton sought a recommendation from the National Institutes of Health Embryo Research Panel for guidelines that would govern federal funding for embryo research. The panel recommended that research on the embryo was acceptable until the appearance of what is called "the primitive streak," which appears at roughly fourteen-days development. Panel members rejected the idea of cloning with the transfer of a cloned embryo to a uterus, the gestation of human embryos in animals, research on embryos beyond twenty-one-days development and research involving fetal eggs and transfer to a uterus. They suggested that embryos should be entitled to "profound respect" without granting the moral and legal rights of full adult persons. The panel also adopted a pluralistic approach to the personhood of embryos that gave some moral weight to the embryo's unique status, but at the same it time allowed for most research to proceed unimpeded, which called into question the panel's view of embryos and how they could have it both ways; treating the embryo with profound respect yet using it for research purposes. Bioethicist Daniel Callahan remarked in his response to the panel's report that "I have always felt a nagging uneasiness at trying to rationalize killing something for which I claim to have profound respect."[27] The panel even recommended that creation of embryos solely for research purposes was appropriate—as opposed to simply using embryos left over from infertility treatments—a recommendation that was eventually rejected by the president.[28] The debate over embryo research and the panel's recommendations have become more critical now that scientists are able to isolate stem cells from human embryos. Stem cells are the undifferentiated cells in early embryonic development. This technology shows promise for creating organs and tissue that are currently in short supply. Stem cell research has put increasing pressure on opponents of embryo research due to the new possibilities for human benefit, yet still at the cost of destroying embryos, for which the researchers claim to have "profound respect."

Technological Assistance in Procreation Within Substance-Dualist Parameters

A final practical question remains for couples who are contemplating technologically assisted reproduction. How can a couple take advantage of the available technology for procreation without stepping outside the moral boundaries set by a Thomistic substance-dualist view of a human person? In other words, how can a couple use reproductive technologies without violating the rights of persons in an embryonic stage of development? It would be naive to suggest that this is a simple thing, since there are parts of the IVF process that are impossible to predict with certainty. But a couple does have some control over the process. They are not bound to the standard operating procedure of most infertility clinics, which includes harvesting all the eggs produced in a given cycle, fertilizing as many eggs as possible, implanting at least four and possibly more eggs to obtain the highest probability of a pregnancy and using cryopreservation of unused embryos and selective termination should the couple so desire. The couple can request that the process be tailored to their specific ethical specifications, as long as there is no medical reason why their request should not be followed. The clinic will likely attempt to encourage them to follow the standard procedure, since it was designed to minimize the cost to the couple and the physical burden on the woman. The couple should understand that the infertility industry is a highly competitive industry, so if their current physician and clinic refuse their request to have the procedures within their moral guidelines, they can simply go to another clinic.

Surplus embryos. The most simple solution to the problems of surplus embryos and selective termination would be to freeze the eggs rather than the embryos. This would still accomplish the objectives of minimizing the costs and burdens to the couple, and it would circumvent the problem of surplus embryos. It would further minimize the need for multiple embryo implantations, or lifeboat implantations, with the resulting prospect of selective pregnancy termination. Unfortunately, egg freezing is still experimental. There are encouraging results from current research around the world, and infertility specialists predict that egg freezing is likely to be widely available in the near future.[29] Once this becomes more routine, women undergoing IVF can still receive hormone treatments to enable maximum egg harvesting, and the eggs can be frozen and thawed when the couple wants to fertilize them. They can be fertilized individually. One of the drawbacks to the current technology is that the thawed eggs must be fertilized by sperm injection, a different and much more expensive process than normal IVF. Only one to three embryos need be implanted, since there are more eggs available to be fertilized. This minimizes the risk of multiple births and "litter" births, in which the woman gives birth to four or more children. It further reduces the need for selective termination, since the number of embryos implanted is lower and the corresponding risk of multiple pregnancies is lower, particularly those multiples that would place the woman or the children at risk.

From a Thomistic substance-dualist view of a person, egg freezing is clearly the ideal. But until it becomes widely available, using these technologies within moral parameters is more complex. One option that can eliminate the prospect of surplus embryos and selective termination is to use the procedure known as GIFT, where eggs are harvested but fertilization occurs inside the body instead of in the lab. The normal procedure is for the clinic to fertilize the rest of the eggs not used in the GIFT procedure (four eggs are generally used for the procedure) and to place the number that successfully fertilize in storage for later use should the initial GIFT procedure fail to produce a pregnancy. The couple can instruct the clinic that they do not want any other eggs fertilized, and thus they avoid having embryos in storage. However, if they fail to achieve a pregnancy, then they must start the procedure again from the beginning. A further drawback to this option is that some women may not be good candidates medically for GIFT. For example, if there is a blockage in a woman's fallopian tubes, then she is a better candidate for IVF, since in that procedure the embryos are placed in the uterus instead of the fallopian tubes.

Using ZIFT or IVF is a complex option for couples with a Thomistic substance-dualist view of a human person. Though they may not understand the technical specifics of this view, many Christian couples regard embryos and fetuses as human persons, and they regard human personhood as beginning at conception. What makes this complex is the uncertainty about the number of eggs that will be fertilized successfully in the lab. If it could be assumed that all the eggs could be fertilized, then the couple would have more control over the process. But one never knows how many of the eggs that are harvested will be fertilized. This is why the clinics routinely attempt to fertilize all the eggs that are harvested and then place the surplus in cryopreservation storage. So if a couple wants to avoid having surplus embryos, they cannot simply suggest that to the clinic. The physician will tell them that it's not that simple. The couple's goal is either to minimize the number of surplus embryos or not to use the procedure at all. If they choose to minimize the number of embryos, they are taking the chance that very few, and possibly none, of the eggs will fertilize. They will have endured the process of egg harvesting for nothing. If they desire to keep the number of surplus embryos to a small number, then they should limit the number of eggs fertilized and allow for some eggs that will not be fertilized. If they manage the procedure in this way, they run the risk of having a surplus of embryos. Should that happen, they would be morally obligated to give those embryos a chance at maturing. They should either implant them themselves—a most unattractive option for couples who have had multiple births through IVF or ZIFT—or they can donate them to another infertile couple, the equivalent of putting children up for adoption. The only difference is the time at which the child is given up. As difficult as this sounds, especially with multiple embryos, a good case can be made for doing adoption this way since it gives the woman who will raise the child the chance to experience the bonding that comes with pregnancy. There is greater continuity for the child, since the woman who gestates and gives birth to the child is the same woman who will raise the child.

Selective termination. Any couple using these technologies should implant only the number of embryos that the woman could carry safely or the number of children the couple is willing to raise. This may not give the greatest probability for achieving a pregnancy, but it avoids the scenario in which selective termination might be considered. There may be cases in which multiple embryos have been implanted and four or more pregnancies have resulted. One can make the case that in order to save some of the embryos, selective termination could be justified, since with no intervention, most will likely not survive pregnancy or they will be delivered so prematurely that they will have a lifetime of severe health problems. However, there are a number of cases of successful multiple births, where women give birth to quads or more. Though multiple births are difficult, the babies grow up healthy. The way to avoid this kind of scenario is to limit the number of embryos implanted to three or four maximum. Even for someone who believes that abortion is morally justifiable, selective termination in these circumstances appears to be particularly callous. The couple has intentionally created a host of human persons through ZIFT or IVF, and more embryos are implanted than the woman can safely carry or than the couple desires to raise, so they contemplate ending some of the pregnancies because they don't like the outcome. This scenario seems different from an accidental pregnancy in which birth-control mechanisms failed, where the couple was genuinely attempting to avoid conception and nature overruled their efforts. Though abortion is not justifiable in circumstances when the pregnancy is not planned, in ZIFT or IVF all the embryos were conceived by design and implanted purposely. Yet they are routinely aborted at the couple's discretion should the couple end up with more pregnancies than they wanted.

Lifeboat implantations. Limiting the number of embryos implanted also avoids the problematic notion of "lifeboat implantations" in which more embryos are implanted than can possibly develop. This is sometimes done in the clinic when couples have had repeated failures to achieve pregnancy through ZIFT or IVF. We would argue that this is the moral equivalent of abortion and that if every embryo created in the lab has the right to a developmental environment, then procedures involving the implantation of anywhere from five to nine embryos are morally problematic. In essence, when a high number of embryos are implanted, some have virtually no chance at developing. This would appear to be the equivalent to throwing people off lifeboats because not everyone can survive. Though women do, at times, give birth to large number of children—as many as seven in the celebrated 1997 case of the McConaghey septuplets—the uterus was not designed to carry a litter, unlike the wombs of many animals. Placing an abnormally high number of embryos in the woman's body in order to achieve the best chance of a pregnancy is the equivalent of condemning some (or even a majority) of the embryos to a virtually certain demise, simply because the womb cannot normally accept such a large number of implanted embryos. If by chance an unusually high number of embryos (four or more) do successfully implant, it may be that their survival is jeopardized by the presence of the others. As a result the couple may be forced to consider selective termination in order to save some. However, this is the equivalent to throwing some off the lifeboat later rather than sooner, and the wise couple who uses these technologies will request that the clinic avoid such possibilities.

Freezing embryos. A further difficulty for IVF and ZIFT is that cryopreservation of embryos is not a perfect procedure. That is, not every embryo that is frozen survives the process of thawing and preparation for implantation. Couples should be very careful about placing embryos in storage using cryopreservation, since there may be some casualties in the process. However, it may be that embryos that cannot survive the thawing process could not be successfully implanted and would naturally miscarry once placed in the body, thereby making freezing embryos per se less of a problem. The possibility of inadvertently destroying embryos in thawing them out argues further for the use of GIFT if medically appropriate and for caution in the use of IVF or ZIFT. The concerns are to prevent not only intentional destruction of embryonic persons by discarding leftover embryos, but also unintended destruction of such persons in the thawing process. These difficulties suggest that the couple who wants to use ZIFT or IVF ethically limit the number of eggs to be fertilized so that enough are available for one round of implants and that they limit the number of embryos implanted to the number that the woman can safely carry to term.

What are we to make of the process of freezing embryos from a metaphysical perspective? Since we are arguing for the existence of the soul from the embryonic phase, how is it possible to speak of cryogenically preserving a soul? Might this not suggest that the naturalist is correct about the human person? We have already addressed this in chapter six, but we are now in a position to add more details to that discussion. What occurs during cryopreservation of embryos in an infertility clinic is that the speed with which the molecules are colliding decreases with the dramatic drop in temperature, and as a result the embryo is temporarily unable to develop. This is because its development is dependent on the interactions of the molecules and atoms in the embryonic cells. By freezing the embryo the lab technician is, in effect, suspending time. Geneticist Jerome Lejune argues that by freezing the embryo we are simply suspending any chemical exchanges between the molecules and atoms. Thus when it is carefully thawed, the temperature is raised and the chemical interactions can begin where they were suspended. The embryo can continue to develop from that point on.[30] Another way to see this is to insist, as we have done, that the embryo has all the ultimate potential for organic life and maturity. It is simply not actualized since it is yet to be in an environment suitable for this development. In fact, the reason the environment is not appropriate for development is due to the fact that the temperature inside the canister where the embryos are stored is so low that molecular interaction cannot occur. That is, the directions that the soul provides to the genetic material temporarily cannot be carried out. However, it does not follow that the soul is not present in the embryo. There is no reason why a being must be conscious in order for it to possess a soul. In this way an embryo is parallel to an acorn. It has all the capacities necessary to become an oak tree, if it is placed in the proper environment. In fact, if an acorn is frozen it will not actualize its capacities for much the same reason that an embryo cannot actualize its capacities. The fact that scientists in the lab can suspend the molecular interaction in an embryo in no way implies that the soul is not resident in the embryo.

Conclusion

From a Thomistic substance-dualist perspective, extracorporeal embryos—whether used for infertility or for research purposes—are simply persons at a very early stage of development. They have the same internal essence as do fetuses, newborns and adult human beings. All embryos should have the chance to mature and express their capacities. All they need is the proper environment. Scientists and bioethicists often speak of "pre-embryos," embryos at a very early stage of development, in a way that suggests that they have no value. Yet the fertilized egg in its one-cell stage is the most complex cell the body will ever have. Lejune, testifying as an expert witness at the Davis frozen-embryo-disposition trial, argued:

> I think it's important because some people would believe that a pre-embryo does not have the same significance as an embryo. On the contrary, a first cell knows more and is more specialized than any cell which is later in our organism. . . . Now the reason that a fertilized egg is the most specialized cell under the sun is because it has a special indication underlining segments of DNA which shall be expressed and others that shall not be expressed. No other cell will ever have it during the life of this individual. . . . In the beginning it was written really not only what is the genetic message we can read in every cell, but it was written the way it should be read from one sequence to another one. . . . That is written in the first cell; it's not written progressively in the other cells.[31]

There appears to be something entirely unique about the fertilized egg that should give us pause about minimizing its significance.

We used to think our fate was in the stars.
Now we know, in large measure, our fate is in our genes.[1]

JAMES D. WATSON

Just as the Christian soul has provided an archetypal concept
through which to understand the person and the continuity of self,
so DNA appears in popular culture as a soul-like entity,
a holy and immortal relic, a forbidden territory.[2]

DOROTHY NELKIN AND
M. SUSAN LINDEE

In their endeavors to fashion new legal safeguards,
legislatures and courts should not succumb to the influence of the popular,
but ultimately irrational, idea that DNA is the essence of human personality.[3]

HUGH MILLER III

CHAPTER 9

Genetic
Technologies &
Human Cloning

*I*N THIS CHAPTER WE ENTER THE BRAVE NEW WORLD OF BIOTECH-
nology. Genetic therapies, testing and technologies present an
array of exciting new possibilities for the detection and treatment
of genetic diseases. What was spoken of as scientific speculation thirty
years ago is now being done in laboratories across the United States, Canada and Western Europe. Even something as unusual as human cloning,
which has been portrayed in films as the ultimate biotechnical science fiction,[4] has been successfully done with human embryos.[5] With the first
successes in animal cloning,[6] researchers now speak of cloning an adult
human being as being only a matter of time.

Though it may actually be some time before scientists are able to clone
adult human beings, the Human Genome Project (HGP) is ahead of
schedule and nearing completion.[7] This ambitious project, which is
attempting to map the entire human genetic code, began in the early
1990s. The practical goal was to identify as many genetic links and predispositions to disease as possible. Some diseases have a clear genetic link
such that if you have the gene for a particular disease, you will develop the
symptoms. For example, Huntington's disease, Down syndrome and cys-

tic fibrosis are all common genetic diseases in which there is a direct link between possession of the gene and development of the disease.

But many genetic "links" are merely predispositions, which do not guarantee a person will develop the disease. A predisposition means that the person has a higher risk of developing a certain condition. Various kinds of cancers, such as colon and breast cancer, fit into the category of genetic predispositions. Once such a link was discovered, then researchers could develop a diagnostic test and eventually a treatment. More than five thousand medical conditions have been traced to defective or inoperative genes.[8]

Gene therapies and genetic engineering are in their infancy, but they are raising difficult moral questions and contributing to the underlying discussion of personhood. Gene therapies are still very new and are generally used to offset the harmful effects of defective genes or to provide the functions of inactive genes. Most people think of gene replacement when they think about genetic engineering. Gene replacement, often called genetic surgery, is a procedure in which the defective gene is "surgically" replaced in the body. This technology is still in development, and many scientists believe this technology is used most productively with human embryos.

Prenatal genetic testing is widespread and is now a part of routine prenatal care, particularly for women over the age of thirty-five. Many genetic abnormalities can be detected through noninvasive ultrasound technology. More sophisticated invasive and risky genetic tests, such as amniocentesis, are now offered for unborn children who are at risk of specific diseases due to family history. Infertility researchers and practitioners are now capable of screening embryos for genetic anomalies. Couples who have a history of genetic disease are now counseled to use IVF to conceive and to have the resulting embryos screened for the defective gene prior to implantation. Embryos with the defective gene are discarded. Genetic testing is now available for adults as well—for those who are at risk for a variety of types of diseases. For example, the HGP recently uncovered a genetic predisposition for breast cancer in women. A diagnostic test is now available to enable women to determine whether they are carrying the defective gene that gives them a higher risk factor for developing breast cancer. Other similar tests are undoubtedly forthcoming.

All these technological developments raise important questions about the concept of human personhood. For example, what are we to make of human cloning? Is the entity that is cloned, either from embryos or from adult cells, a person, with the same immaterial part for which we have argued in the first section of this book? Does a cloned human being have a soul, or is it a "soulless" being? If the latter is the case, it would appear to lend support for the physicalist view of a person. Should cloned human beings have the same rights and protections as persons procreated by normal sexual relations or by an infertility treatment such as IVF? What does the fact of cloning suggest about personal identity? Is there such a thing as a right to one's own unique identity? If so, does cloning violate that right? We argue in this chapter that cloned human beings are full persons with souls and should have all attendant rights of an adult person. We will further argue that human cloning technology is not per se problematic, but there are few if any morally acceptable reasons to clone a person. Though it could threaten the notion of one's own unique identity, we argue that one does not have a right to one's own unique identity, so cloning does not pose a violation of any such right.[9]

The HGP has raised critical questions about what is to be done with the plethora of new genetic information that is now available to society. Questions of privacy and access to this information dominate the ethical discussion of the HGP, and there is a widespread consensus that this information ought to remain private.[10] It should not be disclosed to one's employer or insurer due to the likelihood of genetic discrimination. Such discrimination surely fits the traditional definitions of discrimination, which is based on nonbehavioral factors such as race and gender. Surely one's genetic code is analogous to one's race or gender in that it is part of one's endowment from God, and thus it should not be the basis for discrimination.[11]

However, that is not the only reason why there is a consensus that encourages protection of one's genetic privacy. The other reason is the popular notion, fueled by the scientific community, that the essence of personal identity can be reduced to one's genetic code.[12] This makes one's genetic blueprint legal "hallowed ground" and suggests that if such a claim is true, then violations of genetic privacy constitute the most egregious violations of a person's sense of personal identity. This kind of genetic reductionism is prevalent in the scientific community, and it is consistent with its physicalist view of the world, which reduces reality to that which is material.[13] Thus all human functions and attributes must be explainable in terms of the physical. The enormous advances in genetics that have resulted from the HGP have given support to such a materialist view of a human person. We will argue that such a view of a person does not follow from the recent advances in genetics and that human beings are not fundamentally reducible to their genetic material.

The widespread use of genetic-testing technology, particularly on pregnant women and their unborn children, has also raised questions about the personhood of the unborn child. This is especially the case when such testing is combined with prospects for treatment, surgery and even gene therapy—all of which are either performed or proposed for developing children in utero. These aspects of prenatal testing and treatment often make conflicting assumptions about the personhood of the unborn child. For example, it is widely assumed that if a prenatal genetic test comes back with indications of genetic abnormality, the couple will end the pregnancy, which at least implicitly regards the genetically defective unborn child as less than a full person. Similarly, the prospect of treating conditions and even genetic anomalies in the womb suggests the unborn child is regarded as a patient with interests that can and should be protected. We will argue that the presumption toward abortion in the case of genetic abnormality is unethical and is premised on a defective and unjustified view of a human person.

Personhood and Human Genetics
The amount of genetic information available about a person has increased exponentially in the past decade with the progress of the HGP. This has led to numerous diagnostic tests for genetically linked diseases and the prospect of gene therapy to provide treatment for previously untreatable diseases. The development of gene therapy raises a variety of ethical issues. For example, there has been progress in what is called *germ-line therapy*, in which a genetic alteration is passed along to the next generation in procreation. There are concerns about this kind of therapy, as opposed to what is called *somatic-cell therapy*, in which the genetic material introduced into the patient's body only affects that patient and cannot be passed down to succeeding generations. In addition, there are con-

cerns raised about use of gene therapy to enhance already existing traits as opposed to providing treatment for conditions produced by defective or inactive genes. Theologians have raised concerns about scientists' tampering with the human genome, suggesting that they might be "playing God" by usurping a prerogative that belongs only to God.[14] Finally, eugenic concerns are always a part of the discussion of any gene therapy, especially given the history of eugenics in the West.[15]

This explosion in the amount of available genetic information has led to the discovery of numerous genetic links and predispositions for various diseases. It has also surfaced the genetic contribution to certain behavioral conditions such as schizophrenia, bipolar disorder and depression.[16] Further, there is evidence that genes or groups of genes are associated with behaviors such as shyness.[17] These discoveries have revived the discussion of nature versus nurture in the development of a person's identity.[18] But further, they have raised questions about the nature of a human person and what constitutes the essence of human nature.

The genetic revolution is the most recent chapter in the ongoing discussion of what constitutes a human person. Are persons, in some sense, reducible to a physical entity, as is held by the naturalist? The explosion of genetic information and the contribution of genes or groups of genes to conditions of personality have suggested anew that the essence of human beings can be reduced to their genetic material—that the core of a human person is now found in his or her genetic code.

This view of a human person is not unusual in the community of scientists working on the HGP. We cannot survey every scientist working on the project, and there will undoubtedly be exceptions to this general rule. But numerous genome researchers and some the leaders of the project have written publicly on their role in the project and how they view human nature as a result of their work. Some of the most prominent leaders have backed away from earlier and more radical statements about genetics and the human person, but there is no reason to believe that the basic materialistic assumptions about human personhood have changed.[19] Sociologist M. Susan Lindee and historian of science Dorothy Nelkin summarize the views of the genome research community when they suggest that "just as the Christian soul has provided an archetypal concept through which to understand the person and the continuity of self, so

DNA appears in popular culture as a soul-like entity, a holy and immortal relic, a forbidden territory."[20]

For example, Harvard molecular biologist Walter Gilbert has called the genome the "holy grail" of human identity,[21] and he suggests that understanding the human genome provides the ultimate answer to the commandment to "know thyself."[22] He suggests that as a result of the genome project, our philosophical views of a human person will change. Clearly reflecting a materialist view of the world—which implies that human personhood is reducible to genetics—he argues that "to recognize that we are determined, in a certain sense, by *a finite collection of information* [our genetic content] that is knowable will change our view of ourselves"[23] (emphasis added). Gilbert paints the scenario in which, at the completion of the genome project, a person could store all her genetic information on a single compact disk. He concludes that "three billion bases of sequence can be put on a single compact disk, and one will be able to pull a CD out of one's pocket and say, 'Here is a human being, it's me.'"[24] Gilbert clearly sees the essence of a human person in the genetic material to be unearthed by the HGP such that, when the project is finished, society will have "closed an intellectual frontier, with which we will have to come to terms."[25] He puts this even more clearly when he suggests that "knowing the complete human genome, we will know what it means to be human."[26]

James D. Watson and Francis Crick, who together discovered the double-helix structure of the DNA molecule in the 1950s, have expressed similar views. Crick has suggested that "you, your joys and your sorrows, your memories and your ambitions, your sense of personal identity and free will, are in fact no more than the [genetically determined] behavior of a vast assembly of nerve cells and their associated molecules."[27] That is, in his view, everything that makes a human being a person is determined by biological processes driven by one's genetic structure. Watson, his long-time colleague, has argued that the HGP has as its ultimate aim the search for "ultimate answers to the chemical underpinnings of human existence."[28] That statement taken by itself, when referring to the *chemical* underpinnings of human existence, is not necessarily indicative of a kind of genetic reductionism. But Watson further suggests that "we used to think our fate was in the stars. Now we know, in large measure, our fate is in our genes."[29] Such a statement makes it clear that he holds to genetic reductionism.

More subtle ways of expressing this assumption about a human person's being reducible to his genetic material appear in the way the genome researchers talk about the project. The metaphors and figures of speech they employ to describe their task suggest a reductionistic view of the human person.[30] For example, molecular biologists routinely describe life processes that they investigate in terms of information, messages and codes. DNA is commonly referred to as a program, text or, more frequently, as a code by which the machinery of the body operates. Cells are commonly referred to as chemical factories operated by the computer program of DNA. Organisms become information systems analogous to computer systems in the storage of, and activity based on, the information available to it from the master molecule, DNA. Cells, then, become machines that run according to the genetic instructions given to them.

The researchers' use of these figures of speech to describe their work reflects a physicalist view of the world, and genetic reductionism as the best way to capture that view. Sociobiologist Howard Kaye has suggested that the way in which molecular biologists see life in terms analogous to a computer represents a worldview that sees life in materialistic terms. He argues that "the reduction of all of biology, all of the behavioral characteristics and fundamentals of living things to molecular mechanisms of life betrays a *metaphysical ambition* to demonstrate that organisms really are machines, and that all of life can be accounted for in this way"[31] (emphasis added). This view of the world is neither objective nor empirically verifiable, and it drives the investigation of the genome project. To be sure, there are some who are involved in the project who do not share such a view of the world, and there are others who are only interested in the clinical application of the project's findings.[32] But it is clear that this worldview is widely shared in the genetics community and that it has an influence on the work being done. Such a view has created a paradigm shift in genetics and contributed to the public's accepting this reductionistic view of a human person.

A further and subtle indication of genetic reductionism is found in the way that those involved with the project reduce social problems to genetics. For example, Daniel Koshland, the influential editor of *Science,* has argued for the genome project because of its potential to help not only those suffering from widely accepted genetic diseases but also others such as the poor. He stated in an address at the first human genome conference that "to withhold support [for the genome project] is to commit the immorality of omission, the failure to apply a great new technology to aid the poor, the infirm and the underprivileged."[33] To be sure, the HGP has revived the debate over the respective influences of nature and nurture on the development of a person's identity and sense of self. But it is clear that nature is emerging as the dominant force in that determination, and in some sense this is correct. However, the trend within the project is to reduce social problems to genetics, suggesting that genetics has the primary if not full explanatory power for major social ills. Even the U.S. government's Office of Technology Assessment has suggested that the genome project will provide new knowledge about "the determinants of the human condition" and will provide information about the factors that determine human diseases, even those diseases that "that are at the root of many current *social* problems"(emphasis added).[34]

Perhaps reflecting a kind of genetic determinism, a new confidence in the genetic basis for a growing number of behavioral conditions can be found among researchers. Geneticist Robert Plomin argues that "the role of inheritance in behavior has become widely accepted, even for sensitive domains as IQ."[35] Watson made a more specific application to the genetic basis for manic-depressive disorder, suggesting that medicine and psychiatry is lost in the search for treating manic depression without finding the genetic component."[36] University of California at Berkeley philosopher and historian of science Evelyn Fox Keller has concluded that "in the terms that increasingly dominate contemporary discourse, culture has become subsumed under biology."[37] There seem to be clear indications of a widely held view in the HGP community that human beings are reducible to their genetic material and that social problems can increasingly be spoken of in genetic terms. This would suggest by implication some sort of determinism, which would undermine important notions such as libertarian free will and moral responsibility. This is particularly the case as applied to behavioral genetics, the genetic links to behaviors such as depression and alcoholism.

As we have argued throughout this book, such a conception of a human person is both philosophically problematic and inconsistent with biblical teaching on the nature of human persons. The essence of human personhood cannot be reduced to one's genetic material any more than it can be reduced to any other physical property. The scientists who are making claims about personhood are making a fundamental methodological error in expecting biological data to provide the foundations for metaphysical questions. Biology and biochemistry provide the raw material for biological and biochemical questions; they cannot decisively answer what are ultimately metaphysical questions. When molecular biologists make such metaphysical claims about the nature of personhood, they are no longer practicing molecular biology. They have become philosophers and are inappropriately extending their expertise from biology to philosophy. One simply cannot extrapolate metaphysical conclusions from biological and biochemical data without leaving one's scientific field. The scientists arguing for some sort of genetic reductionism are imposing their worldview on their work and are drawing metaphysical conclusions that simply cannot be drawn from their field of expertise.

The genetic-reductionism model for human identity, illustrated by the "computer program" analogy, assumes causality between genotype and phenotypical expression of one's genetic code. But it is becoming clearer that there is no direct cause-and-effect relationship between the two. Rather, the genotype specifies a range of possible phenotype expressions. The genetic code for any given individual does not constitute a fixed life script. A variety of factors, including environment and nurture, influence how any given genetic pattern will be expressed in the individual. This is particularly the case with behavioral genetics. Far from giving a person a genetically determined set of behaviors, how or whether a given part of a person's genotype will be expressed depends on a variety of other nongenetic factors. Evidence of this comes from cases of identical twins.[38] Although they have the same genotype, they are very different persons. They are clearly shaped by their developmental environment and life experiences.

This is significant given the recent claims made by HGP scientists concerning behavioral genetics. If determinism follows from genetic reductionism, as would seem to be the case, then the variability of the expression of one's genotype especially in the area of behaviors would suggest a serious limit in how the model of genetic reductionism can be applied to human beings. Since two people can share the identical genetic blueprint and still develop into two very different persons, it follows that possession of DNA alone is not a sufficient condition for personal identity. At the least, one's identity is determined by one's freely made choices.[39] One's genetic code simply sets the parameters within which there are a range of possibilities for behavior and personal identity. It is the raw material that plays a role in the determination of identity—but only that. It may even play a more significant role than anyone has anticipated. But genetic reductionism does not follow from the increasingly significant role of the genetic code, particularly given the uncertainties surrounding the actual expression of genetic patterns in the person.

That is not the only shortcoming of the model of genetic reductionism. The activity of genes suggests what we have described earlier as an organocentric view of a human organism, in which the organism is the fundamental unit of control and information. The operation of DNA presupposes the organism as a unity prior to its functioning.[40] The organism as a whole, which is greater than its constituent parts, drives the activity of the DNA. This view is strikingly consistent with the Thomistic substance dualism that we have advocated throughout this book.

The mechanistic or reductionistic view of the human genome suggests that DNA molecules are self-starters. That is, if the DNA contains the fundamental building blocks of life and if the core elements of a human person can be reduced to one's genetic code, then DNA must have the capacity within the molecule to initiate the complex set of chemical reactions necessary for cellular growth and development. However, French geneticist Francois Jacob suggests that DNA needs a driver.[41] He argues that "outside the cell, without the means to carry out the plans, without the apparatus necessary for copying or transmitting, [the genetic program] *remains inert*. No more than memory of a computer can the memory of heredity act in isolation. Able to function only within the cell, *the genetic message can do nothing by itself*. It can only guide what is being done" (emphasis added).[42] Jacob does not elaborate on what that driver might be, but it should be clear that he is describing something like a substance in which the DNA is an important part that needs instructions from some other part of the organism. We would argue that this leaves the door open for consideration of an immaterial part of a person, such as the soul, that drives the DNA to perform its necessary biochemical functions.

Geneticist Barbara McClintock suggests an alternative to the mechanistic and reductionistic views of her colleagues on the genome project by showing the shortcomings of such a model. She states that "the genome is a highly sensitive organ of the cell that monitors genomic activities and corrects common errors, senses unusual and unexpected events, and responds to them often by restructuring the genome. We know about the components of genomes that could be made available for such restructuring. We know nothing, however, about how the cell senses danger and *instigates responses to it that often are truly remarkable*"[43] (emphasis added). It is difficult to see how the phenomena McClintock describes can be consistent with a mechanistic and reductionistic view of genetics and the human person. Though what she has observed does not establish that an immaterial part of the person is necessary as an instigator, it surely leaves open the possibility for such a consideration.

A third concern about the genetic reductionism that is often characteristic of the genome project has to do with the moral and social implications of such a worldview. The way in which people are held morally and criminally responsible for their actions strongly suggests that they possess libertarian free will, and thus a concept of moral desert has meaning. That is, people make genuinely free choices, for which they deserve praise or blame. Society's notion of criminal justice is premised on such a view of a human person. Genetic determinism (like other forms of naturalistic determinism) undermines these important notions of free will and moral and criminal responsibility. The concept of character is premised on freedom to make one's choices, choices that thereby contribute to shaping one's identity. Even given the genetic contribution to various behaviors, genetics merely fixes a set of possibilities out of which the person makes either morally praiseworthy or morally blameworthy choices. Taking determinism seriously, as a naturalist view of a human person seems to imply we should, would undermine critical moral and legal notions of personal and criminal responsibility. Our assignment of these responsibilities strongly suggests a substance view of a person as one who has libertarian free will and who can be held responsible for his or her choices.

Personhood and Human Cloning

In the past few years human cloning has emerged from the realm of science fiction and into the highest levels of bioethical discussion.[44] Though cloning adult human beings is still far from accomplished technologically, scientists have made significant progress toward that goal in the past five years. The first human cloning was successfully performed in 1993, when infertility researchers at George Washington University Medical School cloned human embryos, essentially duplicating in the lab what occurs in the body when identical twins or triplets are produced.[45] The technical term for this type of cloning is *blastomere separation*. This refers to the earliest developmental stage of the embryo, known as the *blastomere stage,* at which time the embryo is cloned. These embryos were not intended for implantation and were defective, only surviving roughly seven to ten days. The original intent for attempting such research was to help infertile couples use IVF more effectively and with less cost to the couple. The researchers who cloned the embryos received an enormous amount of criticism for their work, primarily from people who accused them of "playing God."[46] To date, embryo cloning has receded into the background and does not attract much public attention.

The more celebrated form of cloning is more technologically complicated and is more analogous to the science-fiction view of human cloning. This is called *somatic-cell nuclear transfer.* This occurs when the cells of an adult human person are removed and placed in an egg, which has had its nucleus removed, where they are allowed to grow and develop. The genetic material of the adult has been copied and can develop according to its kind. This was first done successfully with animals in the well-known example of Dolly, the sheep produced by somatic-cell cloning by researchers in Scotland.[47] Cloning has been repeated using sheep and with other types of animals, but no one has yet attempted to perform it on human beings. There are those who have publicly admitted that they will, such as Chicago infertility researcher Dr. Richard Seed. The state of the science is still very much experimental, and researchers admit there are still significant technological bugs to be worked out before it should be attempted on human beings. The National Bioethics Advisory Commission (NBAC) on human cloning recommended a ten-year moratorium on federal funding for cloning research, and there is competing bill pending in Congress that would place an outright prohibition on cloning. At present, no federal law prohibits privately funded cloning research, though some states have passed laws preventing it.

The NBAC recommended against somatic-cell nuclear transfer due to safety concerns both for the developing embryo and for the woman who would carry the embryos to term.[48] The commission suggested that "at this time, the significant risks to the fetus and physical well being of a child created by somatic cell nuclear transplantation cloning outweigh arguably beneficial uses of the technique."[49] This is the primary concern of the commission, on which there was virtually full agreement. What makes this interesting is that the commission is very concerned about the welfare of the developing embryo and fetus that will result from cloning. The concern has to do with the welfare of the child who will develop, or fail to develop, out of the cloning process. (In fact, this concern about cloning is the overriding consideration in the NBAC's recommendation against federal funding for cloning.)

This is a striking contrast to the National Institutes of Health Embryo Research Panel's recommendations on extracorporeal embryo research (mentioned in chapter eight). There the panel suggested that the embryo was owed "profound respect" but could be the subject of experimental procedures that will result in its destruction, either in the process of research or after it is concluded and the embryos are discarded. Why is there so little regard for embryonic and fetal welfare in the public policy on embryo research and such significant concern for the developing embryo or fetus (still extracorporeal at the time of cloning) in the public policy on cloning?

This odd dichotomy in the views of the personhood and rights of embryos and fetuses further illustrates the ambivalence in the bioethics community about the moral status of embryos. The answer to this dichotomy might be to insist that in cloning there is the intent to produce a child, which is not the case in embryo research. This is consistent with the widely held view in the abortion debate that the rights of the fetus are determined by whether the mother desires to keep the child. Clearly cloning would be done in order to raise an identical twin. But as was pointed out in chapter seven, to rest one's view of personhood, which undergirds rights, in such a subjective notion as the intent to keep the child is putting personhood on very shaky philosophical ground. The reason for this is that the desire to keep the child is entirely unrelated to the essence of the entity developing in the womb. Whether a pregnant woman or a recipient of a cloned human being desires to keep the developing child is irrelevant to its basic nature. Whether or not this notion accounts for the difference in the approaches to embryo research and cloning is not clear from the reports by the commission and the panel. But the radical difference in concern for the developing embryo or fetus is striking, and it suggests a lack of clarity about the essence of the embryo or fetus.

What exactly occurs when a person is cloned? Actually "cloning a person" is somewhat misleading, since the person cannot be cloned. It is only the genetic material of the person that is duplicated. Virtually everyone in the cloning discussion admits that a clone would be a different person than the person from whom the genetic material came. This is analogous to the way in which identical twins are nevertheless two different persons. Genetics only partially shapes persons into who they become. Environment contributes significantly, such that a person is a mixture of both nature and nurture. The relative contribution of each has been and will continue to be sharply debated, but there is virtual consensus that both are significantly involved in shaping the whole person. Thus researchers are not cloning whole persons. That would involve duplication of the person's genes, environment and experiences, and more pointedly, duplication of the soul, which are not possible even under the most controlled circumstances. Researchers are simply duplicating the genetic material, producing delayed identical twins.

A variety of issues must be addressed in order to have a coherent position on cloning. These include issues of parental identification and rights, concerns about rights to one's own unique genetic identity, the impact on the notion of the family, commodification of cloned human beings, potential abuses of the process (such as use of clones for organ farming) and concerns about abuses that might lead to eugenics.[50] In addition, there are a variety of theologically motivated issues such as whether cloning constitutes "playing God," whether cloning violates essential human dignity and whether cloning violates biblical norms relating to procreation within the context of marriage.[51] These are all complicated and worthy issues for discussion, on which there is no current consensus in the bioethics community.

Our more narrow focus in this section is on how the notion of personhood relates to human cloning. Specifically, would a cloned human being constitute a person, and if so, on what basis? Further, would a cloned human being possess a soul? Do the questions of the soul and the apparent impossibility of cloning a soul suggest that the materialist might be right about the human person?

First, assuming that a human being were someday successfully cloned, would such a being be a full person? The widespread consensus in the bioethics community is that cloned human beings should be regarded as full persons, with all the attendant rights.[52] There is legitimate concern that cloned persons might be viewed as less than fully human and consequently be used for either dangerous or degrading tasks.[53] The key question here is whether or not cloned human beings ought to be regarded as persons, in terms of metaphysics.

From a naturalistic perspective—in which adherents assume that the genetic material constitutes the basic building blocks of life—there is no reason not to regard a cloned human being as a full person. Possession of the human genome would be sufficient to regard the entity as both living and human, similar to the way in which human embryos and fetuses are viewed. But that does not settle the personhood issue. It only tells us that the entity is alive and human. Whether or not a cloned person would be regarded as a full person from the earliest points of his or her development is another question. To be consistent, those taking a nonessentialist view of a human person would have to subject the cloned person to the same functional criteria for personhood, which we have critiqued in earlier chapters. These include functions such as self-consciousness, awareness of one's environment and sentience. That is, as the cloned person develops in utero, it would achieve the functions deemed necessary for conferral of personhood. Then it would be recognized as a person in the same way as an unborn child who was conceived naturally is recognized. For the naturalist this way of viewing a cloned human person makes sense and is consistent with their assignment of personhood to human beings in utero irrespective of how they were conceived.[54]

If genetics were all that mattered in the determination of personhood, the personhood of cloned human beings would be a relatively simple matter. Since cloning is by definition the duplication of another's genome, cloned human beings would have the same moral status as the person from whom the genetic material was copied. This assumes that the cloned human being would have developed to the same point as the person from whom the genome came. Assignment of personhood at the specific point of development, particularly in utero, would further depend on the criteria one uses for that assignment. Thus if one views personhood as beginning at conception (for which we have argued throughout this work), then the cloned human being would be a person from that point forward, similar to other unborn children, since they possess the human genome. If one views personhood in terms of function, then the function, not the genome, would determine the point at which the human being becomes a full person. The genome would be the necessary minimum for personhood. Some would reject that the human genome sets the parameters, and some only accept functional criteria. The result of this would be some form of animal rights, in which advanced animals would be seen as also having meet the functional criteria for personhood.[55] Of course, we would insist that such a separation of a human being and a person is highly problematic. In our view, if one recognizes an entity as a human being, it should concomitantly be seen also as a person. The point of this discussion is to show that for the naturalist, the issue of personhood of cloned human beings is neither difficult nor problematic.

However, for those (such as ourselves) who hold to an immaterial part of a person, such as a soul, cloning raises other and more complicated questions. Is it reasonable to suggest that cloned persons have souls? If not, how can they be full persons? If so, how can we understand the transmission of the soul in the process of cloning, since clearly souls cannot be cloned?[56]

First, we would insist that if a cloned person were to have no soul, then he or she is not a person. In view of our understanding of the soul in theological perspective and from the view of a Thomistic substance dualist, one cannot be a person without a soul. The immaterial aspect of a person is that which embodies his essence. Our nature is fundamentally bound up with our soul. Since human persons are essentially souls— which are embodied in a body formed through the complex set of interactions in the human genome—it is impossible to speak of a person without a soul: to speak of a "soulless person" is clearly an oxymoron.[57] For any human being at any stage of development to be a person, the soul must be present. To be sure, the degree to which the soul's capacities are actualized at any given time can vary widely. But as we have previously noted, actualization and possession of capacities are two different issues. One cannot draw any conclusions about the possession of higher-order capacities from observations about lower-order capacities that fail to be actualized.

To take this further, we would argue that if a person has no soul, he or she cannot be alive. We would hold that this is consistent with our previous discussion of the soul.[58] Theologically, death is the point at which the soul departs from the body. In view of this, a soulless body would actually be a corpse, and it would only be a person from the perspective of memory. That is, when the soul has departed, the only thing living about the person in this world is the memories of the person that survive with his or her loved ones. Thus, for a human body to be soulless is tantamount to its being dead.

We can take this further in regard to cloning. As we have argued in the first section of the book, the soul is that which animates the body, even directing the DNA molecules to produce the elements necessary for one's physiology and personality to flourish. Without the soul, the body is lifeless; there is no "breath of life" coursing through it. This is why we have argued earlier that animals have souls, though theirs are of a different qualitative kind than human persons.[59] For the process of cloning to effectively produce a human person, the soul must be present. In our view, if the soul is somehow not present in a cloned human being, then not only is that entity not a person, the process of cloning has not worked.

DNA molecules require a driver for their direction, which we have suggested is the soul. This is the organocentric view of DNA, for which we have argued in chapter six. The genetic materials that compose the DNA molecules are simply tools incapable of providing a sense of direction for themselves. Direction must be provided by some sort of internal nature, which provides a species-specific principle of development. This is consistent with a substance view of a human person and suggests that without a soul, there is nothing available to the DNA molecules to function as the driver. In the absence of this it is difficult to see even conceptually how cloning can successfully produce a human being. Thus for cloning to work, the cloned human persons must have souls. As a result, they should be regarded no differently than any other person, with the same rights and respect due any member of the human community.

These conclusions raise the difficult question of how the soul is transmitted from the "parent" (which in cloning is technically the sibling, the identical twin) to the "child" (the new sibling). It is difficult to draw with certainty any conclusions on this question, but such ambiguity about the origin of the soul should not undermine confidence in the Thomistic substance-dualist view of the soul put forth so far. This is not fundamentally a question that science can decide, but our conclusions should be consistent with what is established scientific fact.

At first glance it would seem that a creationist view of the soul would make more sense in view of human cloning. That is, the soul is created ex nihilo at the point at which the physical-reproductive conditions exist for development of the new person. Clearly a Thomistic (not a Cartesian) creationism is preferable, as we have argued in chapter six. In view of the fact that there is no union of sperm and egg in cloning, it is difficult initially to see how a soul could be transmitted through a reproductive process that has not occurred. That is not to say that a soul can be transmitted only through such a reproductive process, either naturally or through IVF. We simply have never had to attempt to explain the origin of the soul for persons procreated apart from union of sperm and egg.

However, a traducian view can explain what may occur if and when human cloning becomes a technological reality. If one accepts this view of the soul's origin, then one must hold that sperm and egg have potentialities to actualize a soul when the proper physical-reproductive conditions exist, whether in natural or technological reproduction. When sperm and egg unite, the two different entities come together and form a new one, and out of the soulish potentialities of sperm and egg a new soul emerges, which then is the driver for the development of the person.

What we may be on the verge of discovering with the advances in human cloning is that virtually any cell, not just the sex cells in sperm and eggs, has these soulish potentialities. When the proper physical-reproductive conditions exist for cloning—that is, when the cloned cells are placed in the enucleated egg and it begins to develop—the soulish potentialities are actualized to form a new soul. This would be analogous to the way a starfish can build a new organism out of a part that has been disconnected from the original whole.[60] In view of the successes in animal cloning, what occurs when a starfish "reproduces" itself seems very similar to, though much less complex than, the process of animal cloning. We would say that the starfish has been cloned. That cloned starfish has a soul in the same way the original starfish did. Somehow the parts of that organism have the potential to develop soulish capacities when in the proper physical environment. What appears to be the case with animal souls could be parallel to the human soul in the instance of human cloning. Each human cell could have the capacity for the development of a soul, actualized in the proper conditions. This would be consistent with our view of how the soul is intimately related to the body. The soul permeates the body and cannot be isolated from any particular part of it. Though it may not be clear yet how the soul is transmitted in cloning, both the Thomistic creationist and traducian views can adequately explain what could occur.

Personhood and Prenatal Genetic Testing

In the past decade genetic testing for pregnant women has become a normal part of prenatal care. Unless there is a medical reason for more sophisticated types of testing, most pregnant women receive a blood test known as the alpha-fetoprotein (AFP) test, which can detect types of severe abnormalities such as neural-tube defects like spina bifida. Ultrasound technology is generally used at least once during most pregnancies to view the features of the unborn child. This is normally a thrilling moment for the pregnant couple, when they are able to see the heart beating and detect many of the key features of their unborn child. This contributes significantly to the couple's excitement with the pregnancy and their sense of bonding to their child. In fact, it is not uncommon for couples to request a video recording of their first ultrasound, taken at roughly the halfway point of the pregnancy. Ultrasound is capable of spotting evidence of a variety of fetal abnormalities, including many genetic anomalies, such as Down syndrome and hydrocephalus. In the hands of a skilled practitioner, ultrasound can be very effective in ruling out specific problems with the unborn child.

For women over the age of thirty-five or for those women with a family history of genetic disease, more invasive and more reliable tests are routinely offered. The most common of these is amniocentesis. In this test the physician inserts a needle into the abdomen of the pregnant woman in order to draw out amniotic fluid. The unborn child has sloughed off cells into the fluid, and the physician can examine the genetic structure of those cells by obtaining them from the amniotic fluid. These tests carry a one to two percent risk of miscarriage and are considered much more invasive and uncomfortable for the woman.

As these tests become more routine and as the number of detectable conditions increase, the genetic-counseling industry has arisen to meet the needs of couples who are suddenly faced with the crisis of discovering that their unborn child has a genetic abnormality. Imagine the trauma that these couples, who desperately want a child and who are thrilled with the news of their pregnancy, must face when they hear the bad news that comes back from their genetic testing. At this point the couple can benefit from insight and perspective from professionals trained to deal with genetic information and with the decisions based on it that the couple must make.

Issues of personhood emerge at three different points in the discussion of genetic testing. First, they come out in a routine viewing of an ultra-sound by an expectant couple. With improvements in the technology, physicians can see features of the unborn child more clearly and earlier in the pregnancy than ever before. Though appearance of humanness is not a criterion for personhood, couples who experience a bonding to the child they see on the ultrasound monitor nevertheless have an intuitive sense that what they are seeing is qualitatively different from an organ or piece of tissue. They no longer view the fetus as a "product of concep-tion" but rather as a living human being. Of course, it could be argued that prospective parents who are planning on keeping their child are pre-disposed to view the child as a person. But the clarity with which medi-cine has enabled parents to see their unborn children is compelling even to some of the most committed prochoice advocates. These advocates are encouraging their colleagues in the movement to finally admit what is intuitively obvious (and made so by the use of ultrasound): the fetus in the womb is not simply a nameless, faceless product of conception; it is a living, breathing human being with the potential to actualize all of its capacities to function in a fully human way.

This is why the essay "Our Bodies, Our Souls" by feminist Naomi Wolf is such a powerful testimony to the intuitive recognition that the unborn child is special and distinct because of its humanness and potential for full development. She and other feminists are arguing that the emphasis of the prochoice movement must stop denying what most people now intuitively accept because of technologies like ultrasound. She suggests that we must now admit that an abortion is more than simply ending a pregnancy: "Increasing knowledge is increasing the awe and respect which we have for the unborn and is causing us to regard the unborn baby as a real person long before birth."[61] She points out that whether or not the child is wanted is irrelevant in view of the vivid visual images of what this child is. It is no longer feasible to suggest that the developing fetus is merely "uterine material" and that abortion is only removing such material. Rather it is taking the life of a human being who, if left alone to develop normally, would become a fully functioning adult like the rest of us. She and her colleagues now argue that there are conditions under which it is morally acceptable to kill an unborn human being, and with this knowledge they still attempt to continue the safeguards for the right to abortion.[62]

The counterargument to their claim (that conditions exist under which it is morally acceptable to kill an unborn human being) is that once one recognizes that a person is in the womb, only self-defense can justify taking its life. When life conflicts with a pregnant woman's liberty to order her life as she chooses, life has virtually always taken precedence in the legal and moral tradition of the West. Even if a woman did not want to have the child because the child would severely disrupt her life, the logical step would be for her to put the child up for adoption, not for her to have an abortion. Once one admits that in abortion a woman is killing a person, only in the most extreme circumstances can she justify taking its life, circumstances in which the presence of the unborn child brings a mortal danger to the pregnant woman. Given the current state of obstetrical technology, it is exceedingly rare for a pregnant woman ever to be in the condition where continuing the pregnancy or delivering the child will pose a mortal threat to her life.

The point of this discussion is not to revisit the abortion debate discussed in chapter seven. Rather it is to highlight how prenatal examination technology is making it increasingly more difficult to hold that the unborn child is not a person. Denying that there is a person in the womb—or denying at least that there is the potential for full development while in the womb—is becoming more difficult in light of medicine's growing ability to enable us to look into the womb. We grant that this does not settle the debate. We only point out here that equating the fetus with a product of conception or uterine material and then justifying abortion on that ground is increasingly more difficult to do given what medicine can demonstrate about life in the womb.

Once a pregnant woman gets beyond ultrasound and into tests like amniocentesis, issues of personhood emerge again. Imagine that the couple receives the results of a genetic test that indicates their child will suffer from Down syndrome. They are clearly distressed by that news; perhaps their worst nightmares are materializing. They discover that the child will require lifelong care, and though they were prepared for their lives to change when they had a child, they did not expect that having a child would be as burdensome as it will be. As they process this news with the genetic counselor, they discover that the counselor seems to be assuming that they will end the pregnancy. Though the counselor has not come out and said it directly, it is a subtle undercurrent in their discussions. The counselor assures them that ending the pregnancy is a reasonable thing to do under the circumstances and that no one would fault them for choosing to avoid a lifetime of caring for a very burdensome child. Their friends and neighbors empathize with them and assure them that any reasonable couple would consider ending the pregnancy an understandable and acceptable option.

This couple is correct in discerning that much of the professional and nonprofessional thinking about prenatal genetic testing expects a couple will abort an imperfect pregnancy. It is widely assumed that if the couple were to get bad news about their child's genetic makeup, they would end the pregnancy. But consider what that assumption indicates about the view of a human person. This kind of presumption about prenatal genetic testing suggests that personhood and the attendant rights to life are dependent on the child's possessing an acceptable genetic makeup. What constitutes such an acceptable makeup would be entirely up to the subjective preferences of the parents. It is solely the genetic anomaly that, in the minds of the parents, renders the fetus as less than a full person, since without the child's anomaly, the parents would undoubtedly consider ending the pregnancy with their wanted child as immoral.

The fact that couples would end a pregnancy on the basis of genetic abnormality assumes that the fetus in the womb is not a full person. Without that assumption, there would be no morally significant difference between ending the pregnancy when a woman is carrying a genetically defective fetus and ending the life of a genetically handicapped adult. Society and the law take the latter as absurd, and in fact the argument is commonly made that the law owes even greater protection to the genetically handicapped because of their vulnerability. If personhood is denied based on genetic abnormality, then there is no justification for protecting the adult genetically handicapped population, which faces physical, mental and genetic challenges. Prenatal genetic testing and the corresponding assumptions about ending the pregnancy indicate a deeply flawed view of a human person. Further, that assumption about what constitutes a person is illogical, since it cannot be applied evenly to all segments of the population.

Our expectant couple might have another option available to them if they have a history of genetic disease and are concerned about passing deleterious genes to their children. If the couple is willing to use IVF and create embryos in the lab, the infertility clinic can screen the embryos prior to implantation. The couple can then elect to implant only the embryos that are free of the defective gene.[63] This would give the couple a much higher probability of having a child free of genetic disorders, and it would seem at first glance to be a very responsible way of procreating children for couples with a history of genetic disease.

However, on further reflection there does not seem to be any morally significant difference between this procedure and ending the pregnancy of a genetically anomalous child. If it is true that embryos, whether extracorporeal or implanted, are persons (as we have held in this work and as is consistent with a Thomistic substance-dualist view of a human person), then the stage of development at which their lives are ended is not morally relevant. Whether their existence is terminated at the preimplantation stage or in the second trimester of pregnancy, the fact remains that the life of a human person has been taken. In this case, the couple would still be aborting because of genetic defect, the only difference being the stage at which the unborn person's life is ended. This testing and selecting based on genetic abnormality is not morally different from using amniocentesis and aborting based on genetic abnormality. Though we empathize with couples who have a history of genetic disease, the cost of insuring a healthy child includes, in our view, the intentional destruction of genetically defective embryonic persons. To be consistent with our view of fetuses and embryos as substances with an essence that endures through the different stages of development, this type of testing is morally problematic.

Suppose our expectant couple in question discovers through their prenatal care that their unborn child is suffering from a condition that can be corrected while in utero. Perhaps it is a condition requiring surgery on the child while in the womb. Or it may even be that the unborn child could benefit from in utero gene therapy. Let's suppose the parents discover this news about their child and the prospects for treatment at roughly the midpoint of the second trimester of pregnancy, that is, at approximately the halfway point.

Some have raised questions about the pregnant woman's moral obligation to undergo invasive procedures for the benefit of her unborn child.[64] This is similar to the arguments made against forcing women to undergo cesarean-section deliveries in cases where physicians deem it medically necessary.[65] It is commonly held that the pregnant woman is not morally obligated to suffer invasions of her body against her will in order to benefit her unborn child. We would take issue with such a view on the ground that the pregnant woman has a higher obligation to seek the best interests of her unborn child because that unborn child is totally dependent on the mother for its existence and nurture, and this dependence heightens the obligation to care for the unborn child. Further, suppose the unborn child will be harmed by not having the treatment or surgery. The pregnant woman no doubt will be inconvenienced temporarily due to the physicians' having to go through her to treat her unborn child. However, the mother will be not harmed in any way proportionate to the harm incurred by the unborn child should the child not receive the proposed treatment or surgery. Under these conditions she is morally obligated to consent to the treatment for her unborn child.

The most significant part of this discussion is not the pregnant woman's moral obligation to consent to the proposed treatment. Rather it is the way in which the unborn child is viewed in the discussion. In the second trimester of pregnancy the pregnant woman can end her pregnancy for virtually any reason she chooses. The unborn child is not considered a person and has no rights under the law. Yet the child is perceived by the physician as a patient with legitimate health interests that everyone recognizes. Again the issue of personhood surfaces: it is very curious that the unborn child can be a patient and not yet a person. We grant that this alone does not establish the personhood of the unborn child;[66] however, this certainly does indicate the ambivalence with which science and culture view the unborn child. We find it strikingly ironic that an unborn child in the womb, prior to viability, can receive treatment or surgery to save its life and be regarded as a patient in his or her own right, separate and distinct from its mother. At the same time and even in the same procedure, the physician can take the life of the unborn child in a fully legal abortion procedure. We view it as tragic and absurd that at almost any given point in pregnancy, one unborn child either can have its life saved as a patient or can have its life taken in an abortion and be regarded as a nonperson.

Regarding the property-thing versus substance depiction of human persons, only a substance view—which suggests a continuity of personal identity and attributes personhood apart from the stage of functional development and the desires of the parents—can provide a consistent view of the personhood of the unborn. Only a substance view can account for our intuitions that suggest a qualitative difference between the fetus and other body parts. Prenatal technologies that enable one to peer into the womb and treat unborn children in utero are strengthening these intuitions.

Conclusion

In this chapter we have resisted genetic reductionism because it is not consistent with the observations of how genes work. Nor is it consistent with widely held notions of libertarian free will or of moral and criminal responsibility. We have suggested that the soul provides the necessary driver, or instigator, for the chemical reactions of the otherwise inert DNA molecules. We have suggested that cloned human beings are full persons and that each cell may have soulish capacities. The notion of a soulless person is an oxymoron, and possession of the soul is critical for animating the life processes of any given person. We have tried to point out how assumption of the nonpersonhood of in utero unborn children is part of the genetic testing and counseling environment, and we have suggested that aborting the genetically anomalous child is morally equivalent to taking the lives of genetically challenged adults.

Further, our view of a human person is important because of its implications for moral and criminal responsibility. A property-thing view of a person is implausible since roughly every seven years, every atom in the human body is replaced. On a materialistic view of the person, if the person is essentially the "stuff" of which he is made, then the person becomes someone different every seven years. Logically, on this view, who you are would change from day to day as the parts of the property-thing are replaced. Stanford University philosopher John Perry illustrates the tension in the property-thing view when he suggests that "if O. J. Simpson had tried to get off by mounting appeals for seven years, then saying: Gee, you've taken so long to convict me that I'm not the same person, that would be bull. . . . We're not trying the atoms. We're trying the person."[67] We believe that a Thomistic substance-dualist view of a human person is a reasonable way to capture Perry's insight.

*The sanctity of life ought to be interpreted as protecting life
in the biographical sense and not merely life in the biological sense.*[1]

JAMES RACHELS

*When an individual becomes permanently unconscious,
the person has passed out of existence, even if biological life continues.*[2]

ROBERT N. WENNBERG

CHAPTER 10

Euthanasia, Physician-Assisted Suicide & Care of Persons at the End of Life

. . . .

*J*OHN IS WASTING AWAY FROM A TERMINAL CASE OF STOMACH cancer. The cancer cannot be treated, and he has less than three months to live. These final months will likely be filled with the kind of suffering that only a dying person can experience. He will likely be racked with pain, and his physicians will be unable or unwilling to administer sufficient amounts of pain medication to make him comfortable. He is already virtually unable to take care of himself and relies on various nurses and family members to care for him, reducing a once proud and independent man to a man totally dependent on others. He is alert only periodically, and when he is lucid he only laments his dismal state. He no longer has any hopes, dreams, aspirations or goals except to die, hopefully in peace and in as little pain as possible. He has a very limited capacity for human interaction, which will continue to diminish as the cancer runs its course. His physicians predict that as he nears the time of his death, he will probably slip into a coma and die shortly after that.

His children look at their father and wonder what happened to the person they once knew. They have gradually come to admit that he is not the person that he once was. They can hardly believe that their once vigorous father has been reduced to such a shell of a person. They are aware that the law in their state of Oregon allows for physician-assisted suicide. They wonder whether that would be a good option for their father, since he will continue to waste away over the next few months. Their Christian view of the world tells them that innocent people have a right to life and should not be killed. They oppose abortion and consider it the killing of an innocent person. But when they consider their father, they wonder how it can be said that their father is still a person; or if they don't think that yet, they know he may reach the point when he will resemble more closely a body kept functioning rather than a person who is living. They wonder whether having a physician assist him in suicide would actually be killing a person. It seems difficult for them to see how their father is much of a person when virtually all of the things that made life important to him, and actually made it life for him, are either gone or will be gone shortly.

Or consider Don and Judy, who are into the third year of maintaining their twenty-one-year-old son, Jim, on life support. Jim is lucky even to be alive, having survived a terrible auto accident that tragically left him in a permanent vegetative state. The only part of his brain that continues to function is the brain stem, which controls the involuntary functions of the body such as respiration, heartbeat and digestion. Neurologists insist that Jim will never regain any higher brain function. He will never wake up, never regain consciousness, never communicate with another person and never realize any of his life's hopes and dreams. In the neurologists' view, he is no longer a person; he is just a body that is maintained by medicine until he meets the state's definition of being dead—the irreversible loss of all brain function, not just higher brain activity. Don and Judy often wonder whether the neurologists are right. Is their son no longer a person? Is he simply a body? Is there any point to maintaining his body through medical means? Has the person died, even though the body remains functioning?

Questions of personhood come not only at the beginning edge of life but also at the ending edge. Though there are many other arguments advanced in favor of physician-assisted suicide (PAS), one primary question in the debate over euthanasia and PAS that needs to be resolved is the question of the personhood of the imminently dying, the irreversibly comatose and those patients in a permanent vegetative state (PVS).[3] Are the patients in these conditions full persons with the rights to dignity and life? Or are they less than full persons, and thus killing them, or assisting in their suicides, is not morally problematic?

Even though the U.S. Supreme Court has not recognized a constitutional right to die, significant debate over PAS in the United States and Europe remains. The decision of the Supreme Court in *Washington v. Glucksburg* and *Vacco v. Quill* in 1997 did not end the debate in the United States. Rather the Court gave states the freedom to make their own laws in this area, insuring that the debate will continue.[4] With the growing notoriety of aggressive PAS advocates such as Dr. Jack Kevorkian and grassroots movements such as the Hemlock Society and Compassion in Dying, the issue is sure to remain in the news for the foreseeable future.[5] Though most of the arguments advanced by these PAS advocates involve considerations of mercy and autonomy, the notion of personhood lies beneath the surface of these arguments. PAS will likely be on the ballot in different states in future elections, leaving it up to voters to decide on the morality and legality of PAS in their state. With the right to refuse life-sustaining treatment now firmly (and, we think, rightly) established in the law and in bioethics,[6] advocates for the terminally ill can be expected to continue to move the discussion forward and to demand the terminally ill person's right to enlist a physician's assistance in ending his or her life. Though the issue of the end-stage terminally ill patient's personhood does not dominate the PAS discussion, some advocates such as philosopher James Rachels have suggested that such patients do not meet the criteria for personhood. Thus assisting in their suicides or administering active euthanasia cannot, in their view, violate moral norms that prohibit the killing of innocent people. We will address Rachels's view of the person, particularly his distinction between biological and biographical life, in this chapter.

Perhaps the more difficult area in the discussion of personhood at the end of life is the moral status of patients who are in an irreversible coma or a PVS. According to the best neurological evidence, PVS patients will never recover any higher-brain function and do not have any conscious awareness of their environment. Nor are they able to communicate, feel any sensations, such as pain, or experience life in any sense except to lie on their beds or be propped up in a chair. They cannot take nutrients or water by mouth and must be fed and hydrated through medically provided means, such as a gastrotomy tube surgically inserted into the lining of the stomach.

Many of these patients could remain in such a state for many years— that is, until their bodies age and they die of natural causes. The law currently protects the rights of these patients, or the rights of their surrogate decision makers, to refuse any medical treatment, including food and water.[7] It is widely held that the PVS patient does not meet the criteria for personhood, and proponents of this view commonly distinguish between a human being and a person: the PVS patient is regarded as being fully human but not fully a person. Though there are other arguments apart from those relating to the personhood of the PVS patient that are important for the moral issue of providing food and water for such patients, the notion of personhood is an important part of this debate, and it is often an unexpressed undercurrent.[8]

The continuing debate over the criteria for death reflects this notion and, in fact, was likely driven by the increase in the number of PVS patients. Those who propose a change in the criteria for death—from whole-brain death to higher-brain death—do so in part to deal with the PVS patient.[9] Should the criteria for death be changed from whole-brain to higher-brain death, physicians would be able to declare the PVS patient clinically and legally dead. At that point there would no longer be any debate concerning the necessity of sustaining these patients, including the provision of medically provided food and water. This same criteria would also apply to anencephalic newborns, which would allow for harvesting of their organs prior to whole-brain death.

The personhood of the PVS patient has been debated not only in the bioethics arena in general but also in Christian bioethics circles. We will interact with the work of two evangelicals who have done thoughtful work in this area: philosopher Robert N. Wennberg and theologian Robert V. Rakestraw, both of whom suggest the PVS patient is no longer a person and no longer bears the image of God. We will argue that their views imply a property-thing view of a human person because they use functional criteria for personhood, which conflicts with the substance-dualist view of a person developed here. Simply because one accepts an essentialist view of a person does not obligate one to ethical vitalism, the view that one must maintain a person's life at all costs and under any circumstances. A good argument can be made for the morality of removing medically provided nutrition and hydration from the PVS patient without denying the personhood of these patients.

Personhood and Physician-Assisted Suicide

To be sure, the denial of the personhood of the patient is not the only argument used to support PAS. For example, there is an argument from mercy, which says that assisting someone in suicide is sometimes the most merciful action physicians can perform for a dying person.[10] Advocates of PAS insist that given the options of either letting someone die a painful death or granting assistance in suicide, it is clear which is the most merciful.[11] Rachels even applies the golden rule in cases like these and suggests that the religious person (who presumably holds to something like the golden rule) who opposes PAS is inconsistent with this central teaching of Jesus.[12] Rachels suggests that if we were faced with the choice between dying in pain and dying by PAS, we would clearly prefer PAS; thus we should not deny such an option to other similarly situated dying persons. However, as the science of pain management is making clearer, there are very few instances in which a patient's pain cannot be adequately controlled. Even Rachels admits that "the moral issue is whether mercy-killing is permissible *if* it is the only alternative to this kind of torment. We may readily grant that in any particular case where suffering can be eliminated, the argument for euthanasia will be weaker."[13] We would argue that the number of cases in which pain management cannot be adequate are so small that the argument for euthanasia on that basis is very weak.[14] It is true that at times the regulatory environment has militated against physicians who desire to administer adequate amounts of opioids for long-term pain management. But in many states, the law is changing, and regulatory agencies are allowing physicians more latitude to manage pain using their best medical judgment and for the patient's best interests.[15]

A second argument commonly used in favor of PAS is the argument from utility.[16] That is, PAS allowed with patient consent promotes the best interests of all the parties in the patient's life, particularly the patient. The patient dies with dignity and comfort, avoiding a long, expensive and painful dying process; the family members can grieve appropriately and get on with their lives, avoiding a drawn-out, emotionally taxing and perhaps financially draining dying process for their loved one. It is clearly better for the caregivers, who do not have to witness the demise of such a deteriorating person. It is a better stewardship of scarce medical resources, since end-of-life care is often the most expensive kind of medical treatment and care. However, even on utilitarian grounds (which we reject as the sole basis for making moral choices), one must account for the long-term as well as the short-term consequences of allowing PAS. Further, one must account for a wider group of affected parties than simply the immediate patient, family and caregivers. A growing body of empirical evidence suggests an increase in the incidence of nonvoluntary euthanasia. This would indicate that opening the door to PAS and euthanasia in general has harmful consequences, particularly when the terminally ill or those in a PVS are administered euthanasia without their consent.[17]

A third argument used by advocates of PAS is an argument from autonomy: that is, the right to privacy protects individuals from state intervention into the most private and personal decisions about one's life. It is argued that the state should not be allowed to intrude on decisions relating to marriage, family, procreation, child rearing and a host of other private decisions. The argument suggests that decisions about the timing and manner of one's death surely count among the most personal decisions someone can make. Traditionally, however, autonomy has been limited when there is evidence of harm that results from the exercise of such autonomy. Given the empirical evidence from around the world on the incidence of nonvoluntary euthanasia and of the people who are harmed as a result of such a practice, this would seem to be more than adequate grounds for limiting someone's liberty in this area. The privacy of the decision is irrelevant to the morality of it, particularly if harm results from the exercise of liberty.[18]

One of the arguments made by proponents of PAS and euthanasia concerns the personhood of the terminally ill and imminently dying person. Irrespective of how it is used in the contemporary PAS debate, it is the central issue here. For if the terminally ill are not persons, society should have no reservations about the practice of PAS. Even nonvoluntary euthanasia would not violate widely held norms against killing innocent persons. Nor would consent for PAS be necessary, for the patient would not be a person with rights worthy of protection. PAS would not violate the commandment "Thou shalt not kill." The arguments from mercy, utility and autonomy all presuppose that the patient is a person with rights and interests to be protected. If the imminently dying are not persons—or, to put it another way, do not have a life (as opposed to simply being alive)— then arguments about their state of pain, best interests and liberty are at best supplementary and at worst irrelevant to the issue. If these patients are not full human persons, then they have the same rights as the unborn under the law as it stands, which are none. We propose a view of the dying patient that is consistent with a substance-dualist view of a human person and that gives the same rights to the imminently dying as to the unborn.

In the discussion of PAS there is perhaps no clearer statement of the distinction between being a human being and being a person than that of Rachels, one of the most influential advocates for legalizing PAS. He carefully distinguishes between being alive and having a life, between one's biological life and one's biographical life. Thus one can be alive physiologically but have no life in the morally relevant sense. A person can be functioning biologically but, either through illness or injury, have lost those aspects of life that make it meaningful to the person. For Rachels this is the morally relevant aspect of life. Therefore, when a person has lost biographical life, he or she has died in the morally significant sense, even though the body may continue to function for some time. He applies this concept of personhood to both the beginning and ending edges of life, and he attempts to be consistent in his application of personhood to the unborn, to defective newborns and to the terminally ill. He has gone a bit further than others in his attempt to apply his notion of personhood at the end of life, since many who advocate PAS do not accept his concept of the personhood of the terminally ill.[19]

Rachels is intent on challenging the traditional notion of the sanctity of life, in which all biological life is deemed worthy of protecting. He presents an alternative view, which suggests that

> there is a deep difference between *having a life* and *being alive*. Being alive,
> in the biological sense, is relatively unimportant. One's *life*, by contrast, is
> immensely important; it is the sum of one's aspirations, decisions, activities,

projects and human relationships. The point of the rule against killing is the protection of *lives* and the interests that some beings, including ourselves, have in virtue of the fact that we are subjects of lives. . . . In deciding questions of life and death, the crucial question is: Is a life, in the biographical sense, being destroyed or otherwise affected? If not the rule against killing offers no objection.[20] (emphasis original)

With this distinction, Rachels proposes a new concept of the sanctity of life in which lives, not mere functioning bodies, are protected with the right to life. He argues that "the sanctity of life ought to be interpreted as protecting lives in the biographical sense and not merely life in the biological sense." He goes on to say only biographical life is worth protecting, and one's biological life is inconsequential, except that it enables one to have a biographical life: Rachels insists that "there is nothing important about being alive except that it enables one to have a life."[21] He does acknowledge that being alive is important, but it is so only as a means to having a life and not as an end in itself.[22] Rachels has clearly distinguished between a human being and a person, concluding that only those with biographical lives are full persons with all the attendant rights of personhood. Of course, until the past few years in which medicine could keep people alive in increasingly poor quality-of-life circumstances, such a distinction between biological and biographical life could not be made. In the past, once someone lost what Rachels calls biographical life, they would likely have also died biologically.

What might a person with no biographical life look like? Perhaps the clearest and most well-known examples of people who have no biographical life are those who are not even conscious. People who are in a long-term coma, such as Karen Ann Quinlan, or in a PVS, such as Nancy Cruzan, would not have any prospect of biographical life, since they do not have any awareness of their environment or the ability to have any kind of human interaction. But someone like Matthew Donnelly is a good example of Rachels' distinction between biographical and biological life. He was in the end stages of terminal skin cancer, having spent his professional life as a physicist, working with the effects of x-rays. He had tumors throughout his body. He was deteriorating and had lost part of his jaw, upper lip, nose and left hand; tumors had also been removed from other parts of his upper body. He was blind and in constant pain, and his physicians could do nothing for him except continue to remove tumors and give him pain killers. His physician considered that he had roughly one year to live. Donnelly asked his brother to shoot him, which he did.[23] Rachels suggests that the only difference between Donnelly's life when his brother shot him and his life as it would have been a year later, when he would have died of natural causes, was minimal, except that he would have lived one year longer. Thus in Rachels' view, legalizing euthanasia in cases such as Donnelly's would not violate his conception of the sanctity of life, since killing Donnelly would not have ended his biographical life. That is, his life, in the morally relevant sense, had not been destroyed, even though he had been killed in the biological sense. Thus euthanasia in this case did not violate the prohibition against killing innocent persons, since Donnelly was no longer a person. The person had died prior to the end of his biological life.

Or consider the case of Dax Cowart, a case widely discussed in bioethics circles. Cowart was burned severely over the majority his body from an exploding gas line that killed his father, who was with him. He was left blind, deaf and crippled, without fingers or much use of his hands. He was kept alive in the burn unit of a hospital by a series of extraordinarily painful treatments, which he repeatedly demanded be stopped. He clearly wanted to die, and he expressed it numerous times throughout his hospitalizations. He wanted to be released from the hospital so that he could commit suicide. He was eventually released, and he attempted suicide but was unable to handle the gun with which he wanted to shoot himself. Rachels suggests that Cowart had lost his biographical life, and thus for him, administering euthanasia would not have been killing a person. Rachels puts it this way when he describes Cowart's case: "What his injury had done, from his point of view, was to destroy his ability to lead the kind of life that made him the distinctive individual he was. Donald's [Dax's] position was that if he could not lead that life, he didn't want to live."[24]

As the story unfolded, Cowart did take up a different kind of life. He married, went to law school and began a practice in which he devoted himself to protecting the rights of patients. He rebuilt his biographical life, but he insists that his physicians were still wrong not to assist him in his attempt to commit suicide. To be sure, one can argue that the physicians should not have forced painful burn treatment on him against his will, and today that would not likely have been done. But that is a different issue from the issue of whether euthanasia should be permitted, and it is a very different issue from whether Cowart was a person when he considered his biographical life lost.[25]

Or consider the case of L. C. Morris. He was shot in the head when police mistook him for a sniper. He suffered extensive brain damage, lived the rest of his life in a nursing home and had to be fed through a tube surgically inserted into his stomach. He had private nursing care around the clock, and even turning him regularly did not prevent extensive bedsores from developing. His wife's health deteriorated from the strain of coping with her husband. When told that he might live another few years, she responded that he had died at the time of the gunshot wound. She recognized that his biographical life was gone even though he kept on living biologically. According to Rachels, in the morally relevant sense Morris had no life and was not a person. Accordingly, administering euthanasia to him would not violate any moral standards prohibiting killing innocent persons.[26] According to Rachels, death is an evil precisely because it closes the door on the possibilities for having a biographical life, "because it frustrates desires, hopes and aspirations; and because it leaves parts of lives pointless and whole lives incomplete."[27]

Rachels' view of a human person is clearly at odds with the portrait of a person we have attempted to present here. His view presupposes a set of functions that are necessary in order for someone to have a biographical life. It is clear that someone must have consciousness and awareness of one's surroundings in order to have goals, aspirations and dreams about one's life. But in our view, consciousness and self-awareness are sufficient but not necessary for biographical life. Rachels thus takes his functional view of a person further than does someone like Bonnie Steinbock, who insisted that someone must have interests in order to have rights.[28] For her, possession of interests presupposed sentience. For Rachels it is similar, though consciousness and self-awareness are not adequate criteria by themselves to establish personhood.

Rachels's view of personhood thus suffers from the same flaws that other functional views of a human person suffer from. The capacity to have a biographical life—far from rendering biological life irrelevant—

actually presupposes it. That is, a person's biographical life is grounded in his or her biological life by virtue of being of a particular kind, a human being. What makes biographical life possible is a set of capacities grounded in one's essence. A human being has an essence that is capable of constructing those elements of biographical life. To put it in the terms we have attempted to use and defend in this work, a thing has first-order capacities (those necessary to develop biographical life) because of its higher-order capacities (being a human being, with a soul and created in God's image). Simply because the first-order capacities are not developed yet—or never develop or have been lost—is irrelevant to the possession of the higher-order capacities in which the first-order capacities are grounded. Simply because those capacities can no longer be expressed, it does not follow that the essence in which they are grounded has also been lost. Personhood is not lost when the ability to express the capacities is lost. Thus it does not follow that someone who has lost the capacities necessary to "have a life," as Rachels puts it, is no longer a person.

We can illustrate the flaw in a functional view of personhood as applied at the end of life by considering someone who is in a temporary and reversible coma.[29] At that point the person has lost all the necessary functions of personhood, and according to Rachels, has no biographical life. Thus an individual in such a condition would not meet the criteria for personhood and, by implication, would have no interests or rights worthy of protection. Thus for Rachels to be consistent, euthanasia would be acceptable for such a patient; it would not be killing a person and thus would not be a violation of the fifth commandment. But such a conclusion is absurd, and it would be resisted by insisting that the coma is only temporary. But such an objection is self-defeating for a functional view of personhood. To make such an objection the functionalist must appeal to some other criteria for personhood and protection of that patient besides the particular functions deemed necessary for personhood. But in doing so one must admit that the functions are not the *sina qua non* for personhood. One must appeal to some essential quality, which may or may not be expressed at any given time. In other words, functionalists are implicitly appealing to higher-order capacities, which they deny are critical for determining personhood.

A further criticism of the distinction between biographical and biologi-

cal life is our inability to live consistently with its implications. For example, if biographical life is that which gives life its value and if when it is
gone only a body can be said to exist, then what is to prevent us from
stripping that body (the biologically functioning corpse in such a view) of
all of its rights? If biographical life is lost, can we bury the "person" and
treat him like a corpse, assuming proper respect for the dead? Can we take
his organs with the consent of next of kin? Can we experiment on him,
again with appropriate proxy consent? If the essentials of one's life and
one's rights are tied up with biographical life and that life is lost, there
does not seem to be any consistent way of preventing these scenarios, as
long as they are done with the appropriate respect for the dead. One
could even argue that if one's personhood and rights have been lost with
biographical life, then consent would not be necessary for the administra-
tion of euthanasia. Yet virtually everyone who favors legalizing euthanasia
insists that it only be done with the consent of the patient. Surely such
insistence on consent suggests that the terminally ill patient, no matter
how incapacitated and no matter how much of her biographical life is lost,
is still a person with rights to be respected. In fact, the moral outrage at
the episodes of nonvoluntary euthanasia reinforces this notion. If biographical life is the determinant of personhood such that when it is lost,
we are not killing a person, then there is no reason to be outraged when
euthanasia is performed without someone's consent or even without their
knowledge.[30]

By extending the functional view of personhood to his concept of biographical life, Rachels has opened himself up to the criticism that his view
leads to subjectivity when it comes to valuing one's biographical life. In
his view, it seems biographical life is independent of any normative standards of validity. That is, there do not seem to be any parameters dictating
that some biographical lives are intrinsically more valuable than others. In
his view, one's biographical life is valuable simply because it is one's own.
It does not appear that one can make any normative judgment about the
validity of any person's biographical life. But surely some biographical
lives are dehumanizing and inconsistent with widely held norms of
decency. For example, consider the person whose goal in life is to be the
most effective administrator of torture in his country. Or take the prosti-
tute whose goal is to be the best provider of sadomasochistic sex for her

clients. We would certainly insist that the biographical lives constructed around such goals are inconsistent with membership in the human community, and these goals would actually devalue someone's life instead of giving it value. Yet Rachel's definition of biographical life as revolving around one's hopes, goals and aspirations has nothing in it to keep biographical life from demeaning life as well as enhancing it.

The subjectivity and fluidity of the notion of biographical life ironically make it possible for someone to regain her biographical life after it has been lost. Rachels's use of the example of Dax Cowart's case illustrates this precisely. Rachels acknowledges that Cowart regained a biographical life by rebuilding his life in a way that had some value for him. Rachels suggests that "we may applaud the courage he [Cowart] eventually showed in making a new life for himself, but we shouldn't miss noticing that his old life was gone."[31] In fact, the possibility of Cowart's rebuilding his life and regaining his biographical life motivated his physicians to continue to treat him against his will. In Cowart's view, the fact that he built a new life did not vindicate the physicians, who wronged him by treating him.

Though Cowart is likely correct that he should have been allowed to refuse treatment, that is not the same thing as insisting on a right to assistance in suicide. Though we do applaud Cowart for his courage in re-creating a new biographical life, the important point that should not be missed is that one can, curiously, "regain" biographical life after it has been lost. Whether Cowart agrees with his physicians on his ability to rebuild his life so as to have value for him, though not comparable to his life prior to his accident, is irrelevant. If biographical life is the critical element of personhood such that when it is lost there is no longer a person, it seems odd, to say the least, that biographical life can be recovered. Surely this suggests a notion such as biographical life is not an adequate determinant of personhood. Further it suggests that biographical life (or the first-order capacities) is grounded in something else, namely the ultimate capacities of being a human being created in God's image. The fact that biographical life can be lost and regained implies that personhood should be grounded in the stable notion of an essence, which remains despite the functional expression or lack thereof of one's lower-order capacities. We would argue that a Thomistic substance-dualist view of a human person provides such a notion.

Personhood and the Persistent Vegetative State

Perhaps the most complicated area in the discussion of end-of-life issues concerns the personhood of patients who are in a PVS, what neurologists call an "eyes-open unconsciousness."[32] The president's commission on bioethics defines the PVS as the state in which "all components of mental life are gone, including self-awareness, thought, emotion, feeling and sensation."[33] Such patients are technically awake, but they are not aware of their environment. They experience normal times of wakefulness and have cycles sleeping and waking. However, they cannot feel pain and indeed are not sentient at all. The reason they are in this state is that they have lost all function of the higher centers of the brain, the cerebral cortex. The brain stem is intact and still functioning, which explains why their involuntary functions such as breathing, heartbeat and digestion still are ongoing. Patients who are in a PVS have lost all higher-brain function due to a traumatic head injury such as one that would result from a serious automobile accident. The person who is in this state is not dead, however, and in general only needs artificial nutrition and hydration in order to remain alive. That is, they can generally breathe on their own without any assistance from medical technology.

Patients in a PVS are not in a coma either. Coma is a state of eyes-closed unconsciousness. A patient in a coma would also have suffered extensive damage to the brain stem, which makes involuntary functioning difficult and often requires ventilator support. Such problems resulting from damage to the brain stem usually result in medical complications that will lead to their death within a period of a few weeks or months. It is very unusual that these patients live more than a year or so. These patients are regarded as terminally ill, and it is generally considered ethically appropriate to withdraw life-sustaining treatment from them on the grounds that it is futile.[34]

The consensus in the neurological community is that patients in a PVS or in a permanent coma do not have the first-order capacity to experience any sensation, namely, pain and suffering.[35] Sentience requires consciousness, and the PVS patient has suffered total loss of all higher-brain function, thus making consciousness impossible (at least while the patient is embodied). Consciousness and the capacity to experience pain are clearly functionally related to the neocortical part of the brain. This is an established fact of neuroanatomy and neurophysiology. Thus PVS patients cannot by definition experience pain. However, it does not follow from this that they cannot be harmed. We would hold to a substantial difference between the experience of harm and its reality.

A further class of patients that fits in the general group of people suffering permanent loss of consciousness while embodied is the anencephalic infant.[36] This kind of child is born with only a brain stem, a severe congenital condition in which the cerebral cortex does not develop. They resemble the PVS patient since they have eyes-open unconsciousness, but they also have an abnormal brain stem and usually die from numerous complications within a few weeks, if not a few days. Like the patients in a permanent coma, those with brain-stem damage can be considered terminally ill, for death is imminent. There is no obligation to treat these patients, since any treatment would be futile. Providing palliative care, or relief of pain, is not an issue due to their inability to experience pain. However, dignity is owed to these patients. They cannot be abandoned, but as they die, they must be treated as the persons they are.

One well-publicized example of a person in a PVS was Nancy Cruzan, whose case came before the U.S. Supreme Court. Cruzan was rendered in a PVS as a result of a serious auto accident in 1983, when she was in her twenties. As a result, she had to be fed through a tube that was surgically inserted into the wall of her stomach, and her doctors estimated that she could live in a PVS for a long time, possibly thirty years or more. Her family and physician claimed that the continuation of artificial feeding was intrusive, futile and against her wishes, which she had communicated to her parents. The hospital refused to allow her feeding tubes to be removed, and her parents sued in order to have the state force the hospital to grant the parents' wishes. The case was finally decided by the Supreme Court in 1990, which ruled that medically provided nutrition and hydration could be discontinued from patients (not only those in a PVS) if there was clear and convincing evidence that this was the patients' wish. The Court ruled that no such evidence existed in this case, and thus they found in favor of the hospital. However, later that year the Cruzan's parents brought the case before the lower court with additional evidence of their daughter's wishes, and the court ruled in favor of the family, saying that they had met the Supreme Court's standard of clear and convincing evidence. This case opened the door to discontinuing the artificial feeding of those in a PVS and allowing them to die.[37] This decision potentially affected roughly ten thousand patients—the number of persons in a PVS in the United States today. Given the advances that can be expected in life-sustaining treatments, it is likely that this number will increase as time goes on.

In questions about treatment of PVS patients, the issue of personhood often arises: how can a patient who has lost all consciousness, sentience, self-awareness and the ability to relate at all to her surroundings be a person? This patient is different from the terminally ill person who is in the last stages of illness, can still relate to her world, is still conscious and is still very capable of experiencing pain and suffering. It is easier to envision this type of patient as merely a body kept alive physiologically by medical technology. It is harder to see how the PVS patient can actually be a person. It is argued that these types of patients are actually living corpses, or merely shells of a person. All the important aspects of someone's life are gone with neocortical destruction, even though her body continues to function.

In addition, these patients will never recover these functions. They are permanently lost through injury or illness. Thus these patients are not analogous to preconscious unborn children, who, given normal development in the womb, will certainly develop higher-brain function. In the unborn the functions associated with a life instead of a mere unconscious existence are only temporarily latent. In a PVS those aspects are permanently latent with no prospect of ever being actualized while the person is embodied. Is it accurate to insist that these patients are indeed persons? Does it make a moral difference that consciousness will never be recovered in the PVS patient, that it is permanently gone as opposed to only temporarily unexpressed in the preconscious fetus?

The view that consciousness is necessary for personhood is an extension of the interests view, in which consciousness was presupposed as a foundation for a person's having interests.[38] Just as it was argued on this view that the preconscious fetus does not have interests and thus is not a person, so it is suggested that the postconscious PVS patient cannot have—will never again have—interests and thus cannot be a person. It is further argued that the difference between the preconscious fetus and the

PVS is morally significant. Thus even if one grants personhood to the pre-conscious fetus on the grounds of potentiality, one cannot make a similar claim for the PVS patient. There is a distinction, then, made between a human being and a human person. A PVS patient, according to this argument, is a good example of a living human being who is not a human person.

This distinction between a living human being and a human person is described by neurologist and bioethicist Ronald E. Cranford and law professor David Randolph Smith; they argue that "consciousness is the most critical moral, legal and constitutional standard, *not for human life itself, but for human personhood.* Thus we believe that permanent loss of all consciousness is just as significant as the loss of all brain functions in determining the moral and legal status of a human being."[39] They suggest that the PVS patient is in a peculiar class of patients, having characteristics of both the living and the dead. But they resist calling the patients dead and suggest that changing the definition of death from a whole-brain view of death (the current standard in the law) to a higher-brain view (in which death is defined as the loss of all neocortical function) is problematic, since that involves a radical shift in the conception of death and encounters major problems in the certainty of the diagnosis of PVS. This is different from the traditional notions of death, such as cardiopulmonary notions and the accepted view of whole-brain death.[40]

Revealing their empiricist view of the world, Cranford and Smith suggest moral views of personhood can be understood based on medical reality and experience. They argue that "once society fully understands the medical reality of permanently unconscious patients, certain legal and moral positions will follow logically."[41] It is difficult to see how medical facts alone can resolve what is fundamentally a philosophical problem. In fact, those who advocate nonpersonhood for PVS patients are making a set of philosophical assumptions about personhood, which we have attempted to address in the first section of this book. These assumptions include a functional view of personhood, in which consciousness is a critical function, as opposed to an essentialist view, which would suggest personhood for all patients regardless of their medical condition, up until their death.

Cranford and Smith resist changing the conception of death and are opposed to taking organs from PVS patients prior to their death.[42] Rather, they suggest changing the notion of personhood and separating a human being from a human person. Thus in their view PVS patients are living human beings but not persons, and PVS patients have no rights since they are incapable of exercising or experiencing those rights.[43] Because the PVS patient is not conscious, he or she has no will. Thus legal rights for these patients, in their view, can have no reference because the PVS patient is not a person. Thus they are meaningless.

The criticism of this view of the PVS patient is similar to the critique of Steinbock's interests view, presented in chapter seven. It seems clear that those who advocate the view that consciousness is necessary for person-hood are taking a property-thing view of a person. Possession of certain properties—or in this case, one particular property of consciousness—is the determinant of personhood. Yet as we have argued consistently throughout this book, the property-thing view of a human person fails because it cannot account for the continuity of personal identity through change, does not leave room for libertarian free will and cannot give a coherent account of moral responsibility. Possession of any given function cannot determine personhood, particularly if it is based on medical grounds, since medical facts cannot determine metaphysical realities. Functional views of personhood fail because expression of lower-order capacities is grounded in the possession of higher-order capacities, namely being a human person made in God's image.

Lacking functional expression of any particular capacity does not sug-gest that the higher-order capacities are gone. Rather they are simply unexpressed at a particular time. It is irrelevant that the ability to express those functions is permanently lost due to the PVS, since func-tion does not determine personhood; personhood is determined by essence. The proper functions of a human person are grounded in the essence of human personhood, and they cannot stand alone apart from a human nature in which these critical functions are grounded. Losing the essence of personhood does not follow from having lost the functions one deems critical to being a person. A Thomistic substance-dualist view of a human person suggests that as long as the person is living, he or she is a person. Indeed, personhood continues to constitute the essence of an individual human even after death. That is why absolute personal identity is sustained in the afterlife.

It is somewhat odd that many medical observers such as Cranford are uncomfortable with taking organs from PVS patients (although perhaps not from anencephalics) or with treating them like physiologically functioning corpses. We can address the same questions here that we addressed earlier in the case of the terminally ill adult. If these PVS patients are not persons and have no rights, then why can't their organs be taken? Why cannot they be buried? Why cannot medical science experiment on them, with consent of next of kin? Why can't they be treated consistently with what it is argued that they are—nonpersons, whose status as living human beings is irrelevant? To be sure, some are willing to suggest that organ donation from PVS patients is appropriate, but few are willing to apply the denial of personhood consistently to these patients. Cranford and others are correct in their hesitation to change the legal definition of death, and there are those who do not want to change the notion of personhood but rather change the criteria for determining death, from whole-brain to higher-brain criteria.[44] Generally, those who suggest changing the definition of death want to say that the PVS patient is dead, not that he or she is still living and not a person.[45]

It is not only members of the medical community who suggest that the PVS patient is not a person. Some in the evangelical world also make this separation between a human being and a human person. In doing so, they seem to suggest a functional view of a human person, which seems to assume a property-thing instead of a substance view of a person. In our earlier discussion of the biblical teaching on theological anthropology, we made the case for the Bible's supporting a substance view of a person. In our view, an attempt to separate the notion of personhood from biological life is problematic both philosophically and biblically.

For example, consider the following view:

> Those operating within a Christian belief system may be attracted to the conclusion that death is the total and irreversible loss of the capacity to participate in God's creative and redemptive purposes for human life. For it is reasonable for Christians to believe that it is precisely this capacity which endows human life with its special significance. More specifically, it is the capacity to shape an eternal destiny by means of decision-making and soul-making, and not mere organic functioning. Indeed it is reasonable to

suppose that human organic life has no value in its own right but receives its significance from the fact that it can make possible and sustain personal consciousness, and thereby make possible the capacity to participate in God's creative and redemptive purposes. However, when the human biological organism can no longer fulfill that function, its significance has been lost. . . . When an individual becomes permanently unconscious, the *person* has passed out of existence, even if biological life continues. There cannot be a person where there is neither the capacity for having mental states nor even the potentiality for having that capacity (as with infants). For persons are beings who have the capacity (potentially or actually) to think, will, affirm moral and spiritual ideals, love and hate, desire, hope, plan and so forth. *Where no such capacities exist at all due to permanent loss of consciousness, there we no longer have an individual who commands the special respect due a person, because we no longer have a person.*[46]

Such a view is a theologically oriented example of the separation of a human being and a human person, which in our view is both philosophically and biblically inconsistent. One who holds to a view like this could hold, for example, that someone in a PVS (like Cruzan) actually died when she had her accident, even though she was still biologically alive and could remain so for some time.[47] This view reflects the property-thing view of a human person, in which specific functions, or lower-order capacities, are the primary criteria for personhood. But as we have argued in this section, loss of lower-order capacities does not involve loss of the higher-order ones, even if the loss of these first-order capacities is irreversible. This is because functional expression of capacities is related to the possession of higher-order capacities. It does not follow that when the functional expression of first-order capacities is no longer possible, the higher-order capacities are also lost.

The distinction between higher- and lower-order capacities is helpful when considering a person who has temporarily lost the function of lower-order capacities, as is the case when a person is in a deep sleep or under general anesthesia. In order to maintain the personhood of such a person, one must appeal to something else besides the possession of the first-order capacities deemed important to personhood (such as consciousness and awareness of one's environment) in order to maintain that the individual who has temporarily lost those functions is still a person. In other words, one must appeal to one's continued possession of ultimate capacities even when lower-order functional expression has been lost. The PVS patient is a full person because of her essence or inner nature as a human person. This is consistent with the substance view of a person for which we have been arguing throughout this book.

The substance view of a person, which we are defending, also fits well theologically with the notion of eternal life, in which God simply restores the lower-order capacities that were lost at one's death (or prior to it) rather than creating a new person. Theologically, it is clear that in eternity believers in Christ are given resurrected bodies in which functions lost due to aging, illness or injury are restored. Nowhere does Scripture indicate that God creates new persons ex nihilo in the eternal state. Rather, we are the same persons, but we have full functional expression of all our lower-order capacities, since the presence of sin in the world does not restrict the ability to actualize our capacities.

To be sure, it is not easy emotionally to insist that a person in a PVS is indeed a full person with all attendant rights. After all, the PVS patient is not conscious, cannot relate to anyone or anything and at best only makes reflex reactions, which can actually mislead family members into thinking that he is aware when that is not the case. For many people it is counterintuitive to think that a PVS patient who will never regain any voluntary function (at least prior to the eternal state) can be a person with rights worthy of protection. However, the fact that such a person cannot experience or exercise those rights is irrelevant to the fact that he possesses them. If one accepts that a person has an essential nature, then the functions lost through the injury that caused the PVS are not ultimate functions but lower-order capacities. These capacities are grounded in the possession of ultimate ones, and the failure to actualize such lower-order capacities does not signal loss of one's essential human nature.

In addition, if personhood is dependent on the actualization of a specific lower-order capacity, then it follows that personhood is a degreed property. Since in the property-thing view the essential capacities for personhood can be expressed in varying degrees, it would appear that personhood and its attendant rights could also be similarly possessed. Those who advocate such a view admit there is some threshold of function, however imprecisely one can pinpoint it, that is decisive for personhood.

However, it is clear that persons continue to develop long after that threshold is reached. This raises the question of what precisely is developing as the person grows and matures. If one answers that what is developing are the properties that constitute personhood, this answer is problematic and self-defeating, since on what basis can one say personhood is achieved if one continues to grow in the expression of those capacities? According to a substance view, one does not become something else as one develops; one matures according to one's kind.

This is why in the view expressed above there is a distinction between fetuses and infants who lack sufficient expression of capacities to be considered a person but who have the potential for such expression, and the PVS patient who has no such potential. This is actually a truncated view of degreed personhood, in which only the permanent loss of the key aspects of personhood signals the end of personhood. Interestingly, this distinction, which is based on potential, actually reflects a substance view of a person; for one's temporarily latent capacities, which will be expressed at some point given normal development, are important for personhood. This suggests that something besides those functions are critical for personhood, pointing one toward an underlying essence that governs the expression of those capacities.

This view has implications for the end of life as well. If personhood is a degreed property, then it is lost in one's declining years commensurate with one's loss of functions. The PVS would actually be the culmination of loss of those functions. This is why some have argued for changing the basis of the definition of death to higher-brain function as opposed to whole-brain function. It is not difficult to see why advocates of a property-thing view would be inclined to support such a definition of death. The property-thing view separates the human being from the human person until the threshold of function is either reached or lost. On this view, mental, not biological, functioning is critical. Thus, when neocortical function is lost, the PVS patients can no longer exercise any of the key functions deemed nonnegotiable for a person. A substance view, on the other hand, takes more into account than mental function for a view of a human person. Biological functioning is important to a substance view since it holds that the human person is an organic unity grounded in an individuated essence. This is why a substance view cannot be consistent with any separation of a human being and a human person.

This is not to say that those who hold a substance view must define death as the irreversible loss of all functions, including cardiopulmonary ones. The whole-brain definition of death is consistent with a substance view of a person since once the entire brain ceases to function, heartbeat and respiration will cease as well. It is true that medical technology can keep a person's heart beating and lungs moving after a declaration of brain death. In fact, this is often done when the family members designate organ donation. But once that technology is removed, cardiopulmonary function will stop, since nothing is functioning in the brain to give direction to the heart and lungs. Whole-brain definitions of death are most consistent with a substance view of a person, in which the person is a unity of biological, mental and spiritual components, grounded in an individuated essence—one's human nature.

Recognizing the personhood of the PVS patient does not obligate one to offer all necessary treatments to keep such a patient alive. To be sure, what is driving both the movement to change the definition of death and the separation of a human being and a person in the case of PVS patients is the desire to be free of the obligation to administer futile treatment to these patients. Take the case of anencephalic infants, who are born without a cerebral cortex, which is analogous to the case of the adult PVS patient. With the anencephalic there is the added motivation to use these children as organ donors, since vital organs for newborns and small children are in very short supply. This has created pressure for a higher-brain definition of death so that these children could be regarded as nonpersons. In our view, such a radical philosophical shift is not necessary for relieving one of the obligation to offer futile treatment to these patients.

The reason that there is no obligation to offer all treatments necessary to keep a person alive is because clearly some of them are futile, and even if not, they still may be refused. One example of a treatment that can be refused is nutrition and hydration for a PVS patient. In our view, medically provided nutrition and hydration are treatments that a competent patient or proxy decision-maker may refuse. In many cases physicians must surgically insert a feeding tube into the wall of the patient's stomach. This procedure must be performed by licensed physicians in properly

338 ───────────────────────────────── B O D Y & S O U L

licensed medical facilities. Health insurance carriers and Medicare regard it as a type of treatment, for which they reimburse hospitals and physicians. "Medically provided nutrition and hydration" is the correct term for what takes place when a PVS patient is fed by medical means. This procedure has all the indications of a type of medical treatment, and it does not resemble the "cup of water" compassionately administered by a loved one to a dying person. Though less invasive than a ventilator, medically provided nutrition and hydration in principle function the same way. Through mechanical and medical means, the technology performs a basic human function that the body can no longer do for itself as a result of injury or illness.

Very few people question the morality of removing ventilator support from patients who request it or for whom it is futile. Yet surely getting air to breathe is as basic to human functioning as is getting nutrition and hydration. In cases in which it is morally appropriate to remove a ventilator, it is similarly appropriate to withdraw medically provided nutrition and hydration, for withdrawing medically provided nutrition and hydration is not starving someone to death any more than removing a ventilator is suffocating someone. In both cases the underlying disease or injury, not the removal of the treatment, is the cause of death. Removing treatment allows the disease or condition to take its course, and in many cases death does not occur immediately. Medically provided nutrition and hydration are forms of treatment that may be refused and need not be provided if they are futile, if they bring on a greater burden than benefit to the patient or if refused. In the absence of clear evidence that the patient does not desire medically provided nutrition and hydration, then as is true with other types of treatments, there is a presumption to provide it.[48] Thus one does not need to deny that PVS patients are persons in order to justify their liberty to refuse such treatment. It does not follow from their moral status as persons that one is necessarily obligated to provide them with treatment that is widely considered futile.

Caring for Human Persons at the End of Life

If it is true that personhood is not a degreed property, that human persons are full persons throughout their lives regardless of their medical condition and that human persons have value and dignity by virtue of being made in God's image, then it follows that at a person's most vulnerable point in life—the approach of death—he or she is owed compassionate and dignified care to enable her to face death with the self-respect that her status as human person suggests she deserves. This is even more the case for the caregiver who is giving care out of a Christian view of the world, since the Bible places special emphasis on the vulnerable among us and thus reveals that those who care for them have a higher responsibility to protect their interests.

In the late 1980s and early 1990s, a landmark study on care of the dying was conducted. The SUPPORT study, when published in 1995, brought care of the dying to the forefront of bioethical discussion.[49] This study measured critical aspects of the experience of dying in the hospital such as the frequency and severity of pain experienced by the patient; communicating with the physician about the patient's preferences on CPR, if and when DNR (do not resuscitate) orders were written; and days spent in the ICU or on mechanical ventilation. The principal investigators of the study concluded that "we are left with a troubling situation. The picture we describe of the care of seriously ill or dying persons is not attractive."[50] The findings of the study suggest that care of the dying was far from optimal, prompting one prominent bioethicist to conclude that "if dying patients want to retain some control over their dying process, they must get out of the hospital they are in, and stay out of the hospital if they are out."[51] Since the vast majority of people still die in a hospital setting, the data gleaned from the SUPPORT study suggests that the general experience of dying in the hospital has numerous shortcomings, some of which are the result of that hospital's having inadequate resources to provide optimal care for all terminally ill patients.

What then does compassionate care for dying persons involve? First, it involves respecting their wishes, which are expressed either verbally or more formally in some sort of advance directive. Since the Patient Self-Determination Act of 1991, advance directives have become more common, though a relatively small percentage of people have completed them. Frequently, patients at the end of life desire only comfort care—or what is known as palliative care—and choose to forego aggressive therapies and life-sustaining interventions such as CPR and ventilator support. Even though there is a strong legacy of patient autonomy and support for this notion in the law, it is not uncommon for a patient's advance directive to be ignored either by physicians or more commonly by family members who represent the patient, who do not want to "let go" of their loved one. Physicians at times accede to these requests for futile interventions for fear of litigation and out of a desire not to give up. When a person's wishes concerning care at the end of life are ignored, their dignity is violated, and they are often subjected to treatment that can be more burdensome than beneficial. This is not to say that a particular intervention should be provided simply because a dying person desires it: for example, some patients at the end of life do desire assistance in suicide, though as we have argued, it is unethical to provide it. However, terminally ill patients at times do not receive the best care that medicine can provide. Society is increasingly recognizing that hospices are the best places for terminally ill persons to receive care that is consistent with their dignity and their wishes for how they want to live out their remaining days. It may be that a dying person's wishes can best be respected by a hospice or by home hospice care. These are not places where "people go to die" but rather places where the terminally ill can maximize their remaining time prior to their death.

A second critical element in compassionate care for the dying is adequate pain management. One of the most glaring revelations of the SUPPORT study was that roughly half the patients in the study experienced moderate to severe pain in the last few weeks prior to their death. Among the reasons for inadequate pain relief is physician's fear of regulatory scrutiny should he or she prescribe adequate amounts of opiods (the most potent form of pain medication) such as morphine. Public health authorities are justifiably concerned about the abuse of such powerful drugs, but in many states the law is changing to give physicians more latitude to administer sufficient doses of these very effective pain medications.

One of the most emotionally compelling arguments in favor of PAS is the argument from mercy. This argument suggests that assisting someone in easing into a death with dignity is the most merciful and compassionate thing that medicine can do for a suffering patient. The reality that people are dying in pain is one of the principal forces behind the drive to legalize PAS. However, those times in which medicine cannot effectively control pain are rare. Thus the answer to a very real problem of people's dying in pain is not to legalize PAS but to empower physicians to more effectively manage the pain of their patients. There may be situations in which the dosage of medication necessary to control a person's pain may slow their heartbeat and respiration and thus hasten their death, but that is far different from the intentional overdoses that characterize PAS.

Physicians are morally obligated to manage their patient's pain adequately, and if such pain management hastens death, then that is justifiable based on the principle of double effect. This principle suggests that the anticipated but unintended side effects of otherwise morally justifiable actions do not undermine the action itself. So if physicians intend simply to relieve pain and not to cause death, they may prescribe a sufficient dosage of pain medication to do precisely what they intend. If that hastens the patient's death, then that anticipated but unintended (a key concept) effect does not render the action of relieving pain unethical. Intending to relieve pain and intending to cause death are two very different things. Effective pain management is a moral imperative, but intentionally causing death is unethical.

For PVS patients, for whom pain does not appear to be an issue, offering comfort care would be unnecessary. But that does not mean these patients can be abandoned. One writer has compared PVS to a form of exile, one in which the patient exists but is totally separate from the rest of the human community.[52] Though physicians are not obligated to provide the PVS patient with medically provided nutrition and hydration, they are obligated to provide dignity care. This would include measures such as keeping the patient groomed and bathed or providing ice chips for the patient's face and lips to alleviate the effects of dehydration.

A third element in compassionate care for the dying is effective and timely communication with patients and their families. Patients generally want to know the true diagnosis and prognosis, though this does vary according to some cultures.[53] Patients and their families generally take communication as a sign of caring. Patients often have relational "unfinished business," and it is critical that they know they are approaching their death so that they can take care of such business with loved ones. Patients also want to be sure that their wishes are known and understood, which can only happen with clear and timely communication. This type of communication is often difficult to maintain since it forces everyone involved to face their own mortality. But a significant part of respecting the dignity of dying patients is to be forthright and consistent in one's communication with them.

Conclusion

Medical technology makes it increasingly possible for people to prolong their lives or their dying process by the use of life-sustaining treatments and technologies. Tragically, the result is often that people's lives are prolonged in an undesirable quality of life. Medical ethics and the law have made important advances to empower patients to refuse any type of life-sustaining treatment they so desire. They may speak directly or, when they become incompetent, their proxy decision-maker can speak on their behalf, reflecting their wishes. Medicine is under no obligation to provide futile treatment or treatment in which the burden to the patient outweighs the benefits.[54]

However, none of these protections would have been possible without the undergirding principle that these patients are full persons, with all the rights of conscious patients and physically well persons. The medical community has rightly sought to protect the rights of the elderly, arguably some of the most vulnerable persons in the population today. The reason those rights are important is precisely because these patients *are* persons, regarded as having a continuity of personal identity throughout their lives and particularly during their dying days. They are entitled to dignity because of their personhood. Denying the personhood of these patients is not only unnecessary but sets a dangerous precedent of separating a human being from a human person.

CONCLUSION

*I*N THIS WORK WE HAVE ATTEMPTED TO MAKE A CASE FOR A VIEW
of a human person that is both consistent with biblical teaching
and that makes philosophical sense. Our perspective, that of Thomistic substance dualism, suggests that a human person should be viewed
as a substance and not as a property-thing. That is, the person is more
than the material components that constitute the body. The essence of a
person is more than one's genetic makeup, but it is identified with the
immaterial soul. The existence of the soul, in our view, is clearly taught by
Scripture. It is the soul that governs the lawlike development of the body
and enables the substantial person to maintain absolute personal identity
through change and developmental stages.

We have further argued for a libertarian view of free will and moral
responsibility. Moral responsibility is not a utilitarian fiction that is required to maintain social and moral order. Rather it is rooted in a view of
a person in which libertarian freedom, not compatibilism, makes the most
sense. Many physicalists will admit that this notion of moral responsibility
is somewhat problematic for them, since their physicalism implies a form
of event-causation that rules out a moral agent's having active power,

which appears necessary for genuine moral responsibility. In our view, the notions of both moral responsibility and criminal justice presuppose a libertarian view of freedom that, in turn, has a substance view of a human person as the best model of the agent.

We have attempted to avoid having this work be solely an abstract metaphysical treatise, divorced from the real-life issues that individuals and public policy makers face. One need only look periodically at the newspaper to see the kinds of issues at the forefront of public debate, issues in which the view of a human person makes a difference. In many of these issues the view of a human person is tantamount to the trump card that effectively ends the debate. Some issues in bioethics—such as abortion, fetal-tissue research and embryo research—have the notion of personhood at the center. In fact, in several of these debates, some will rightly admit that the notion of personhood is philosophically or theologically rooted, but they will also suggest that because personhood is not scientifically verifiable, it cannot have a role in the debate. All the while, such a view is itself a physicalist perspective on human personhood, rooted in scientism and a naturalistic view of the world. Our substance view of a person is consistent with the notion of continuity of personal identity taught in Scripture, and this view suggests that there is no morally or ontologically significant break in the process of development from conception onward. Thus, in our view, abortion is the killing of an innocent person, and both fetuses and embryos (the latter whether extracorporeal or not) are deserving of full moral status as persons with all the protections therein.

Other issues where personhood is important include genetic technologies and human cloning. We have argued that the identity and essence of a human person are the soul and its nature, not the genes, and that human personhood cannot be reducible to or taken as supervenient upon one's genetic makeup. It is indicative of the physicalism that dominates the academy, particularly the sciences, when one's genetic components can be said to be the Holy Grail of human identity and the answer to the commandment "Know thyself." We think there is evidence that the genetic makeup is, by itself, inert and that it needs the activity of the soul to give it direction and organization.

Human cloning—perhaps the most controversial of all the genetic technologies—has raised unique challenges to the notion of personhood. We hold that a substance view can adequately account for the phenomena of cloning. Human cloning does not result in the creation of soulless persons, a concept that we consider an oxymoron. Some argue that euthanasia and physician-assisted suicide at the end of life do not violate the sanctity of life because those at the end of life, particularly those in a persistent vegetative state, are no longer persons. In such a view these patients may be biologically alive, but the person has passed away. We reject such a dichotomy between a human being and a human person and hold that a substance view requires that a patient is a person until he or she has died; at that point, the soul goes to be with God (or to be separated from him), and the body awaits future resurrection. Patients at the end of life, because they are persons, are deserving of the best care medicine has to offer, which may or may not include aggressive treatment depending on the patients' prognosis.

We are aware that our view of a human person is not popular in much of the academy today and that it is being challenged increasingly by Christian philosophers and theologians. Yet we hold that a Thomistic substance-dualist view of a human person is both theologically consistent and philosophically defensible. Our goal has been to make our contribution to restoring a fully biblical view of the world and to resist the prevailing winds of secularity, scientism and physicalism.

Notes

Introduction
[1]Compare Edmund Husserl, *The Crisis of European Sciences* (Evanston, Ill.: Northwestern University Press, 1970), pp. 3-65, appendix 3.
[2]Dallas Willard, *The Divine Conspiracy* (San Francisco: Harper, 1998), p. 82.
[3]Ibid., p. 92; cf. pp. 75, 79, 134, 184-85.
[4]Allen C. Guelzo, "Soulless," *Books & Culture,* January-February 1998, p. 23.
[5]Ibid.
[6]Edward O. Wilson, "The Biological Basis for Morality," *Atlantic Monthly,* April 1998, pp. 53-70.

Chapter 1: Establishing a Framework for Approaching Human Personhood
[1]H. D. Lewis, *Christian Theism* (Edinburgh: T & T Clark, 1984), p. 125.
[2]J. K. Howard, "The Concept of Soul in Psychology and Religion," *Faith and Thought* 98 (1970): 74; cf. pp. 75-76.
[3]Alvin Plantinga, "Advice to Christian Philosophers," *Faith and Philosophy* 1 (July 1984): 264-65.
[4]Augustine *On the Immortality of the Soul* 16.25.
[5]Thomas Aquinas *Summa Theologica* 1.Q75.
[6]Blaise Pascal, *Pensées,* Lafuma edition (1951), p. 427.
[7]Another position on the mind-body problem is called *personalism:* the person is a distinct, irreducible metaphysical category all its own, and mind and body are two irreducible "aspects" of persons. We will not consider personalism in this book because (1) it is very close to substance dualism in spirit if not letter and (2) the notion of an "aspect" is too metaphysically vague to be satisfactory compared with the metaphysical categories of substance, property, relation and event.
[8]Even Christians like Aquinas, who argued that the soul is "simple" and thus not capable of ceasing-to-be by dissolution, held that the soul depends on God to sustain it in being.
[9]Wolfhart Pannenberg, *What Is Man?* (Philadelphia: Fortress, 1970), pp. 47-48.
[10]John W. Cooper, *Body, Soul and Life Everlasting* (Grand Rapids, Mich.: Eerdmans, 1989).
[11]John Calvin *Institutes of the Christian Religion* 1.1.1.
[12]Franz Delitzsch, *A System of Biblical Psychology* (1899; reprint, Grand Rapids, Mich.: Baker, 1977), p. 55.
[13]Plantinga, "Advice to Christian Philosophers," pp. 264-65.
[14]Boethius *Against Eutyches and Nestorius* 3.
[15]We are assuming here that God-talk (and angel-talk) is either univocal or analogical (with a univocal element) and not equivocal.
[16]Warren S. Brown, Nancey Murphy and H. Newton Malony, preface to *Whatever Happened to the Soul?* (Minneapolis: Fortress, 1998), p. xiii.
[17]Bruce Reichenbach, *Is Man the Phoenix?* (Grand Rapids, Mich.: Eerdmans, 1978).
[18]Murray Harris, *Raised Immortal* (Grand Rapids, Mich.: Eerdmans, 1983).
[19]Ibid., p. 126.
[20]Joel B. Green argues against a certain employment of a word-study approach to understanding biblical anthropology. See Joel B. Green, "'Bodies—That Is, Human Lives': A Re-Examination of Human Nature in the Bible," in *Whatever Happened to the Soul?* ed. Warren S. Brown, Nancey Murphy and H. Newton Malony (Minneapolis: Fortress, 1998), pp. 152-53. Roughly, Green claims that such an approach fails because (1) lexical

meaning derived from one text can become a distorting presupposition for determining usage in another text and (2) this distorting tendency is exaggerated by the fact that biblical conceptions of human nature are not tied to a specific vocabulary, that biblical anthropological terms are not highly specialized and that word study fails to focus adequately on the appropriate context in which a specific word is being used. Our use of word studies here is not guilty of any of these charges. We take it that word studies themselves should be derived from holistic context sensitivity, that word studies create a field of meaning for a term that can be helpful but not determinative of usage in a specific passage and that biblical anthropological terms, though plastic, are not so fuzzy that one cannot get a fairly clear idea as to what they mean in a given text. Moreover, we agree that biblical anthropology is not tied to a specific vocabulary, and we will take into account below other factors relevant to its formulation.

[21]See Robert A. Morey, *Death and the Afterlife* (Minneapolis: Bethany, 1984), pp. 45-51.

[22]Francis Brown, S. R. Driver and C. A. Briggs, *A Hebrew and English Lexicon of the Old Testament* (reprint edition, Oxford: Clarendon, 1972), p. 220.

[23]Hans Walter Wolff, *Anthropology of the Old Testament* (Philadelphia: Fortress, 1974), p. 20.

[24]See Morey, *Death and the Afterlife,* pp. 51-53; Wolff, *Anthropology of the Old Testament,* pp. 32-39.

[25]John Hick, *Death and Eternal Life* (San Francisco: Harper & Row, 1976), pp. 55-60.

[26]Cooper, *Body, Soul,* pp. 75-76, 81-103.

[27]Compare ibid., pp. 81-103.

[28]The structure of our argument from New Testament teaching is heavily indebted to Cooper, *Body, Soul,* pp. 104-95.

[29]For an alternative interpretation favoring the immediate-resurrection view, see Harris, *Raised Immortal,* pp. 219-26. For a response, see Cooper, *Body, Soul,* pp. 155-63.

[30]Compare George Eldon Ladd, *A Theology of the New Testament* (Grand Rapids, Mich.: Eerdmans, 1974), p. 457.

[31]Howard, "The Concept of Soul," p. 74; cf. pp. 75-76.

[32]Arthur R. Peacocke, *Theology for a Scientific Age* (Minneapolis: Fortress, 1993), p. 3.

[33]Ibid., pp. 6-7.

[34]Ibid., pp. 60-61, 72-80, 140, 144-45. Compare Arthur R. Peacocke, *God and the New Biology* (San Francisco: Harper & Row, 1986), pp. 88-93.

[35]Karl Giberson, "Intelligent Design on Trial: A Review Essay," *Christian Scholar's Review* 24 (May 1995): 469; cf. *Worlds Apart* (Kansas City: Beacon Hill Press, 1993); J. P. Moreland, "Theistic Science and the Christian Scholar: A Response to Giberson," *Christian Scholar's Review* 24 (May 1995): 472-78.

[36]John Searle, *The Rediscovery of the Mind* (Cambridge: MIT Press, 1992), pp. 3-4.

[37]If someone is tempted to claim that an issue that cannot be settled by scientific investigation amounts to excess metaphysical baggage fit only for idle speculation, then he or she should be aware that this epistemic posture plays directly into the hands of antirealist understandings of science like the one offered by Bas C. van Fraasen. See Bas C. van Fraasen, *The Scientific Image* (Oxford: Oxford University Press, 1980). Van Fraasen argues that those aspects of scientific theories that go beyond the proper goal of science (i.e., "saving the phenomena") involve one in irrelevant metaphysical speculation. For those complementarians like Peacocke who adopt some form of scientific realism, consistency would seem to require that they cannot dismiss metaphysical argumentation *tout court.*

[38]Instructive in this regard is a careful study of debates about the nature of human persons during the rise of contemporary scientific study of matter in general and the brain and human body in particular. It becomes clear from such a study that the central issues and

348 —————————————————————————— BODY & SOUL

their resolution were largely philosophical and theological and only secondarily scientific. See John W. Yolton, *Thinking Matter: Materialism in Eighteenth-Century Britain* (Minneapolis: University of Minnesota Press, 1983).

[39]Alvin Plantinga, "When Faith and Reason Clash: Evolution and the Bible," *Christian Scholar's Review* 21 (September 1991): 29-31.

[40]Stephen T. Davis, "The Resurrection of the Dead," in *Death and Afterlife,* ed. Stephen T. Davis (New York: St. Martin's Press, 1989), p. 141.

[41]See George Bealer, "The Philosophical Limits to Scientific Essentialism," in *Metaphysics,* vol. 1 of *Philosophical Perspectives,* ed. James E. Tomberlin (Atascadero, Calif.: Ridgeview, 1987), pp. 289-365; and "On the Possibility of Philosophical Knowledge," in *Metaphysics,* vol. 10 of *Philosophical Perspectives,* ed. James E. Tomberlin (Cambridge, Mass.: Blackwell, 1996), pp. 1-34.

[42]Joshua Hoffman and Gary S. Rosenkrantz, *Substance: Its Nature and Existence* (London: Routledge, 1997), p. 7; cf. pp. 77-79. Unfortunately, Hoffman and Rosenkrantz fail to follow their own advice, or so it seems to us. For they claim that although souls are intelligible and, thus, possibly exist, there is no sufficient reason to postulate their existence, given the natural scientific view of living organisms and their place in the natural world (cf. pp. 6-7). But this judgment reverses the epistemic order between science and "folk" ontology, and it removes the burden of proof about the soul that science has not met, and perhaps cannot meet, given the nature of the issue. For at least three reasons, a substantial soul is every bit as much a part of folk ontology as substances in general: (1) the substantial soul is something we know immediately and, therefore, substance dualism is not first and foremost a postulate but a descriptive report that finds a place in folk ontology; (2) the issues for which substance dualism is, in fact, a postulate largely turn on considerations that may count against scientism but for which science is largely silent; (3) the emergence and existence of mental states and their connection with physical entities is inexplicable on a scientific naturalist picture of the world (as Hoffman and Rosenkrantz admit) but intelligible in a theistic substance dualist world-view. For more on this last point, see J. P. Moreland, "Searle's Biological Naturalism and the Argument from Consciousness," *Faith and Philosophy* 15 (January 1998): 68-91.

[43]Roderick Chisholm, "Coming into Being and Passing Away: Can the Metaphysical Help?" in *On Metaphysics* (Minneapolis: University of Minnesota Press, 1989), p. 49.

[44]Bealer, "On the Possibility of Philosophical Knowledge," p. 1.

[45]Alvin Goldman, "The Psychology of Folk Psychology," *Behavioral and Brain Sciences* 16 (1993): 15-28.

[46]Thomas V. Morris, introduction to *Divine and Human Action* (Ithaca, N.Y.: Cornell University Press, 1988), p. 3.

Chapter 2: Human Persons as Substances or Property-Things

[1]W. Norris Clarke, *Explorations in Metaphysics* (Notre Dame, Ind.: University of Notre Dame Press, 1994), p. 105.

[2]Richard J. Connell, *Substance and Modern Science* (Notre Dame, Ind.: University of Notre Dame Press, 1988), p. 69.

[3]Richard H. Bube, *Putting It All Together* (Lanham, Md.: University Press of America, 1995), pp. 124-25.

[4]Tibor Machan, "Abortion: Does the Pro-Life Argument Emerge from the Nation's Documents?" *Orange County Register,* May 14, 1995.

[5]Robert N. Wennberg, *Life in the Balance* (Grand Rapids, Mich.: Eerdmans, 1985), p. 29.

[6]For more on properties, see J. P. Moreland, "Issues and Options in Exemplification," *American Philosophical Quarterly* 33 (April 1996): 133-47; "How to Be a Nominalist in

Realist Clothing," *Grazer Philosophische Studien* 39 (summer 1991): 75-101; "Keith Campbell and the Trope View of Predication," *Australasian Journal of Philosophy* 67 (December 1989): 379-93; and "A Critique of Campbell's Refurbished Nominalism," *Southern Journal of Philosophy* 35 (summer 1997): 225-46.

[7]For more on this, see Alvin Plantinga, *The Nature of Necessity* (Oxford: Clarendon, 1974), pp. 44-69; Michael J. Loux, ed., *The Possible and the Actual* (Ithaca, N.Y.: Cornell University Press, 1979), pp. 15-64; Kenneth Konyndyk, *Introductory Modal Logic* (Notre Dame, Ind.: University of Notre Dame Press, 1986).

[8]For a defense of the existence of relations, see Reinhardt Grossmann, *The Existence of the World* (London: Routledge, 1992), pp. 51-57.

[9]Gustav Bergmann, *Realism* (Madison: University of Wisconsin Press, 1967), p. 54.

[10]D. M. Armstrong, *A Theory of Universals*, vol. 2 of *Universals and Scientific Realism* (Cambridge: Cambridge University Press, 1978), p. 172.

[11]D. M. Armstrong, *Universals: An Opinionated Introductión* (Boulder, Colo.: Westview, 1989), pp. 43-44, 55, 100.

[12]Compare Lawrence Brian Lombard, "Event Theory," in *A Companion to Event Theory*, ed. Jaegwon Kim and Ernest Sosa (Oxford: Blackwell, 1995), pp. 140-44; Jaegwon Kim, "Events as Property Exemplifications," in *Action Theory*, ed. M. Brand and D. Walton (Dordrecht: D. Reidel, 1976), pp. 159-77; Jonathan Bennett, *Events and Their Names* (Indianapolis: Hackett, 1988).

[13]See Saul Kripke, *Naming and Necessity* (Cambridge: Harvard University Press, 1972); Thomas V. Morris, *Understanding Identity Statements* (Aberdeen, U.K.: Aberdeen University Press, 1984).

[14]See John Searle, *The Rediscovery of the Mind* (Cambridge: MIT Press, 1992), pp. 111-26; Jaegwon Kim, *Philosophy of Mind* (Boulder, Colo.: Westview, 1996), pp. 211-40; Paul Teller, "Reduction," in *The Cambridge Dictionary of Philosophy*, ed. Robert Audi (Cambridge: Cambridge University Press, 1995), pp. 679-80; Ernest Nagel, *The Structure of Science* (New York.: Harcourt, Brace & World, 1961), pp. 336-97; Sahotra Sarkar, "Models of Reduction and Categories of Reductionism," *Synthese* 91 (1992): 167-94. Compare J. P. Moreland, "Should a Naturalist Be a Supervenient Physicalist?" *Metaphilosophy* 29 (January-April 1998): 35-57.

[15]Still useful in this regard is Walter T. Marvin, *An Introduction to Systematic Philosophy* (New York: Columbia University Press, 1909), pp. 38-56.

[16]Nagel, *Structure of Science*, pp. 336-97.

[17]For a helpful treatment of issues in mereology and physical constitution, see Michael Rea, ed., *Material Constitution: A Reader* (Lanham, Md.: Rowman & Littlefield, 1997).

[18]For excellent treatments of the notion of substance in the Aristotelian/Thomist tradition, see David Wiggins, *Sameness and Substance* (Cambridge: Harvard University Press, 1980); Etienne Gilson, *From Aristotle to Darwin and Back Again* (Notre Dame, Ind.: University of Notre Dame Press, 1984); Joshua Hoffman and Gary S. Rosenkrantz, *Substance: Its Nature and Existence* (London: Routledge, 1997); Michael J. Loux, *Substance and Attribute* (Dordrecht: D. Reidel, 1978); C. J. Ducasse, *Nature, Mind and Death* (La Salle, Ill.: Open Court, 1951), pp. 161-73; W. E. Johnson, *Logic Part III* (New York: Dover, 1924), pp. 78-101; C. D. Broad, "The 'Nature' of a Continuant," in *Examination of McTaggart's Philosophy* (Cambridge: Cambridge University Press, 1933), 1:264-78; Connell, *Substance and Modern Science*. We advocate a full-blown theory of substance, and some contemporary advocates of substance would not accept all of the things we claim characterize a substance (e.g., irreducible teleology). However, we think that our view is defensible and that it is an accurate representation of the traditional position.

[19]There are certain differences between them in this area of their thought, and not all phi-

350 ─────────────────────────────────────── B O D Y   &   S O U L

losophers are agreed as to the precise interpretation of every facet of these thinkers' overall positions about the metaphysics of substance. Nevertheless, Aristotle and Thomas Aquinas are sufficiently clear and united in their views to label their positions as the traditional view. For a brief treatment of Aquinas's view of substance, see Clarke, *Explorations in Metaphysics,* pp. 102-22. For a treatment of two main rival notions of substance (the Lockean bare substratum view and the bundle theory), see Loux, *Substance and Attribute,* pp. 107-52. For a critique of Loux's own alternative, see Moreland, "How to Be a Nominalist," pp. 75-101.

[20]Compare Ian Hacking, "Individual Substance," in *Leibniz: A Collection of Essays,* ed. Harry G. Frankfurt (Notre Dame, Ind.: University of Notre Dame Press, 1972), pp. 137-53; Michael Ayers, "Substance: Prolegomena to a Realist Theory of Identity," *Journal of Philosophy* (February 1991): 69-90.

[21]For a recent emphasis on this aspect of substance, see chaps. 1-2 of Hoffman and Rosenkrantz, *Substance* (esp. pp. 65-69). Hoffman and Rosenkrantz offer a distinctive understanding of the key trait of a substance in terms of its independence.

[22]For an emphasis on this aspect of substance, see Connell, *Substance and Modern Science,* esp. chaps. 6-8, 11-13, 18, 20-21.

[23]For a recent emphasis on this aspect of substance, see Wiggins, *Sameness and Substance,* chaps. 1-2.

[24]This aspect of substance is also emphasized in Wiggins, *Sameness and Substance,* chaps. 2-3.

[25]This aspect of substance is emphasized in Loux, *Substance and Attribute.*

[26]In biology there is a three-way debate about the nature of the unity of biological classification groups: pheneticism (unity is wholly grounded in similarity relations among members), cladism (unity is wholly grounded in geneological relatedness) and evolutionary systematics (a combination of both pheneticism and cladism). In the next chapter we will see why evolutionary theory makes the existence of essences unlikely. Now, if similarity is grounded in identity (i.e., if a is similar to b, then there exists some property F, such that both a and b have F), then given that living organisms are like gold in certain Twin Earth thought experiments (e.g., they resemble other members of their natural kinds in essence and not merely in surface features), it follows that (1) pheneticism entails that organisms have natures and (2) cladism is the most likely view, given evolutionary theory. For more on Twin Earth cases, see Kripke, *Naming and Necessity;* Hilary Putnam, *Reason, Truth and History* (Cambridge: Cambridge University Press, 1981), pp. 18-19, 22-25. For a defense of the claim that similarity is grounded in identity in the context of natural "classes," see D. M. Armstrong, *Nominalism and Realism,* vol. 1 of *Universals and Scientific Realism* (Cambridge: Cambridge University Press, 1978), pp. 36-57.

[27]Because of evolutionary theory, a number of contemporary advocates of substance reject irreducible teleology as part of the doctrine of substance. See Hoffman and Rosenkranz, *Substance,* pp. 91-149, esp. pp. 93-99; Wiggins, *Sameness and Substance,* p. 133. For a recent emphasis on this aspect of substance, see Gilson, *From Aristotle to Darwin.*

[28]Hoffman and Rosenkrantz, *Substance,* pp. 98-99.

[29]By "properties" here we mean "pure properties." An impure property (being identical to Socrates, being to the left of the tree) requires reference to a particular in order to be described. Pure properties (being red, weighing twenty-five pounds) requires no such reference.

[30]For a defense of bare particulars as individuators, see J. P. Moreland, "Theories of Individuation: A Reconsideration of Bare Particulars," *Pacific Philosophical Quarterly* 79 (1998): 251-63.

[31]There are two different uses of *substance:* the count sense (in which a whole cow counts as

one substance and of which we may ask, e.g., "How many cows are in the field?") and the mass or quantity sense (in which the amount of a certain kind of material or stuff is in view and of which we may ask, e.g., "How much cow did you eat, five or ten ounces?"). Property things can be treated as structured stuff or as a structured set of substances taken in the count sense (e.g., a ring is a structured collection of gold atoms taken as individual substances or as a structured amount of stuff).

[32]Bube, *Putting It All Together,* pp. 124-25.

Chapter 3: Human Persons in Naturalist & Complementarian Perspectives
[1]John Searle, *The Rediscovery of the Mind* (Cambridge: MIT Press, 1992), pp. 86-87.
[2]Arthur R. Peacocke, *Theology for a Scientific Age* (Minneapolis: Fortress, 1993), pp. 37-38.
[3]David Hull, *The Metaphysics of Evolution* (Albany: State University of New York Press, 1989), pp. 74-75.
[4]Compare John Rawls, *A Theory of Justice* (Cambridge: Harvard University Press, 1971); Kai Nielsen, *Ethics Without God* (Buffalo, N.Y.: Prometheus, 1989).
[5]David Papineau, *Philosophical Naturalism* (Oxford: Blackwell, 1993), p. 1.
[6]Jaegwon Kim, "Mental Causation and Two Conceptions of Mental Properties" (paper presented at the American Philosophical Association, Eastern Division meeting, Atlanta, Ga., December 1993), pp. 22-23.
[7]John Bishop, *Natural Agency* (Cambridge: Cambridge University Press, 1989), p. 5.
[8]Searle, *Rediscovery of the Mind,* esp. chaps. 1 and 4.
[9]Compare Alex Rosenberg, "A Field Guide to Recent Species of Naturalism," *British Journal for the Philosophy of Science* 47 (1996): 1-29.
[10]John Post, *Metaphysics: A Contemporary Introduction* (New York: Paragon , 1991), p. 11.
[11]William Lyons, introduction to *Modern Philosophy of Mind* (London: Everyman, 1995), p. lv. In context, Lyons's remark is specifically about the identity thesis, but he clearly intends it to cover physicalism in general.
[12]Malcolm A. Jeeves, "Brains, Mind and Faith," in *Real Science, Real Faith,* ed. R. J. Berry (Eastbourne: Monarch, 1991), p. 149.
[13]Wilfred Sellars, *Science, Perception and Reality* (London: Routledge & Kegan Paul, 1963), p. 173.
[14]Steven J. Wagner and Richard Warner, *Naturalism: A Critical Appraisal* (Notre Dame, Ind.: University of Notre Dame Press, 1993), p. 1.
[15]Papineau, *Philosophical Naturalism,* p. 3.
[16]Robert C. Stalnaker, *Inquiry* (Cambridge: MIT Press, 1984), p. 6.
[17]Post, *Metaphysics,* p. 121.
[18]D. M. Armstrong, "Naturalism, Materialism and First Philosophy," *Philosophia* 8 (1978): 262.
[19]Howard Robinson points out that historically materialism was the view that the only substances existing are material ones but that a duality of properties and abstract objects were allowed. Today, says Robinson, physicalists agree that whatever exists is physical, but they disagree about what *physical* designates: (1) whatever is exhaustively described in the language of physics and chemistry, (2) extend the first sense to include sciences like biology, (3) extend these to include common sense (e.g., secondary qualities). See Robinson, ed., *Objections to Physicalism* (Oxford: Clarendon, 1997), pp. 1-3. In our view, two things are at issue here: adopting a sense of *physical* most consistent with the naturalist epistemic attitude (e.g., the unity of science) and accounting for both the existence and emergence of the properties in the second and third senses within the constraints of the naturalist etiology. It is not enough simply to point to or describe a hierarchy of part-whole systems and their so-called emergent properties because without a naturalist explanation of their exist-

ence and origin, announcing that such emergent entities (and the various relations they sustain to lower-level "systems") are natural begs the question. One of us has argued elsewhere that supervenient physicalism should not be taken as an option for a contemporary naturalist. See J. P. Moreland, "Should a Naturalist Be a Supervenient Physicalist?" *Metaphilosophy* 29 (January-April 1998): 35-57.

[20]See William Rowe, *Thomas Reid on Freedom and Morality* (Ithaca, N.Y.: Cornell University Press, 1991), esp. chaps. 2 and 4.

[21]Papineau, *Philosophical Naturalism,* p. 16.

[22]Compare Richard Swinburne, *The Evolution of the Soul* (Oxford: Clarendon, 1986), pp. 234-37. Our own use of STF differs from but is similar to a principle employed by Swinburne.

[23]Kim, "Mental Causation," p. 21, and *Philosophy of Mind* (Boulder, Colo.: Westview, 1996), pp. 226-33.

[24]Searle, *Rediscovery of the Mind,* pp. 86-87.

[25]E. Mayr, *Populations, Species and Evolution* (Cambridge: Harvard University Press, 1970), p. 4.

[26]Hull, *Metaphysics of Evolution,* pp. 74-75.

[27]Bruce Aune, *Metaphysics: The Elements* (Minneapolis: University of Minnesota Press, 1985), p. 35.

[28]Armstrong, "Naturalism," p. 263. Compare his *Nominalism and Realism,* vol. 1 of *Universals and Scientific Realism* (Cambridge: Cambridge University Press, 1978), pp. 126-35.

[29]Kim, *Philosophy of Mind,* pp. 3-4.

[30]Bruce Reichenbach and V. Elving Anderson admit that "interactive dualism" provides a clear solution to the metaphysical problem of what grounds libertarian freedom. See Reichenbach and Anderson, *On Behalf of God* (Grand Rapids, Mich.: Eerdmans, 1995), pp. 280-84. But they claim that this solution "faces severe difficulties." The only ones they list are (1) the problem of how mind and brain interrelate and (2) interactive dualism's failure to account for the significant degree to which biophysical factors affect the mind. Regarding (2), they admit that a savvy dualist will admit a causal relation between mind and body, and thus (2) does not refute interactive dualism. This leaves (1). It is hard to see how a theist can take this to be a "severe difficulty." For dualist responses to the problem in interaction, see Keith A. Yandell, "A Defense of Dualism," *Faith and Philosophy* 12 (October 1995): 551-53; J. P. Moreland, "A Defense of Substance Dualism," in *Christian Perspectives on Being Human: A Multidisciplinary Approach to Integration,* ed. J. P. Moreland and David M. Ciocchi (Grand Rapids, Mich.: Baker, 1993), pp. 75-77; Mark Bedau, "Cartesian Interactionism," in *Studies in the Philosophy of Mind,* vol. 10 of *Midwest Studies in Philosophy,* ed. Peter A. French, Theodore E. Uehling Jr. and Howard K. Wettstein (Minneapolis: University of Minnesota Press, 1986), pp. 483-502; John Foster, "In Defense of Dualism," in *The Case for Dualism,* ed. John R. Smythies and John Beloff (Charlottesville: University Press of Virginia, 1989), pp. 1-25.

[31]Some philosophers would embrace strict physicalist forms of supervenient physicalism, but they are in the minority and, in any case, the only version of supervenient physicalism relevant to our concerns here is property dualism.

[32]Compare Kim, *Philosophy of Mind,* pp. 9-13.

[33]Sometimes emergent and structural supervenience are called *causal* and *constituitive* supervenience, respectively.

[34]For more on this contrast, see Timothy O'Connor, "Emergent Properties," *American Philosophical Quarterly* 31 (April 1994): 91-104; D. M. Armstrong, *A Theory of Universals,* vol. 2 of *Universals and Scientific Realism* (Cambridge: Cambridge University Press,

1978), pp. 68-71.

[35] Paul M. Churchland, *Matter and Consciousness* (Cambridge, Mass.: MIT Press, 1984), p. 21.

[36] Arthur R. Peacocke and Grant Gillett, eds., *Persons and Personality* (Oxford: Blackwell, 1987), p. 55.

[37] Papineau, *Philosophical Naturalism*, p. 11; cf. pp. 9-32.

[38] The argument also assumes that naturalists reject the overdetermination of physical events by both mental and physical states—that is, that some effect has both a sufficient mental event and a sufficient physical event as a cause.

[39] Supervenience physicalism is actually a form of dualism if the emergent entities are taken to be intrinsically and irreducibly mental (and this is the standard way to take the doctrine), so the name is misleading and should instead be *supervenience dualism*. (This is different from another form of property dualism, e.g., the direct bundle theory of dualism according to which there are no mental substances yet mental properties exist and are directly bundled together in such a way that they are not states of, nor do they in any sense belong to, the body, though they may sustain direct causal relations to that body.)

[40] See esp. essay 14 in Jaegwon Kim, *Supervenience and Mind* (Cambridge: Cambridge University Press, 1993), pp. 265-84; Papineau, *Philosophical Naturalism*, pp. 21-23.

[41] Howard Robinson, *Matter and Sense* (Cambridge: Cambridge University Press, 1982), p. 2. Compare Searle, *Rediscovery of the Mind*, pp. 3-4.

[42] See Richard Swinburne, *The Existence of God* (Oxford: Clarendon, 1979), chap. 9; *Evolution of the Soul*, pp. 183-96; *Is There a God?* (Oxford: Oxford University Press, 1996), pp. 69-94; "The Origin of Consciousness," in *Cosmic Beginnings and Human Ends*, ed. Clifford N. Matthews and Roy Abraham Varghese (Chicago: Open Court, 1995), pp. 355-78; Robert Adams, "Flavors, Colors and God," in *Contemporary Perspectives on Religious Epistemology*, ed. R. Douglas Geivett and Brendan Sweetman (New York: Oxford University Press, 1992), pp. 225-40; J. P. Moreland, "Searle's Biological Naturalism and the Argument from Consciousness," *Faith and Philosophy* 15 (January 1998): 68-91.

[43] Swinburne, *Evolution of the Soul*, chaps. 8-9. We part company with Swinburne's Cartesian dualism in favor of Aristotelian or Thomist dualism. See J. P. Moreland, "Humanness, Personhood and the Right to Die," *Faith and Philosophy* 12 (January 1995): 95-112; and J. P. Moreland and Stan Wallace, "Aquinas Versus Locke and Descartes on the Human Person and End-of-Life Ethics," *International Philosophical Quarterly* 35 (September 1995): 319-30.

[44] Thomas Nagel, *The View from Nowhere* (New York: Oxford University Press, 1986), p. 27.

[45] Robinson, *Matter and Sense*, p. 2. See also Searle, *Rediscovery of the Mind*, p. 10.

[46] Roderick Chisholm, "Human Freedom and the Self," in *On Metaphysics* (Minneapolis: University of Minnesota Press, 1989), p. 14.

[47] John Searle, *Minds, Brains and Science* (Cambridge: Harvard University Press, 1984), p. 98.

[48] Bishop, *Natural Agency*, p. 1.

[49] For an instructive study in just how serious the problem of the substantial self and self-control are for the naturalist, see Daniel Dennett, *Elbow Room* (Cambridge, Mass.: MIT Press, 1984), pp. 74-100. If something like Dennett's view is the price one must pay to be a naturalist, then the price is too high.

[50] William Provine as cited in Phillip Johnson, *Darwin on Trial*, 2d ed. (Downers Grove, Ill.: InterVarsity Press, 1993), p. 127.

[51] Searle, *Minds, Brains and Science*, p. 92.

[52] Bishop, *Natural Agency*, p. 40. An interesting implication of Bishop's view is that naturalism cannot allow for there to be a first event in the absolute sense of not being preceded by other events because all events are caused by prior events or else they are simply uncaused.

In the latter case, the "coming to be" of the event cannot be "natural" since it is just a brute fact. In the former case, this means that if the kalam cosmological argument is correct and there was a beginning to the universe, then the beginning itself was not a natural event, nor was its cause, if it had one.

[53]Compare Dallas Willard, *Logic and the Objectivity of Knowledge* (Athens: Ohio University Press, 1984), pp. 180-81.

[54]Nancey Murphy, "Human Nature: Historical, Scientific and Religious Issues," in *Whatever Happened to the Soul?* ed. Warren S. Brown, Nancey Murphy and H. Newton Malony (Minneapolis: Fortress, 1998), p. 7.

[55]See Robert Larmer, "Mind-Body Interaction and the Conservation of Energy," *International Philosophical Quarterly* 26 (September 1986): 277-85.

[56]Searle, *Minds, Brains and Science,* p. 92

[57]Kim, *Philosophy of Mind,* p. 12.

[58]Papineau, *Philosophical Naturalism,* p. 122.

[59]Richard H. Bube, *Putting It All Together* (Lanham, Md.: University Press of America, 1995), pp. 124-25.

[60]Richard H. Bube, *The Human Quest* (Waco, Tex.: Word, 1971); *Putting It All Together;* and Bube, ed., *The Encounter Between Christianity and Science* (Grand Rapids, Mich.: Eerdmans, 1968). Bube has also published a number of pieces through the years in *Perspectives on Science and Christian Faith* (previously called the *Journal of the American Scientific Affiliation*).

[61]Arthur R. Peacocke, *Creation and the World of Science* (Oxford: Clarendon, 1979); *God and the New Biology* (San Francisco: Harper & Row, 1986), and *Theology for a Scientific Age.*

[62]Malcom Jeeves, *Psychology and Christianity* (Downers Grove, Ill.: InterVarsity Press, 1976); *Mind Fields* (Grand Rapids, Mich.: Baker, 1994); and *Human Nature at the Millennium* (Grand Rapids, Mich.: Baker, 1997).

[63]Nancey Murphy, *Anglo-American Postmodernity* (Boulder, Colo.: Westview, 1997); preface and chaps. 1 and 6 in *Whatever Happened to the Soul?* ed. Warren S. Brown, Nancey Murphy and H. Newton Malony (Minneapolis: Fortress Press, 1998); and Murphy and George F. R. Ellis, *On the Moral Nature of the Universe* (Minneapolis: Fortress, 1996).

[64]D. M. Mackay, *Christianity in a Mechanistic Universe* (London: Inter-Varsity Press, 1965); *The Clockwork Image* (Downers Grove, Ill.: InterVarsity Press, 1974); *Human Science and Human Dignity* (Downers Grove, Ill.: InterVarsity Press, 1979); and "Complementarity II," in supplementary vol. 32 of *Proceedings of the Aristotelian Society* (1958): 105-22.

[65]David G. Myers, *The Human Puzzle* (San Francisco: Harper & Row, 1978); and Myers and Malcolm A. Jeeves, *Psychology Through the Eyes of Faith* (San Francisco: Harper & Row, 1987).

[66]Bube, *Putting It All Together,* p. 124; cf. p. 179.

[67]Compare Peacocke, *Theology for a Scientific Age,* pp. 38, 63-67; *God and the New Biology,* pp. 52-53, 144; and *Creation and the World of Science,* pp. 58-160.

[68]Peacocke, *Theology for a Scientific Age,* pp. 60-61.

[69]Ibid., p. 161; and *God and the New Biology,* p. 91.

[70]Peacocke, *Creation and the World of Science,* pp. 120-21.

[71]See Murphy, *Anglo-American Postmodernity,* pp. 13-14, 19-35, 193-97; Murphy and Ellis, *On the Moral Nature of the Universe,* pp. 4-7, 19-38.

[72]Murphy allows for the possibility that a strong identity and not a functionalist version of physicalism may be adequate to deal with mental states such as pains. See Murphy, "Human Nature," p. 10. In our view, the argument we are advancing works against both views. For more on this, see Saul Kripke, *Naming and Necessity* (Cambridge: Harvard

University Press, 1972), esp. lecture 3.

[73]First-person knowledge of one's own self and its states has always been a problem for functionalist views of mental events or properties, but it is even more so for Murphy's specific version of functionalism, which has it that a mental property supervenes not on the relevant brain property along but on the brain property combined with the relevant circumstances. Now these circumstances are usually external to the subject such that the subject has no direct awareness of them. In this case the subject may have no access to that which constitutes the pain as a pain. In response it will do no good to cite cases where two subjects with different expectations may have different experiences resulting from the same physical stimulation: e.g., two subjects with different expectations will experience a small electrical shock differently, as either a burning or as ice. Each subject will still be able to know the subjective texture of his or her own mental state by direct awareness of its intrinsic features and not by knowing the circumstances relevant to their obtaining. For a critique of a view relevantly similar to Murphy's regarding its inability to allow for a priori justification, see Lawrence Bonjour, *In Defense of Pure Reason* (Cambridge: Cambridge University Press, 1998), chap. 6, esp. pp. 164-80.

[74]For arguments that identify the soul and the self, see Nancy S. Duvall, "From Soul to Self and Back Again," *Journal of Psychology and Theology* 26 (spring 1998): 6-15; J. P. Moreland, "Restoring the Substance to the Soul of Psychology," *Journal of Psychology and Theology* 26 (spring 1998): 29-43.

[75]Peacocke, *Creation and the World of Science,* p. 130.

[76]See Bube, *Putting It All Together,* pp. 22-25, 120-25, 172-75, 182-87.

[77]Bube, *Human Quest,* p. 143. More recently, Bube has claimed that when we use *soul/spirit* to refer to the person's "identity" maintained in the afterlife, this identity rests in and depends on God's holding a memory of the person in his mind. See Bube, *Putting It All Together,* pp. 184-85.

[78]Murphy and Ellis, *On the Moral Nature of the Universe,* p. 35. Compare Nancey Murphy, "Nonreductive Physicalism: Philosophical Issues," in *Whatever Happened to the Soul?* ed. Warren S. Brown, Nancey Murphy and H. Newton Malony (Minneapolis: Fortress, 1998), pp. 138-39.

[79]Robert N. Wennberg, *Terminal Choices: Euthanasia, Suicide and the Right to Die* (Grand Rapids, Mich.: Eerdmans, 1989); and *Life in the Balance* (Grand Rapids, Mich.: Eerdmans, 1985).

[80]Wennberg, *Terminal Choices,* p. 176.

[81]See John Locke, "Of Identity and Diversity," chap. 27, bk. 2 of *An Essay Concerning Human Understanding.* Though Locke was somewhat inconsistent, the standard way to understand him is to note that he distinguished the identity of being human, which consists in the "continuity" of a living organized body, from the identity of a person, which consists in the "continuity" of consciousness and psychological traits, especially memory. It is important to note that, for Locke, continuity of a person is not continuity of a substance that has consciousness but continuity of consciousness itself.

[82]Wennberg, *Life in the Balance,* p. 49.

[83]Wennberg, *Terminal Choices,* p. 159.

[84]Ibid., p. 160. Compare Wennberg, *Life in the Balance,* pp. 31-46.

[85]Wennberg, *Terminal Choices,* pp. 171, 159.

[86]Wennberg, *Life in the Balance,* pp. 36, 39-40, 52.

[87]Ibid., p. 29.

[88]Wennberg, *Terminal Choices,* pp. 159, 168.

[89]Wennberg, *Life in the Balance,* pp. 27-28, 34, 124-25. On p. 124 Wennberg falsely implies that traditional sanctity-of-life advocates identify being human with falling under

the biological classification *Homo sapiens*. But this is not so because traditionalists view humanness as a theological and metaphysical notion that goes beyond biology.

[90]Ibid., pp. 33, 36, 42, 127.

[91]Ibid., pp. 43-44, 117-19, 130; Wennberg, *Terminal Choices,* pp. 159, 161, 163, 165, 169.

[92]It could be argued that our view renders the existence of human nonpersons impossible, and this is too strong because, even if the view is false, it is surely possibly the case that one could be a Cartesian creationist regarding the soul, holding that God creates the soul and, thus, the person, at viability and that prior to this the fetus was a human nonperson. In response, we return to a distinction mentioned in chapter two between metaphysical and epistemological possibility. Given that our view is true—that *humanness* is a species of the genus *personhood*—then the Cartesian view just mentioned is de re impossible in a metaphysical sense though it is epistemologically possible in that one could hold that the Cartesian view may, indeed, be the correct position and that ours the incorrect one. In the current context, we are primarily explicating our view and not arguing for it, so the metaphysical and not the epistemological sense of possibility is the relevant one.

Chapter 4: Substance Dualism & the Human Person: Free Agency

[1]Roderick Chisholm, "Human Freedom and the Self," in *On Metaphysics* (Minneapolis: University of Minnesota Press, 1989), p. 14.

[2]John Bishop, *Natural Agency* (Cambridge: Cambridge University Press, 1989), p. 1.

[3]Thomas Nagel, *The View from Nowhere* (New York: Oxford University Press, 1986), p. 110.

[4]For biblical and theological defenses of libertarian agency, see Charles W. Carter, ed., *Biblical, Systematic and Practical,* vol. 1 of *A Contemporary Wesleyan Theology* (Grand Rapids, Mich.: Zondervan, 1983); Jack Cottrel, *God the Creator* (Joplin, Mo.: College Press, 1983); Cottrel, *God the Ruler* (Joplin, Mo.: College Press, 1984); Cottrel, *God the Redeemer* (Joplin, Mo.: College Press, 1987); Roger T. Forster and V. Paul Marston, *God's Strategy in Human History* (Wheaton, Ill.: Tyndale House, 1973); John Miley, *Systematic Theology,* vols. 1-2 (New York: Eaton & Mains, 1894); Clark H. Pinnock, ed., *Grace Unlimited* (Minneapolis: Bethany, 1975); Clark H. Pinnock, ed., *The Grace of God, The Will of Man* (Grand Rapids, Mich.: Zondervan, 1989); H. Orton Wiley, *Christian Theology,* vol. 2 (Kansas City: Beacon Hill, 1952).

[5]As we are using the term, *event causation* includes the notion that all events are caused by prior events according to the relevant laws. Stewart Goetz is an advocate of a noncausal libertarian view who denies agent causation, accepts event causation for human acts and holds that a free act involves an uncaused event (e.g,, an exercise of active power) that event-causes an effect (e.g., the raising of the hand) for a teleological end (e.g., to vote). See Stewart Goetz, "Libertarian Choice," *Faith and Philosophy* 14 (April 1997): 195-211.

[6]This is not quite correct because sometimes an agent performs an intentional action by simply allowing a certain sequence of events to take place. Here an agent gives a sort of passive permission and does nothing to stop a sequence of events that accomplish the agent's intent. The agent refrains from endeavoring.

[7]Some have denied that the ability to have done differently is a necessary condition for free action on the grounds that what are called *Frankfurt-type counterexamples* (named after the philosopher Harry G. Frankfurt) have shown this to be the case. Here is a Frankfurt-type counterexample: A mad scientist places an electrode in Baker's brain and had the ability to read Baker's deliberative processes. If Baker voluntarily chooses to shoot Holmes, the scientist will do nothing. But if Baker decides not to shoot Holmes, the scientist will hit a button that activates the electrode and produces a volition in Baker to shoot Holmes. Now, in this case, if Baker voluntarily shoots Holmes while the scientist does nothing, then he acts freely even though he could not have done otherwise (since the scientist would

have activated the electrode if Baker had decided otherwise). In response, we point out that in Frankfurt-type counterexamples, there is still a dual ability: the ability for Baker to have exercised his own power to shoot Holmes or for Baker to have refrained from exercising his own power to shoot Holmes (in which case the scientist would produce the volition to shoot Holmes). What the Frankfurt examples show is that the ability condition is really grounded in a type of "internal control" possessed by free agents. This type of "internal control" is easy to capture on a substance-dualist view of human persons—it is an active mental power that constitutes the immaterial self—but it is hard to see how it can be described in scientific, physical terms or possessed by a system of particles.

[8]Actually the free act of the driver of car ten is the real cause, but we identify car ten itself for the purposes of illustration.

[9]Thus, a necessary condition for libertarianism (but not for compatibilism) is that persons are substances, not property-things (as complementarianism requires).

[10]Moreover, there would be no guarantee that the statistical indeterminacy of microevents could be directed down a specific macropathway by a mental act (e.g., of willing to raise one's arm to vote). Such an act may well require causing a chain of events outside the bounds of causal potential set by micro level indeterminacy.

[11]Bishop, *Natural Agency*, p. 40.

[12]Thus, claims that quantum indeterminacy provide critical aid in resolving problems of free will are simply mistaken. For an example of such a claim, see Michael E. Kellman, "Science and Free Will," *First Things*, May 1994, p. 5.

[13]Nagel, *View from Nowhere*, p. 114.

[14]John Searle, *Minds, Brains and Science* (Cambridge, Mass.: Harvard University Press, 1984), p. 98.

[15]John Foster, *The Immaterial Self* (London: Routledge, 1991), p. 267. Compare Tibor Machan, "What Free Will Is, and Why It Matters," *Orange County Register*, January 4, 1998; Bishop, *Natural Agency*, pp. 58, 72, 69, 95-96, 103-4, 110-11, 114, 126-27, 140-41, 144; Robert Kane, *The Significance of Free Will* (Oxford: Oxford University Press, 1996), p. 4.

[16]J. A. Cover and John O'Leary-Hawthorne, "Free Agency and Materialism," in *Faith, Freedom and Rationality*, ed. Jeff Jordon and Daniel Howard-Snyder (Lanham, Md.: Rowman & Littlefield, 1996), p. 51.

[17]Goetz, "Libertarian Choice," pp. 197-99.

[18]Daniel Dennett, *Elbow Room* (Cambridge, Mass.: MIT Press, 1984).

[19]See Donald Davidson, "How Is Weakness of the Will Possible?" in *Essays on Actions and Events by Donald Davidson* (Oxford: Clarendon, 1980), pp. 21-42.

[20]Bishop, *Natural Agency*, pp. 113-14.

[21]Ibid., p. 120.

[22]For the details of this dialectic, see Bishop, *Natural Agency*, esp. chaps. 4-6.

[23]Nancy Holmstrom, "Firming Up Soft Determinism," *The Personalist* 58 (January 1977): 47.

[24]Two other objections against libertarianism are that it is inconsistent with naturalism and that it turns free actions into completely random events. Clearly, the first criticism begs the question, and, in one way or another, the first six chapters are a response to it. For a treatment of the second criticism, see Stewart Goetz, "A Noncausal Theory of Agency," *Philosophy and Phenomenological Research* 49 (December 1988): 303-16; and "Libertarian Choice," pp. 195-211.

[25]William Rowe, *Thomas Reid on Freedom and Morality* (Ithaca, N.Y.: Cornell University Press, 1991), pp. 30-40, 145-61.

[26]If the question is raised as to why the agent did x for reason r as opposed to doing y for

reason *s*, it may be possible to cite another reason for the agent's choosing to act for *r* and not *s*. But at some point the regress of explanations will just stop. We will simply say that it is a brute fact that the agent did what he did for such and such reason and that this is just the way it should be given the nature of free agency. In this sense, asking for a reason for an agent's ultimate, brutely selected reason, is like asking for a reason or a cause for God's existence.

[27]Nagel, *View from Nowhere,* p. 113.

[28]Barry Stroud, "The Charm of Naturalism," *Proceedings and Addresses of the American Philosophical Society* 70 (1996): 44.

[29]Randolph Clarke, "Toward a Credible Agent-Causal Account of Free Will," *Nous* 27 (1993): 201. In fairness to Clarke, his remarks are in connection with his own quite unique version of libertarianism. For a criticism of Clarke, see J. P. Moreland, "Naturalism and Libertarian Agency," *Philosophy and Theology* 10 (1997): 351-81.

[30]Compare Tibor Machan, "What Free Will Is"; Timothy O'Connor, "Agent Causation," in *Agents, Causes and Events,* ed. Timothy O'Connor (New York: Oxford University Press, 1995), pp. 178-80; and Timothy O'Connor, "Emergent Properties," *American Philosophical Quarterly* 31 (April 1994): 91-104.

[31]See Goetz, "Libertarian Choice," pp. 196-99.

[32]For a slightly different way of describing the problem, see Cover and O'Leary-Hawthorne, "Free Agency," pp. 58-66.

[33]In their article Cover and O'Leary-Hawthorne consider and accept the notion that the following is a logically consistent triad: (1) a family *A* supervenes on family *B;* (2) family *B* does not supervene on family *A;* (3) some member of *A* is causally relevant to/responsible for some member of *B* (see ibid., pp. 60-61). They claim that while the triad is logically consistent, it nevertheless presents serious problems for naturalism (cf. ibid., pp. 64-66). We are in substantial agreement with their analysis of this issue, but we want to make explicit something that is, at best, implicit in their treatment: limiting our discussion to the emergence of *AP,* the only way the triad is broadly logically consistent is if we take members of set *A* (in this case, the property or properties of exercising active power) to be structural properties composed out of members of set *B*. For example, one can work out a sort of top-down causation for functionalist structural views of mental properties that are realized by the relevant brain states. Let some brain state bs_1 be a member of set *B*, and say that bs_1 both realizes and partially constitutes functional state m_1, which is a member of set *A*. Further, let us specify that m_1 includes both causal inputs to the organism containing the brain with bs_1 and a structural pathway for directing the causal chain towards bs_1 and on to the relevant outputs. In this case, a member of set *B* (i.e., bs_1) realizes a member of set *A* (i.e., m_1), and m_1 (structurally) supervenes on bs_1, yet m_1 is causally relevant to bs_1. However, this is a sort of outside-in causation and not a real case of top-down causation. As far as I can see, the triad is consistent only for examples of structural supervenience or in cases where the subvenient entity is included in the set of supervenient entities. But in neither case is supervenience a genuine type of emergence, and that is what is relevant for the problem of the supervenience of libertarian agency.

[34]See ibid., p. 65.

[35]John Searle, *The Rediscovery of the Mind* (Cambridge, Mass.: MIT Press, 1992), pp. 124-25.

[36]Nagel, *View from Nowhere,* p. 111.

[37]David Papineau, *Philosophical Naturalism* (Oxford: Blackwell, 1993), pp. 29-32.

[38]Nagel, *View from Nowhere,* p. 111. As David Chalmers notes about conscious experiences in general, "There is an explanatory gap between the physical level and the conscious experience. If this is right, the fact that consciousness accompanies a given physical process is a further fact not explainable simply by telling the story about the physical facts. In a sense,

the accompaniment must be taken as brute." See David Chalmers, *The Conscious Mind: In Search of a Fundamental Theory* (Oxford: Oxford University Press, 1996), p. 107.

[39]Nagel, *View from Nowhere*, p. 111.

[40]Terence Horgan, "Nonreductive Materialism and the Explanatory Autonomy of Psychology," in *Naturalism: A Critical Appraisal*, ed. Steven J. Wagner and Richard Warner (Notre Dame, Ind.: University of Notre Dame Press, 1993), pp. 313-14.

[41]Bruce Reichenbach, *Is Man the Phoenix?* (Grand Rapids, Mich.: Eerdmans, 1978), p. 111. Compare Bruce Reichenbach and V. Elving Anderson, *On Behalf of God* (Grand Rapids, Mich.: Eerdmans, 1995), pp. 250-95.

[42]John Foster, *The Immaterial Self* (London: Routledge, 1991), p. 280.

Chapter 5: Substance Dualism & the Human Person: Personal Identity

[1]Thomas Reid, "Of Identity," in *Thomas Reid: Inquiry and Essays*, ed. Ronald E. Beanblossom and Keith Lehrer (Indianapolis: Hackett, 1983), pp. 214-15.

[2]Richard Swinburne, *The Evolution of the Soul* (Oxford: Clarendon, 1986), p. 160.

[3]Howard Robinson, *Matter and Sense* (Cambridge: Cambridge University Press, 1982), p. 2.

[4]John Calvin *Institutes of the Christian Religion* 1.1.1.

[5]Our characterization of a thought is related to what philosophers call *propositions*. In our view, when an event of thinking takes place in the self, the self—more specifically the event of thinking in the self—exemplifies a proposition. The proposition is an intentional quality or property that is predicated of the mind in an act of thinking. Thus, propositions are properties that can be exemplified by minds, and propositions are the immanent content of thinking events. For more on this, see Dallas Willard, *Logic and the Objectivity of Knowledge* (Athens: Ohio University Press, 1984).

[6]The supposed vagueness of quantum states prior to their measurement is irrelevant here for two reasons: (1) Whatever else a sensation is, it is not a quantum state of some sort, and (2) quantum vagueness is most likely epistemological and not ontological.

[7]For a helpful survey of the literature on and defense of the knowledge argument, see David J. Chalmers, *The Conscious Mind: In Search of a Fundamental Theory* (Oxford: Oxford University Press, 1996), pp. 140-46.

[8]David Papineau, *Philosophical Naturalism* (Oxford: Blackwell, 1993), pp. 103-14; Paul M. Churchland, *Matter and Consciousness* (Cambridge, Mass.: MIT Press, 1984), pp. 33-34.

[9]Geoffrey Madell, *Mind and Materialism* (Edinburgh: Edinburgh University Press, 1988), p. 83.

[10]So either intentionality is an abnormal relation (as Reinhardt Grossmann argues in *The Existence of the World* [London: Routledge, 1992], p. 94) or it is an unusual monadic property (as Dallas Willard contends in *Logic and the Objectivity of Knowledge*). In our view, intentionality is not a relation but a monadic property.

[11]John Searle, *Minds, Brains and Science* (Cambridge, Mass.: Harvard University Press, 1984), pp. 32-33. Compare John Searle, "Minds, Brains and Programs," *The Behavioral and Brain Sciences* 3 (1980): 417-24.

[12]For a devastating critique of the three main physicalist attempts to analyze intentionality within physicalist constraints, see Madell, *Mind and Materialism*, pp. 11-36.

[13]Nancey Murphy, "Human Nature: Historical, Scientific and Religious Issues," in *Whatever Happened to the Soul?* ed. Warren S. Brown, Nancey Murphy and H. Newton Malony (Minneapolis: Fortress, 1998), p. 17; cf. pp. 13, 27, 139-43.

[14]Richard Bube, *The Human Quest* (Waco, Texas: Word, 1971), p. 143. See also his discussion of *soul/spirit* as postmortem identity based in God's memory, in Richard Bube, *Putting It All Together* (Lanham, Md.: University Press of America, 1995), pp. 184-85.

[15]Paul Tidman, "Conceivability as a Test for Possibility," *American Philosophical Quarterly* 31 (October 1994): 297-309.

[16]See James van Cleve, "Conceivability and the Cartesian Argument for Dualism," *Pacific Philosophical Quarterly* 64 (1983): 35-45; Charles Taliaferro, *Consciousness and the Mind of God* (Cambridge: Cambridge University Press, 1994), pp. 134-39.

[17]A. D. Smith points out that if we sever our beliefs in possibility entirely from conceivability, we shall land in extreme Megareanism, where the possible and the necessary collapse into the actual. See A. D. Smith, "Non-Reductive Physicalism," in *Objections to Physicalism,* ed. Howard Robinson (Oxford: Clarendon, 1997), p. 243. Critics of substance dualism use conceivability as a test for modality in various contexts. Thus Christian physicalist Nancey Murphy argues for the supervenience of moral properties on nonmoral ones on the grounds that "we cannot imagine [she means 'conceive'] a possible world like this one in all nonmoral respects but differing only in moral respects." See Nancey Murphy, "Nonreductive Physicalism: Philosophical Issues," in *Whatever Happened to the Soul?* p. 134 n. 14.

[18]Compare Keith A. Yandell, "A Defense of Dualism," *Faith and Philosophy* 12 (October 1995): 548-66; Charles Taliaferro, "Animals, Brains and Spirits," *Faith and Philosophy* 12 (October 1995): 567-81.

[19]Some have argued that part of what it means to be a body is to be a physical thing but that a body is more than a physical thing and, moreover, that a body is not essentially a physical thing. Thus, the body could exist even if no physical thing existed. See Trenton Merricks, "A New Objection to A Priori Arguments for Dualism," *American Philosophical Quarterly* 31 (January 1994): 81-85. The argument we state explicitly is one that sets this issue aside. The parallel argument we suggest but do not develop is a weaker claim, and it allows for the possibility that one could exist with no physical object existing but still be identical to one's body if one's body were not essentially a physical thing.

[20]Kathleen Wilkes has raised objections against the use of thought experiments in philosophy generally and in personal identity arguments specifically. See Kathleen Wilkes, *Real People: Personal Identity Without Thought Experiments* (Oxford: Clarendon, 1993), pp. 1-48. In our view, Wilkes's views about thought experiments in this area rest on two claims: (1) philosophical thought experiments should conform to scientific thought experiments because philosophy is continuous with science, and (2) "being a person" is not a natural kind, thus, it is a vague notion that easily sparks misleading intuitions. We cannot respond in detail to Wilkes's claims here. Suffice it to say that her views on this matter are an expression of a naturalist view of philosophical method, and the first six chapters of this book are an attempt to provide a detailed description and defense of an alternative view.

[21]In normal life, one may be focusing on speaking kindly and be unaware that one is scowling. In extreme cases (multiple personalities and split brains), one may be fragmented in one's functioning or incapable of consciously and simultaneously attending to all of one's mental states, but the various personalities and mental states are still all one's own.

[22]We also point out that if one is possibly such that one can exist (and may actually exist as Paul may well have done) disembodied, it follows that one is not identical to one's body nor is one's body essential to one irrespective of whether or not the body is essentially physical or essentially a body.

[23]For a more detailed response, see Charles Taliaferro, "Possibilities in Philosophy of Mind," *Philosophy and Phenomenological Research* 58 (March 1997): 127-37.

[24]We also believe there is a burden of proof on those who claim that we are identical to our bodies, that our bodies are composed of separable physical parts and yet the body is not essentially physical. We believe advocates of this view must do at least the following:

(1) explain New Testament teaching (cf. chapter one) that counts against this view, especially teaching that argues in favor of a disembodied intermediate state and against an extinction or recreation view of the afterlife, and (2) offer a more detailed account of the body than has been forthcoming to date. We believe such an account will have difficulty avoiding an identification of a person (i.e., a person's body) with some collection of relational, structural entities. If this is so, then it will be difficult to retain the substantial sort of primitive unity a substance view offers for depicting the self. We also suspect that any such account will reintroduce a new sort of dualism. For now the body will be at least but not only physical. What this means is that an ontology of the body will have to go beyond being physical (whatever that amounts to in any particular analysis). If this is so, then it is not clear in what sense the account is "physicalist" as opposed to offering some sort of duality between different entities that make up the body (the physical and nonphysical aspects of the body). Surely it will come as a shock to most physicalists to be told that they should hold that a body is not essentially physical.

[25]It is likely that neither ship is the original on the grounds that something cannot exist, cease to be and come into existence a second time. Therefore, the ship of Theseus may not be the best example to illustrate the issues here. However, if we assume for the sake of argument that one of the two ships is the original, no harm will be done, because it is the intuitions about the nature of material constitution for property-things that are at issue, not whether something can come to be twice. For more on this, see Michael Rea, introduction to *Material Constitution: A Reader* (Lanham, Md.: Rowman & Littlefield, 1997), pp. xv-lvii.

[26]Compare Swinburne, *Evolution of the Soul,* pp. 145-73.

[27]For a recent example of this objection, see John Searle, *The Rediscovery of the Mind* (Cambridge, Mass.: MIT Press, 1992), pp. 95-100, 143-44.

[28]For more on this argument, see Madell, *Mind and Materialism,* pp. 103-25; and *The Identity of the Self* (Edinburgh: Edinburgh University Press, 1981).

[29]An exception would be *now.* If one accepts an *a* series view of time, then *now* is a basic indexical along with *I.*

[30]See Swinburne, *Evolution of the Soul,* pp. 145-60.

[31]Compare Thomas Nagel, "Brain Bisection and the Unity of Consciousness," in *Mortal Questions* (Cambridge: Cambridge University Press, 1979), pp. 147-64, esp. pp. 154-55.

[32]See J. P. Moreland, "An Enduring Self: The Achilles Heel of Process Philosophy," *Process Studies* 17 (fall 1988): 193-99.

[33]For a developed version of this approach to the problem of knowledge of other minds, see Swinburne, *Evolution of the Soul,* pp. 11-16. For a survey of other approaches, see Alvin Plantinga, *Warrant and Proper Function* (New York: Oxford University Press, 1993), pp. 65-77; see pp. 48-57 for Plantinga's treatment of self-knowledge, which he takes to warrant the belief that we are not our bodies, our brains or computer programs.

[34]Compare Peter van Inwagen, *Material Beings* (Ithaca, N.Y.: Cornell University Press, 1990), esp. chaps. 2 and 9; and "Dualism and Materialism: Athens and Jerusalem?" *Faith and Philosophy* 12 (October 1995): 475-88; Lynn Rudder Baker, "Need a Christian Be a Mind/Body Dualist?" *Faith and Philosophy* 12 (October 1995): 489-504; Trenton Merricks, "The Resurrection of the Body and the Life Everlasting," in *Reason for the Hope Within,* ed. Michael J. Murray (Grand Rapids, Mich.: Eerdmans, 1999), pp. 261-86; and Merricks, "A New Objection," pp. 81-85; Kevin J. Corcoran, "Persons and Bodies: The Metaphysics of Human Persons" (Ph.D. diss., Purdue University, 1997).

[35]This may actually be false, because in separating large extended parts of clay from each other, one may actually destroy some of the simple parts that lie on the boundary between those large parts prior to their separation. However, not everyone believes that extended

parts of wholes contact each other by having simple parts on the boundaries of those extended parts that coincide.

[36]For purposes of exposition we set aside those who would claim that nothing can come into existence twice and survive a gap in existence and those who would claim that the watch (taken as a sort of sum) continues to exist when disassembled.

[37]For more on this, see John D. Kronen, "The Substantial Unity of Material Substances According to John Poinsot," *The Thomist* 58 (October 1994): 599-615.

Chapter 6: Substance Dualism & the Body

[1]John W. Cooper, *Body, Soul and Life Everlasting* (Grand Rapids, Mich.: Eerdmans, 1989), p. 55.

[2]Brian C. Goodwin, *How the Leopard Changed Its Spots* (New York: Simon & Schuster, 1994), pp. 176-77.

[3]See Richard Levins's statement in Werner Callebaut, *Taking the Naturalistic Turn* (Chicago: University of Chicago Press, 1993), p. 249.

[4]For more on René Descartes's dualism, especially as it relates to the thought of Thomas Aquinas, see Theresa M. Crem, "A Moderate Dualist Alternative to Cartesian Dualism," *Laval thaeologique et philosophique* 35 (June 1979): 153-75; John Mourant, "Cartesian Man and Thomistic Man," *Journal of Philosophy* 54 (June 1957): 373-82; Albert G. A. Balz, "Concerning the Thomistic and Cartesian Dualisms: A Rejoinder to Professor Mourant," *Journal of Philosophy* 54 (June 1957): 383-90; J. P. Moreland and Stan Wallace, "Aquinas Versus Descartes and Locke on the Human Person and End-of-Life Ethics," *International Philosophical Quarterly* 35 (September 1995): 319-30. For helpful treatments of Aquinas, see Brian Davies, *The Thought of Thomas Aquinas* (Oxford: Clarendon, 1992), pp. 207-26; Anthony Kenny, *Aquinas on Mind* (London: Routledge, 1993).

[5]See Richard Swinburne, *The Evolution of the Soul,* rev. ed. (Oxford: Clarendon, 1997); John Foster, *The Immaterial Self* (London: Routledge, 1991); Cooper, *Body, Soul;* Peter Kreeft and Ron Tacelli, *Handbook of Christian Apologetics* (Downers Grove, Ill.: InterVarsity Press, 1994), pp. 227-56. Though she is not happy with the term, Eleanore Stump defends a version of Thomistic substance dualism that has many (but not all) things in common with the view we are defending. See Eleanore Stump, "Non-Cartesian Substance Dualism and Materialism Without Reductionism," *Faith and Philosophy* 12 (October 1995): 505-31. William Hasker develops a different view that, although different from traditional versions of substance dualism, is certainly closer to substance dualism than to physicalism or property dualism. See William Hasker, "Emergentism," *Religious Studies* 18 (December 1982): 473-88; "Brains, Persons and Eternal Life," *Christian Scholar's Review* 12 (1983): 294-309, "Brains and Persons," in *The Reality of Christian Learning,* ed. by Harold Heie and David L. Wolfe (Grand Rapids, Mich.: Eerdmans, 1987), pp. 181-203; and "Concerning the Unity of Consciousness," *Christian Scholar's Review* 12 (October 1995): 532-47.

[6]Compare Howard Robinson, "Aristotelian Dualism," in *Oxford Studies in Ancient Philosophy* (Oxford: Oxford University Press, 1983), pp. 123-44.

[7]For more on this, see Richard Connell, *Substance and Modern Science* (Notre Dame, Ind.: University of Notre Dame Press, 1988), pp. 89-118, 185-201.

[8]See Alvin Plantinga, *Warrant and Proper Function* (New York: Oxford University Press, 1993), pp. 194-215, esp. pp. 199-211.

[9]We are setting aside further qualifications (e.g., the presence of the proper environment in which the organism and its properly functioning part is placed) for brevity of exposition. See Plantinga, *Warrant,* p. 236 note 26 for more details about proper function. We have modified his presentation to take into account the role of an organism's essence in unpacking the notion of proper function.

[10]Jonathan Wells, "The Dogma of DNA," *Bible-Science News* 31, no. 8 (1993): 15.

[11]Goodwin, *How the Leopard,* p. 3. Compare J. M. Barry, "Informational DNA: A Useful Concept?" *Trends in Biochemical Sciences* 11 (1986): 317-18; Brian C. Goodwin, "What Are the Causes of Morphology?" *BioEssays* 5 (1985): 32-36; Michael Locke, "Is There Somatic Inheritance of Intracellular Patterns?" *Journal of Cell Science* 96 (1990): 563-67; Michael Polanyi, "Life's Irreducible Structure," *Science* 160 (June 1968): 1308-12; Richmond T. Prehn, "Cancers Beget Mutations Versus Mutations Beget Cancers," *Cancer Research* 54 (October 1994): 5296-300; Jonathan Wells, "The History and Limits of Genetic Engineering," *International Journal on the Unity of the Sciences* 5 (summer 1992): 137-50.

[12]Wells, "Dogma of DNA," p. 13.

[13]For a critique of evolution, see J. P. Moreland, ed., *The Creation Hypothesis* (Downers Grove, Ill.: InterVarsity Press, 1994).

[14]H. F. Nijhout, "Metaphors and the Role of Genes in Development," *BioEssays* 12 (September 1990): 442.

[15]Goodwin, *How the Leopard,* pp. xi-xii, 3, 37, 39-40, 43-44, 77-78, 172, 175-76, 177-79, 186, 196-200.

[16]Compare Etienne Gilson, *From Aristotle to Darwin and Back Again* (Notre Dame, Ind.: University of Notre Dame Press, 1984).

[17]Jeffrey H. Boyd has shown in detail that there is a modern translational tendency to remove *soul* from our renderings of relevant scriptural texts. See Jeffrey H. Boyd, *Affirming the Soul* (Cheshire, Conn.: Soul Research Institute, 1994), pp. 217-25.

[18]For more on this, see Swinburne, *Evolution of the Soul,* pp. 11-16, 180-96, 200-219.

[19]Compare ibid., pp. 203-19; Moreland, *Creation Hypothesis,* chap. 7.

[20]See J. P. Moreland, "Searle's Biological Naturalism and the Argument from Consciousness," *Faith and Philosophy* 15 (January 1998): 68-91; John Haldane, "The Mystery of Existence," *Aristotelian Society* 96 (1996): 261-67.

[21]See John Gilmore, *Probing Heaven* (Grand Rapids, Mich.: Baker, 1989), pp. 130-33.

[22]Thomas S. Hall, *Ideas of Life and Matter* (Chicago: University of Chicago Press, 1969), pp. 285-87. Compare Maurice Merleau-Ponty, *The Structure of Behavior* (Boston: Beacon, 1963), pp. 145-60; Gilson, *From Aristotle to Darwin,* chaps. 1-2, 5; David Hull, *Philosophy of Biological Science* (Englewood Cliffs, N. J.: Prentice-Hall, 1974), pp. 125-41; William Coleman, *Biology in the Nineteenth Century* (Cambridge: Cambridge University Press, 1977), pp. 146-59; Timothy Lenoir, *The Strategy of Life* (Chicago: University of Chicago Press, 1989), pp. 9-12.

[23]Both Cartesian and Thomistic substance dualisms provide tremendous resources to capture much of what contemporary psychological theory says about the self and its functioning. See Nancy S. Duvall, ed., "Special Issue: Perspectives on the Self/Soul," *Journal of Psychology and Theology* 26 (spring 1998).

[24]Compare A. A. Howsepian, "Who or What Are We?" *Review of Metaphysics* 45 (March 1992): 483-502.

[25]Creationism is fairly familiar to most people today. For an analysis of traducianism, see C. A. Dubray, "Traducianism," in *The Catholic Encyclopedia,* ed. Charles G. Herbermann et al., (New York: Encyclopedia Press, 1912), pp. 14-15; J. E. Royce, "Soul, Human, Origin of," in *New Catholic Encyclopedia* (Washington, D.C.: McGraw-Hill, 1967), 13:470-71; P. B. T. Bilaniuk, "Traducianism," in *New Catholic Encyclopedia,* 13:230; William G. T. Shedd, *Dogmatic Theology,* vol. 2 (1888; Grand Rapids, Mich.: Zondervan, 1988), pp. 3-94; Charles Hodge, *Systematic Theology,* vol. 2 (Grand Rapids, Mich.: Eerdmans, 1975), pp. 65-78.

[26]Aquinas himself believed that as the fertilized egg developed, it was animated first by a purely vegetative, then by a sensitive and finally by an intellectual, human soul. See his *Summa Theologiae,* 1.A.Q.118, article 2, reply obj. 2.

[27]Compare Swinburne, *Evolution of the Soul,* p. 199.

[28]For defenses of dualist interaction, see Keith Yandell, "A Defense of Dualism," *Faith and Philosophy* 12 (October 1995): 551-53; J. P. Moreland, "A Defense of Substance Dualism," in *Christian Perspectives on Being Human: A Multidisciplinary Approach to Integration,* ed. J. P. Moreland and David M. Ciocchi (Grand Rapids, Mich.: Baker, 1993), pp. 75-77.

[29]For a defense of this view of chemical change, see Connell, *Substance and Modern Science,* pp. 81-87; cf. Enrico Cantore, *Atomic Order* (Cambridge, Mass.: MIT Press, 1969), pp. 254-80; J. Van Brakel, "Chemistry as the Science of the Transformation of Substances," *Synthese* 111 (June 1997): 253-82.

[30]Lawrence Becker, "Human Being: The Boundaries of the Concept," in *What Is a Person,* ed. Michael F. Goodman (Clifton, N.J.: Humana, 1988), p. 60 (originally published in *Philosophy and Public Affairs* 4 [1975]: 334-59).

[31]See Robert N. Wennberg, *Life in the Balance* (Grand Rapids, Mich.: Eerdmans, 1985), p. 118.

[32]Compare J. P. Moreland and John Mitchell, "Is the Human Person a Substance or Property-Thing?" *Ethics and Medicine* 11 (1995): 50-55. This article contains a response to the view that the properties of personhood are threshold properties.

[33]It is important to note that DNA cannot solve this problem because a DNA molecule has the same features possessed by the human body in this regard: it is a multiplicity in need of organic unification, and it has a distinctively human set of capacities and properties owned by and grounded in the human soul. For more on this, see the discussion below.

[34]Swinburne, a Cartesian dualist, argues that persons still exist while asleep in that the sleeping body will again, by normal processes (or by events like being shaken), give rise to a conscious life that is the life of the person existing before sleep. He adds to this the idea that a person still exists while the soul is not functioning just in case normal bodily processes or available artificial techniques will, in a fairly speedy way, restore or give rise to functioning. See Swinburne, *Evolution of the Soul,* pp. 176-79. Note that the soul's functioning is spelled out strictly in terms of mental functioning (e.g., having desires, thoughts, beliefs, volitions, sensations). Absent is the soul's role in sustaining bodily functioning. It would appear that this omission is what gives Swinburne's discussion an aura of arbitrariness, which he himself acknowledges.

[35]John Locke *An Essay Concerning Human Understanding* (Dover ed.) 2.28.22.

[36]Ralph Cudworth, as cited in John Yolton, *Thinking Matter: Materialism in Eighteenth-Century Britain* (Minneapolis: University of Minnesota Press, 1983), p. 122.

Chapter 7: The Moral & Metaphysical Status of the Unborn
[1]Bonnie Steinbock, *Life Before Birth: The Moral and Legal Status of Embryos and Fetuses* (New York: Oxford University Press, 1992), p. 5.

[2]Naomi Wolf, "Our Bodies, Our Souls," in *The Abortion Controversy: Twenty-Five Years After Roe v. Wade,* ed. Louis P. Pojman and Francis J. Beckwith, 2nd ed. (Belmont, Calif.: Wadsworth, 1998), p. 405 (originally published in *The New Republic,* October 16, 1995, pp. 26-35).

[3]Some have suggested that the notion of the immaterial soul is not necessary for many of the protections of vulnerable persons and that, in some cases, it may even be harmful in the effects that such a view produces. For example, Stephen G. Post has argued that belief in the soul contributed significantly to such moral anathemas as slavery, denial of pleasure in sex and patriarchy in gender relations. However, these practices had their roots in a gnostic view of the soul, which substantially downplayed the place of the body, making it

irrelevant at best and an obstacle to growth of the soul at worst. We would hold that slavery and patriarchy represent a deeply flawed understanding of dualism. The dualism we
are defending does not downplay the body. We would suggest that in the Scripture, there
is just as much hope for the body as there is for the soul (see, e.g., 1 Cor 6:18-20). The
body is not in any way inferior to the soul, and any practices that are premised on such an
understanding of the body are not consistent with biblical teaching. Simply because one
believes in the existence of the soul does not commit one to a gnostic view of the body.
Institutions such as slavery clearly do not follow from belief in the soul. For further discus-
sion, see Stephen G. Post, "A Moral Case for Non-Reductive Physicalism," in *Whatever
Happened to the Soul?* ed. Warren S. Brown, Nancey Murphy and H. Newton Malony
(Minneapolis: Fortress, 1998), pp. 195-212. For a work similar in design to *Whatever
Happened* but defending a substance dualist view of human nature, see J. P. Moreland and
David Chiocchi, eds., *Christian Perspectives on Being Human: A Multidisciplinary
Approach to Integration* (Grand Rapids, Mich.: Baker, 1993).

[4]See, e.g., the statement by Gerald M. Edelman that "clothing consciousness studies with
ethical restraint is one of the largest challenges of our time" (Allen C. Guelzo, "Soulless,"
Books and Culture [January-Febuary 1998], p. 23). The clear implication is that providing
adequately grounded moral parameters for people within a physicalist view of the person
has yet to be done satisfactorily. Others such as Daniel Dennett (*Consciousness Explained*
[New York: Little Brown, 1991]) and Francis Crick (*The Astonishing Hypothesis: The Scientific Search for the Soul* [New York: BasicBooks, 1991]) reject the traditional notion of
moral responsibility, and it is not clear precisely what they propose in its place.

[5]Francis Brown, S. R. Driver and C. A. Briggs, *Hebrew and English Lexicon of the Old Testament,* 5th ed. (Oxford: Oxford University Press, 1977).

[6]Of course, there is more to the theological understanding of the personhood of the
unborn than the continuity of personal identity. The doctrine of the incarnation, e.g., suggests strongly that the image of God is possessed by the unborn at the earliest stages of
pregnancy. The Gospels point out the significance of the incarnation not only at Jesus'
birth, but also at the first indication that Mary was pregnant with him. In Luke 1:39-45,
Mary visits her sister Elizabeth, when Mary is only a few weeks pregnant. Elizabeth and
her son, John the Baptist, whom she is carrying in the womb, both recognize the significance of Mary's pregnancy. That is, the momentous nature of the incarnation was recognized at Jesus' conception and Mary's first awareness of her pregnancy, not solely at his
birth. For further discussion of this, see Scott B. Rae, *Ethical Issues in Embryo and Fetal
Research and Experimentation* (Philadelphia: Crossroads, 1997), pp. 6-18.

[7]For more on this text, see Umberto Cassuto, *Exodus* (Jerusalem: Magnes, 1967), p. 275;
Gleason Archer, *Encyclopedia of Bible Difficulties* (Grand Rapids, Mich.: Zondervan,
1982), pp. 246-49.

[8]Bruce K. Waltke, "Reflections from the Old Testament on Abortion," *Journal of the Evangelical Theological Society* 19 (1976): 3.

[9]Some philosophers and bioethicists suggest that newborns up to a few months or even up
to one year old do not meet the criteria for personhood. We will discuss the work of some
who hold these views, such as Michael Tooley, Peter Singer and Helga Kuhse, later in this
chapter.

[10]Recently the focus of the abortion debate has shifted slightly from the personhood of the
unborn to the autonomy of the pregnant woman in making choices about her body. We
will address this modification of the pro-choice argument later in this chapter.

[11]*Roe v. Wade,* 410 U.S. 113 (1973).

[12]Viability actually is different for each unborn child, and medical technology has successfully pushed viability back to as early as twenty-weeks gestation. An unborn child is gener-

ally considered viable at roughly twenty-four to twenty-six weeks.

[13] *Doe v. Bolton,* 410 U.S. 179 (1973).

[14] *Doe v. Bolton,* 192-93.

[15] For example, a California abortion practitioner testified before the California legislature that his practice provided partial-birth abortions in most cases for birth-control reasons unrelated to the health risks to the mother of continuing the pregnancy. See Katherine Dowling, "What Constitutes a Quality Life?" *Los Angeles Times,* August 28, 1996, p. B9.

[16] Until 1989, the Court struck down virtually every attempt to limit a woman's access to abortion. The exceptions to this include the *Webster* decision (*Webster v. Reproductive Health Services,* 109 S. Ct. 3040 [1989]), which allowed states to deny public funding and the use of public facilities for abortion, and the *Casey* decision (*Planned Parenthood v. Casey* 112 S. Ct. 2791 [1992]), which allowed states to impose a twenty-four-hour waiting period and parental consent for a minor child. However, both these decisions strongly affirmed the constitutional right of a woman to an abortion.

[17] The law in Minnesota provides this: Minnesota Statutes, 609.2661(1), 609.2662(1). The Minnesota Supreme Court ruled that the fetal-homicide law is consistent with the Constitution. See *State v. Merrill* (C7-89-766).

[18] Steinbock, *Life Before Birth,* pp. 89-90. In Massachusetts, see *Commonwealth v Cass* (392 Mass. 799, 467 N.E. 2d 1324 [1984]). Many states do not share the view of the Massachusetts Supreme Court, however. I am indebted to Steinbock's discussion of the legal status of unborn children for this section.

[19] *Craig v. IMT Insurance Co.* (118/86-535) (Iowa).

[20] Tamar Lewin, "South Carolina Justices Expand Child Abuse to Fetus," *New York Times,* November 1, 1997, p. A1. Other state supreme courts (Florida, Kentucky, Nevada, Ohio and Wisconsin), however, have struck down similar laws.

[21] George F. Will, "Fetuses as Carolinians," *Newsweek,* June 8, 1998, 78.

[22] See the decision of the New York Supreme Court in *Kelly v. Gregory* 282 A.D. 542d, 125 N.Y. S. 2d 696 (1953).

[23] Steinbock, *Life Before Birth,* p. 101. Steinbock admits and fears that the recognition of fetal personhood in these cases might lead to further protection of fetal rights with, in her view, disastrous consequences for pregnant women.

[24] See the discussion of this point in Thomas A. Shannon, "Fetal Status: Sources and Implications," *Journal of Medicine and Philosophy* 22, no. 5 (1997): 415-22.

[25] See, e.g., the recently issued report on human cloning and its public-policy recommendations. The National Bioethics Advisory Committee, commissioned by President Clinton, suggested that "for the purposes of recommending public policy in a democratic society, the Commission was also interested in the extent to which moral arguments in the various religious traditions rest on premises accessible to others outside those traditions. . . . Some theological analyses provide answers to their adherents, but are incapable of serving as the sole basis for policy making in a religiously diverse nation committed to the separation of church and state" (*Cloning Human Beings: Report and Recommendations of the National Bioethics Advisory Commission* [Rockville, Md.: National Bioethics Advisory Commission, June 1997], pp. 39, 93).

[26] See, e.g., the National Institutes of Health Human Embryo Research Panel's report, in which the panel says, "Public policy employs reasoning that is understandable in terms that are independent of a particular religious, theological *or philosophical* perspective, and it requires weighing of arguments and evidence in light of the best available information and scientific evidence" (*Report of the Human Embryo Research Panel* [Washington, D.C.: National Institutes of Health, September 27, 1994], pp. 50-51, emphasis

added).

[27]For further discussion on this complicated area of religion and public policy, see the classic work by Richard John Neuhaus, *The Naked Public Square* (Grand Rapids, Mich.: Eerdmans, 1983), and the debate in Robert Audi and Nicholas Wolterstorff, *Religion in the Public Square: The Place of Religious Convictions in Political Debate* (Lanham, Md.: Rowman & Littlefield, 1997), esp. pp. 67-120.

[28]The term *inconvenience* does not do justice to the difficulty of the abortion decision that must be made when the child does not fit into the life plans of the pregnant woman.

[29]For a helpful compendium of the various positions on abortion, including those related to the personhood of the unborn, see Louis P. Pojman and Francis J. Beckwith, eds., *The Abortion Controversy: 25 Years Later* (Boston: Jones & Bartlett, 1998). Many of these classic and contemporary readings can be found in a variety of bioethics anthologies, and many of these influential articles are still included in the most up-to-date anthologies. See, e.g., Thomas A. Mappes and David DeGrazia, *Biomedical Ethics,* 4th ed. (New York: McGraw-Hill, 1996).

[30]Mary Ann Warren, "On the Moral and Legal Status of Abortion," in *Social Ethics: Morality and Social Policy,* ed. Thomas A. Mappes and Jane Zembaty, 5th ed. (New York: McGraw-Hill, 1997), pp. 11-12. Originally published in *The Monist* 57, no. 1 (1973): 43-61.

[31]Warren, "On the Moral and Legal Status," p. 440.

[32]Joseph Fletcher, "Indicators of Humanhood: A Tentative Profile of Man," *Hastings Center Report* 2 (1972): 1-4; and "Four Indicators of Humanhood: The Enquiry Matures," *Hastings Center Report* 4 (1974): 4-7. These are cited in Scott B. Rae, "Views of Human Nature at the Edges of Life: Personhood and Medical Ethics," in *Christian Perspectives on Being Human: A Multidisciplinary Approach to Integration,* ed. J. P. Moreland and David M. Ciocchi (Grand Rapids, Mich.: Baker, 1993), pp. 235-56, esp. p. 239.

[33]Warren, "On the Moral and Legal Status," p. 440.

[34]Ibid.

[35]Ibid., pp. 440-41.

[36]Ibid., p. 441.

[37]Ibid., p. 442. Warren draws an analogy to a space explorer who is captured and whose captors want to use his body parts to generate other human beings. His right to life gives him the right to escape his captors, even if it means denying the right to life of the potential people who would be created by this process. Here Warren's key analogy clearly fails, since it is only analogous to those very rare cases in which the pregnant women's life is threatened by the pregnancy. Further she confuses potential and future people, or those not yet conceived. Surely there is a difference between fetuses, who are actualizing capacities in development, and people who exist only in the imagination.

[38]Ibid., p. 443.

[39]Ibid.

[40]Here she cites the example of primitive cultures existing in subsistence conditions in which infanticide is practiced as a matter of survival. Warren is hesitant to condemn those peoples for such a practice.

[41]Ibid., p. 444.

[42]This view is commonly attributed to philosopher Joel Feinberg, "The Rights of Animals and Unborn Generations," in *Philosophy and Environmental Crisis,* ed. William T. Blackstone (Athens: University of Georgia Press, 1974), pp. 43-68.

[43]Michael Tooley, "In Defense of Abortion and Infanticide," in *The Abortion Controversy: A Reader,* ed. Louis P. Pojman and Francis J. Beckwith (Boston: Jones & Bartlett, 1994), p. 209 (originally appeared in Joel Feinberg, *The Problem of Abortion* [Belmont, Calif.: Wads-

worth, 1984]). Tooley's original argument was made and refined in "Abortion and Infanticide," *Philosophy and Public Affairs* 2 (1972): 37-65; 3 (1973): 419-32.

[44]Tooley, "In Defense," pp. 209-10.

[45]Ibid., pp. 199-200.

[46]Peter Singer and Helga Kuhse, *Should the Baby Live?* (New York: Oxford University Press, 1985), pp. 121-32.

[47]Ibid., p. 133.

[48]Steinbock, *Life Before Birth*, p. 5. Steinbock, like Tooley, is applying the interests of Feinberg (see n. 40 above), and she admits her debt to Feinberg on pp. 10, 14.

[49]Ibid., pp. 5, 15.

[50]This view is echoed by Ronald E. Cranford and David Randolph Smith, "Consciousness: The Most Critical Moral (Constitutional) Standard for Human Personhood," *American Journal of Law and Medicine* 13 (1987): 233-48.

[51]Steinbock, *Life Before Birth*, pp. 14-15.

[52]Ibid., p. 41.

[53]Ibid., p. 25. Steinbock takes this point from Joel Feinberg, *Harm to Others* (New York: Oxford University Press, 1987), p. 34.

[54]Steinbock, *Life Before Birth*, p. 26.

[55]Ibid., p. 37.

[56]We would not want to argue for this point, however.

[57]Ibid., p.57.

[58]Ibid.

[59]Even someone with a radical view such as Singer's admits this point. He cites all the proposed decisive moments during gestation and admits that none provide adequate grounding for personhood. Of course, he does not suggest a view like ours. See Peter Singer, *Rethinking Life and Death: The Collapse of Traditional Ethics* (New York: St. Martin's Press, 1994), pp. 100-103. For further critique of these various decisive moments, see Scott B. Rae, *Brave New Families: Biblical Ethics and Reproductive Technologies* (Grand Rapids, Mich.: Baker, 1996), pp. 96-100.

[60]This is Steinbock's counter to the illustration she poses: She maintains that this illustration suggests the argument from potential has persuasive force. She suggests that "we extend moral status to the temporarily unconscious neonate because she is like a normal infant in all respects save one, and that deficiency can be easily remedied" (Steinbock, *Life Before Birth*, pp. 60-62). The other difference she suggests has nothing to do with personhood: it is the fact that the fetus needs the womb of the mother as its life-support system, unlike the baby already born. We would argue that this is only a difference in degree of dependence, because the neonate is hardly independent. This argument from a woman's right to her own body was addressed earlier in this chapter, and it was shown that this assumes the conclusion prior to making the argument.

[61]Interestingly, this is a point to which Steinbock admits. In response to the second scenario, she states that "it is hard to think of a fully developed, otherwise healthy baby not having a welfare of her own, simply because she is temporarily unconscious" (ibid., p. 61).

[62]Lawrence Becker, "Human Being: The Boundaries of the Concept," in *What Is a Person?* ed. Michael F. Goodman (Clifton, N.J.: Humana Press, 1988), p. 60. Originally published in *Philosophy and Public Affairs* 4 (1975): 334-59. For further development of this point and critique, see Scott B. Rae and John A. Mitchell, "The Moral Status of Fetuses and Embryos," in *The Silent Subject: Reflections on the Unborn in Society,* ed. Brad Stetson (Westport, Conn.: Praeger, 1995). Steinbock suggests this point when she comments that "a fetus is still in the process of becoming a human being." See Steinbock, *Life Before Birth*, p. 61. This gradualist view is widely held, and it was recently put forth by the

National Institutes of Health Human Embryo Research Panel in their 1994 deliberations on the personhood of embryos. See chapter eight for further discussion of the panel's report.
[63]Becker, "Human Being," p. 60.
[64]Roderick Chisholm, *On Metaphysics* (Minneapolis: University of Minnesota Press, 1989), pp. 59-60.
[65]One representative of this view is Christian Perring, "Degrees of Personhood," *Journal of Medicine and Philosophy* 22 (1997): 173-97. One of the reasons Perring comes to this view and many of its uncomfortable conclusions is that he has rejected substance dualism and the notion of the soul. See esp. pp. 180-81, where naturalism is his starting point.
[66]Perring is certainly right on this point. Perhaps someone like Steinbock is an exception to this point since sentience is more of an all-or-nothing property.
[67]Perring suggests that allowing exceptions to the absolute right to life implies a graded view of personhood, when nothing of the sort is true. See Perring, "Degrees of Personhood," pp. 190-91.
[68]This is essentially the position of philosopher Jane English, "Abortion and the Concept of a Person," in *The Abortion Controversy: Twenty-Five Years After Roe v. Wade,* ed. Louis P. Pojman and Francis J. Beckwith, 2nd ed. (Belmont, Calif.: Wadsworth, 1998), pp. 315-24 (originally published in *Canadian Journal of Philosophy* 5, no. 3 [1975]: 233-43).
[69]Wolf, "Our Bodies," pp. 400-13. Even Singer suggests that to unlock the abortion deadlock the participants need to move beyond the personhood issue to the question of why it is wrong to take a human life. In other words, even if the unborn is a person, it still may be permissible to take its life. See Singer, *Rethinking Life and Death,* p. 105.
[70]Wolf, "Our Bodies," p. 405.
[71]Ibid., p. 408.
[72]This is the classic argument by Judith Jarvis Thomson in which she equates a woman with an unwanted pregnancy to a person who had been kidnapped and hooked up to donate blood to a world-famous violinist. The violinist is totally dependent on the connection to the kidnapped person for his life, and if the kidnapped person were to unplug the intravenous line connecting them, the violinist would die. Therefore the kidnapped person must stay connected to him for nine months. Thomson concludes that most people would regard such a demand as outrageous. Thus she concludes that even if the fetus is a person, its right to life does not give it the right to the mother's body against her will. The response to this argument is that such an analogy only fits the cases in which sex leading to conception is nonconsensual. Also Thomson confuses killing with withholding treatment, which are indeed two very different things. Further, the fetus is anything but a stranger to the mother connected to her. Thus Thomson's analogy fails to make anything more than a narrow point about the legitimacy of abortion in cases of rape or incest. See Judith Jarvis Thomson, "A Defense of Abortion," *Philosophy and Public Affairs* 1 (1971): 47-66. For a response, see Francis J. Beckwith, "From Personhood to Bodily Autonomy: The Shifting Legal Focus of the Abortion Debate," in *Bioethics and the Future of Medicine,* ed. John F. Kilner et al. (Grand Rapids, Mich.: Eerdmans, 1995), pp. 187-98.
[73]See Wolf, "Our Bodies," pp. 409-11, for the striking use of this imagery. She states, "But how one might ask, can I square a recognition of the humanity of the fetus, and the moral gravity of destroying it, with a prochoice position? The answer can only be found in the context of a paradigm abandoned by the left and misused by the right: the paradigm of sin and redemption" (p. 409).
[74]The contours of this debate are beyond the scope of this chapter. For representative positions, see John A. Robertson, "Rights, Symbolism and Public Policy in Fetal Tissue Transplants," *Hastings Center Report* 18 (December 1988): 5-12 (who favor use of fetal tissue with very few restrictions); Alan Fine, "The Ethics of Fetal Tissue Transplants, *Hastings*

Center Report 18 (June-July 1988): 5-11 (which favors use of fetal tissue with restrictions on recipient designation and financial incentives for donation and which is the position of the 1988 report by the National Institutes of Health Panel on Human Fetal Tissue Transplantation); Kathleen Nolan, "Genug ist Genug: A Fetus Is Not a Kidney," *Hastings Center Report* 18 (December 1988): 13-17; Scott B. Rae, "Spare Parts from the Unborn?" *Christian Research Journal* (fall 1991): 28-33 (which argues against the use of fetal tissue).

[75]We should make it clear that the tissue transplants cannot cure any disease, though they can alleviate symptoms and make life more productive for Parkinson's sufferers, for example. This argument on the morality of the use of the tissue is widespread. One example can be found in Steinbock, *Life Before Birth,* p. 171.

[76]LeRoy Walters, "Ethical Issues in Experimentation on the Human Fetus," *Journal of Religious Ethics* 2 (spring 1974): 41-48.

[77]This point is made powerfully by Fr. James T. Burtchaell and James Bopp Jr. in their dissent from the 1988 National Institutes of Health Panel Report on Human Fetal Tissue Transplantation. This part of the panel's report was published as "Fetal Tissue Transplantation: The Fetus as Medical Commodity," *This World* 26 (summer 1989): 65-71, see esp. pp. 67-68.

[78]Even an advocate of the transplants such as Steinbock recognizes the force of the complicity argument. See Steinbock, *Life Before Birth,* pp. 180-83.

Chapter 8: Reproductive Technologies in Substance-Dualist Perspective
[1]Peter Singer, *Rethinking Life and Death: The Collapse of Traditional Ethics* (New York: St. Martin's Press, 1994), p. 97.

[2]George J. Annas, "A French Homunculus in a Tennessee Court," *Hastings Center Report* 19 (November-December 1989): 22. This is also cited in Bonnie Steinbock, *Life Before Birth: The Moral and Legal Status of Embryos and Fetuses* (New York: Oxford University Press, 1992), p. 215.

[3]Surrogate motherhood raises a host of complicated moral and legal issues, but none that are relevant to our discussions of personhood and bioethics. The only exception to this would be when a gestational surrogate is used and in vitro fertilization is necessary to implant the embryos in her womb. For further discussion of surrogacy, see Scott B. Rae, *The Ethics of Commercial Surrogate Motherhood* (Westport, Conn.: Praeger, 1994).

[4]The morality of using donor sperm and donor eggs is beyond the scope of this work. For discussion of those complicated issues and an assessment of most major reproductive technologies from a biblical perspective, see Scott B. Rae, *Brave New Families: Biblical Ethics and Reproductive Technologies* (Grand Rapids, Mich.: Baker, 1996).

[5]Should Chuck and Linda experience repeated failures in GIFT, ZIFT or IVF, they could try implanting more than four embryos. Couples have inserted up to seven or eight embryos on rare occasions.

[6]Rae has argued that Scripture is skeptical of third-party contributors but that Scripture is probably not clear enough on the subject to prohibit it in every case. For further discussion of this important area, see Rae, *Brave New Families,* chap. 1.

[7]Rae has argued that commercial surrogacy is indeed baby selling (*Ethics of Commercial Surrogate Motherhood,* chap. 2). The majority of the states that have passed laws on surrogacy have agreed, prohibiting the practice and the brokers who arrange and monitor the contracts for the couple hiring the surrogate. See also Martha A. Field, *Surrogate Motherhood: The Moral and Legal Issues* (Cambridge, Mass.: Harvard University Press, 1988).

[8]For example, in Rae's work on surrogate motherhood, the overwhelming majority of material in the literature comes from law reviews or law journals. The bioethics literature

contains discussion of these issues, but the best and most thorough treatment typically comes from the legal arena.

[9]See, e.g., John A. Robertson, *Children of Choice: Freedom and the New Reproductive Technologies* (Princeton, N.J.: Princeton University Press, 1994), pp. 100-118. The discussion of reproductive technologies focuses on legal questions such as rights over transfer of embryos, posthumous implantation, resolving disputes over frozen embryos and access to these technologies.

[10]These are both well documented in Rae's *Brave New Families* and *Ethics of Commercial Surrogate Motherhood*. See, e.g., Scott B. Rae, "Parental Rights and the Definition of Motherhood in Surrogate Motherhood," *Southern California Review of Law and Women's Studies* 3, no. 2 (spring 1994): 219-77; Marjorie Maguire Schultz, "Reproductive Technology and Intent Based Parenthood: An Opportunity for Gender Neutrality," *Wisconsin Law Review* 2 (1990): 297-398; Andrea Stumpf, "Redefining Mother: A Legal Matrix for the New Reproductive Technologies," *Yale Law Review* 96 (1986): 197-208.

[11]The opinion of the circuit court is found in *Junior L. Davis v Mary Sue Davis v. Ray King, M.D., d/b/a Fertility Center of East Tennessee,* NO. E-14496, Circuit Court for Blount County, Tennessee, September 21, 1989. The decision of the Tennessee Supreme Court is found in *Davis v. Davis,* 842 S.W.2d 588 (Tennessee 1992). For further discussion of this enigmatic case see George J. Annas, "Crazy Making: Embryos and Gestational Mothers," *Hastings Center Report* 21 (January-February 1991): 35-38; Alexander Morgan Capron, "Parenthood and Frozen Embryos: More than Property and Privacy," *Hastings Center Report* 22 (September-October 1992): 32-33; Jerome Lejune, *The Concentration Can* (San Francisco: Ignatius Press, 1992).

[12]There is a misconception among some in academic bioethics circles on this point. For example, Steinbock, in her recent work on fetuses and embryos, suggests that "most American IVF programs do not fertilize more eggs than they plan to place in the uterus. This avoids the problem of what to do with surplus embryos, but at a price." That price is, of course, the additional financial cost to the couple and the woman's physical burden of having to reharvest eggs. In reality the clinics care very little about minimizing the number of surplus embryos. Steinbock states that "if IVF doctors did not have to worry about discarding surplus embryos, they could extract more eggs, perhaps as many as 20 or 30, and fertilize them all. If the couple did not need the surplus frozen embryos because pregnancy was achieved the first time, the extra embryos could be donated, discarded or used in research." This is precisely what occurs routinely in most infertility clinics, though harvesting twenty to thirty eggs, as Steinbock suggests is the norm, is actually a bit overstated. In fact, most extra embryos are discarded or used in research, and the donation of surplus embryos is still unusual. The reason for this is that most couples, ironically, do not want their "children" being born and raised by some other couple without their knowledge. Steinbock and others have a serious misconception of the routine practice of infertility clinics. See Steinbock, *Life Before Birth,* pp. 198-99 (she appears to be citing John A. Robertson, "Embryos, Families and Procreation: The Legal Structure of the New Reproduction," *Southern California Law Review* 59 [1986]: 948). Robertson appears to have changed his views since the publication of this 1986 article. In his *Children of Choice,* pp. 107-8, Robertson correctly describes the routine way in which infertility clinics perform IVF.

[13]This is referred to as "lifeboat implantations," the morality of which will be discussed below.

[14]We addressed this in chapter six, but we are adding more details to that discussion in this chapter.

[15]Peter Singer and Karen Dawson, "IVF Technology and the Argument from Potential," in

Embryo Experimentation: Ethical, Legal and Social Issues, ed. Peter Singer et al. (Cambridge: Cambridge University Press, 1990), pp. 76-77.

[16]Steinbock, *Life Before Birth,* pp. 59-61. See her chapter six for a more extended discussion of her view.

[17]Ibid., pp. 199-200.

[18]One of the "others" is constitutional law professor Laurence Tribe, who suggests that "it is the natural fate of an embryo *inside a woman* to come to term, making her a mother. The 'natural' fate of an embryo created in a petri dish and stored in the freezer is far less clear." See Laurence Tribe, *Abortion: The Clash of Absolutes* (New York: W. W. Norton, 1990), pp. 234-35.

[19]We are not here suggesting that the notion of "potential persons" should be used, only that it is Singer's term (and Steinbock's). Our view is that the idea of a potential person makes no sense. See the discussion of this in chapter six.

[20]Singer and Dawson, "IVF Technology," p. 87.

[21]See the application of this distinction in chapter six.

[22]Steinbock, *Life Before Birth,* p. 200. See also Singer and Dawson, "IVF Technology," pp. 82-83, where they make this same point.

[23]Annas, "A French Homunculus," p. 22.

[24]Singer and Dawson have changed the imagery slightly to now include embryos produced from natural intercourse and implantation.

[25]Singer and Dawson, "IVF Technology," pp. 79-80.

[26]Ibid., p. 80.

[27]Daniel Callahan, "The Puzzle of Profound Respect," *Hastings Center Report* 25 (January-February 1995): 39.

[28]For further discussion, see the panel's report (National Institutes of Health Human Embryo Research Panel, *Report of the Human Embryo Research Panel* [Washington, D.C.: National Institutes of Health, September 27, 1994]), commentary on the panel report in Erik Parens, ed., "What Research? Which Embryos? *Hastings Center Report* 25 (January-February 1995): 36-45, and a summary and critique of the panel's report in Scott B. Rae, *Ethical Issues in Embryo and Fetal Research and Experimentation* (Philadelphia: Crossroads, 1997), pp. 1-6.

[29]See Jeffrey Kluger, "Eggs on the Rocks," *Time,* October 27, 1997, 105-6; Traci Watson, "Storing Up Eggs for a Rainy Day," *U.S. News and World Report,* June 23, 1997, p. 49.

[30]Lejune, *Concentration Can,* pp. 35-37.

[31]Ibid., pp. 43-45.

Chapter 9: Genetic Technologies & Human Cloning

[1]James Watson as quoted in Leon Jaroff, "The Gene Hunt," *Time,* March 20, 1989, p. 62.

[2]Dorothy Nelkin and M. Susan Lindee, *The DNA Mystique: The Gene as Cultural Icon* (New York: W. H. Freeman, 1995), p. 41.

[3]Hugh Miller III, "DNA Blueprints, Personhood and Genetic Privacy," *Case Western University Health Matrix: Journal of Law-Medicine* 8 (summer 1998): 221.

[4]See, e.g., *The Boys from Brazil,* a film about a group of clones of Adolf Hitler; *Blade Runner,* a film about a population of cloned, soulless and thus subhuman beings who were forced to perform inhumane tasks; and the recent comedy *Multiplicity,* in which a harried husband clones himself three times and assigns each one to a different phase of his life.

[5]Human embryos were successfully cloned in 1993 by infertility researchers at George Washington University Medical School.

[6]See the popular account of the cloning of the first adult sheep, Dolly, in J. Madeline Nash, "The Age of Cloning," *Time,* March 10, 1997, pp. 62-67; Jeffrey Kluger, "Will We Fol-

low the Sheep?" *Time,* March 10, 1997, pp. 68-72. For a more detailed account see Gina Kolata, *Clone: The Road to Dolly and the Path Ahead* (New York: William Morrow, 1998).
[7]For readable and popular accounts of the Human Genome Project, see Jaroff, "Gene Hunt," pp. 62-71; Philip Elmer-Dewitt, "The Genetic Revolution," *Time,* January 17, 1994, pp. 46-57; J. Madeline Nash, "Riding the DNA Trail," *Time,* January 17, 1994, pp. 54-55. For a more extended discussion see Robert Shapiro, *The Human Blueprint: The Race to Unlock the Secrets of Our Genetic Script* (New York: St. Martin's Press, 1991); Daniel Kevles and Leroy Hood, eds., *The Code of Codes: Scientific and Social Issues in the Human Genome Project* (Cambridge, Mass.: Harvard University Press, 1992); George J. Annas and Sherman Elias, *Gene Mapping: Using Law and Ethics as Guides* (New York: Oxford University Press, 1992).
[8]For further discussion of this see C. Thomas Caskey, "DNA-Based Medicine: Prevention and Therapy," in *The Code of Codes: Scientific and Social Issues in the Human Genome Project,* ed. Daniel Kevles and Leroy Hood (Cambridge: Harvard University Press, 1992), pp. 112-135.
[9]The ethics of cloning human beings is beyond the scope of this work. For discussion of this from a biblical perspective see Scott B. Rae and Paul M. Cox, *Bioethics: A Christian Approach in a Pluralistic Age* (Grand Rapids, Mich.: Eerdmans, 1999), esp. chap. 3, "Medical Technology in Theological Perspective."
[10]See, e.g., Ruth Macklin, "Privacy and the Control of Genetic Information," in *Gene Mapping: Using Law and Ethics as Guides,* ed. George J. Annas and Sherman Elias (New York: Oxford University Press, 1992), pp. 157-72; Henry T. Greely, "Health Insurance, Employment Discrimination and the Genetics Revolution," in *The Code of Codes: Scientific and Social Issues in the Human Genome Project,* ed. Daniel Kevles and Leroy Hood (Cambridge, Mass.: Harvard University Press, 1992), pp. 264-80.
[11]This argument is made in more detail in Patricia King, "The Past as Prologue: Race, Class and Genetic Discrimination," in *Gene Mapping: Using Law and Ethics as Guides,* ed. George J. Annas and Sherman Elias (New York: Oxford University Press, 1992), pp. 94-114; and in Macklin, "Privacy and the Control," pp. 157-72.
[12]For extended discussion of this material, see Nelkin and Lindee, *DNA Mystique.*
[13]See, e.g., Walter Gilbert, "Vision of the Grail," in *The Code of Codes: Scientific and Social Issues in the Human Genome Project,* ed. Daniel Kevles and Leroy Hood (Cambridge, Mass.: Harvard University Press, 1992), pp. 83-97.
[14]For discussion of the religiously based issues in genetic technologies in general, see J. Robert Nelson, *On the New Frontiers of Genetics and Religion* (Grand Rapids, Mich.: Eerdmans, 1994).
[15]For a thorough discussion of these concerns about gene therapy in general and a nontechnical description of the technology of gene therapy, see LeRoy Walters and Julie Gage Palmer, *The Ethics of Human Gene Therapy* (New York: Oxford University Press, 1997).
[16]Erik Parens, "Taking Behavioral Genetics Seriously," *Hastings Center Report* 26 (July-August 1996): 13.
[17]Robert Plomin, Michael J. Owen and Peter McGuffin, "The Genetic Basis of Complex Human Behavior," *Science* 264 (1994): 1733-39; C. Robert Cloninger, Rolf Adolfsson and Nedad M. Svrakie, "Mapping Genes for Human Personality," *Nature Genetics* 12 (1996): 3-4.
[18]Evelyn Fox Keller, "Nature, Nurture and the Human Genome Project," in *The Code of Codes: Scientific and Social Issues in the Human Genome Project,* ed. Daniel Kevles and Leroy Hood (Cambridge, Mass.: Harvard University Press, 1992), pp. 281-99.
[19]Evelyne Shuster, "Determinism and Reductionism: A Greater Threat Because of the Human Genome Project?" in *Gene Mapping: Using Law and Ethics as Guides,* ed. George

J. Annas and Sherman Elias (New York: Oxford University Press, 1992), p. 124.

[20]Nelkin and Lindee, *DNA Mystique,* p. 41. The views of the genome-project community are well documented in this fine work.

[21]Gilbert, "Vision of the Grail," p. 83 (also cited in Jaroff, "Gene Hunt," p. 63).

[22]Gilbert as quoted in Miller, "DNA Blueprints, Personhood and Genetic Privacy," p. 180.

[23]Gilbert, "Vision of the Grail," p. 96.

[24]Ibid.

[25]Ibid.

[26]Gilbert as quoted in R. Lewontin, "The Science of Metamorphoses," *New York Review of Books,* April 19, 1989, p. 18.

[27]Francis Crick, *The Astonishing Hypothesis: The Scientific Search for the Soul* (New York: BasicBooks, 1994), p. 3.

[28]James D. Watson, "The Human Genome Project: Past, Present and Future," *Science* 248 (1990): 44-48.

[29]Watson as quoted in Jaroff, "Gene Hunt," p. 67.

[30]This is summarized from a more detailed account in Shuster, "Determinism and Reductionism," pp. 120-21.

[31]Howard Kaye, *The Social Meaning of Modern Biology* (New Haven, Conn.: Yale University Press, 1986), p. 55.

[32]A prime example of a prominent molecular biologist who does not share this materialistic view of the world is the current director of the Human Genome Project, Dr. Francis Collins, who is a Christian.

[33]Daniel Koshland, "Sequences and Consequences of the Human Genome," *Science* 146 (1989): 189. This editorial was based on the address given in October 1989 at the first human genome conference. In his address Koshland argued that the homeless will be one of the major groups benefiting from the information gleaned by the genome project.

[34]U.S. Congress Office of Technology Assessment, *Mapping Our Genes* (Washington, D.C.: U.S. Government Printing Office, 1988).

[35]Robert Plomin, "The Role of Inheritance in Behavior," *Science* 248 (April 13, 1990): 187.

[36]Watson gave these remarks in a speech at California Institue of Technology on May 9, 1990; cited in Keller, "Nature, Nurture," p. 294.

[37]Keller, "Nature, Nurture," p. 297.

[38]Among the numerous studies in this area, see T. J. Bouchard et al., "Sources of Human Psychological Differences: The Minnesota Study of Twins Reared Apart," *Science* 250: (1990): 223-28.

[39]See the extended discussion of libertarian free will in chapter four. A helpful discussion of this applied to the issue of genetic privacy is found in Miller, "DNA Blueprints."

[40]This is a summary of the longer discussion in chapter six.

[41]This is the same term for the activity of the soul in DNA that we employed in chapter six.

[42]Shuster, "Determinism and Reductionism," p. 122.

[43]Barbara McClintock, "The Significance of the Genome to Challenge," *Science* 226 (1984): 792-801.

[44]See, e.g., the National Bioethics Advisory Commission (NBAC) report entitled *Cloning Human Beings* (Rockville, Md.: NBAC, June 1997), which was issued within a few months of the first cloning of an adult mammal.

[45]See Gina Kolata, "Doctor Clones Human Embryos, Creates Twins," *New York Times,* October 24, 1993, p. A1.

[46]For a moral assessment of embryo cloning and a discussion of the technology, see Scott B. Rae, *Brave New Families: Biblical Ethics and Reproductive Technologies* (Grand Rapids, Mich.: Baker, 1996), pp. 169-88.

[47]See the popular discussions of this in Sharon Begley, "Little Lamb, Who Made Thee?" *Newsweek,* March 10, 1997, pp. 53-58; Nash, "Age of Cloning." pp. 62-65.

[48]NBAC, *Cloning Human Beings,* pp. 65-66.

[49]Ibid., p. 65.

[50]On these issues see, e.g., George J. Annas, "Human Cloning: A Choice or an Echo?" *Dayton Law Review* 23 (winter 1998): 247-75; Ronald Chester, "To Be, Be, Be . . . Not Just to Be: Legal and Social Implications of Cloning for Human Reproduction," *Florida Law Review* 49 (April 1997): 303-37; Katheryn Katz, "The Clonal Child: Procreative Liberty and Asexual Reproduction," *Albany Law Journal of Science and Technology* 8 (1997): 1-47; Lori B. Andrews, "Is There a Right to Clone?: Constitutional Challenges to Bans on Human Cloning," *Harvard Journal of Law and Technology* 11 (summer 1998): 643-72; Clarke Forsythe, "Human Cloning and the Constitution," *Valparaiso University Law Review* 32 (spring 1998): 469-542; Rosamond Rhodes, "Clones, Harms and Rights," *Cambridge Quarterly of Healthcare Ethics* 4 (1995): 285-90.

[51]For examples of this discussion see Thomas A. Shannon, "Human Cloning: Examining the Religious and Ethical Issues," *Valparaiso University Law Review* 32 (spring 1998): 773-92; Jan C. Heller, "Revisiting Safety as a Moral Constraint," *Valparaiso University Law Review* 32 (spring 1998): 661-78.

[52]This assumption permeates the NBAC report on cloning mentioned above. There is no direct discussion of the personhood of cloned human beings because it is assumed that the clone is a person.

[53]An example of this is the way colonies of clones were used in the film *Blade Runner.*

[54]We realize that cloned persons are not conceived in the traditional sense or the technological sense, as would be the case with IVF.

[55]One such advocate of animal rights who takes the functional criteria alone to determine personhood and rejects the genome as the minimum is Peter Singer (*Rethinking Life and Death: The Collapse of Traditional Ethics* [New York: St. Martin's Press, 1994]). He accuses those who give weight to possession of the human genome for personhood as "speciesists," or racists according to one's species.

[56]See the popular expression of this question in Robert Wright, "Can Souls Be Xeroxed?" *Time,* March 10, 1997, p. 73.

[57]Rev. Robert H. Schuller, a prominent Protestant pastor, wrote an editorial shortly after Dolly was cloned that suggested human cloning should not be allowed because scientists would be creating soulless people. See Robert H. Schuller, "The Human Soul Is Not for Cloning," *Los Angeles Times,* February 11, 1998, p. B7.

[58]See in particular the discussion of the biblical and theological basis for the soul in chapter one.

[59]See the discussion of this in chapter six.

[60]See the discussion of the starfish and the souls of animals in chapter six.

[61]Naomi Wolf, "Our Bodies, Our Souls," in *The Abortion Controversy: Twenty-Five Years After Roe v. Wade,* ed. Louis P. Pojman and Francis J. Beckwith, 2nd ed. (Belmont, Calif.: Wadsworth, 1998), p. 405 (originally published in *The New Republic,* October 16, 1995, pp. 26-35).

[62]For an elaboration and a critique of this defense of abortion, see Francis J. Beckwith, "From Personhood to Bodily Autonomy: The Shifting Legal Focus of the Abortion Debate," in *Bioethics and the Future of Medicine,* ed. John F. Kilner et al. (Grand Rapids, Mich.: Eerdmans, 1995), pp. 187-98.

[63]For a fuller description of this procedure, see Sheryl Stolberg, "Reproductive Research Far Outpaces Public Policy," *Los Angeles Times,* April 29, 1997: A1, pp. 12-13.

[64]A good example of this discussion is found in Susan B. Mattingly, "The Maternal-Fetal

Dyad: Exploring the Two-Patient Obstetric Model," *Hastings Center Report* 22 (January-February 1992): 13-18.

[65]For examples of this discussion, see George J. Annas, "Forced Cesareans: The Most Unkindest Cut of All," *Hastings Center Report* 12 (June 1982): 16-17, 45; Frank A. Chervenak and Laurence B. McCullough, "Justified Limits on Refusing Intervention," *Hastings Center Report* 21 (March-April 1991): 12-18; Veronika E. B. Kolder et. al., "Court-Ordered Obstetrical Interventions," *New England Journal of Medicine* 316, no. 19 (1987): 1192-96.

[66]For example, we would acknowledge that animals can also be patients for a veterinarian, and that alone does not confer on them the status of persons.

[67]John Perry as quoted in K. C. Cole, "Unsettling Our Sense of Self," *Los Angeles Times,* April 26, 1997: A1, p.13.

Chapter 10: Euthanasia, Physician-Assisted Suicide & Care of Persons at the End of Life

[1]James Rachels, *The End of Life* (New York: Oxford University Press, 1986), p. 26.

[2]Robert N. Wennberg, *Terminal Choices: Euthanasia, Suicide and the Right to Die* (Grand Rapids, Mich.: Eerdmans, 1989), p. 159.

[3]A full treatment of the arguments for and against physician-assisted suicide is beyond the scope of this chapter. For further discussion of this subject, see chap. 7 of Scott B. Rae, *Moral Choices: An Introduction to Ethics,* 2nd ed. (Grand Rapids, Mich.: Zondervan, 2000); J. P. Moreland and Norman L. Geisler, *The Life and Death Debate: Moral Issue of Our Time* (Westport, Conn.: Praeger, 1993).

[4]See *Glucksburg v. Washington* and *Vacco v. Quill,* 117 S. Ct. 2258 (1997), landmark cases in which the Court refused to recognize a constitutionally protected right of the terminally ill to die with a physician's assistance.

[5]In July 1998, Jack Kervorkian's lawyer, Geoffrey Fieger, announced that he had won the Democratic Party's nomination for governor of Michigan.

[6]The case of Karen Ann Quinlan in the mid-1970s provided the legal right for competent patients (or for their surrogate decision-makers acting on their behalf) to refuse any life-sustaining treatment. This was rightly considered a watershed case in the development of patients' rights to decide their course of treatment, including life-sustaining treatment. In *Quinlan* 255A. 2d 665, (1976).

[7]In *Cruzan v. Missouri Department of Health,* 110 S. Ct. 2481 (1990), the U.S. Supreme Court recognized the rights of a PVS patient to refuse life-sustaining treatment, including medically provided nutrition and hydration. The right to refuse treatment is not the same thing as the right to enlist a physician's assistance in suicide. Literature on the issue of the removal of food and water for PVS patients is vast. See, e.g., Joanne Lynn, ed., *By No Extraordinary Means* (Bloomington: Indiana University Press, 1989).

[8]For a summary of the case for and against providing medical means of nutrition and hydration for the PVS patient, see Scott B. Rae, "Views of Human Nature at the Edges of Life: Personhood and Medical Ethics," in *Christian Perspectives on Being Human: A Multidisciplinary Approach to Integration,* ed. J. P. Moreland and David M. Ciocchi (Grand Rapids, Mich.: Baker, 1993).

[9]See, e.g., Robert Veatch, "The Impending Collapse of the Whole-Brain Definition of Death," *Hastings Center Report* 23 (July-August 1993): 18-24.

[10]For further discussion of the argument from mercy, see the section "Caring for Human Persons at the End of Life" later in this chapter.

[11]Rachels is a good example of such advocates. See Rachels, *The End of Life,* pp. 151-54.

[12]Ibid., pp. 158-60.

[13]Ibid., p. 154. We would suggest that the standard for pain management is not elimination of pain but adequate control of pain. Elimination of pain, short of assistance in suicide, is often an unrealistic goal of palliative care.

[14]There is increasing documentation of favorable outcomes for patients who received adequate amounts of appropriate pain-control agents such as opioids. See, e.g., Russell K. Portenoy, "Opioid Therapy for Chronic Nonmalignant Pain: A Clinicians' Perspective," *Journal of Law, Medicine and Ethics* 24 (1996): 296-309; Paul H. Coluzzi, "A Model for Pain Management in Terminal Illness and Cancer Care," *Journal of Care Management* 2, no. 4 (1996): 2-8.

[15]See, e.g., David L. Ralston, "Pain Management: Texas Legislative and Regulatory Update," *Journal of Law, Medicine and Health Care* 24 (1996): 328-37; Shannon Brownlee and Joannie M. Schrof, "The Quality of Mercy," *U.S. News and World Report,* March 17, 1997, pp. 54-67.

[16]Rachels admits that utilitarianism as a moral theory has its flaws, but he holds that if actions improve the general welfare of the parties involved, then that merits serious considerations. See Rachels, *The End of Life,* p. 157.

[17]For empirical evidence on the incidence of nonvoluntary euthanasia, see Herbert Hendin, Chris Rutenfrans and Zbigniew Zylicz, "Physician Assisted Suicide and Euthanasia in the Netherlands: Lessons from the Dutch," *Journal of the American Medical Association* 277, no. 21 (1997): 1720-22; John Keown, "The Law and Practice of Euthanasia in the Netherlands," *Law Quarterly Review* (January 1992): 51-78; John Keown, "On Regulating Death," *Hastings Center Report* 22 (March-April 1992): 39-43; Carlos Gomez, *Regulating Death: Euthanasia and the Case of the Netherlands* (New York: Free Press, 1991).

[18]For more on the limits on autonomy in PAS, see Daniel Callahan, "When Self-Determination Runs Amok," *Hastings Center Report* 22 (March-April 1992): 52-55.

[19]One other philosopher who takes a similar view of personhood and applies it to the terminally ill is Peter Singer. See his *Rethinking Life and Death: The Collapse of Traditional Ethics* (New York: St. Martin's Press, 1994), which is cited throughout chapter seven.

[20]Rachels, *End of Life,* p. 5.

[21]Ibid., p. 26.

[22]Ibid., p. 27.

[23]Ibid., pp. 32-33.

[24]Ibid., p. 54. For more discussion on this landmark case in bioethics, see Lonnie D. Kliever, ed., *Dax's Case: Essays in Medical Ethics and Human Meaning* (Dallas: Southern Methodist University Press, 1989).

[25]Rachels does insist that there is no morally relevant difference between killing and allowing someone to die. That distinction is beyond the scope of this chapter. For discussion of this point in more detail, see Rachels, "Active and Passive Euthanasia," in *Killing and Letting Die,* ed. Bonnie Steinbock and Alastair Norcross (New York: Fordham University Press, 1994) pp. 112-19; J. P. Moreland, "James Rachels and the Active Euthanasia Debate," *Journal of the Evangelical Theological Society* 31 (March 1988): 81-94; and J. P. Moreland, review of *The End of Life,* by James Rachels, *The Thomist* 53 (October 1989): 714-22.

[26]Rachels, *The End of Life,* p. 55.

[27]Ibid., p. 59.

[28]See the discussion of Bonnie Steinbock's views on the personhood of the unborn in chapter seven.

[29]This example is parallel to the example (touched on in chapter seven) given by Steinbock in which a small child will awake from a temporary coma. Even Steinbock is uncomfortable with her interests view in such a situation. The same criticism that we lodged against

Steinbock applies here to Rachels.

[30]The incidence of euthanasia without consent in places like the Netherlands is striking. See note 17 for documentation on this point.

[31]Rachels, *The End of Life,* p. 55.

[32]Ronald E. Cranford and David Randolph Smith, "Consciousness: The Most Critical (Constitutional) Standard for Human Personhood," *American Journal of Law and Medicine* 13, no. 2-3 (1992): 237. For further discussion of the PVS, see Ronald E. Cranford, "Patients with Permanent Loss of Consciousness," in *By No Extraordinary Means,* ed. Joanne Lynn (Bloomington: Indiana University Press, 1989).

[33]President's Commission for the Study of Ethical Problems in Medicine and Biomedical and Behavioral Research, *Deciding to Forego Life Sustaining Treatment* (Washington, D.C.: Government Printing Office, 1983), pp. 174-75.

[34]For further discussion of this, see Ronald E. Cranford, "Termination of Treatment in the Persistent Vegetative State," *Seminars in Neurology* 4 (1981): 36-44. The literature on futile treatment is voluminous. For a summary of the debate see Scott B. Rae and Paul M. Cox, *Christian Perspectives in Bioethics* (Grand Rapids, Mich.: Eerdmans, 1999), pp. 239-40. In our view, treatment can be discontinued from terminally ill patients if it is futile or if it results in a greater burden than benefit to the patient. It can also be removed if it is requested by a competent adult or a surrogate decsion-maker effecting the patient's clear wishes.

[35]American Academy of Neurology, "Position of the American Academy of Neurology on Certain Aspects of the Care and Management of the Persistent Vegetative State Patient," *Neurology* (1989): 125-26.

[36]The following discussion about the personhood of the PVS patient can easily apply to these other two classes of permanently unconscious patients: the permanently comatose and the anencephalic infant.

[37]*Cruzan v. Director, Missouri Department of Health,* 110 S. Ct. 2481 (1990).

[38]See the extended discussion and critique of the interests view of personhood of Bonnie Steinbock in chapter seven.

[39]Cranford and Smith, "Consciousness," pp. 233-34. Many others make a similar case. See, e.g., Michael B. Green and Daniel Wikler, "Brain Death and Personal Identity," *Philosophy and Public Affairs* 9 (1980): 105-6 (emphasis added).

[40]Cranford and Smith, "Consciousness," pp. 234-44.

[41]Ibid., p. 233.

[42]To be fair, it is not clear whether or not Cranford and Smith advocate taking organs from anencephalics prior to their legal death. See ibid., p. 246.

[43]Ibid., pp. 246-47.

[44]See, e.g., Veatch, "Impending Collapse," pp. 18-24.

[45]Whether or not the definition of death should be changed from whole-brain to higher-brain is still debated today. That discussion is beyond the scope of this work. What is important is that those who advocate higher-brain death criteria do not advocate separating the concept of a human being and a human person. They maintain a unity of the concept of personhood and argue that the way in which society should view the death of a human person should change.

[46]Wennberg, *Terminal Choices,* pp. 159-60 (emphasis added). A similar view, though with some differences, is taken in Robert V. Rakestraw, "The Persistent Vegetative State and the Withdrawal of Nutrition and Hydration," *Journal of the Evangelical Theological Society* 35, no. 3 (1992): 389-405; see esp. pp. 401-3. Rakestraw suggests that "as we study the Scriptures on the image of God concept we find that to be the representatives of God on earth presupposes some capacity, either actual or potential, for self-awareness and self-direction, for relationships and for the exercise of authority over creation" (p. 401). Recognizing that

potential for expression of these capacities is important and in our view, undermines the notion of personhood based on the above functional capacities. For to admit that potential for expressing capacities is important is to imply that there is something else besides those capacities that gives value and rights to the person with the potential to develop them. This is particularly the case since Rakestraw rightly rejects the notion of a "potential person." We would argue that the argument for potential suggests a substance view of a person. There is no reason why a preconscious fetus should differ in moral status than a PVS patient. If potential suggests an essence in which the expression of those capacities is grounded, then there is no reason why the PVS patient cannot have the same human nature as the preconscious fetus. Rakestraw goes on to suggest that for a PVS patient, "the body still has some kind of residual life, the person is dead. . . . The Christian, then, has a theological basis for distinguishing between the death of the body, with its residual movements, and the death of the person" (pp. 402-3). In our view, this too reflects this problematic separation of a person and a human being. What is particularly troublesome about such a view is the link between the image of God and these specific functions of personhood. In our view, the image of God is something that is part of the essence of a person and is not primarily related to one's actualized capacities.

[47]For example, see Kenneth Schemmer, "Nancy Cruzan Is Already Dead," *Loma Linda University Medical Center Update* 5 (December 1989): 4-5.

[48]This follows the legal guidelines set down by the U.S. Supreme Court in the *Cruzan* case.

[49]The SUPPORT Principal Investigators, "A Controlled Trial to Improve Care for Seriously Ill Hospitalized Patients," *Journal of the American Medical Association* 274, no. 20 (1995): 1591-98. The study's findings were considered so important that the Robert Wood Johnson Foundation (which funded the SUPPORT study itself) also funded a study by the Hastings Center to address the ethical implications of the study (Ellen H. Moskowitz and James L. Nelson, eds., "Dying Well in the Hospital: The Lessons of SUPPORT," *Hastings Center Report, Special Supplement* 25 [November-December 1995]: S1-S36).

[50]SUPPORT Principal Investigators, "A Controlled Trial," p. 1591.

[51]George J. Annas, "How We Lie," in Moskowitz and Nelson, "Dying Well in the Hospital: The Lessons of SUPPORT," *Hastings Center Report Special Supplement* 25 (November-December 1995): S13.

[52]Lawrence J. Schneiderman, "Exile and PVS," *Hastings Center Report* 20, no. 3 (1990).

[53]See, e.g., Leslie J. Blackhall et al., "Ethnicity and Attitudes Toward Patient Autonomy," *Journal of the American Medical Association* 274, no. 10 (1995): 820-25.

[54]The definition of "futile treatment" is the subject of a great deal of debate. Generally, futile treatment is treatment that cannot reverse the patient's downward spiral toward death or cannot restore an acceptable level of the patient's functioning. The vast majority of people make it clear in their advance directives that they do not desire to have nutrition and hydration medically provided should it become necessary indefinitely. It is a form of treatment that most people would refuse if they were in a PVS.

Index